Labor's Wage Policies in the Twentieth Century

# LABOR'S

# WAGE

# POLICIES

# in the

# TWENTIETH CENTURY

by JAMES S. YOUTSLER

Twayne Publishers　　　　　　　Skidmore College

To Anne

# Preface

It is highly important that a book dealing with the wage policies in the twentieth century appear at this time. It reveals to us that the wage is the very heart of our economic society; therefore the fixing of wage rates is of primary significance. This analysis of wage policies demonstrates the interdependence of the various phases of the economic institution. Wage rates, for example, affect prices, bank rate policies and foreign trade policies, and cause the development of techniques to create steadiness in the area of wages.

In earlier years in fixing wages the general practice was for the various agencies entrusted with this matter to compromise without developing any policies. But because of the seriousness of the wage problem in recent years, attempts have been made to discover criteria for determining a fair wage and to justify any policy that is used for the fixing of wages. It is apparent, however, that as yet there is no agreement on the proper wage policy that should be applied. Also in striving to arrange policies for the setting of wage rates numerous problems have arisen. For instance, the unions have contended that it is unfair to assume that it is possible to determine a fair wage and to neglect or fail to apply the same reasoning to the other factors of production. Also these organizations have bitterly opposed the stabilization of wages without any effort to stabilize profits.

This study clearly shows that in our attempt to discover wage criteria or policies for the determination of wages in the twentieth century the approach has not been narrowly economic. In fact, much emphasis has been placed upon the social and ethical factors. While some attention is placed upon wages in relation to productivity, the author clearly shows that much emphasis has been placed upon need, cost of living, the setting of a minimum wage, and a more equitable distribution of the national income. The trend is to see that laborers have a living wage; that is, an income which would enable them to live on a reasonable comfort level. Also in the fixing of a wage policy the employer's position is taken into consideration when the factors of ability to pay and the going wage in the area are emphasized.

The author points out the fact that the recent federal statutes have played a significant role in the determination of policies or criteria for the setting of wage rates. For example, the National Labor Relations Act and the Taft-Hartley Amendments stress the importance of purchasing power in the maintenance of full employment and industrial peace in our economy. These laws assume that if unions are protected and allowed to function, then workers will receive their fair share of the values produced in the production process. From the functional point of view, this will lead to greater purchasing power and to more employment. From the personal point of view, workers will be more satisfied and their morale will be increased. Consequently, there will be fewer strikes and greater production. The Fair Labor Standards Act assumes that the employer must pay the living wage as outlined in the law or cease to operate because an industry unable to pay this wage is not an asset but a liability to society. No industry, the law assumes, should be subsidized by a low wage.

This book reveals that workers are greatly interested in security on an improved level. This desire for security has resulted in various reactions on the part of the labor unions in the United States. In specific industries in order to maintain employment the demands of the union have been kept within the framework of economic reality. In the textile industry, for example, the union took a wage reduction because its employers were in a disadvantageous position in the area of competition. On the other hand, other unions are putting much emphasis upon the maintenance of wages. This is to be accomplished by shortening the work week in order to spread employment, by increasing the amount of fringe benefits, and by stabilizing employment. The most recent device of unions proposed to assure their income is the annual wage. Whether this will be a reality in the near future is a question. This demand has undoubtedly alerted management to the seriousness of the problem of job security and has caused a number of employers to attempt to stabilize employment. It has also led to a new interpretation of both the cause of unemployment and the responsibility for those who are without work.

It is realized that many of these problems have been created by our philosophy of life in the United States. The environment has been changed so that the principle of freedom has been extended to the workers. Also, our philosophy is that one's "reach should exceed one's grasp"; therefore, every person should try to improve his economic position. As is the way of life, in trying to solve this problem numerous other serious problems have arisen. It is now realized that the values in our economic society must be made so that the workers can react favorably to them or some changes are inevitable.

This book makes a very worthwhile contribution to the literature dealing with the wage problem in America.

WALTER L. DAYKIN,

Professor of Labor, Department of Labor and Management, College of Commerce, State University of Iowa, Iowa City, Iowa

# Acknowledgments

Grateful acknowledgment is made to the following authors and publishers for permission to quote from their copyrighted publications: American Federation of Labor and the Congress of Industrial Organizations for excerpts from convention proceedings and other miscellaneous publications; Harcourt, Brace and Co., Inc., for a passage from *The General Theory of Employment, Interest and Money* by John M. Keynes; Houghton Mifflin Co. for excerpts from *Real Wages in the United States* by Paul H. Douglas; The Brookings Institution for a quotation from *Controlling Factors in Economic Development* by Harold G. Moulton and for a quotation from *America's Capacity to Consume* by Maurice Leven, Harold G. Moulton, and Clark Warburton; McGraw-Hill Book Co., Inc., for a table from *Recent Social Trends in the United States*, Report of the President's Research Committee on Social Trends; the *American Economic Review* for excerpted material from an article, "Demand and Supply Functions for Labor" by John T. Dunlop and a book review, "Unions and Capitalism," by John T. Dunlop; Council of Economic Advisers to the President of the United States for passages from the 1955 Economic Report of the President; U.S. Department of Commerce and Bureau of Labor Statistics, U.S. Department of Labor for excerpts from their publications; the *Southern Economic Journal* for the privilege of reproducing as Chapter VII, with some modification, the article, "Collective Bargaining Accomplishments in the Paper Industry," by James S. Youtsler in April 1955 issue.

It is impossible for me to mention all who have been of assistance in the preparation of this volume. I have drawn upon the opinions of many scholars in the academic field and the labor movement.

I am especially indebted to Professor Walter L. Daykin of the University of Iowa, who stimulated my interest in the social and ethical aspects of labor economics; Dr. Irving Bernstein and Dr. Benjamin Aaron of the Institute of Industrial Relations, University of California, Los Angeles, and Everett V. Stonequist who were helpful as counselors; Professors Coleman B. Cheney and Dr. Fenton Keyes, vice-president of Skidmore College, for reading portions of the manuscript and offering valuable criticism. I also owe much to the interest and encouragement of Dr. Henry T. Moore, President of Skidmore College.

Union research staffs were helpful in making available union records. Their critiques of my work have greatly strengthened the book. Particular recognition should be given to: Dr. Lazare Teper of the International Ladies' Garment Workers' Union; Solomon Barkin and George Perkel of the Textile Workers Union of America; Vice-president Gladys Dickanson and Frieda Shaviro of the Amalgamated Clothing Workers of America; President John P. Burke and Raymond Leon of the International Brotherhood of Pulp, Sulphite and Paper Mill Workers; President Paul Phillips and Russell Allen of the International Brotherhood of Paper Makers; Nat Weinberg and Frank Winn of the United Automobile Workers; Dr. Otis Brubaker of the United Steelworkers of America; David Lasser of the International Union of Electrical, Radio and Machine Workers.

To the members of the staffs of the Industrial Relations Library, Littauer Center, Harvard University; the Labor and Industrial Relations Library, University of California, Los Angeles; New York State Library, Albany; and to Miss Margery Pierpoint of the Lucy Scribner Library at Skidmore College: my appreciation is given for assistance. I have pleasure in recording the help given to me by my wife Anne M. Youtsler in research, editing and indexing.

JAMES S. YOUTSLER

Saratoga Springs, New York
December 1955

# Table of Contents

13

14 *Contents*

# Introduction

The purpose of this study is to trace labor's wage demands in the United States during the first half of the twentieth century. Although occasional references are made to other countries, such data are included to shed light on wages in the United States.

It is the hope of the author that the study will make some contribution to the understanding of the *role of need* in influencing wage demands. Emphasis has been centered primarily on union labor because only through organized labor do we find an articulate expression of the wage earner. It is true that what unions say about wages is much less important than what they do in specific contexts. Labor leaders are usually very skillful in trading. Nevertheless, they serve the important role of crystallizing the support of the union membership, influencing government and the public agencies, creating a sympathetic public opinion, and preparing for more effective negotiation with employers.[1]

In order to indicate the role of need behind the demand of labor, the writer has attempted, when data are available, to correlate the workers' wage with the cost of living, minimum family budgets for maintenance of health and decency, and the distribution of wealth and income.

The first section presents a survey of wage theories in order to provide the reader with the necessary theoretical background. Another equally important reason for the inclusion of this material is to determine the extent to which labor has accepted prevailing wage theories.

The statements of labor's wage demands were obtained from the following sources: adopted resolutions of the American Federation of Labor, the Congress of Industrial Organizations, and the affiliated national unions; pronouncements by labor leaders at the annual meetings of the unions and through union periodicals; mediation and arbitrational decisions; and records of negotiations.

With the mushrooming of the labor movement in the 1930's after the passage of the National Labor Relations Act, labor's wage demands took on added significance. Attention has, therefore, been focused not only on labor's pronouncements, but also on the results achieved through collective bargaining. A sample has been made of AFL and CIO union contracts covering a considerable area of the American economy.

Whatever contribution this study makes to the existing wage literature will result from the more thorough treatment of the *role of need* than has hitherto been made in the determination of wages.

Part One

# INTRODUCTORY

## CHAPTER ONE

# Wage Theories

### INTRODUCTION

Before attempting to trace labor's wage pronouncements and demands, it is appropriate to examine briefly the basic wage theories of the last one hundred and fifty years. Thus, a theoretical context and historical perspective can be applied to our subject and enable us to determine just how far labor has accepted economic theory in its wage demands.

### SUBSISTENCE THEORY—THE IRON LAW OF WAGES

A century and a half ago it was believed that wages could not permanently rise above the subsistence level. The leading exponent of this school of thought was David Ricardo. Ricardo and many of his followers in the nineteenth century had been influenced by the population theory of Malthus. According to Malthus, the population of the world will always increase up to the limits of the food supply. This would be true because of: 1) man's biological possibilities of human fecundity based on rates of population growth, 2) nature's niggardliness, and 3) the law of diminishing returns.[1]

Restating the population theory of Malthus in terms of wages, Ricardo expressed the principle that wages would tend in the long run to be at a subsistence level. A rise in wages would be of no avail to the worker because of the automatic fall of the death rate and the concomitant increase in the number of births. The increased supply of labor in the market would tend to push wages down to the subsistence level. According to Ricardo, labor had its natural and its market price. The natural price is that price which is necessary to enable the worker to subsist and perpetuate the race. The market price is the price which is paid for the service of the laborer by the employer. "It is when the market price of labour exceeds its natural price, that the condition of the labourer is flourishing and happy, that he has it in his power to command a greater proportion of the necessaries and enjoyments of life, and therefore to rear a healthy and numerous family. When, however, by the encouragement which high wages give to the increase of population, the number of labourers is increased, wages again fall to their natural price, and indeed from a re-action sometimes fall below it."[2] Because of the hopelessness of the laborer to enjoy a high standard of living over the long-run period, economics during much of the nineteenth century won for itself the title of the "dismal science."

Few informed people today would accept the population laws of Malthus or the iron law of wages as espoused by Ricardo. The advance in the standard of living of the laboring classes in all industrial nations has been phenomenal. It must be remembered that the early classical writers lived before the full development of the industrial revolution. Yet even by the middle of the nineteenth century there was doubt whether technology had altered the Malthusian-Ricardian doctrines. John Stuart Mill, one of the most widely accepted economists, stated in his book, *Principles of Political Economy* (1848): "Hitherto it is questionable if all the mechanical inventions yet made have lightened the day's toil of any human being. They have enabled a greater population to live the same life of drudgery and imprisonment, and an increased number of manufacturers and others to make fortunes."[3] However, the rate of return to the capitalist would after a while tend to approach zero through the operation of the law of diminishing returns. Thus a stationary society rather than a dynamic one appeared a certainty. But in Mill's time the industrial revolution was still in its infancy, and he could not be expected to perceive the economic significance of coming developments. In every field of economic endeavor the application of science and technology has increased many-fold the productivity of the worker. According to Harold G. Moulton, "instead of diminishing returns from natural resources—agriculture and mining—we have witnessed constantly increasing returns. This outcome . . . is not so much a result of the discovery of new agricultural and mineral resources as of a more efficient use of human resources."[4] There are authorities who differ with Moulton in respect to the productivity of our resources, while others have become concerned over the large increase in the world's population. They foresee lower living standards unless there is a slowing down of the birth rate and a cessation of the wilful destruction of our land.[5]

### THE WAGES-FUND AND RESIDUAL CLAIMANT THEORIES

The subsistence theory of wages placing its emphasis on the supply of labor was distinctly a long-run explanation of how wages were set. Later economists such as John Stuart Mill and Nassau Senior stressed demand as well as supply as a force influencing wages particularly during the short run, as from year to year. The demand for labor was believed to be determined by the amount of capital funds which employers had available to hire workers. The wages-fund theory proved to be just another version of the subsistence theory, because it recognized that wages from the long-run point of view were to be explained by the growth of population and the diminishing food supply.[6]

Another closely related and rigid concept of wages was the residual-claimant theory. The chief exponent was the American author, Francis H. Walker. Walker claimed that although wages may be advanced out of capital, they are paid out of the product of industry. The laboring class would receive the remaining or residual share of the product of industry after payment had been deducted for rent, interest, and profit.[7]

The major weaknesses of the wages-fund theory are:

1. Principle of substitution. The employer constantly balances all the costs of production against each other. Therefore, labor is not a fixed unit, but continually varies in the productive process;
2. It is impossible in mass-production industries to measure with any exactitude the amount of the product which labor or any other factor of production contributes;
3. There is no fixed fund out of which labor is paid. Labor is paid before the product is created, and its cost will be recovered when the product is sold.

As far as the residual-claimant theory is concerned, wages are not the residue but rather profit. Then, too, labor is usually paid in advance of the sale of the product. Therefore, it would be inconsistent to say that it received the residual share.[8]

### MARX'S SURPLUS VALUE-EXPLOITATION THEORY

Karl Marx's theory of wages was based on the classical writers. He believed in a labor theory of value as expounded by Adam Smith and David Ricardo. He accepted the wages-fund concept and paid lip-service to the population principles of Malthus. Marx differed from his contemporaries and predecessors chiefly on how the product created by labor should be divided. According to Marx, if labor represents the value of the product, then it should receive the total value of the product.[9] But in practice, labor is paid only its cost of subsistence while the employer retains the balance which is created by the worker, namely, the surplus value. Hence, the end result is exploitation. Marx's solution was the abolishing of the capitalist class and restoring to the workers the instruments of production. Only then could each person contribute according to his ability and receive his just share of the product.

Marx's theory of wages has appealed to the exploited and to many people living on a bare subsistence level, but it is nevertheless unsound. It ignores the role of management in our productive process, and it overlooks the need of savings necessary to create capital equipment.[10]

### MARGINAL PRODUCTIVITY THEORY OF WAGES

Toward the latter part of the nineteenth century a change occurred in the formulation of value and hence of distribution. The classical theory of Ricardo and Mill emphasized production, supply, and cost; the new theory is more concerned with consumption, demand, and utility. The marginal utility concept was introduced to effect this shift of emphasis. The marginal productivity theory of wages is an outgrowth and integral part of the marginal productivity theory of values.

The first generation of modern marginal utility theorists included William Stanley Jevons, Carl Menger, Léon Walras, and Hermann Heinrich Gossen. It was, however, Alfred Marshall of the second generation of marginalists who was responsible for the refinement and classification of the theory of value and distribution. To Marshall it took two blades of a pair of scissors to make value, namely, supply and demand. Behind demand is marginal utility reflected in the demands of buyers and hence in prices of goods purchased. Behind supply is marginal effort and sacrifice, reflected in supply price, that is, prices of goods and services supplied in the market. The final price or value will be determined in the market where demand and supply are equated.[11] In other words, price and value depend on what buyers are willing to pay for the last or marginal unit which is produced and sold, and what the suppliers or producers are willing to accept for the last or marginal unit supplied.

Let us turn our attention to distribution, or the payment to be made to the factors of production, land, labor, capital, and management. According to the theory, each will be paid in conformity with its contribution, or what the last or marginal unit contributes. The employer's aim is the maximization of his returns, and he must discover and maintain the most advantageous combination of the productive factors. This will require addition or subtraction of the factors employed until the price that is paid for the last (marginal) unit or factor employed is just equal to the value of the last (marginal) product that is produced. The price of any factor, or the amount which each will receive, is thus determined by the product yielded by the last or marginal unit of the factor employed. And the price or worth of each factor is also determined by the "law of diminishing returns," because as additional units of a factor are employed, with other factors remaining constant, the contribution of further applications of the variable factor will naturally decline.

It should be kept in mind that the marginal productivity of labor, and hence its price, like that of other factors, is dependent upon its relative abundance or scarcity. For when the supply of labor is small proportionate to its demand, and the relative supply of the other factors are large, the price of labor will be high—and vice versa.[12] Assuming constancy in the "state of the arts," that is, technology and inventions, and similarity or uniformity in the workers' skill and effort, competition for the factors of producton (free labor market), and competition in the sale of the products (free product market), then wages would be set by "marginal productivity" under the laws of demand and supply.

*In the short run:* On the demand side, each employer will consider a demand schedule for labor, which will be based on the abundance of labor and the other factors that are available. Substitution, or addition, and subtraction, will follow. According to the "law of diminishing returns," when units of labor are changed while the other factors are held constant, each additional unit of a given type of labor applied will result in a smaller increment than the preceding one. The employer will find it to his advantage to add or subtract a number of workers of each class until the wage he must pay the last (marginal) worker is just equal to the last (marginal) amount produced by that last employee. At this point the marginal labor cost (MLC) equals marginal revenue (MR). The accompanying diagram depicts this process.

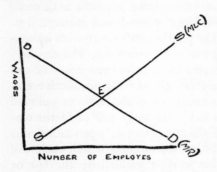

The employers' demand-curve for labor may be thought of as the marginal revenue-curve for the product manufactured and sold. The supply-curve represents the supply of labor offered to the employer and may be termed marginal labor cost. It will be based on the effort or sacrifice involved by the workers in performing labor, and what they could be paid elsewhere. Equilibrium is reached when MLC equals MR. At that point the rate of pay is uniform for each class of employees in the market area, and there will be no inducement for the workers to transfer to other employers.

The pricing process for the labor market as a whole would be similar to that of the single employer. Here the demand-curve would be composed of all the separate demand-curves for each class of labor, and the supply-curve would be the sum of the employee supply-curves for each individual market. The market would be in equilibrium at the point of the intersection of the sum of demand and supply, and the price of labor would be set at this point.[13]

*In the long run:* The level of wages would be determined by the proportion of capital to labor used in the productive process. If the capital equipment is high relative to labor, the productivity of labor will be high, and wages will correspondingly be high. If the capital investment ratio is low, productivity will be low and wages will be small.[14] According to Harold G. Moulton, the increasing productivity of labor since 1900 has come mainly from new types of machines and equipment, from improvement in the quality of tools and materials, and from the increased size of plant and equipment.[15] Higher wages, of course, will stimulate still greater capital investment in an effort to reduce costs and maximize total returns to the firm. High wages since World War II have undoubtedly been responsible in part for the rapid introduction of labor-saving devices. The relatively high wages in the United States in comparison with other countries may be explained chiefly by this country's continued high capital investment.

## LIMITATIONS OF THE MARGINAL PRODUCTIVITY THEORY OF WAGES

The theory assumes competition in the labor market and competition among employers in the product market. At the present time there are between 16,000,000 and 17,000,000 members of trade unions in the United States. The individual worker instead of competing with his fellow laborers for his wage now lets the union bargain for the group. Then, too, the union may place restrictions on the number who may enter the trade. One purpose of the union is to create a degree of monopoly in labor so as to influence the price of labor and to effect general improvement in the conditions of work. Professor Sumner H. Slichter has stated: "Unions have tremendous power. No longer do they cover a small fraction of the work force. About seven million jobs in American industry may be held only by men who are union members or whom unions are willing to accept as members. About eleven million employees who work in union shops or closed shops or under maintenance-of-membership clauses hold their jobs only so long as they keep in good standing in the union. No longer are most unions underdogs. The strongest unions . . . are the most powerful organizations which the country has ever seen."[16] Collective bargaining, as a result, will affect both the structure and behavior of wages. "One may expect the structure of wages under collective bargaining to reflect not the skill and responsibility required of workers in different occupations and industries or the relative supply of labor and the demand for it, but, on the one hand, the differing bargaining power of the 50,000 local unions or the 190-odd national unions and, on the other hand, the bargaining power of the employer or the employer associations."[17]

As there is now little competition among employees in the labor market so, as Professor Phelps points out, there is little competition among the buyers of labor. The labor market in many communities represents monopsony or oligopsony rather than competition. Our larger industrial corporations are labor markets in themselves, with their own labor pools, reserves, and wage systems, influenced only slightly by other firms in their territory. The mammoth concern may frequently set the standard for wages in both the industry and the locality in which it resides, as it may be one of several large concerns in the industry which will have a major market influence on the general pattern of wages in both the industry and the respective communities in which these firms are located.[18]

Let us turn now to monopoly in the product market. The employer demand-curve in an imperfect competitive market is sloping which gives him an incentive to restrict his output in order to maximize his total returns. Because of the sloping demand-curve, the amount added by the marginal worker to the total revenue is somewhat less than the marginal product manufactured. According to Professor Chamberlin, the employer will subtract from the marginal worker's product the loss from lowering his price on the other units of the product. Thus, under imperfect competition the employee may not obtain the marginal product achieved by his labor.[19] It is possible monopoly may also depress wages by forcing labor, which could be used in the monopolistic industries, into the competitive areas. In doing so, an oversupply is created in the more competitive fields which may reduce the marginal productivity and wages.[20]

Professor Shister takes a somewhat different point of view on monopoly. He points out that the assumption of the employer maximizing his profits in the long-run period does not hold indiscriminately. In more instances than one, other objectives of a non-pecuniary aspect are observable such as the desire for power, recognition, and respect. Employers have been found who were satisfied to earn what they believed a satisfactory return rather than try to increase profits by expansion policies. Employers have kept some plants in operation even though it was unprofitable to do so.[21]

Another criticism of the marginal productivity theory is the assumption that the wage of the marginal worker and the price of the marginal product may be calculated. But large manufacturing concerns do not vary the last unit of labor employed to equal the amount of the worker's contribution to the company's receipts. The difficulty of such calculation may be realized by the fact that companies do not maintain constant production, but rather vary the scale of operations so that the cost of production differs from time to time. Also when a company produces and sells more than one product, joint costs are involved which would make it impossible to calculate the marginal product; and when production includes a number of processes, the value of the contribution of any one worker is practically indistinguishable.[22]

The marginal productivity theory is open to criticism in respect to the problem of units. The theory assumes that the units of labor are uniform and homogeneous, and that they are added or subtracted in increments of a single unit. In reality, these are false assumptions, for no two workers are of the same quality. Therefore, the amount produced as well as the quality of work will vary. In our large mass-production industries labor is not added or released in single unit, but in groups. Under such circumstances, the calculation of the marginal product would be extremely difficult.[23]

To the foregoing criticisms must be added the lack of mobility, full knowledge of the labor market, and price quality for the standardized units of labor. Anyone who is at all familiar with the labor market realizes that labor is very immobile. Labor is frequently ignorant of the opportunities in other markets. Likewise, there is no price equality for like units of labor, as observed in the many collective bargaining contracts between employers and unions in the same market and throughout the country as a whole.

Finally, the theory breaks down in respect to the supply-curve of labor. A normal supply-curve is positive in character, sloping upward from left to right, signifying that the higher the wage, the larger the number of units of labor that will be supplied. But, according to Professors Douglas and Lester, in the short-run period there is a high negative correlation between hourly wages and the quantity of labor offered.[24] That is, the higher the price paid for labor, the less labor will be supplied, and lowering the price for labor will cause a larger number of workers to seek employment. The reasons advanced for this phenomenon are as follows: as the family's real income rises, workers will seek a shorter work-week and more leisure, women will become less eager to seek employment, young people will enter the labor market at a later age, and older people will retire sooner. The opposite tendency will occur as the family's real income falls. It would appear then that over the short-run period in some markets the labor supply-curve would be negatively inclined, i.e., sloping downward from right to left, signifying that a larger number of laborers will become available at lower rates of pay and a lesser number at higher wages. According to Professor Phelps, a negatively sloped supply-curve for labor would greatly undermine a competitive theory of wages, which has as its strongest point a constant tendency toward a stable equilibrium with full employment and maximum return to each employee. For example, it could easily result in the disastrously unstable situation where competitive bidding for personnel by employers drives wages further away from the point of intersection of the curves, increases the gap between the quantity demanded and that supplied, and leaves personnel needs unsatisfied.

Below the spurious equilibrium point, competitive bidding by employees will drive wages down and increase the unemployment gap.[25]

In conclusion, the marginal productivity theory of wages, which is based on the neo-classical emphasis of the interaction of supply and demand for labor in a competitive market, has proved to be false and entirely inconsistent with the pricing of labor in the short-run period. Over the long run, marginal productivity may be an important influence, particularly in determining the upper limits of wages that labor may enjoy.

### BARGAINING THEORY OF WAGES

Because of the unreality of the basic assumptions of the marginal productivity theory of wages when applied to the industrial processes, and especially since the mushrooming of unionism into a powerful movement since the early 1930's, it became apparent that wage rates are determined more by conscious human decision than by impersonal market forces. Therefore, the bargaining theory of wages was introduced as a partial answer to the labor theorists' dilemma.

The bargaining theory is not an innovation. It was recognized by Adam Smith in his book, *The Wealth of Nations*.[26] Professor John Davidson in 1898 was one of the first economists who emphasized the theory in concise terms.[27] Later Alfred Marshall and Maurice Dobbs admitted that it played a role in the distribution of income.[28] The discard of the marginal productivity theory was slow, as evidenced by J. R. Hicks in his book, *The Theory of Wages*. Professor Hicks incorporated bargaining into his general theory of distribution by saying that collective bargaining could determine wages but marginal productivity accounted for the volume of employment.[29]

According to the bargaining theory, it was believed there is no single wage rate which is determined by the forces of demand and supply in the marketplace. There is instead a range of possible wage rates between the "upper and lower limits." The upper limit is the highest wage the employer will pay, and the lower limit is the lowest wage the worker will accept. Just where the actual wage will be set between the two limits depends upon the bargaining strength of the union and the employer. Among the influences affecting the bargaining are: the necessity of retaining a sufficient capital in the business; the percentage of labor cost to the total costs; possibility of substituting capital or land for labor; competitive conditions in the market for both the product and the factors of production; shifts in consumer demand; the financial status of the employer; the quality of union bargaining representatives against that of the employers'; cyclical fluctuations in the level of prices, output, and employment; the ability of the union to conduct successfully a strike; the productivity of the workers; and the like.

CRITICISM OF THE BARGAINING THEORY

The theory has many weaknesses and consequently does not give the final answer on how wages are determined. The assumption that capital investment must be maintained in the firm or industry as an influence in determining bargaining has been challenged by Arthur M. Ross in the coal and railroad industries. The unions in these two areas do not always regard it as their obligation to protect the "capital and business power" of the employer.[30] Secondly, it is believed that the theory has placed an undue emphasis on the union as a seller of labor and the maximizing of the total wage bill. Mr. Ross holds that the political role of the union in many instances is more important than its economic function. The wage settlements are influenced more by the union leader's necessity of maintaining the union and his leadership against rival cliques, competitive unions, and the employer.[31] Professors Shultz and Myers take issue with Mr. Ross in his over-emphasis on the political environment of the union. It is their opinion that the economic pressures under which the union functions affect policy decisions no less than the political. This is particularly true in those industries which experience strong competition for their products and those which are not completely organized. The unions in these cases give considerable weight to the employment effect of their wage demands except in periods of full employment and rising prices.[32] Professor Dunlop concurs with Shultz and Myers on the economic role of the unions. Much stress is laid on non-income objectives such as: allocating the available work among prospective wage earners; requests for benefits in the form of vacations, health insurance, pension benefits; controlling the rate of introduction of technical innovations; improvement in working conditions such as hours, differential rates for different shifts, Sundays and holidays; control of entrance to a trade by differential rates paid to apprentices and learners, etc.[33]

The wage patterns in the economy are not determined so much by the myriad local unions and employers through bargaining negotiations. More and more, wage rates appear to be influenced and determined by key bargains between the unions and large corporations, or between the union and the industry. Professor Dunlop states: "There are a limited number of key bargains in the system which act as wage leaders. The fixing of these rates will lead to the adjustment of the rest of the wage structure to these growth points. These wage leaders are centers in the economy where all the factors customarily regarded as relevant to wage setting get focused—anticipations regarding the business outlook, past increases in living costs, and level of profits. These factors are operative in an industrial relations context where willingness to fight or settle—aside from money calculations—may also be important. Money wage rates are raised at these key bargains either when the cost of living has risen significantly over the past period (with the expectation of no sharp decline) or when the expectation is widely held of profit levels higher than normal for an indefinite period ahead. The cost of living may be viewed as a push and the profits influence a pull on wage rates. Money wage rates are reduced via the following mechanism: decreases in income lead to falls in prices at certain points in the economy; the reduced profit margins force wage reductions which may then spread to the nearest key bargains; as these bargains are reduced, the general wage level declines. It is the decline in product price rather than unemployment which brings about the reduction. Wage cuts do not appear typically where prices are held rigid. These suggestions on the process of change in money-wage-rate levels require further abstraction to yield a few tractable relationships for a model of the total system."[84]

### KEYNESIAN THEORY OF WAGES

J. M. Keynes in his book, *The General Theory of Employment, Interest and Money*, rejects the classical theory's assumption that the natural forces of supply and demand for labor in a free market would always maintain continous full employment. Wages under the natural operation of the marketplace would be flexible—responding to the demand and supply of labor. If the supply of labor in a given market is greater than the demand, wages would fall, and vice versa. According to the classical writers, the drop in wages would be a stimulus to employers to hire more labor and thereby help to maintain full employment. Keynes pointed out that the self-adjusting flexible wages may leave an adverse effect on investment and consumption by reducing purchasing power and thus may decrease the volume of output and employment.[85]

In a place of a flexible wage policy based on collective bargaining in the market, Keynes favored an inflexible wage policy based on government regulation. His objective was to avoid fluctuation in employment and output. "I am now of the opinion that the maintenance of stable general level of money-wages is, on a balance of considerations, the most advisable policy for a closed system; whilst the same conclusion will hold for an open system, provided that equilibrium with the rest of the world can be secured by means of fluctuating exchanges. There are advantages in some degree of flexibility in the wages of particular industries so as to expedite transfers from those which are relatively declining to those which are relatively expanding. But the money-wages level as a whole should be maintained as stable as possible, at any rate in the short period. This policy will result in a fair degree of stability in the price-level; greater stability, at least, than with flexible wage policy."[36]

A government-administered wage policy for the entire economy is not a novelty in the United States. During World War II the National War Labor Board administered wages. It worked quite satisfactorily in spite of labor's criticisms of the "Little Steel Formula." But such a policy in peacetime would be repugnant to both labor and management. Nevertheless, the government does influence wage determination during peacetime both indirectly and directly. It sets minimum wage standards in many occupations and, of course, it sets wages for its own employees. By requiring contractors and suppliers dealing with the government to pay at least a given minimum wage it can indirectly affect wages. It can compete with private business firms in public construction programs and contribute to a rise in wages.[37]

## CONCLUSION

As Walton Hamilton and Stacy May comment: "There are just as many theories of wages, reputable and disreputable, as there are books and articles upon the subject."[38]

"Despite the numerous studies," says Professor Lester, "our knowledge of wages has remained largely superficial."[39] It is obvious that there is need for more research. Many of the assumptions have not corresponded to reality, and many of the hypotheses have lacked empirical testing. As a result of the abstract and unrealistic nature of conventional wage theory, it is questionable whether management and union officials have been benefited by the labor theorists. Although many useful studies have been and are being made, they have raised more questions than they have answered. It appears that collective bargaining is the most significant force in the determination of wages, but it is a mistake to assume that either political or economic factors are the most important influences. Undoubtedly, wages are greatly affected by what Dunlop calls key bargains between the unions and the large corporations and through industry-wide bargaining. Marginal productivity is a factor particularly in the long run. The contribution and effort of the individual worker in the small non-unionized plant may exert a force in determining his wage, but it would be negligible in the large plant and even in the smaller non-unionized plants. The role of government is also an influence in wage determination, but its influence is only a minor and indirect one in the United States in peace time.

# Part Two

# LABOR'S WAGE DEMANDS 1900–1930

## CHAPTER TWO

# Labor's Wage Emphasis from 1900 Through the First World War

Wage demands were almost negligible in the historical labor litera-ture because the trade union movement in the United States prior to the turn of the twentieth century was largely local in character and primarily embraced skilled workers. It is true that the Knights of Labor did include both the unskilled and skilled workers and had an estimated membership of possibly 700,000 at the height of power in 1886. Although the Knights did win some notable wage victories during the period of the "great upheaval" in 1885–86, they soon lost much of their power. The trade unions became indifferent toward the movement because of its ineffectiveness and centralized charac-ter. Moreover, the mingling in some local assemblies of workers of many trades acted as an impediment to the effective concentration of economic strength. Membership in the Knights declined to around 200,000 in 1888, and to less than 100,000 members by the 1890's.

After the disintegration of the Knights the trade unions evidenced little progress in the growth of membership and economic power. The aggregate membership of all unions affiliated with the AFL from 1893 to 1897 was around 275,000. The AFL in 1892 possessed only 40 national unions. Total membership in all unions was only 440,000 in 1897 and grew slowly to 791,000 by 1900.[1]

An examination of the annual proceedings of the AFL during the 1880's and 1890's shows that this organization did not press for wage demands to an appreciable extent but rather appeared more in-terested in a reduction in the hours of labor (demand for an eight-hour day); organization of female labor; adoption of the union label; restriction of the power of the courts in issuing injunctions against labor; prevention of the use of convict labor against free labor in the open market; opposition to lack of immigration laws; the abolition of letting out government work by contract; the prevention of child

35

labor, etc. Although this program did not express itself in direct wage demands, it did embody the ideal of "protection of the job" particularly against competition or the arbitrariness of employers, and thus would indirectly enhance the trade union wage and improve working conditions.[2]

Soon after the opening of the twentieth century, the United States suffered a drop in business activity. Concomitant with this decline was the statement on the part of management that wage reductions might need to be adjusted downward. Samuel Gompers immediately responded with what appears to be one of the earliest AFL statements in respect to general wage policies. Mr. Gompers felt that the policy of reducing wages during a period of declining business would reduce consumer buying-power and would prolong and intensify the crisis.[3] This early wage enunciation may be likened to the purchasing-power theory concept which was used by labor intermittently during the 1930's and 1940's.

In 1906 the AFL went on record as opposing wage reductions not on the basis of maintenance of purchasing power but rather on the premise that labor is not a factor of production to be treated like the other inanimate materials in the production process. "Trade-unionism should declare in form, as it has in fact, that the labor seller is not an inert piece of merchandise, but the product of all civilization has given to the world, with the power to think and to act. The higher thought has taught him to reach out for the things which make life worth living. He refuses to be longer juggled with by mercantile and speculative acrobats. He says, Make your future profits out of something else than my flesh and blood. I am going at least to keep what I have got and to get as much more as I can. Reckon it, then, as a fixed factor in your business calculations that labor's share in the joint product shall never more be scaled downward."[4]

With the oncoming of the depression in 1907, organized labor as voiced by the AFL concurred in its emphasis on no wage reductions. It was felt that a decline in wages would not only worsen the condition of the employee but also the employer. The worker would be deprived of a living wage, and the employer would receive no profit.[5]

### FAIR WAGE AND THE LIVING WAGE

"Fair wage" and "living wage" demands appeared soon after the turn of the twentieth century. John Mitchell of the United Mine

Workers Union stated: "What we seek to do is to fix a reasonable fair rate of wages for all men who work in the mining industry, so as to give them a wage that will enable them to live in a manner comfortable to American standards and put something away for old age or infirmity."[6]

Samuel Gompers of the AFL, in revealing the fallacy of wage reductions, also enunciated the fair wage. "The old theory that the selling price of an article shall determine the wages paid to the workmen is hollow, shallow, and unnatural. The order must be reversed and the first consideration in the selling price of an article must be a fair wage to labor. Wages must dominate prices, not prices dominate wages."[7]

James M. Lynch of the International Typographical Union in commenting about wages stated: "Our members working by the piece and on time . . . are expected to perform a fair day's work for a fair day's pay."[8]

James O'Connell, representing the International Association of Machinists, likewise stressed the belief in fair wages. "The organization that I represent requires its members to perform a fair day's work for a fair day's pay, and we recognize that one man is capable of producing more than another."[9]

A perusal of the early union trade literature evidenced that there was no appreciable difference between the fair wage and the living wage pronouncements. Statements pertaining to the living wage received more emphasis at the time of the establishment of minimum wage laws around 1916 and during the period of the First World War, largely because of the rise in the cost of living.

The "living wage" probably had its origin in England in the latter part of the nineteenth century in the attempt to establish minimum wage laws and in state arbitration decisions. However, the establishment of a living wage had always been one of the main purposes of the English trade unions' efforts. The miners' strike of 1893 was fought to maintain the principle of a living wage. It was then that the phrase became popular and received much discussion in the journals and reviews. A long series of labor disputes over the deplorable wages and living standards had taken place in England between 1883 and 1893. The inquiries of government commissions and committees all showed the miserable conditions of factory workers. The outcome was a series of public health and factory acts. The London School Board was the first public body to insist that the standard rate of wages should be paid for work under its jurisdiction. In 1889 it adopted what is known as the Fair Wage Resolution. The London County Council followed its example, and within five years over 150 local authorities had adopted a similar policy. The House of Commons in 1891 and in 1893 passed resolutions in favor of the adoption by the state of the principle of the "living wage" for laborers in its employment.[10]

At the beginning of the century the living wage demand in the United States, as in England a number of years earlier, grew out of the depressed living conditions of the working class. In particular, the unskilled workers suffered greatly, and a large percentage of them did not receive an income sufficient to maintain a decent standard of living. Being largely unorganized, they lacked sufficient power to obtain any substantial increase in earnings. The influx of immigrants from Southeastern Europe tended to keep wages down, and the large corporations seemed to be more interested in the output of the workers than in their financial well-being.

The average full-time weekly earnings in all manufacturing industries (skilled and unskilled) in 1900 were $12.74 which compares with $15.84 in 1914, while the average annual earnings were $435 in 1900 which compares with $580 in 1914. In the bituminous coal mining industry the average annual earnings in 1900 were $410 compared to $549 in 1914. In land transportation industries $554 were the average annual earnings in 1900 while in 1914 they increased to $787. Government employees in the District of Columbia received average annual earnings of $1,033 in 1900 compared to $1,140 in 1914. Farm laborers were at the bottom of the list, receiving an average annual wage of only $247 in 1900 and $351 in 1914, while school teachers were a close second with $328 and $564 average salaries respectively for the two years. Looking at the average yearly earnings of workers in all industries, with the exclusion of farm labor, we find that $503 was received by the wage earner in 1900 compared with $673 in 1914.[11]

It should be noted that the averages are compiled for all workers—single as well as married men, women, and young people. They do not show exclusively the earnings of heads of families. However, the United States Bureau of Labor in 1903 made a study of incomes of male heads of families which covered 25,000 wage-earning families. It revealed that four per cent of the male heads of families received less than $300 income a year, 30 per cent obtained less than

$500, 48 per cent less than $600, 65 per cent less than $700, and 82 per cent less than $800.[12]

What gains, if any, did the employed workers obtain in their scale of living from 1900 to 1914? Reducing the average annual earnings of wage earners in all industries to an index number, Professor Douglas found that the relative earnings, using 1890–99 as the base, advanced from 105 in 1900 to 140 in 1914. The cost-of-living index, on the other hand, rose from 106 to 139. Dividing the index of money earnings by the index of living costs, the real wage, or the purchasing power of the earnings of the wage earner, was 101 in 1914 compared to 99 in 1900, which represents a two per cent increase. We conclude then that the employed laborer did not secure any significant permanent gains. His increase in money income was swallowed by commensurate advances in the cost of living.[13]

Because of the deplorable wage conditions, the idea began to develop that a "living wage" should be an irreducible minimum. This minimum was first recognized as a "subsistence level." Wages should be enough to provide for at least the bare physical needs of the worker and his family. Samuel Gompers insisted that the "living wage" must be a demand from employers and society.[14]

As was to be expected, social and charitable workers also saw the necessity for the head of the family to receive sufficient income to cover the minimum requirements for family subsistence. Budgetary studies were made of the minimum subsistence requirements of an average unskilled worker's family. A study made by Dr. R. C. Chapin of 642 working men's families in New York City in 1907 showed that an annual income of $900 or over was necessary to maintain a subsistence standard for a wage earner's family of five members.[15] In the same year an investigation conducted for the New York State Conference of Charities and Corrections of the budgets from 391 families in New York City set the cost of living for a normal family in New York City at approximately $825. But it was believed by competent authorities that $876 a year was a more valid estimate for New York City and $772 for Buffalo.[16] In 1911 Professor Streightoff estimated that $650 was the extreme low limit for a family budget for northern, eastern, and western cities in the United States,[17] while in 1913 Dr. Nearing concluded that $700–$850 was the bare subsistence budget depending on the particular location.[18]

Comparing the above minimum budgetary requirements with the average yearly earnings of industrial workers during the period from

1900 to 1914 as computed by Professor Douglas, the conclusion is apparent that the average adult male worker had a difficult time to support a standard family at a subsistence level. It was necessary for the wife and children to seek employment in order to supplement the earnings of the head of the family.[19]

MINIMUM WAGE LAWS

It began to dawn upon people that low wages had a definite correlation with health, strength, and morals, particularly of women workers. The successful operation of the Australian system of minimum wage legislation and the enactment of minimum wage laws in England in 1910 convinced people that industry could pay its workers a sufficient wage to maintain a minimum level of health and decency. Massachusetts was the first state to enact minimum wage legislation in 1912 and was followed by California, Colorado, Minnesota, Nebraska, Oregon, Utah, Wisconsin, and Washington in 1913. Fifteen states had minimum wage legislation by 1923. However, these laws covered only female labor and minors under eighteen years of age. Public opinion was still too individualistic in character to sanction the regulation of adult male workers. Organized labor during the earlier years was opposed to wage regulation for adult males. This opposition was based on the fear that too much state paternalism would do the labor movement more harm than good. The workers preferred the policy of "getting things for ourselves."[20] The majority decision of the United States Supreme Court in refusing to uphold a New York State law limiting the hours of adult males in a private bakery establishment on the grounds of violating the freedom of contract was an additional stumbling block to similar laws regulating adult male wages.[21] Even though social workers, economists, and members of other professional groups continued to advocate minimum wage and hour laws for all workers, organized labor remained skeptical of state interference especially for male workers. Labor preferred to adhere to the spirit of laissez-faire and rugged individualism when applied to wages and even to some extent to hours of work.

RECOGNITION OF LIVING WAGE IN RAILWAY ARBITRATION DECISIONS

Professor Stockett reveals that in a number of disputes involving lower-paid employees on railways in the United States and Canada prior to the First World War, the living wage demand frequently occurred. In most cases, the workers demanded an increase in wages based on the advanced cost of living so that they could maintain their real wage. In 1910 the telegraphers on the Missouri Pacific Railroad were granted a living wage by an arbitration board. The maintenance-of-way-employees on the Canadian Pacific and Canadian Northern received increases in wages in 1911. In the year 1912 an arbitration board granted the telegraphers and station agents of the Canadian Pacific a 10 per cent increase on the ground that a living wage could be maintained. Numerous arbitration boards favored the payment of a living wage even without regard to the ability of the railroad to pay.[22]

### LIVING WAGE DEMANDS DURING THE FIRST WORLD WAR

The outbreak of World War I in 1914 stimulated the rise in prices because of the heavy demand for American products from the European nations, but wages did not rise equivalent to the increased family budgets. It was not until the entrance of the United States into the war that wages jumped forward. However, prices did not stop their rapid advance so that the disparity between earnings and cost of living became wider and wider and developed into one of the principal reasons for the great prevalence of strikes during the war period.

Table I, depicting the trend in cost of living and union wages, clearly illustrates the variance between these indices. The decline in purchasing power of the wage earner's dollar is revealed in the fact that the cost of living from 1913 to 1918 rose 30 per cent but the weekly union wage rate increased only 11 per cent, leaving the workers with a loss of 19 per cent in purchasing power. In 1918 the wage earner lost still more ground, and no improvement was experienced during the next year in spite of the substantial increase of wages. It was not until after the war that wages finally caught up with prices.

There are no data exclusively of non-union wages during the war years. Non-union earnings, as a whole, probably did not share as much advance as union wages, but non-organized workers in many trades and localities experienced a greater percentage increase in wages than the organized laborers.[23]

The earnings of workers in some specialized occupations as, for example, the manufacture of armaments, the garment industry, building of cantonments, and the like, rose as rapidly and sometimes more rapidly than did prices. In general, the advance in wages was less pronounced in other occupations. Government employees, clerical and professional workers, pensioners, and others on fixed income were the hardest hit and contributed a larger share to the cost of the war than the manual workers.

It has been estimated that in order to maintain a standard family on the level of health and decency during the years 1917 and 1918, it would have required, as an average over the country, an income be-

TABLE I[24]

Index Numbers of the Cost of Living, Weekly Wages, and Real Earnings in Union Manufacturing Industries and Building Trades 1913–1925. 1913 = 100

| Year | Cost of Living | Rates of Wages Per week Full Time | Real Earnings |
|------|---------------|-----------------------------------|---------------|
| 1913 | 99  | 99  | 100 |
| 1914 | 100 | 100 | 100 |
| 1915 | 98  | 100 | 103 |
| 1916 | 107 | 104 | 98  |
| 1917 | 129 | 110 | 87  |
| 1918 | 157 | 123 | 82  |
| 1919 | 178 | 141 | 82  |
| 1920 | 206 | 184 | 87  |
| 1921 | 177 | 190 | 108 |
| 1922 | 165 | 179 | 109 |
| 1923 | 168 | 194 | 116 |
| 1924 | 169 | 208 | 124 |
| 1925 | 173 | 215 | 126 |

tween $1,475 and $1,500. In 1920, $2,125 to $2,200 was a minimum.[25] The average annual earnings during this period made it impossible for the average worker to meet the health and decency standard. In 1917 the average annual earnings of employed wage earners in all industry was $794, in 1918—$997, in 1919—$1,144, and in 1920—$1,337.[26] The conclusion seems clear that most wage earners' income was insufficient to maintain a living standard throughout the period of the First World War. This explains why it was necessary in many cases for other members of the family, such as the wife and children, to supplement the income of the head of the family. But even with the additional help, the total income was still insufficient. This was revealed by a study conducted by the United States Bureau of Labor Statistics in 1918 of 12,750 family incomes in various parts of the United States. The average family earnings were only $1,455.[27]

The mounting cost of living during the war period and the con-comitant inadequacy of income resulted in labor's demand for a liv-ing wage. Typical of many unions, the National Brotherhood of Operative Potters approved several resolutions in 1918 demanding an increase of 25 per cent in wages for all trades.[28] The Glass Blowers Association in 1918 approved an increase from 20 to 35 per cent for workers in various grades of glass ware.[29]

A careful study of strikes throughout the war indicates the demand for higher wages was by far the most common cause for striking. The demand for increased wages alone accounted for 43.4 per cent of all the strikes in 1916, 54.9 per cent in 1917, and 51.4 per cent in 1918. The percentage of strikes having wage advances as one of the demands was as follows: 66 per cent in 1916, 63 per cent in 1917, and 66.8 per cent in 1918. It is interesting to note that although the num-ber of strikes declined in 1918, yet the demand for higher wages was greater than in 1917.[30]

The "living wage" principle, encompassing a modest comfort and health level, slowly evolved from 1917 and finally became accepted as one of the chief principles and policies which guided the National War Labor Board in its relations between management and labor. It was first enunciated in the wage arbitration case in 1917 be-tween the street railway companies and their employees in Seattle, Washington, and in Oakland, California. Health and modest comfort budgets were prepared for a standard family of five. On the basis of these budgets the arbitration boards gave their approval of the living wage.[31] After the United States was officially in the war, capital and labor agreed to maintain the prewar status in regard to industrial rela-tions. In respect to wages, this meant that prewar standards of real wages were to be maintained. This required that wages should be ad-justed at stated intervals in accordance with fluctuations in the cost of living. The wage adjustment boards in the various industries fol-lowed this principle as best they could. An exception to the main-tenance of prewar standards of real wages was evidenced in those cases where the rates of pay before the war were too low to main-tain the health and modest comfort standard. Here the cost-of-living factor was to be given only secondary consideration.

With the establishment of the National War Labor Board on April 8, 1918, the above principles were given formal sanction as the basis for wage determination for the balance of the war. The "liv-ing wage" principle was enunciated as follows: "1) The right of all workers to receive a living wage; 2) In fixing wages, the minimum rates of pay should be established which will insure a subsistence of health and reasonable comfort for the worker and his family."[32]

A study of the awards of the Board reveals that bargaining relationships and the establishment of the principle of a living wage were the two most far-reaching concepts that were effected. The principle that the worker is entitled to a living wage sufficient to maintain his family in reasonable comfort was emphasized in the Board's attempt to set up a minimum wage based upon studies of the cost of living. As the minimum wage differed with the cost of living in various localities, it did not establish an all-inclusive minimum. The decisions of the Board indicated that it believed in the principle of adjusting wages as the cost of living changed. In the majority of cases involving a demand for higher wages, it granted the request of labor. The Board met with a high degree of success in carrying out its wage awards and thus improved labor's living standards during the latter part of the war. Nevertheless, the average earnings of workers in American industry continued to be inadequate to maintain a family with a modest standard of comfort and health.

## CHAPTER THREE

# The Period of the 1920's

The signing of the Armistice in 1918 found the United States unprepared to handle the industrial problems in the transition to peace, and, as a result, much confusion and unrest occurred. A large segment of management desired to return to prewar anti-union industrial relations. Many spoke out in favor of reducing wages on the pretense that higher wages would merely add to higher prices. The Executive Council of the American Federation of Labor immediately took the following stand in respect to the position of labor on wages: Wages must be maintained and advanced at all hazards. Wages paid today are not too high, but on the contrary are still too low in many industries. To enjoy continued progress, the individual must have a higher standard of living.[1]

The wage position of the Executive Council of the AFL was further substantiated by the following recommendations of the reconstruction committee of the AFL: "1) The American standard of life must be maintained and improved. The value of wages is determined by the purchasing power of the dollar. There is no such thing as good wages when the cost of living in decency and comfort equals or exceeds the wages received. There must be no reduction in wages; in many instances wages must be increased. 2) The workers of the nation demand a living wage for all wage-earners, skilled or unskilled, a wage which will enable the worker and his family to live in health and comfort, provide a competence for illness and old age, and afford to all the opportunity of cultivating the best that is within mankind."[2]

On December 13, 1919, a conference of officers of national and international unions and representatives of farmers' organizations convened for the purpose of giving expression to the best thought of the trade union movement. A resolution was adopted which pointed out labor's grievances, opposed any reduction in the standard of living of workingmen, and denounced the belief that wages should be fixed on a cost-of-living basis. "It means putting progress in chains and liberty in fetters. It means fixing a standard of living and a standard of life and liberty which must remain fixed. America's workers can not accept that proposition. They demand a progressively advancing standard of life. . . They discard and denounce a system of fixing wages solely on the basis of family budgets and bread bills. Workers are entitled not only to a living, but modern society must provide more than what is understood by the term 'a living.' It must concede to all workers a fairer reward for their contribution to society, a contribution without which a progressing civilization is impossible."[3]

In the short postwar depression of 1920–21 a deflation of wages was temporarily adopted in spite of the opposition of organized labor. However, the greatest reduction was experienced among the unskilled workers who were largely unorganized. The average full-time weekly earnings of union labor in manufacturing industries and building trades declined from $44.10 in 1920 to $42.95 in 1922, slightly more than two per cent, while the unskilled workers suffered a drop from $25.50 to $19.38, or about three per cent.[4]

The cost of living during the 1920–21 depression also declined, dropping from 206 to 165 or 24.8 per cent. Because the decline in the cost of living was greater than that of wages a substantial gain in real wages was achieved for employed persons. However, in a wage study of twelve industries by the National Industrial Conference Board, Professor Douglas disclosed that for 1920 eleven out of the twelve industries did not pay sufficient wages to support a family at the so-called Philadelphia standard of $1,803.[5] To have attained this minimum standard would have necessitated an increase of 27 per cent in the wages of these eleven industries.[6]

In the intervening years between the postwar depression and 1930 labor's wages rose slowly. Table II depicts the average annual earnings of several selected groups of wage earners between 1921 and 1926.

The rise in the cost of living tended to swallow up the increase in yearly earnings as shown in Table II. Living costs advanced from a low of 165 in 1922 to 174 in 1926, representing about five per cent increase.

During the prosperous twenties it has been estimated that between $1,500 and $1,800 was necessary to maintain a family at a minimum standard of health and decency; between $1,100 and $1,400 to provide a minimum subsistence level; and between $2,000 and $2,400 to provide for a minimum comfort level, or the so-called American standard of living.[7]

An examination of the average annual earnings of selected groups of wage earners shows that only the workers in the building trades were able to meet the minimum health and decency standard. The average earnings of the wage earners in manufacturing, coal mining, transportation, and the average earnings of the unskilled workers were

TABLE II[8]

Average Annual Earnings of Selected Groups of Wage Earners
1921–1926

| Year | Manufacturing, Coal Mining, Transportation | Building Trades | Unskilled Workers |
|------|------|------|------|
| 1921 | $1,008 | $2,404 | $1,014 |
| 1922 | 1,027 | 2,247 | 988 |
| 1923 | 1,256 | 2,479 | 1,118 |
| 1924 | 1,196 | 2,654 | 1,132 |
| 1925 | 1,262 | 2,751 | 1,170 |
| 1926 | 1,304 | 2,933 | 1,184 |

not sufficiently large to maintain themselves above the poverty level until 1923, and in no year were these workers able to obtain the minimum comfort level. There may be some distortion in these figures due to the fact that these averages include all employees, comprising minors, women, and partly incapacitated workers. Then, too, some industries paid higher wages than others. The average annual earnings per worker for 1925 and 1926 in the following industries were: iron and steel, $1,659 and $1,687; motor vehicles, $1,652 and $1,590; petroleum refining, $1,602 and $1,587; newspaper and periodical printing, $1,859 and $1,914.[9]

In respect to labor's earnings from 1926 to 1929, Professor Douglas in his sequential study to his earlier work has expressed the real and money annual earnings relative to the 1914 base of 100. As shown in Table III, the trend of real earnings showed an improvement, registering a gain of five per cent.

The average annual earnings of employed workers in manufacturing in 1927 were $1,129 compared to $1,325 in 1928; in the railroad industry $1,627 was the average in 1927 and $1,647 in 1928; in the public utility industry the average annual earnings were $1,440 in 1927 and

$1,447 in 1928; and in the coal industry, $1,197 in 1927 and $1,239 in 1928.[10]

Although more workers were probably able to enjoy a higher standard of living during the latter part of the 1920's than in any previous period, on the whole the great mass of workers had insufficient earnings to support an average family on the minimum level of health and decency. The American standard of living was still in the distant future.

TABLE III[11]

Real Annual Earnings of American Workers, 1926–1928

| Year | Including Farm Labor | Excluding Farm Labor |
|------|----------------------|----------------------|
| 1926 | 126 | 124 |
| 1927 | 128 | 126 |
| 1928 | 132 | 130 |

THE SOCIAL WAGE DEMAND

In the mid-1920's, a period of business prosperity and rapid technological changes coupled with relatively stable living costs, organized labor began to recognize that a more aggressive philosophy and policy was required. During the 1925 and 1926 conventions of the AFL we find what is known as the "social wage" demand. This new slogan appeared to be a reaction against the cost-of-living emphasis during the war and early postwar period. In fact, this protest first appeared in a statement of the Executive Council of the AFL at the 41st annual convention of the AFL in 1921, in which it was said: "The practice of fixing wages solely on a basis of the cost of living is a violation of the whole philosophy in progress and civilization . . . what we find as a result of practice, so far as it has gone, is that there is a constant tendency under it to classify human beings and to standardize classes, each class having a presumptive right to a given quantity of various commodities . . . To measure the life possibilities of a highly civilized people in terms of yearly allowance, or so many pounds and yards of commodities, is a conception which the American labor movement can not tolerate and which it must remove from the realm of practice.[12] At this early date the AFL felt it was necessary to have further research and study before laying down a definite policy regarding wage measurement, but by 1925 the AFL came to the conclusion that productivity should be the basis for granting wages. It emphasized that "social inequality, industrial instability and injustice must increase unless the workers' real wages, the purchasing power of their wages, coupled with a continuing reduction in the number of hours making up the working day are progressed in proportion to man's increasing power of production."[13] At the 1926 Annual Convention the AFL adopted the report of the Executive Council on the productivity theory of wages. In order to augment labor's wage on the basis of labor's contribution, it recommended the need for increasing the efficiency of management and perfecting techniques for measurement of individual output.[14]

The emphasis on productivity led organized labor to a study of government statistics in order to ascertain whether labor was receiving its rightful share of the increased national income.[15] A number of studies by outstanding social scientists have been made in respect to labor's share in the national income or physical production. We shall examine the following tests: real earnings and physical product, relative value of the product and real earnings, functional distribution of the national income by shares, and labor's share of the value created by manufacturing industries.

Professor Douglas, utilizing Dr. Thomas's index of physical production in manufacturing, has compared the movement of real earnings with physical productivity per employee in all manufacturing as shown in Table IV. From 1899 to 1926 the real earnings increased 30 per cent as compared with a 54 per cent increase in productivity. In only one of the five-year periods (1914–1919) did relative real wages increase more than the physical product for the worker, and in the period 1923–1925 the physical productivity far surpassed the relative real earnings of employees.

For the remainder of the 1920's and for the depression years of the 1930's the evidence shows that there was a lag in real earnings with the rapid rise in productivity. From 1925 to 1929 output per person increased from 138.3 per cent to 149.5 per cent or about 11 per cent while average real earnings of workers in all industry advanced from 122 in 1925 to 130 in 1926 or four percent.[16]

From 1930 to 1934, according to a study of the National Bureau of Economic Research, the output per wage earner employed declined about three or four per cent while the output per man-hour increased between 25 and 30 percent.[17] Real hourly earnings in a majority of industries during the depression years showed some increase, while real weekly earnings remained fairly constant. It was in physical output that the phenomenal advances occurred. Professors Montgomery and Millis have stated that the unavoidable conclusion in comparing the movement of real earnings and physical productivity per employee in manufacturing is that: "Since the turn of the century real earnings have lagged behind physical product the greater part of the time, and in recent years this lag seems to have become greater than less."[18]

## TABLE IV[19]

### Comparative Movement of Real Earnings and Physical Productivity Per Employee in All Manufacturing

| Year | Average Annual Earnings (in dollars) | Relative Real Earnings | Relative Physical Productivity Per Employee | Percentage Divergence of Real Earnings from Physical Production |
|------|------|------|------|------|
| 1899 | 437 | 100 | 100 | 0 |
| 1904 | 496 | 101 | 110 | − 8 |
| 1909 | 548 | 106 | 117 | − 9 |
| 1914 | 631 | 106 | 116 | − 9 |
| 1919 | 1,246 | 118 | 113 | + 4 |
| 1921 | 1,236 | 117 | 117 | 0 |
| 1923 | 1,319 | 132 | 138 | − 4 |
| 1925 | 1,330 | 130 | 154 | −16 |

Another indication of the workers' share in the national income is a comparison of the relative value of the product per worker with his real earnings. Professor Douglas has made this comparison for nine major groups of manufacturing as shown in Table V.

The table indicated that not until 1925 did the relative value product per employee exceed relative real earnings. This excess of the relative real earnings over the value of the product is in marked contrast to the lag of relative real earnings to that of the relative physical product per employee, and may be accounted for by the decline of the exchange ratio of manufactured products. While there was an excess of relative real earnings to that of the value of the product per employee of 26 per cent in 1919, the margin decreased steadily in the 1920's, and by 1925 the value of the product per employee was in excess of the relative real earnings per worker. Although no comparable studies are available from 1925 to 1930, there is every reason to believe that there was a further lag in real earnings compared to the value of the product per employee.[20]

The functional distribution of the national income by share to the various claimants in the productive process is a third test of labor's progression or regression. As indicated in Table VI, page 52, labor's share of the total income produced has, on the whole, increased from 1900 to 1930.

After the First World War the percentage increase was very sharp, and although it dropped somewhat after 1921, the latter part of the 1920's showed labor's share as more than 63 per cent. However,

TABLE V[21]

Comparison of Relative Value of Product per Employee with Real Earnings for Nine Major Groups of Manufacturing (1899 = 100)

| Year | Relative Real Earnings Per Employee | Relative Value Product Per Employee | Percentage Deviation of Relative Real Earnings from Relative Value Product |
|---|---|---|---|
| 1904 | 101 | 98 | + 3 |
| 1909 | 105 | 97 | + 8 |
| 1914 | 105 | 96 | + 9 |
| 1919 | 116 | 92 | +26 |
| 1921 | 115 | 105 | +10 |
| 1923 | 128 | 121 | + 6 |
| 1925 | 125 | 126 | − 1 |

labor's increased share of the national income is attributable in part to a shift from unpaid employment to remunerative employment and to a reduction in the number of partnership and proprietorship firms. There was a corresponding increase in the number of wage earners and salaried workers as the corporation became more and more important.[22]

A fourth test of labor's share in the national income is its share of the value created by manufacturing industries. Table VII shows the distribution of the value product between wages, wages and salaries, and overhead and return to capital from 1899 to 1930.

It is of interest to note that from 1899 to 1921 labor tended to receive a slight increase in the total value product of manufacturing industry. After 1921 the opposite tendency began to be evidenced, and labor's return decreased markedly from 1925 through 1929. These conclusions were also confirmed by Professor Paul H. Douglas in an earlier study.[23] Although the percentage decline in labor's share may be attributed in part to the decrease in the number of workers employed in manufacturing during the 1920's, the percentage decline

## TABLE VI

### Relative Shares of Major Claimants in Income from Current Production of Goods and Services, 1900-1929
#### (As Percentages of Total Income Produced)

| Year | Total | Employees[a] Wages | Salaries | Individual Enterprisers[b] Total | Agric. | Non-Agric. | Investors[c] and Property Holders | Business Savings |
|------|-------|--------|----------|-------|--------|-----------|----------|---------|
| 1900 | 53.2 | | | | | | | |
| 1909 | 54.4 | 38.0 | 15.6 | 26.2 | 12.6 | 13.6 | 14.7 | 4.7 |
| 1910 | 55.8 | 38.8 | 16.0 | 24.9 | 12.6 | 12.3 | 15.4 | 3.9 |
| 1911 | 56.8 | 39.0 | 16.9 | 24.8 | 10.9 | 13.9 | 16.0 | 2.4 |
| 1912 | 55.6 | 38.3 | 16.5 | 25.2 | 11.6 | 13.6 | 15.3 | 3.9 |
| 1913 | 56.5 | 39.1 | 16.5 | 23.8 | 10.3 | 13.5 | 15.5 | 4.2 |
| 1914 | 57.4 | 38.4 | 18.0 | 25.0 | 10.5 | 14.5 | 15.8 | 1.8 |
| 1915 | 55.0 | 37.3 | 16.8 | 24.1 | 10.7 | 13.4 | 14.9 | 6.0 |
| 1916 | 51.3 | 35.7 | 14.5 | 23.9 | 10.8 | 13.1 | 13.6 | 11.2 |
| 1917 | 50.3 | 34.6 | 14.9 | 27.1 | 13.5 | 13.6 | 13.4 | 9.2 |
| 1918 | 56.9 | 36.0 | 19.8 | 27.4 | 15.3 | 12.1 | 12.2 | 3.5 |
| 1919 | 55.4 | 36.1 | 18.1 | 25.5 | 14.3 | 11.2 | 12.3 | 6.8 |
| 1920 | 62.8 | 43.9 | 17.4 | 22.8 | 11.6 | 11.2 | 12.3 | 2.1 |
| 1921 | 68.7 | 44.3 | 22.5 | 21.3 | 7.6 | 13.7 | 15.1 | −5.1 |
| 1922 | 63.3 | 41.2 | 20.2 | 20.3 | 7.8 | 12.5 | 13.6 | 2.8 |
| 1923 | 62.7 | 42.0 | 19.2 | 20.7 | 7.8 | 12.9 | 13.0 | 3.6 |
| 1924 | 63.6 | 41.5 | 20.3 | 21.1 | 8.1 | 13.0 | 13.2 | 2.1 |
| 1925 | 61.7 | 40.5 | 19.8 | 21.0 | 8.4 | 12.6 | 13.5 | 3.8 |
| 1926 | 63.8 | 41.8 | 20.5 | 19.2 | 7.1 | 12.1 | 14.1 | 2.9 |
| 1927 | 64.6 | 41.3 | 21.7 | 19.7 | 7.4 | 12.3 | 14.4 | 1.3 |
| 1928 | 63.5 | 40.4 | 22.1 | 18.9 | 6.8 | 12.1 | 14.6 | 3.0 |
| 1929 | 65.1 | 42.1 | 21.7 | 17.3 | 6.8 | 10.5 | 14.9 | 2.7 |

SOURCE: Leven, M., Moulton, H.G., Warburton, C., *America's Capacity to Consume*, The Brookings Institution, Washington, D.C., 1934, p. 158.

[a] Includes pensions, workmen's compensation, etc.

[b] Includes return on owned capital as well as "labor income" of entrepreneurs.

[c] Interest, dividends, rents, and royalties. This is the share realized. Obviously, the portion retained in business as corporate surplus also accrues to the investor.

in the number of employees was much less than the decrease in the percentage of value added to employees. Between 1919 and 1929 the decline in the number of employees was 2.3 per cent, as compared to approximately 11 per cent decline of value added to workers.[24]

TABLE VII[25]

Percentage That Wages, Salaries, Overhead, and Return to Capital Were of the Total Value Added by Manufacturers, 1899–1929

| Year | Wages | Wages and Salaries | Overhead and Return to Capital | Year | Wages | Wages and Salaries | Overhead and Return to Capital |
|------|-------|--------------------|--------------------------------|------|-------|--------------------|--------------------------------|
| 1899 | 41.6  | 49.5 | 50.5 | 1921 | 44.7 | 57.5 | 42.5 |
| 1904 | 41.5  | 50.6 | 49.4 | 1923 | 42.6 | 53.4 | 46.6 |
| 1909 | 40.2  | 51.2 | 48.8 | 1925 | 40.0 | 51.0 | 49.0 |
| 1914 | 41.3  | 54.1 | 45.9 | 1927 | 39.3 | 51.3 | 48.7 |
| 1919 | 42.4  | 53.8 | 46.2 | 1929 | 37.2 | 48.6 | 51.4 |

The conclusion of the studies on labor's share in the national income seems obvious. Although labor did increase its real earnings during the period from 1899 to the First World War and then again during the 1920's, the worker in manufacturing industries suffered a relative loss. He did not share proportionately with capital in the increased productivity, particularly during the prosperous period of the 1920's. Labor's demand for higher wages based on labor's increased contribution appears to have been well justified. Capital, rather than labor, was obtaining a larger proportionate share in the total product.

Part Three

# LABOR'S WAGE DEMANDS 1930-1953

## CHAPTER FOUR

# The AFL and CIO Federation Wage Policies

The wage policies of the AFL and CIO, the primary federations among the nation's organized workers, are significant, because they influence the decisions of their affiliated members as well as all other working groups in the society. It should be borne in mind that the economic policies formulated by these loose federations of independent and autonomous unions are not necessarily the policies that will be adopted by the affiliated unions.

## THE AFL WAGE POLICIES DURING THE

## GREAT DEPRESSION

### THE MAINTENANCE OF WAGES

A perusal of the records of the AFL during the year 1930 shows that the Federation was much concerned about the downturn in business activity and its threatening effect on wages and employment. Representatives of the AFL, railroad brotherhoods, and business gathered at the White House to express their opposition to wage cutting. The employers gave President Hoover their pledge against initiating any movement for wage reduction. The AFL went on record as saying: "This definite repudiation of wage cuts as the method of meeting business depression was a constructive achievement. It means a definite effort to maintain standards and to prevent the foundations of buying power from being completely undermined. It added a new element of security to wage earners' status. It was recognition of the principle that misfortunes of business are not to be handed over to wage earners in the form of wage deductions."[1]

With the worsening of the depression, the following program recommended by the AFL Executive Council was approved by the national convention:

> 1. Maintenance of wages—Wage levels should be maintained as a preventive measure against further deepening of the depression, as the lowering of wages would cause a competitive wage and price reduction;
> 2. Reduction of work hours—The shortening of work hours and establishment of the five day week so as to divide the available work as equitably as possible among all workers;
> 3. Stimulation of employers to hire additional workers;
> 4. Public works to create work;
> 5. Encouragement of young persons to remain in school in order to avoid competition for jobs;
> 6. Preference for workers with dependents.[2]

### AFL OPPOSES TYING WAGES TO PRICES

The AFL was disturbed in the year 1933 because of the reduction in wages of federal government employees through various economy cuts. Legislation permitted wage reductions based on lower costs of living. In an adopted resolution the AFL pointed out that the freezing of wages to the standards of any given year was contrary to the principle of the AFL that the worker shall share in all benefits flowing from social and economic progress. Wages should be adjusted to continuously rising standards.[3]

### DEMAND FOR SHORTER WORK WEEK

During the years of the Great Depression the AFL increasingly demanded a universal five-day week and a six-hour day and the maintenance of wages as the best solution to obtaining business recovery. In a resolution adopted at the 1932 convention the AFL demanded the early adoption of the 30-hour week throughout industry. "If we are to measurably match production and consumption, wages must go up and the hours of labor be progressively lessened as the only answer to the machine era in which we live. No program of social or economic reform can hope to attain success that does not embrace this economic truth as a corner-stone of its reasoning."[4]

## THE NRA EXPERIMENT

The enactment of the National Industrial Recovery Act in 1933 was welcomed by the AFL as an opportunity for labor to develop collectively industrial policies for the improvement of business. President Green strove for the inclusion of the six-hour day and the five-day week in industry codes. Equally important was the need for providing an adequate annual living wage. Wages should be raised to increase the mass purchasing power and to keep buying power ahead of living costs.[5] There should be no differentials in regional wage rates nor discrimination in wages because of color or sex.

Although the NRA gave lip service to the concept of the decent living wage, the ideal was not achieved. Nevertheless, minimum wage rates were achieved which tended to approximate the minimum of the better paying concerns in the industries. This helped to raise the total labor income and made for equality of wage rates among competing employers. Although all codes stipulated that female employees performing the same work as males should receive the same rates of pay, many codes embodied a lower rate for women workers. In respect to regional wage differentials, more than half the codes had variances in minimum wage rates in different regions or divisions of the industry. Between the North and South the average differential was 6.8 cents per hour.[6] The AFL believed that the hours of work embraced in the codes were much too long to absorb the millions out of jobs. The minimum wages were so low that purchasing power continued to lag behind production.[7]

### AFL AGAIN DEMANDS SHORT WORK-WEEK

In the year 1934 the Executive Council of the AFL reported to the membership that the achievement of prosperity necessitated a shortening of the hours of work and a substantial increase in wages. The latter was deemed necessary to provide sufficient purchasing power to accelerate the rate of production of goods and services.[8] In 1935 the AFL repeated its warning that unemployment could not be overcome unless the work week was shortened and wages increased to match the rise in productivity. At the 1935 convention of the AFL a resolution was adopted reaffirming the five-day six-hour work-week and urging its universal adoption without delay.[9]

THE EFFECT OF THE GREAT DEPRESSION AND SUBSEQUENT
RECOVERY ON LABOR 1929-1936

The Great Depression substantially weakened the AFL. Its membership declined from 2,934,000 in 1929 to 2,127,000 by 1933. Financially, its members also lost ground. As shown on Table X, page 84, average gross weekly earnings in manufacturing fell from $25.03 to $16.73 during the same period, representing a 33 per cent decline. Average gross hourly earnings in manufacturing industries dropped from .566 to .422 cents or 21 per cent. The larger decline in weekly earnings was attributable largely to part-time employment. From the standpoint of real wages, real average weekly earnings in manufacturing establishments deteriorated approximately 11 per cent, but real hourly earnings increased about three per cent. These figures clearly show that the decline in the workers' income during the Great Depression was not due so much to the reduction of wage rates but rather to the shorter work-week. Labor's total income fell from $50,904,000,000 in 1929 to $26,386,000,000 in 1933, a shrinkage of 48 per cent. According to Professors Millis and Montgomery, the decline in labor's income was caused by partial or complete unemployment rather than by low wage rates. Between the third quarter of 1929 and the first quarter of 1933 it was estimated that about 40 per cent of the wage earners in manufacturing were laid off.[10]

The recovery of business in 1933 was reflected in improvement in labor's position. AFL membership soon regained its loss from the depression years, surpassing the three million mark by 1935 and 1936. Much credit for the growth of union membership was due to the active sponsorship of labor unions by the federal government through the National Industrial Recovery Act of 1933 and the National Labor Relations Act of 1935. Hourly and weekly earnings also experienced an upward movement as revealed by Tables IX and X, pages 83–4. Average hourly earnings in manufacturing industries advanced from .442¢ to .556¢ between the years 1933 and 1936, while average weekly earnings rose from $17.05 to $21.78. Real earnings also participated in the rise as the index of consumer prices rose considerably less than did wages as depicted in Table XI, p. 85. Millis and Montgomery believe that the gain of the working classes as a whole was considerably greater than indicated by the improvement in real earnings, because a much larger number of people were employed.[11]

THE AFL AND CIO WAGE POLICY DURING THE RECESSION OF 1937–1938

Although the CIO had been in existence only one year prior to the recession of 1937–1938, nevertheless it exerted an important influence on the wage policy of the nation. Through aggressive organizing drives it made large gains in the establishment of industrial unions in the mass-production industries and by 1937 comprised almost four million members.

Both the CIO and the AFL insisted on the maintenance of wage rates during the business recession of 1937–1938. Although several of the CIO unions were not strong at this early period, they resisted attempts by employers to reduce wages. The efforts of both the AFL and CIO to maintain wages appeared successful. Average hourly manufacturing wages were .624¢ in 1937, .627¢ in 1938, and increased to .633¢ in 1939. Average weekly earnings dropped from $24.05 in 1937 to $22.30 in 1928, but by 1939 they rose to $23.86. Although the consumer price index declined, weekly earnings dropped more, resulting in some loss of purchasing power to the wage earner.

In a resolution adopted at the first constitutional convention of the CIO in 1938, the organization gave itself credit for its successful efforts to maintain wage rates. It pledged itself to continue to insist upon the maintenance and improvement of wage rates.[12]

The purchasing power doctrine of wages was expressed during the early history of the CIO. President John L. Lewis in his report to the first CIO convention said: "Full production in the modern economy is based on effective consuming power. Consuming power must at all times be able to absorb the full product of our economy. Broadly speaking it is the lack of adjustment between consuming power and productive capacity which brings us face to face with the paradox of plenty on the one hand, and on the other, people ill housed, ill clothed and ill fed."[13]

The CIO in common with the AFL opposed the principle of relating wages to the cost of living because of labor's inadequate standard of living. In support of an adopted resolution against basing wages on living costs, John L. Lewis stressed the tenet of wages based on increased productivity.[14]

At the 1938 AFL convention the Federation reiterated its endorsement of the 30-hour week. Its insistence on the shortening of the work week during a time when weekly wages had shrunken rested on the continued increase in productivity and the need to absorb the unemployed into jobs.[15]

## WAGE POLICIES DURING THE
### DEFENSE PROGRAM

The stimulus to business through the defense program in 1939 was soon reflected in wages. Hourly wages rates in manufacturing increased from .627¢ from 1938 to .661¢ in 1940 while weekly earnings rose from $22.30 to $25.20. As consumer prices remained almost stationary, there was a substantial gain in real wages. Notwithstanding the improvement in the workingman's position, the AFL and CIO were not satisfied. The AFL purported to show that the majority of American wage earners do not earn enough to support a family at an adequate living standard. Budget studies cited by the federation revealed that it took about a 70¢ hourly wage and a working week of 40 hours throughout the year to support a family of four at a bare subsistence level and a $1 hourly wage with a 40-hour work week to support a family of five at a health and efficiency standard.

Other arguments employed by the AFL in its drive for higher wages included the ability to pay and labor's failure to share equitably in the increased productivity of the economy. It pointed out that many businesses were earning exceptional profits through enhanced productivity and the stimulus of the defense program. Companies participating in defense production could well afford to pay $1 hourly wage. The affiliated unions were urged to study the financial reports of those companies with which they had contracts, and to work out a program whereby their members receive a just part of the increased income resulting from greater productivity. Cooperation between the workers and management was stressed. Formal committees were suggested as a proper means of increasing efficiency in order that there be a larger income to be divided between the employers and the employees.[16]

The AFL Executive Council in its report to the annual convention of the Federation in 1941 repeated its stand on wage increases: "Wage earners base their demands for increased wages upon a justified claim to share in increased productivity and increased income which has been created by the production expansion developments arising out of the application of the defense program. Increasing productivity, savings in production costs, reduced unit selling costs, economies which accompany expanding production all along the line have made it possible in general to pay higher wages without reducing individual profits."[17]

Through President Philip Murray's 1941 report to the federation the CIO demanded an increased share in the national income. The report stated: "Underlying the economic policy of the CIO and its affiliates has been the fundamental conviction that the working people of the nation should receive a greater share of the national income. The vigor and success of the CIO has grown from its steadfast adherence to this principle . . . The CIO policy must continue to be based upon securing for the working people an increased share of the national income. This policy enforced by all possible efforts to expand national production to a maximum is essential to the maintenance of national morale and the attainment of maximum industrial output . . .[18]

### THE AFL AND CIO POSITION ON WAGES DURING WORLD WAR II

Upon entrance of the United States in the Second World War the Executive Council of the AFL issued the following statement on wages: "Wage policy in wartime requires . . . that workers be treated fairly and justly in comparison with other groups in American society. If the income of farmers and business men is permitted to increase, then similarly workers' wages must be permitted to increase. If workers are required to sacrifice the wage gains they would secure in normal times, then equal sacrifices must be required of other groups.

. . . Every effort must be made to level up wages of lower income groups. This has a double purpose: to provide an adequate living standard and to prevent wage inequalities in different plants from causing pirating or migration of workers from one plant to another."[19]

The Executive Council placed much emphasis on the raising of the workers' living standards through higher wages. It justified its demand on the ground that: 1) war production would be enhanced because of the improved physical and psychological condition of the worker; 2) the worker would be enabled to purchase war bonds which would provide needed purchasing power for business prosperity after the termination of the war.[20] The "saving" concept of wages was therefore another rationalization for increased wages.

The CIO position on wages in a war economy, like that of the AFL, was intransigent in demanding fair treatment of the workers compared with other groups in the society. With the establishment of the National War Labor Board and its jurisdiction over wages, the CIO unions brought to the attention of the Board the need for an upward adjustment of wages due to increased living costs and the raising of sub-standard wages.[21]

An examination of earnings during the years 1940 to 1942 reveals that average hourly earnings in manufacturing establishments rose from .661¢ in 1940 to .853¢ in 1942, representing a 29 per cent increase. Weekly earnings advanced during the same period from $25.20 to $36.65 or 45 per cent. The much larger gain in weekly earnings was due to the longer work-week with its accompanying overtime rates. Although consumers' prices rose substantially, both real hourly and weekly earnings showed marked gains. The former increased about 11 per cent, while the latter advanced 25 per cent.

In spite of the economic improvement in labor's status, the AFL continued to press for higher wages. In support of its demands it cited the results of a study of workers' annual incomes by the OPA in 1942. The report indicated that nearly two-thirds of all non-farm families receive less than $2,500 and 29 per cent of this number receive less than $1,500. On the other hand, budgetary studies of the Heller Committee of the University of California showed that a yearly income of $2,500 was essential for an industrial wage earner to maintain his family at a minimum standard of health and efficient living. The AFL Executive Council stated: "Until wage rates are lifted to a much higher level, the vast majority of workers' families must live on a very inadequate budget in normal times."[22]

When the War Production Board requested union management cooperation at the beginning of the war as a means of stimulating greater production, the AFL immediately indicated its approval. While the principle of union-management cooperation had been endorsed by the AFL since 1923, it had not been welcomed by management, on the whole. The Federation believed that the war program presented an opportunity to build up a democratic structure in industry which would carry over into the postwar years. In a resolution unanimously approved at the 1942 convention the AFL urged every union to exercise its fullest efforts in the establishment of labor-management committees in companies with which they had collective agreements.[23]

The CIO strongly advocated its "Industry Council Plan" as a means of promoting the defense effort. The plan would create industry councils in each basic industry to deal with problems of production and labor relations. Each council would consist of an equal number of representatives of employers and employees with a government representative to act as chairman. A central policy-making board would be established to coordinate the work and plans of the councils. The CIO believed that the "Industry Council Plan" would be valuable in preventing unemployment after the war: "by providing the means for economic planning, for pooling the nation's productive brains, and for giving labor its full place in our industrial setup."[24] Government and industry appeared cool to the CIO plan, and it won little following outside the CIO.

With the establishment of price controls in the summer of 1942 it became obvious to both the AFL and the CIO that wage controls would be necessary. In July 1942 President Green presented to the President of the United States the following declaration on wages and inflation and an accompanying program of inflation control: "Every American working for wages is personally and vitally concerned in the nation's effort to avert inflation. Every wage earner is equally concerned in the nation's wage policy and the effect of this policy on the workers' contribution to maximum war production. Every American worker will do his very utmost to help his country win. But he will insist that our common sacrifice be equal, fair and just."[25]

The inflation control program to achieve this goal should include:

1. Wage adjustment through collective bargaining except that covered by wage stabilization agreements;
2. Voluntary wage stabilization agreements in key industries;
3. Establishment of a wage policy commission to coordinate and unify wage policies;
4. Payment of wage increases in war bonds to be cashable after the war;
5. A fiscal control program built around taxation of excess profits, progressive income taxation, and the voluntary purchase of war bonds;
6. Effective price control and rationing;
7. Control of costs on war contracts.[26]

The Federation criticized the inflation control program of the President of the United States for its failure in regard to the principle of equal sacrifice. It felt that wages were the only return effectively subject to control.

Concerning the CIO's stand, President Murray in his report to the 1943 convention pointed out the following needed adjustments to the national wage policy:

1. Government commitment to roll back prices to the level of September 15, 1942, or make up the price level difference by adjustment of wage rates;
2. Authority granted to the War Labor Board to make necessary wage adjustments in order to eliminate inequalities in wage rates;
3. Equal pay for similar work.[27]

The CIO criticized the national wage policy for its inequitable treatment of labor. Special interests had prevented effective steps to stabilize the economy. Wages had been frozen, but Congress refused to curb profits. Congress had impeded and prevented effective control over prices.[28]

THE FEDERATION'S OPPOSITION TO THE
"LITTLE STEEL FORMULA"

Although Congress directed the President of the United States to stabilize wages on October 2, 1942, it was not until the spring of 1943 that effective wage stabilization was instigated through the President's hold-the-line executive order. In implementing the President's order the National War Labor Board issued the "Little Steel Formula" in May 1943 which became the measuring rod for all wage problems. Under the formula the Board approved general wage increases of 15 per cent over straight-time wage rates on January 1, 1941. The Board was permitted some flexibility in order to correct for inequalities in wages within industries and plants, to deal with substandard wages, and to make for the effective prosecution of the war.

At the 1943 conventions of the AFL and CIO resolutions were adopted voicing opposition to the "Little Steel Formula," because it reduced the standard of living of the workers and increased the profits of business. The AFL demanded either the abolition of the formula or its modification to permit wages to be increased from 15 per cent to 25 per cent above the levels of January 1941. The CIO demanded the outright elimination of the "Little Steel Formula" and the restoration of collective bargaining. Other demands included the lifting of substandard wage rates to minimum levels of decency, a vigorous price control and rationing policy, and a program of equitable taxation.[29]

The AFL Executive Council reported to the membership in 1944 that the wage freeze was holding wage rates at a dangerously low

level. With advancing living costs, hourly wage rates were not sufficient to support most American workers at a decent standard of living. Citing the War Labor Board's study of straight-time average
hourly earnings of January 1944, the Executive Council emphasized
that 25 million workers, or 92 per cent of all employed in private
industry received less than $1.30 an hour, and 16,600,000 or 60 per
cent received less than 85 cents an hour. The Council believed that
$1.30 an hour or $52.00 for a 40-hour week was the minimum amount
necessary to support a worker and his family in health and efficiency,
and 85 cents an hour or $34.00 a week was the minimum for bare exis-
tence. The Heller Committee budget for 1944 required $52.15 per
week or $2,712 a year to support a family of four at a minimum health
and decency standard.[30] As shown on Tables IX and X, pp. 83–4,
both hourly and weekly manufacturing wages failed to reach this
standard in 1944. Average hourly earnings were $1.019, and weekly
earnings $46.08.

The AFL thought that the low wage levels were of further significance to the nation, because 1) the workers and their families after
the war would be condemned to live at poverty levels as no appreciable reduction in living costs could be expected; 2) consumer buying power would not be sufficient to maintain full production and employment.[31] The following report of the AFL Executive Council was
unanimously adopted at the 1944 annual convention of the Federation: "The American Federation of Labor has a definite part to play
in the national effort to bring full production and full employment.
Our task is to see that wage rates are high enough to provide a good
living and furnish the necessary buying power, which alone can make
full production possible. . . . Substantial wage increases for all union
members must be secured. But our task will not be ended there.
Millions of low paid, unorganized workers must also have their wages
raised. Full production and full employment will not be possible
unless they too receive very substantially higher wages. To secure
the necessary wage increases throughout industry we commend the
following program:

1. That all unions affiliated with AFL make a concerted drive
for wage increases for all workers;
2. That the necessary legislative action be taken to raise substantially the wage floor provided in the Fair Labor Standards
Act;

3. That a concerted drive under Federation leadership be carried out during the coming year to assist international unions in organizing workers in their jurisdictions in the low paid industries and in raising their pay; and where there are no international unions having jurisdiction that the workers be organized in federal unions and the necessary wage increases secured."[32]

During the year 1944 the CIO and its affiliated unions were busy prosecuting cases before the National War Labor Board to obtain adjustments in wages beyond the limits of the "Little Steel Formula," to eliminate substandard wages and the wage bracket system, to demand the guaranteed annual wage, etc. The most outstanding case from the point of view of its ramifications was that of the United Steelworkers of America and the steel industry. President Murray and other representatives of the CIO and the United Steelworkers emphasized the injustice that had been dealt to labor through the wage freeze. The precipitous rise in the cost of living because of an inadequate stabilization program had destroyed the peacetime standard of the workers. On the other hand, corporation profits had soared through an inadequate taxation system. It was important that wage adjustments be granted not only to restore real wage standards but also to avoid disaster at the termination of the war. The cutback and cancellation of war contracts would sharply reduce the purchasing power of the wage earners. The raising of wages would assure the continued mass purchasing power necessary to encourage the production of peacetime goods. Mr. Murray requested that the Board grant the principle of the guaranteed annual wage as a necessary step for full employment. If the worker were able to figure his income in yearly terms, the mass purchasing power which is necessary for increasing prosperity would be assured.[33]

Growing pressure for a modification of the "Little Steel Formula" caused the National War Labor Board to appoint a special panel to hear the AFL arguments. Secretary-Treasurer Meany presented the AFL case. He declared the wage freeze a great injustice to labor because consumer prices were never controlled. He alleged that living costs had risen more than 15 per cent since the adoption of the "Little Steel Formula," that there were many deficiencies in the B.L.S. consumers' price index, and that consequently prices were considerably higher than revealed by the index. He urged the Board to request the President to modify the formula to the more realistic conditions existing in the year 1944. The Federation felt that the President should permit employers to apply for an increase in wages without the Board's approval.[34]

In October 1944 the AFL members of the Board introduced a resolution that the Board request the President to issue an executive order to adjust the "Little Steel Formula" in keeping with the increased cost of living and to permit management and labor to make adjustments in wages by voluntary agreement and without permission of the Board. The resolution was defeated, as the majority of the Board felt they had insufficient data on the effects of a modification of the "Little Steel Formula" on the national economy. However, the Board did adopt a resolution to submit to the President through the Economic Stabilization Director a report setting forth data in respect to the relationship of wages to the cost of living, and an appraisal of the nature and extent of inequities in wages.

The labor members of the Board, angered by this action, issued a statement: "It is an admission by the public members of the Board that they are not competent to perform their duties. They are specifically charged with the responsibility of administering the wage policy of the government, and they ought to be in a better position than any other single group of men in the country to have informed opinions as to any necessary changes in the country's wage policy. . . . . The only conclusion we can draw on the action of the Board today is that it deems that no change in the 'Little Steel Formula' should be recommended."[35]

A resolution was approved at the 1944 convention of the AFL that President Green appoint a committee to call upon the President of the United States and request him to issue an executive order to adjust the "Little Steel Formula" to correspond to the increased cost of living and to permit labor and management to put into effect the new policy without submission to the Board. The CIO in convention in November 1944 adopted a resolution condemning the action of the National War Labor Board in its refusal to: 1) submit a recommendation to the President for a revision of the "Little Steel Formula," 2) eliminate the abominable wage bracket system, 3) raise minimum rates of pay in order to correct substandard wages.[36]

Although the AFL and CIO were not successful in breaking the "Little Steel Formula," they asserted that their members on the National War Labor Board did help to bring about more flexibility in the Board's wage policies. For example, on February 21, 1945, the Board approved a minimum rate of 55 cents per hour to correct substandards of living in the textile industry. This rate was later generalized to all employees without the Board's approval. On March 8, 1945, the Board was given authority by the Economic Stabilization Director to approve certain non-basic wage adjustments. Shortly, these adjustments were liberalized to include: vacations of one week after one year's service and two weeks after five years' service; shift differentials; reclassifications and job evaluations; adjustments in wages in accordance with industry or area practice.[37]

### AFL AND CIO WAGE POLICY DURING THE POSTWAR PERIOD

With the termination of the National War Labor Board in December 1945, the wage stabilization functions were transferred to the National Wage Stabilization Board. By executive order, wage or salary increases could be made lawful without government approval, except in the building construction industry and agriculture. Employers desiring price relief to meet increased labor costs were permitted to apply to the Wage Stabilization Board. If the petition was rejected, the applicant could apply to the OPA after a period of six months. The following new basis was established for the approval of voluntary increases in wages: 1) increases necessary to bring wages up to prevailing rates in the industry or area; 2) increases necessary to bring rates up to a point where the average earnings of workers in an appropriate unit would be 33 per cent above average earnings of January 1941.

In February 1946 the President issued Executive Order 9697 which established a new principle in the wage stabilization program, namely, the "general pattern standard." Under this principle wage increases made in accordance with a government recommendation in a wage controversy may be applied to other companies in the industry. Where no "general pattern" was available as a guide, the order provided for the approval of wage increases which were necessary to correct wage or salary inequities, substandard wages or salary conditions, or disparities between the cost of living and wages. Wage adjustments not affecting price ceilings or increased costs to the government still remained free of government control. Any employer who desired to use a wage increase as a basis for a price increase was required to seek approval of the Board.

The AFL Board members opposed the new "general pattern standard." They believed that the government's wage policy reflected a general wage pattern only for those workers who were on strike and closed the door on millions of workers who would rather follow the orderly procedure of collective bargaining. A wage policy should provide for equity of treatment for all workers in all industries.[38]

The Federation at its 1946 convention severely criticized the government's wage policy as unduly interfering with free collective bargaining, as employers were given an unfair advantage by making collective bargaining agreements contingent upon receiving approval of price relief. The Federation declared that a premium was placed on strikes. The tying of wages to prices was considered highly inflationary and denied workers the benefits of wage increases. Resolutions were approved, reaffirming the AFL belief in collective bargaining, and requesting the President to revoke Executive Order 9697 and to remove the Wage Stabilization Board and the Wage Adjustment Board.[39]

The AFL Executive Council's report to the Federation in 1946 emphasized the need for higher wages to restore prewar living standards. The Heller Committee budget for industrial families in June 1946 revealed that $3,079 yearly income was necessary to support a family on a minimum level of health and efficiency. To achieve this income a worker should receive $1.50 an hour which would be equivalent to $60 for a 40-hour week. Despite substantial wage raises during the first half of 1946 the workers' average take-home pay in the heavy industries was lower than under the wage freeze in 1943 and 14 per cent below the wartime peak.

The report concluded with the following statement on wage policy: "With the year's rapid price increases there is grave doubt whether workers' buying power is adequate to maintain industrial production at full employment levels. . . . Progress for workers and all others requires that wage increases be paid for by increasing output per man hour. Where collective bargaining exists and a relationship of square dealing and good faith has developed between management and union, cooperation of the two groups to promote efficiency and increase production per man hour will contribute greatly to the progress of both. Such cooperation should lead to a genuine partnership between management and workers, to the end that the income to pay wage increases will be created, wages will be increased and workers will receive a just and equitable division of profits that accrue from the wealth they produce."[40]

The CIO postwar policy was similar to that of the AFL in demanding substantial wage increases to preserve the living standards of the workers and to increase their purchasing power. The spiraling of prices following their decontrol deteriorated the living standards of employees, while, on the other hand, profits had continued to soar. The following resolution approved at the 1946 convention is indicative of the CIO postwar wage policy: "Under present conditions it is imperative that American industry in collective bargaining give substantial wage increases. Our people must have sustained purchasing power and a decent living wage to avert the swift economic tragedy which now confronts us. This is the important task for CIO unions in their approaching collective bargaining conferences."[41]

The CIO recognized that security was of equal importance to wages. Security against ill health in the form of health and hospitalization insurance, security against old age through adequate pensions, and security against loss of job through the guaranteed annual wage was a protection enjoyed by relatively few people. In an unanimously adopted resolution at the 1946 convention the CIO went on record to develop immediately a broad social security program through collective bargaining in order to provide for adequate pensions, health and hospitalization plans, group insurance programs and guaranteed annual wage.[42] Again in 1947 and 1948, the CIO emphasized that collective bargaining must remain the workers' primary bulwark against insecurity. It resolved to intensify collective bargaining in order to bring to its members a coordinated program of security and economic benefits and urged the affiliated unions to embark on a vigorous campaign to secure pensions, health and welfare benefits.[43]

President Murray in 1948 was dissatisfied with labor's gains since the end of the war. In spite of three rounds of wage increases the income of the workers had not kept pace with rising prices. Real earnings were now only 30 per cent greater than in 1939, while profits had increased over 400 per cent and industrial production 80 per cent. He believed that the trade union movement must fight more aggressively on the political front to elect a Congress whose objective would be to promote a full-production and a full-employment economy. At the same time the CIO's efforts must not lag on the industrial front. The CIO must pledge itself to the achievement of a strong and powerful trade union movement which would forge ahead simultaneously on both fronts.[44] In a resolution passed at the 1948 convention the CIO approved Mr. Murray's wage policy as follows: "1) The CIO reaffirms as one of its basic and fundamental tenets the ever improving standard of living of American workers; and that

2) we declare that it is the continual objective of the CIO to build a high consumption level economy wherein wage earners' real income is continually increasing; and that 3) it is essential in a dynamic economy for wages to be ever increasing and for the wage segment of our national income to be enlarging through taking a greater share of an ever increasing national income; and that 4) it is possible for wages to increase and living standards to improve within the framework of a reasonable profit structure for American Industry."[45]

The CIO pledged itself to build a stronger trade union movement by continuing to organize the unorganized workers. It empowered the National Executive Board to investigate and to take appropriate action of affiliates that had failed to bring about effective organization of the workers within their jurisdictions.[46]

The year 1949 was historic for the CIO and the entire labor movement. The CIO United Steelworkers of America went on strike against the steel companies for their refusal to accept a pension and security program recommended by the President's fact-finding board. From the standpoint of the CIO, the steelworkers were fighting to end the double standard which provided large pensions on a non-contributory basis to the steel executives while refusing modest pensions to the workers. The CIO pledged the United Steelworkers and the members on strike its moral, organizational and financial support in the strike.[47]

At the 1949 convention the CIO reiterated its stand on the question of security and wages of the workers. In respect to security, it resolved that as long as the government social security program failed to meet standards of adequacy it was necessary for unions to bargain collectively to supplement the government security benefits. It affirmed that security protection is a legitimate cost of doing business and must be financed entirely by employer contributions. As to wages, the CIO repeated its belief that a disproportionately large share of the national income was going to business and a lesser portion to the wage and salary earners. Since the achievement of full employment results in improved living standards, it pledged that its continual objective must be to increase the share of national income going to the wage earner.[48]

In conclusion, the AFL and CIO wage policy which emerged at the termination of the war on VJ Day and which continued throughout the postwar period was aimed at substantially higher wages and fringe benefits in the form of welfare payments. The CIO was much more outspoken and aggressive in its demands for social security programs than the AFL. The federations justified their demands, to wit:

1. The obligation to maintain take-home pay as overtime declined and as workers were downgraded and transferred to lower paid jobs;
2. The need for wage earnings to keep pace with rising prices;
3. "Ability to pay" as measured by excess profits;
4. The increased productivity of the worker and his declining share in the national income;
5. The necessity to raise the purchasing power of the workers in order to prevent a depression.

Social security was a cardinal principle in the program of the CIO. As long as the government was derelict in providing adequate protection against the vicissitudes of life, it was felt that management must assume these legitimate business costs. Although the CIO went on record for an immediate social security program in 1946 through collective bargaining, it was not until 1949 that it forced its demands through the use of the strike. In previous postwar years, 1946-1949, higher wages were given priority, but with the downturn in business in 1949 and the concomitant lowering of living costs, fringe benefits gained ascendancy. The guaranteed annual wage, first demanded during the latter part of the war, continued to be pressed by the CIO. Meeting opposition by business, the CIO was willing to settle for other gains.

An examination of wage earnings, living costs, corporation profits, and the distribution of the national income reveals propriety in the AFL and CIO demands. Although average hourly wages in manufacturing establishments rose from $1.023 in 1945 to $1.401 in 1949 and average weekly earnings increased from $44.39 to $54.92, the abrupt rise in consumer prices largely erased labor's gains as shown on Table XI, p. 85. Table X, p. 84, shows that the termination of the war with its loss in overtime work had an adverse effect on weekly take-home pay. The decrement among the heavy industries was considerably greater than in others, as could be expected. Table XII, p. 86, indicates that labor's share in the national income remained quite stable fluctuating from 58.9 per cent in 1945 to a high of 60.8 per cent in 1947, then declining to 59.1 per cent in 1948, but rising to 60.6 per cent by 1949. Corporate profits, on the other hand, enjoyed the largest gain in the distributive process. Obtaining 13.2 per cent of the private national income in 1945, they dropped sharply to 11.6 per cent in 1946, but thereafter rose abruptly to 15.6 per cent in 1948 and 1949. It appears that organized labor had some justification for demanding a larger share of the national income, but the landowner and the lender of capital likewise had a grievance.

### AFL AND CIO WAGE POLICY DURING THE KOREAN WAR

With the outbreak of the Korean hostilities the Executive Council of the AFL took the position that price controls of some sort were necessary but protested against wage controls. If events proved that wage controls were needed, they should be flexible, permitting adjustments for wage inequities, rising living costs, and increases in productivity. In a resolution adopted at the 1950 convention the Federation emphatically rejected any rigid wage formula which would tie wages to the cost of living. Another resolution that was approved urged Congress to amend the Fair Labor Standards Act increasing the minimum wage from 75¢ to $1.00 and extending the coverage of the Act to exempt workers.[49]

The CIO through its President, Mr. Murray, opposed the Defense Production Act. He believed that the Act's provision for price controls on defense items and simultaneous regulation of wages was both inequitable and unworkable. The establishment of price controls on vital defense products would freeze the wages of the workers manufacturing the products while at the same time the cost of living would be permitted to rise.[50]

At its 1950 convention the CIO approved a resolution strengthening the Wages-Hour and Public Contracts Act. Like the AFL, it believed that the minimum wage should be raised to $1.00, and that all exempt workers should receive coverage. In addition, the officers of the CIO were directed to restore the overtime provisions of the Act and to work for amendment or enactment of state wage-hour laws so as to bring them in line with federal standards. In respect to the Public Contracts Act, the CIO and its affiliated unions were requested to continue to oppose the efforts of a minority group of employers to: 1) repeal the Act, or 2) to limit its application, and 3) to demand that the Act be applied to all purchasers under the ECA or any other economic and military assistance program.[51]

The CIO during 1950 restated its postwar stand on wages, working conditions and security. The following resolution declared: "The CIO and its affiliated unions will vigorously pursue their objectives of continual improvement in wages, working conditions and security of the American workers. The CIO dedicates itself to further improving the wage standards and real earnings of American workers through the narrowing of the growing inequity between wages and profits."[52]

On January 11, 1951, representatives of the AFL, CIO, and railway brotherhoods presented a joint labor policy statement to the Wage Stabilization Board on the question of wage controls. The statement emphasized the importance of preserving collective bargaining as the basis of wage stabilization, the need for an effective inflation control program, allowing cost-of-living and productivity wage adjustments, the correction of wage inequities, and the raising of substandard wages.

On January 25, 1951, general price and wage controls were invoked followed by a series of general regulations clarifying and amending the general freeze. General wage regulation no. 6 caused a unanimous dissent of labor. This regulation limited general wage increases to 10 per cent above the wage levels of January 15, 1950. All wage increases negotiated since that time were to be offset against the 10 per cent allowance. The cost of fringe benefits which might be negotiated after January 25, 1951, also had to be balanced against the allowable wage increase. The adoption of this regulation precipitated the resignation of the labor members from the Board in protest against the inequities in the wage freeze formula. Their objections were:

1. The formula would invalidate many existing agreements,
2. It disregarded the effects of the increased cost of living on wages;
3. The inclusion of the cost of fringe benefits was unworkable, because most of these costs cannot be accurately measured in advance;
4. The regulation did not include adjustments for inequities.

An executive order by the President on April 21, 1951, reconstituted a new wage stabilization and disputes board which was acceptable to labor. Regulations were soon adopted which modified the previous ones. The permission to negotiate certain fringe benefits and cost-of-living allowances outside the limits of the 10 per cent wage formula was welcomed by labor. Other changes which were later approved comprised: corrections for inter-plant and intra-plant inequities, equal pay for equal work, pension and profit-sharing plans.

In spite of the new wage policies, the CIO and AFL were not satisfied with the wage stabilization program. The CIO charged the Board with delinquency in developing policies on many neglected benefits, with the result that thousands of petitions for approval of collective bargaining agreements had been pending for months. Permission for workers to share in the benefits of increased productivity was withheld. The federations believed that wage stabilization should not be used to deny the benefits obtained through collective bargaining; wage stabilization should not mean wage freezing. Finally, the CIO scored the unequal sacrifice in the defense effort. It felt that businessmen, landlords, and farmers had profited at the expense of labor through inadequate price control legislation.[53] The Executive Council of the AFL issued a warning to Congress in January 1952 that labor would refuse to cooperate with the wage stabilization program unless price controls were strengthened and the cost of living kept down.[54]

During 1952 the AFL laid much stress on basing wage increases on productivity. The Wage Stabilization Board's policy of approving wage increases on the cost-of-living principle was held unfair as it did not guarantee a worker maintenance of his former standard of living because of high taxes and other burdens of the defense program. Capital, in turn, was enjoying a larger share in the fruits of the expanding national product.[55] On June 4, 1952, Boris Shishkin, AFL economist, appearing before the Wage Stabilization Board demanded an immediate approval of 11 per cent increase in wages for all workers. His plea was based on the gains in productivity during the past two years. A productivity increase in wages would not be inflationary, he said, because it is a reflection of more efficiency with resulting higher output.[56]

The AFL Executive Council in its report to the Federation in September 1952, reiterated the demand for productivity wage increases. "It is essential that our country realize its full productive potential and that we do everything possible to increase our productivity and assure equitable distribution of its benefits. It is in increased productivity and in fair distribution of its fruits that lies the secret of our industrial strength and power, and is the greatest factor in constantly improving the living standard of the American people.

. . . "It is essential for workers to know that they will share fully and fairly in the gains resulting from increased productivity so that their full effort can be contributed to it. Present wage stabilization regulations however have prevented workers from increasing their wages proportionately with their increase in productivity. For while production per man is now rising at the rate of 5½ per cent per year, workers' real wages per man hour have risen on the average only slightly more than one per cent per year during the wage stabilization period."[57]

An examination of Table XI, p. 85, shows that labor made meager gains in real earnings during the years 1951 and 1952. Although average hourly and weekly manufacturing wages rose considerably, real wages advanced approximately three per cent. It would appear that the AFL and CIO had grounds for complaint against the wage stabilization policy.

With the suspension of wage controls on February 6, 1953, a return to free collective bargaining once more became the pattern for wage determination. Shortly, the AFL called upon its affiliated unions to press for higher wages to keep pace with rising productivity. It warned that a business slump would be inevitable unless the purchasing power of the wage earner was increased. President Meany of the AFL pointed out that from 1949 through 1952 productivity in the United States had risen 13.2 per cent but real factory wages had advanced only seven per cent. Substantial wage increases were demanded at once to make up for this lag. The Federation called on the membership for political action to elect friends of labor to Congress in 1954, in order to help labor get its fair share of the product it produces. An improved educational program was launched to help the public to recognize that the objectives of labor are beneficial to all.[58]

The AFL made substantial progress during 1953 securing wage increases ranging from five cents to fifteen cents or more and improvements in health and welfare plans, vacations and premium pay and other miscellaneous fringe benefits. The AFL Executive Council felt further wage gains were needed, because of the improvement in productivity, the need of greater purchasing power to sustain business activity, and the failure of most factory workers to meet the Bureau of Labor Statistics "modest but adequate" standard of living. Although the average gross weekly earnings of factory workers rose to $72.04

by June 1953, the real net spendable earnings (after the deduction of price rises and taxes) for a worker with three dependents were only $34.67. According to the BLS estimate, the average city worker with three dependents needed $82.21 a week in June 1953 to provide a "modest but adequate" living standard.[59]

The CIO during 1953 also emphasized basing wages on productivity. This was revealed in the negotiations of the United Automobile Workers and the United Steelworkers. The purchasing power argument, so often used in the past, was reaffirmed by the CIO in 1953. President Reuther in his New Year's statement said: "The philosophy of economic scarcity—'too little and too late'—must yield to the broad concept of an ever expanding productivity capacity geared to the full development of our natural resources. In large measure, the relationship between labor and management will determine the future growth of the American economy, for collective bargaining is the important area in which decisions need to be made to bring purchasing power in balance with our productive power."[60]

An editorial in the January 5, 1952, *CIO News*, "What's Ahead in the Next Four Years," points out that the hopes of continued prosperity lie in increasing the capacity of the American public to buy what the factories produce. Collective bargaining and public policy were enumerated among the six methods to achieve this goal. Higher wages should be sought which exceed the annual productivity gains. This would mean reducing the portion of the high profits now being used for industrial expansion and high dividends.[61]

Improved health and social security provisions in labor contracts were an integral part of the CIO wage program during 1952-1953. On February 2, 1953, Walter Reuther initiated a movement for the improvement of health and social security provisions in collective bargaining contracts of CIO affiliates. The CIO would make this drive, he stated, "in the knowledge that gains on the industrial front through collective bargaining in these vital areas will benefit all citizens who need protection from the hazards of illness, unemployment, and old age."[62] The guaranteed wage became one of the major objectives of the CIO in 1952 and has become increasingly more important during the last two years. At both 1952 and 1953 annual conventions the CIO pledged itself to support its member unions in their negotiation of guaranteed annual wage agreements and to call upon management to recognize its responsibility to formulate plans for guaranteeing workers needed security.[63] The CIO approach to the guaranteed annual wage is being based currently on the following arguments:

1. It will help assure continuing full employment and full production in peacetime;
2. It will stimulate business to find ways to reduce unemployment thereby promoting stability in the economy;
3. The cost of wage guarantees to the employer can be reduced through offsets against unemployment insurance and by limiting the guarantee to the employers' contributions to the guaranteed fund. The CIO believes that with constructive business planning, wise government policies to provide full employment and improved unemployment insurance, the guaranteed wage would not be too costly to the employer;
4. The guaranteed wage will improve the well-being and morale of the workers. When people are working they can plan their purchases in advance without worry about the next week's paycheck and installment payments. When workers are laid off, they will be able to maintain their living standards for a much longer period.[64]

### CONCLUSIONS

During the Korean War 1950-1953 the AFL and CIO opposed the freezing of wages, although acknowledging the necessity for wage controls provided they were flexible. The government disregarded labor's demands by freezing wages on January 25, 1951, and failed to develop an effective inflation control program and to allow for flexibility in wage adjustments. The labor representatives of the Wage Stabilization Board resigned in protest against the stabilization program, but the appointment of a new Board resulted in modification of regulations. A more flexible government wage policy pacified labor for the time being. Dissatisfaction soon arose because:

1. The Board held up for a long period the petitions of labor for approval of collective bargaining contracts;
2. The Board refused to grant workers a share in increased productivity;
3. The government failed to stabilize the whole economy.

Both the AFL and CIO felt that labor was bearing the brunt of the defense effort. While businessmen, landlords, and farmers had prospered, the standard of living of the workers had deteriorated. Labor seemed to have a case in its demand for a more just government wage policy. Although the real earnings of labor increased slightly from 1949 to 1953, profits enjoyed a phenomenal advance.

The tactics or arguments employed by the federations during the three-year period to reinforce their wage demands varied somewhat. While prices were abruptly rising during the early part of the defense program, much stress was laid on the cost of living and ability to pay. Minor emphasis was given to adjustment of wage inequities and to productivity, the raising of substandard wages, and the allowance of fringe benefits.

With the threatened downturn of business and prices in 1952-1953 upon the cessation of the Korean War, the productivity and purchasing power argument was used to justify the claim for higher wages. Basing wages on productivity gains was regarded as a legitimate factor in wage determination and was claimed not to be inflationary. The increasing share of productivity was being withheld from labor, with large profits flowing to business as a result. Higher wages are necessary to enable the workers to buy the expanded flow of goods and services essential for full employment, it was asserted.

Although substantial economic gains were achieved during 1953 as indicated in Table XI, p. 85, the AFL and CIO continued to stress the need for higher wages and improvements in fringe benefits. Labor pointed to the difficulty of the average city factory worker to support his family on even a modest standard of living and the workers' failure to share equitably in the gains from increased productivity.

## TABLE VIII

### Membership in AFL and CIO in Thousands

| Year | AFL Membership | Year | AFL Membership | CIO Membership |
|------|----------------|------|----------------|----------------|
| 1897 | 265   | 1925 | 2,877 |       |
| 1898 | 278   | 1926 | 2,804 |       |
| 1899 | 349   | 1927 | 2,813 |       |
| 1900 | 548   | 1928 | 2,896 |       |
| 1901 | 788   | 1929 | 2,934 |       |
| 1902 | 1,024 | 1930 | 2,961 |       |
| 1903 | 1,466 | 1931 | 2,890 |       |
| 1904 | 1,676 | 1932 | 2,532 |       |
| 1905 | 1,494 | 1933 | 2,127 |       |
| 1906 | 1,454 | 1934 | 2,608 |       |
| 1907 | 1,539 | 1935 | 3,045 |       |
| 1908 | 1,587 | 1936 | 3,422 |       |
| 1909 | 1,483 | 1937 | 2,861 | 3,718 |
| 1910 | 1,562 | 1938 | 3,623 | 4,038 |
| 1911 | 1,762 | 1939 | 4,006 | 4,000 |
| 1912 | 1,770 | 1940 | 4,247 | 3,625 |
| 1913 | 1,996 | 1941 | 4,569 | 5,000 |
| 1914 | 2,021 | 1942 | 5,483 | 4,195 |
| 1915 | 1,946 | 1943 | 6,564 | 5,285 |
| 1916 | 2,073 | 1944 | 6,807 | 5,935 |
| 1917 | 2,371 | 1945 | 6,931 | 6,000 |
| 1918 | 2,726 | 1946 | 7,152 | 6,000 |
| 1919 | 3,260 | 1947 | 7,578 | No consecutive |
| 1920 | 4,079 | 1948 | 7,221 | series of statis- |
| 1921 | 3,907 | 1949 | 7,241 | tics published by CIO since |
| 1922 | 3,196 | 1950 | 7,143 | 1947. Estimated |
| 1923 | 2,926 | 1951 | 7,864 | membership as of September, |
| 1924 | 2,866 | 1952 | 8,098 | 1954 is approxi- |
|      |       | 1953 | 8,655 | mately 6 million |

*Handbook of Labor Statistics,* 1950 edition, p. 139, and *Handbook of Labor Statistics,* 1951 supplement, p. 47, U.S. Dept. of Labor, Bureau of Labor Statistics.

*Proceedings,* 72nd Convention AFL 1953 p. 35, letter to the author from CIO September 22, 1954.

## TABLE IX

Average Gross Hourly Earnings in Selective Industries, 1929-1954

### PERIOD MONTHLY AVERAGE

| Year | Total | Manufacturing | | Bituminous Coal Mining | Building Construction | Class I R. R. |
| | | Durable Goods | Non Durable Goods | | | |
|---|---|---|---|---|---|---|
| 1929 | .566 | Not avail. | Not avail. | .681 | Not avail. | Not avail. |
| 1930 | .552 | Not avail. | Not avail. | .684 | Not avail. | Not avail. |
| 1931 | .515 | Not avail. | Not avail. | .647 | Not avail. | Not avail. |
| 1932 | .446 | .497 | .420 | .520 | Not avail. | Not avail. |
| 1933 | .442 | .472 | .427 | .501 | Not avail. | Not avail. |
| 1934 | .532 | .556 | .515 | .673 | .795 | Not avail. |
| 1935 | .550 | .577 | .530 | .745 | .815 | Not avail. |
| 1936 | .556 | .586 | .529 | .794 | .824 | Not avail. |
| 1937 | .624 | .674 | .577 | .856 | .903 | Not avail. |
| 1938 | .627 | .686 | .584 | .878 | .908 | Not avail. |
| 1939 | .633 | .698 | .582 | .886 | .932 | .730 |
| 1940 | .661 | .724 | .602 | .883 | .958 | .733 |
| 1941 | .729 | .808 | .640 | .993 | 1.010 | .743 |
| 1942 | .853 | .947 | .723 | 1.059 | 1.148 | .837 |
| 1943 | .961 | 1.059 | .803 | 1.139 | 1.252 | .852 |
| 1944 | 1.019 | 1.117 | .861 | 1.186 | 1.319 | .948 |
| 1945 | 1.023 | 1.111 | .904 | 1.240 | 1.379 | .955 |
| 1946 | 1.086 | 1.156 | 1.015 | 1.401 | 1.478 | 1.087 |
| 1947 | 1.237 | 1.292 | 1.171 | 1.636 | 1.681 | 1.186 |
| 1948 | 1.350 | 1.410 | 1.278 | 1.898 | 1.848 | 1.301 |
| 1949 | 1.401 | 1.469 | 1.325 | 1.941 | 1.935 | 1.427 |
| 1950 | 1.465 | 1.537 | 1.378 | 2.010 | 2.031 | 1.572 |
| 1951 | 1.59 | 1.67 | 1.48 | 2.21 | 2.19 | 1.73 |
| 1952 | 1.67 | 1.77 | 1.54 | 2.29 | 2.31 | 1.83 |
| 1953 | 1.77 | 1.87 | 1.61 | 2.48 | 2.48 | 1.88 |
| 1954* | 1.81 | 1.92 | 1.66 | 2.48 | 2.60 | Not avail. |

* Preliminary

Economic Report of the President, Jan., 1955, p. 162, by the Council of Economic Advisers, U. S. Government Printing Office, Washington, D.C., 1955.

## TABLE X

### Average Gross Weekly Earnings in Selective Industries, 1929-1954

## PERIOD MONTHLY AVERAGE

| Year | Manufacturing | | | Bituminous Coal Mining | Building Construction | Class I R. R. |
|------|-------|-----------------|------------------------|------------------------|------------------------|-----------|
| | Total | Durable Goods | Non Durable Goods | | | |
| 1929 | 25.03 | 27.22 | 22.93 | 25.72 | Not avail. | Not avail. |
| 1930 | 23.25 | 24.77 | 21.84 | 22.21 | Not avail. | Not avail. |
| 1931 | 20.87 | 21.28 | 20.50 | 17.69 | Not avail. | Not avail. |
| 1932 | 17.05 | 16.21 | 17.57 | 13.91 | Not avail. | Not avail. |
| 1933 | 16.73 | 16.43 | 16.89 | 14.47 | Not avail. | Not avail. |
| 1934 | 18.40 | 18.87 | 18.05 | 18.10 | 22.97 | Not avail. |
| 1935 | 20.13 | 21.52 | 19.11 | 19.58 | 24.51 | Not avail. |
| 1936 | 21.78 | 24.04 | 19.94 | 22.71 | 27.01 | Not avail. |
| 1937 | 24.05 | 26.91 | 21.53 | 23.84 | 30.14 | Not avail. |
| 1938 | 22.30 | 24.01 | 21.05 | 20.80 | 29.19 | Not avail. |
| 1939 | 23.86 | 26.50 | 21.78 | 23.88 | 30.39 | 31.90 |
| 1940 | 25.20 | 28.44 | 22.27 | 24.71 | 31.70 | 32.47 |
| 1941 | 29.58 | 34.04 | 24.92 | 30.86 | 35.14 | 34.03 |
| 1942 | 36.65 | 42.73 | 29.13 | 35.02 | 41.80 | 39.34 |
| 1943 | 43.14 | 49.30 | 34.12 | 41.62 | 48.13 | 41.49 |
| 1944 | 46.08 | 52.07 | 37.12 | 51.27 | 52.18 | 46.36 |
| 1945 | 44.39 | 49.05 | 38.29 | 52.25 | 53.73 | 46.32 |
| 1946 | 43.82 | 46.49 | 41.14 | 58.03 | 56.24 | 50.00 |
| 1947 | 49.97 | 52.46 | 46.96 | 66.59 | 63.30 | 55.03 |
| 1948 | 54.14 | 57.11 | 50.61 | 72.12 | 68.85 | 60.11 |
| 1949 | 54.92 | 58.03 | 51.41 | 63.28 | 70.95 | 62.36 |
| 1950 | 59.33 | 63.32 | 54.71 | 70.35 | 73.73 | 64.14 |
| 1951 | 64.71 | 69.47 | 58.46 | 77.79 | 81.47 | 70.93 |
| 1952 | 67.97 | 73.46 | 60.98 | 78.09 | 88.01 | 74.30 |
| 1953 | 71.69 | 77.23 | 63.60 | 85.31 | 91.76 | 76.33 |
| 1954* | 71.64 | 77.01 | 64.59 | 79.95 | 94.19 | Not avail. |

\* Preliminary

*Economic Report of the President*, Jan., 1955, p. 163, by the Council of Economic Advisers, U. S. Government Printing Office, Washington, D.C., 1955.

## TABLE XI

Indexes of Consumers Price, Average Hourly and Weekly Manufacturing
Wages, and Real Hourly and Weekly Manufacturing Earnings
1929-1954  (1935-'39=100)

| Year | Consumer Price Index | Average Hourly Earnings | Average Weekly Earnings | Real Hourly Earnings* | Real Weekly Earnings* |
|---|---|---|---|---|---|
| 1929 | 122.5 | 95 | 112 | 77 | 91 |
| 1930 | 119.4 | 92 | 104 | 77 | 87 |
| 1931 | 108.7 | 86 | 93 | 79 | 86 |
| 1932 | 97.6 | 75 | 76 | 76 | 78 |
| 1933 | 92.4 | 74 | 75 | 79 | 81 |
| 1934 | 95.7 | 89 | 82 | 93 | 86 |
| 1935 | 98.1 | 92 | 90 | 94 | 92 |
| 1936 | 99.1 | 93 | 97 | 94 | 98 |
| 1937 | 102.7 | 104 | 107 | 102 | 104 |
| 1938 | 100.8 | 105 | 100 | 104 | 100 |
| 1939 | 99.4 | 106 | 106 | 107 | 107 |
| 1940 | 100.2 | 111 | 112 | 110 | 112 |
| 1941 | 105.2 | 122 | 132 | 116 | 125 |
| 1942 | 116.6 | 143 | 164 | 122 | 140 |
| 1943 | 123.7 | 161 | 192 | 130 | 156 |
| 1944 | 125.7 | 170 | 206 | 136 | 164 |
| 1945 | 128.6 | 171 | 198 | 133 | 154 |
| 1946 | 139.5 | 182 | 196 | 130 | 140 |
| 1947 | 159.6 | 228 | 223 | 143 | 140 |
| 1948 | 171.9 | 226 | 242 | 131 | 141 |
| 1949 | 170.2 | 234 | 245 | 138 | 144 |
| 1950 | 171.9 | 245 | 265 | 143 | 154 |
| 1951 | 185.6 | 267 | 289 | 144 | 156 |
| 1952 | 189.7 | 279 | 302 | 147 | 159 |
| 1953 | 191.3 | 296* | 319* | 155 | 167 |
| 1954 | 191.9 | 303* | 319* | 158 | 166 |

*Compiled by the writer.

*Economic Report of the President,* Jan., 1953, by Council of Economic Advisers, U.S. Government Printing Office, Washington, D.C., 1953.

*Monthly Labor Review,* United States Department of Labor, Bureau of Labor Statistics, April 1955, Vol. 78, p. 506.

**TABLE XII**

**\*PERCENTAGE DISTRIBUTION OF PRIVATE NATIONAL INCOME BY DISTRIBUTIVE SHARES, 1929 - 1950**

| | 1929 | 1930 | 1931 | 1932 | 1933 | 1934 | 1935 | 1936 | 1937 | 1938 | 1939 | 1940 | 1941 | 1942 | 1943 | 1944 | 1945 | 1946 | 1947 | 1948 | 1949 | 1950 |
|---|---|---|---|---|---|---|---|---|---|---|---|---|---|---|---|---|---|---|---|---|---|---|
| Total Private National Income | 100.0 | 100.0 | 100.0 | 100.0 | 100.0 | 100.0 | 100.0 | 100.0 | 100.0 | 100.0 | 100.0 | 100.0 | 100.0 | 100.0 | 100.0 | 100.0 | 100.0 | 100.0 | 100.0 | 100.0 | 100.0 | 100.0 |
| Compensation of Employes | 55.5 | 59.1 | 63.7 | 70.3 | 70.0 | 65.6 | 60.7 | 61.0 | 60.6 | 61.5 | 61.4 | 59.3 | 57.6 | 56.7 | 57.5 | 58.1 | 58.9 | 59.9 | 60.8 | 59.1 | 60.6 | 60.3 |
| Income of Unincorporated Enterprises | 16.9 | 15.7 | 15.4 | 13.5 | 15.2 | 15.6 | 19.7 | 17.6 | 18.6 | 18.3 | 17.6 | 17.5 | 17.7 | 19.1 | 18.8 | 19.4 | 21.5 | 22.4 | 19.6 | 19.5 | 17.4 | 16.7 |
| Rental Income of Persons | 7.1 | 6.9 | 6.8 | 6.9 | 5.9 | 5.0 | 4.6 | 4.7 | 4.8 | 5.6 | 5.4 | 5.0 | 4.6 | 4.5 | 4.3 | 4.3 | 4.3 | 4.2 | 3.9 | 3.7 | 3.9 | 3.7 |
| Corporate Profits and Inventory Valuation Adjustment | 12.5 | 9.4 | 3.1 | 5.5 | 5.8 | 2.6 | 6.0 | 8.7 | 9.4 | 7.3 | 9.0 | 12.6 | 15.7 | 16.5 | 17.0 | 16.1 | 13.2 | 11.6 | 13.7 | 15.6 | 15.6 | 16.8 |
| Net Interest | 8.0 | 8.9 | 11.1 | 14.9 | 14.6 | 11.2 | 9.1 | 7.9 | 6.6 | 7.3 | 6.6 | 5.7 | 4.4 | 3.2 | 2.4 | 2.1 | 2.1 | 1.9 | 2.0 | 2.1 | 2.5 | 2.5 |

\*National income excluding compensation of government and government enterprise employees.

Source: U. S. Department of Commerce, *Supplement to the Survey of Current Business*, *National Income*, p. 17, *Survey of Current Business*, July 1952, p. 12.

**TABLE XIII**

**Profits before and after Tax, All Private Corporations 1929-1954**
*(Billions of dollars)*

| Period | Corp. Profits Before Tax | Corp. Tax Liability* | Corp. Profits after Tax | | |
|---|---|---|---|---|---|
| | | | Total | Dividend Payments | Undistributed Profits |
| 1929 | 9.6 | 1.4 | 8.3 | 5.8 | 2.4 |
| 1930 | 3.3 | .8 | 2.5 | 5.5 | —3.0 |
| 1931 | —.8 | .5 | —1.3 | 4.1 | —5.4 |
| 1932 | —3.0 | .4 | —3.4 | 2.6 | —6.0 |
| 1933 | .2 | .5 | —.4 | 2.1 | —2.4 |
| 1934 | 1.7 | .7 | 1.0 | 2.6 | —1.6 |
| 1935 | 3.1 | 1.0 | 2.2 | 2.9 | —.7 |
| 1936 | 5.7 | 1.4 | 4.3 | 4.5 | —.2 |
| 1937 | 6.2 | 1.5 | 4.7 | 4.7 | ** |
| 1938 | 3.3 | 1.0 | 2.3 | 3.2 | —.9 |
| 1939 | 6.4 | 1.4 | 5.0 | 3.8 | 1.2 |
| 1940 | 9.3 | 2.8 | 6.5 | 4.0 | 2.4 |
| 1941 | 17.0 | 7.6 | 9.4 | 4.5 | 4.9 |
| 1942 | 20.9 | 11.4 | 9.5 | 4.3 | 5.2 |
| 1943 | 24.6 | 14.1 | 10.5 | 4.5 | 6.0 |
| 1944 | 23.3 | 12.9 | 10.4 | 4.7 | 5.7 |
| 1945 | 19.0 | 10.7 | 8.3 | 4.7 | 3.6 |
| 1946 | 22.6 | 9.1 | 13.4 | 5.8 | 7.7 |
| 1947 | 29.5 | 11.3 | 18.2 | 6.5 | 11.7 |
| 1948 | 32.8 | 12.5 | 20.3 | 7.2 | 13.0 |
| 1949 | 26.2 | 10.4 | 15.8 | 7.5 | 8.3 |
| 1950 | 40.0 | 17.8 | 22.1 | 9.2 | 12.9 |
| 1951 | 41.2 | 22.5 | 18.7 | 9.1 | 9.6 |
| 1952 | 37.2 | 20.0 | 17.2 | 9.1 | 8.1 |
| 1953 | 39.4 | 21.1 | 18.3 | 9.4 | 8.9 |
| 1954*** | 35.0 | 17.2 | 17.8 | 9.9 | 8.0 |

*Federal and State corporate income and excess profits taxes.

**48 million dollars.

***Preliminary

*Economic Report of the President*, January 1955, by Council of Economic Advisers, p. 189, U.S. Government Printing Office, Washington, D.C., 1955.

Part Four

# A SAMPLING OF WAGE POLICIES OF AFL AND CIO AFFILIATED UNIONS

## CHAPTER FIVE

# International Ladies' Garment Workers' Union

## INTRODUCTION

The International Ladies' Garment Workers' Union was founded in 1900 and became an affiliate of the AFL. Its roots lead back to the immigration of the eighties, and its members are largely of Jewish and Italian descent.[1] The union is composed of more than 430,000 members distributed among 491 locals, 24 joint boards and 21 departments and regional offices. The joint boards comprise two or more locals in the same industry and locality. Their function is to transact the business of the locals which comprises negotiating, administering and enforcing the collective agreements.

The two largest joint boards are located in the New York City area. One includes the coat, suit and skirt industry; the other the dress industry. The Joint Board of Cloak, Suit, Skirt, and Reefer Makers' Union, popularly known as the Cloak Joint Board, consists of eight locals of the International. It has a membership of over 60,000, most of whom are men. Affiliated with it is the Cloak Out-of-Town Department which is composed of locals of the International whose members reside in the territory contiguous to New York City and who produce coats and suits for manufacturers and jobbers in the metropolis. The Joint Board of Dress and Waistmakers' Union, referred to as the Dress Joint Board, consists of four locals of the International. It has more than 85,000 members covered by its collective agreements, most of whom are women. Affiliated with it is the Eastern Out-of-Town Department and the Northeast Department. These departments are composed of locals whose members are employed elsewhere in New York State, New Jersey, Connecticut, Delaware, Pennsylvania, Rhode Island, and Massachusetts.

The manufacture of women's garments is for the most part an industry of small business men. Entrance into the industry is compara-

91

tively easy, and anyone with little capital, organizing ability and experience can try his hand in the business.[2] This has encouraged the overexpansion of contracting and sub-manufacturing to the delight of the manufacturers and jobbers. The latter have in the past used them to gain unfair advantages which more often than not would redound to hardship on the workers. The industry has always been subject to unpredictable factors of taste, weather and rapid style changes. Style is perhaps the one factor of overshadowing importance and affects every aspect of the business. There is a constant threat of obsolescence even before the garment is produced. Obsolescence is felt not only by the manufacturer but also by the retailer. The retailer does not wish to make large commitments for particular styles without knowing consumer acceptance. As a result the retailer will delay ordering until the last minute. Reorders are usually made upon condition of speedy delivery. Because of the reluctance of the retailers to order very far in advance, the manufacturers and jobbers find it necessary to reduce their risks. They do this by producing the garments to specific orders of retailers rather than for stock. In order to meet the demands of the retailers for immediate deliveries, it has been necessary to maintain a reserve supply of labor, geared to the peak demand rather than an average demand. Following the relatively busy short spring and fall seasons, there is a longer period of reduced hours and widespread unemployment. This has caused not only low annual incomes to the workers but an unhealthy competition among workers for available work and a breakdown of work standards through lower piece rates and hourly rates of pay.

The industry is composed of four types of firms. First, the "inside" manufacturer performs all the main supply functions, including purchase of materials, designing the styles, and manufacturing the garments on their own premises and selling the final product directly to the retailer.[3] Some "inside" manufacturers leave the manufacture of garments to contractors and sub-manufacturers. The second type of firm is known as the "jobber." In function he is similar to the "inside" manufacturer, but differs in that he has no inside factory. The manufacturing of the garments is left to contractors or sub-manufacturers. The third type of firm is the "contractor." He makes up the finished garments out of the cut goods reserved from the jobbers or manufacturers according to their specifications. The last group is the "sub-manufacturer." He performs work similar to that of the contractor, but differs somewhat in that he is also required to cut piece goods in addition to making them up into garments.[4]

During the first decade of the twentieth century the industry was characterized by its notoriously bad labor conditions. Subsistence wages, lack of fixed wage scales, long hours of work and unsafe and unsanitary work shops were widespread. It was indeed a sweat shop industry. The tension among the workers finally resulted in a strike of 20,000 dressmakers in 1909 to be followed by a revolt of 50,000 to 60,000 cloakmakers in 1910. The strike ended in a signing of the Protocol of Peace which represented the first collective agreement between a union and employers covering an entire industry in New York City.

The Protocol marked a turning point in the history of the union. The Protocol was more than a collective bargaining agreement, for "it introduced the notion that labor had a stake in industry beyond wages and hours, a stake in its efficient management, continuous prosperity and social responsibility. The Protocol assumed a benevolent partnership between capital and labor, a sort of joint syndicate of boss and worker.[5] The Protocol established a preferential union shop, a system of voluntary factory inspection, a 50-hour week, double pay for overtime, ten legal holidays with pay, payment of wages in cash; it abolished inside subcontracting and charges for use of work tools, thread and power; and finally it effected a permanent machinery for conciliation and arbitration.[6] The signing of the Protocol ushered in a period of constructive experimentation in collective bargaining. However, it was not long before trouble arose. Some of the "inside manufacturers" began to evade their responsibility to their workers. In effect, many of the "inside manufacturers" abandoned their shops and became jobbers. By contracting with the sub-manufacturer for the production of the garments, they left the workers at their mercy.

The change-over from manufacturing to jobbing resulted in a deterioration of labor standards. A tremendous surplus of contractors and sub-manufacturers appeared. As might be expected, fierce competition resulted in bidding for the work of jobbers and manufacturers. The jobbers aggravated the situation by concentrating their production among a small number of contractors and sub-manufacturers and giving the others a small amount of work in order to keep them in existence. Another unscrupulous practice by the jobbers was the pitting of contractor and sub-manufacturer against each other by giving work to the one who bid the lower. The ability of the contractor to get work was based on how much less than the union scale he could pay his workers. Out of this chaotic situation it was not long before the labor standards in the shops of the legitimate "inside" manufacturers were undermined.

In order to meet the deplorable conditions created by the outside system of production, the International was convinced that it must make the jobbers directly responsible for the subcontractor and contractor. The jobber must be dealt with as an employer on the same terms as a manufacturer. A fixed system of control must be established to ascertain whether a jobber was sending his work to union or non-union shops.[7]

### THE GOVERNOR'S COMMISSION

Shortly before the expiration of the collective agreements in the New York Cloak and Suit industry in 1924, the International and the Cloak Joint Board formulated the following twelve-point program: 1) Each manufacturer and jobber shall employ only such number of contractors or sub-manufacturers as he can supply with work to their full capacity. No manufacturer or jobber may engage any additional contractors or sub-manufacturers so long as those working for him are not fully provided with work; 2) No contractor or sub-manufacturer shall be employed unless his shop consists of at least fourteen machines and unless he employs fourteen operators and a necessary complement of workers of the other crafts; 3) No manufacturer or jobber shall discharge his contractors or sub-manufacturers except for good cause; 4) In the slow season, all available work shall be divided by the manufacturers equitably among his inside shop and all his contractors and sub-manufacturers and their workers, and by the jobbers equitably among all his contractors and sub-manufacturers and their workers; 5) The payment of wages and the observance of union conditions of work on the part of the contractor or sub-manufacturer shall be guaranteed by the manufacturer and jobber; 6) Representation of the jobbers on the Joint Board of Sanitary Control; 7) The adoption of an appropriate union label to be attached to each garment; 8) All workers employed in the industry shall be guaranteed a specific number of full weeks' employment during the year or the payment of the contractual wages for such period; 9) The establishment of an unemployment insurance fund through contributions on the part of the employers and workers; 10) Reduction of hours of labor from 44 to 40 hours per week; 11) An adequate increase in wages; 12) Examination of employers' books and records to detect violations of the agreement on their part and payment of damages for such violations.[8]

The employers in the industry refused to accept the union program, and the International and the Cloak Joint Board threatened to call a strike.[9] The strike was averted by the appointment of a Commission by Governor Alfred E. Smith in June 1924 to investigate the problems involved and to make advisory recommendations for their solution. The Commission handed down its intermediate report on July 8, 1924. The report stated:

"The Commission believes that unless all of the different factors in the industry, union, inside manufacturers, sub-manufacturers and jobbers, are brought together under a harmonious arrangement, there can be no lasting peace in the industry. The question of the recognition of the union is not involved in this controversy. The union has been recognized by both the jobbers and the manufacturers who many years ago decided that it was to their advantage to deal collectively with the union and to maintain union standards in the industry. One point, and that is fundamental, must be emphasized. A group cannot agree to maintain union standards and then be permitted to resort to practices, the only effect of which is to break down and weaken, the very standards they have agreed to maintain and which they profess to regard. The only hope for the future of the industry is to have the four elements mentioned assume mutual obligations that will bring about fair dealing, that will not give one group an unfair advantage over the other and that will tend to restore stability and insure the maintenance of proper labor and sanitary standards in the industry."[10]

The Commission recommended the adoption of several of the proposals previously requested by the International and the Cloak Joint Board in their 12-point program. These included: 1) Reduction in the number of shops in the industry by requiring a minimum of 14 machines; 2) All garments shall be produced in union shops; 3) Although the Commission did not recommend a union label, it urged that an appropriate label by the Joint Board of Sanitary Control be attached to each garment made by firms who had collective agreements with the union; 4) All factors in the industry to be represented on the Joint Board of Sanitary Control; 5) An unemployment insurance fund should be established through contributions of the employers and workers; 6) Jobbers and manufacturers should be responsible to the employees in their contracting shops for one week's wages.[11]

In regard to the demands of the union relating to the jobber, contractor, sub-manufacturer relationships and dealings, the Commission felt that because of the highly complicated and technical nature of the problems it could not pass upon the question immediately. It did, however, recommend an impartial investigation of the problems by a group of experts to report back to the Commission by January 1, 1925. The investigation was launched and continued for almost two years. The report of the experts verified the union's position that in order to improve labor conditions it was necessary to reform the contracting system.[12]

On May 20, 1926, the Commission submitted its final report. In the following statement it gave its approval to the union program for regulating the contracting system:

"We recommend that the parties adopt a system of limitation of submanufacturers with whom a jobber may do business. At definite intervals every jobber shall, in accordance with a standard to be agreed upon between the parties, select and designate the submanufacturers he needs to handle his production . . . He shall not give work to other submanufacturers when his designated submanufacturers are not busy, and shall adhere, so far as practicable, to a policy of equitable distribution of work among the submanufacturers designated by him. The administration of such system would, as cases arise, be subject to equitable interpretation through the impartial machinery.
The foregoing recommendations are intended to apply as well to that part of the business of the members of the Industrial Council which is carried on in outside shops."[13]

Other important recommendations were: establishment of a Labor Employment Bureau to supervise placements and replacements; an increase in minimum wage scales; the development of the Prosanis Label under the supervision of the Joint Board of Sanitary Control; the establishment of a Bureau of Research; the establishment of an impartial chairman for the industry; permission to inside manufacturers with a regular force of 35 or more employees to "recognize" their shops once a year, provided it would not cause displacement in any one year or more than 10 per cent of the workers in the shop, and provided no unfair discrimination was exercised. It is interesting to note that the union objected to this recommendation because it felt that it was an opening wedge against union members.[14]

### THE COAT, SUIT, AND DRESS INDUSTRY 1926-1933

Except for the establishment of an unemployment insurance fund, the adoption of a Prosanis label, and some minor points recommended by the Governor's Commission, most of the recommendations of the Commission were rejected by the manufacturers and jobbers and the Cloak Joint Board. This refusal may be explained chiefly by the fact that communist leaders had gained control of the Cloak and Suit Board. To make matters worse, the Board called a strike because the Commission failed to reduce the work-week and to recommend a guaranteed period of employment. The 26-week strike greatly weakened the Cloak Joint Board. The union failed to obtain the important recommendations of the Commission while in the meantime the unemployment insurance fund was eliminated and the Prosanis label fell into disuse.[15]

In November 1926 collective agreements between the Cloak Joint Board and the employers were obtained which provided for a 42-hour week and wages based on time worked. Unfortunately, the union had not freed itself from communist control which weakened the value of the agreements to the workers. The employers did not adhere to the hours limitation nor did they abide by the contractual wage scales. Workers in over half of the shops were forced to accept piece rate wages with no voice in setting up the standards.[16]

In protest, the Joint Cloak Board called a general strike in July 1929. Franklin D. Roosevelt, then governor of the State of New York, called the representatives of the International, the Cloak Joint Board, and the employers' associations together. Lieutenant Governor Herbert H. Lehman was designated to mediate the problems and to find a solution. An agreement was drawn up which modified the reorganization right of the manufacturers, granted the certification of contractors, the creation of a joint commission with union representation to police the industry, eliminated bootleg production, and instituted strict observation of union standards in all shops.[17]

Just as the union was getting back on the road to health with the communist element defeated, the working conditions greatly improved, and the industry once more stabilized, economic crisis fell across its path. During the Great Depression stabilization and regulation of the industry were forgotten. The lowering of union standards became widespread. The industry was once again experiencing sweat shop conditions.[18] The Cloak Joint Board urged that the evils in the industry could be wiped out if the jobbers and manufacturers accepted the principle of designation of contractors and sub-manufacturers and the responsibility for the labor standards of the workers in the contractor and sub-manufacturing shops. But the jobbers and manufacturers continued to fight against these principles.

In the dress industry chaotic conditions likewise prevailed during the Great Depression. A strike was called by the New York Dress Board in 1930 for the purpose of bringing about collective relationships with the employers. On the surface the strike appeared to have succeeded in its goal, but it was not long before conditions grew worse. The manufacturers, jobbers and contractors, instead of living up to the conditions prescribed in the agreement, began dodging observance of union work rules and showed no inclination to help the union to establish orderliness and sanity in the industry. The evils of the jobber-contractor-sub-manufacturer relationship in the dress industry and the problems experienced closely resembled those of the coat and suit industry. There has always been a surplus of contractors which enabled the jobber to play off one contractor against the other in his desire to get the lowest possible cost. Since the contractor's labor cost was his principal item of expense, lower prices to the contractors resulted in lower wages to the workers. In order to increase his income the contractor was under constant pressure to lower wages.

To meet the problems, the Dressmakers Joint Board demanded that: the Jobbers' Association withdraw work from non-union shops, and assume full responsibility for union standards in contractor shops; the introduction in the entire industry of a price settlement system based on schedules of piece-prices for all parts of the garments and minimum hourly rates of pay; a minimum guarantee of earnings to all piece workers; extra compensation for overtime to piece workers; no Saturday work; preference of work to inside shops; disciplinary fines for employers failing to comply with decisions.[19]

The employers turned down the union demands, and a strike followed. Under the terms of settlement the union won a significant victory which included many of the requests sought by the union.[20] After the agreement was signed in 1932, the dress industry suffered a severe economic collapse because of a poor spring and fall season. The result was that the agreed minimum hourly wage schedules were not followed and labor standards generally were ignored.[21]

By the time of the renewal of the collective agreements in August 1933 between the Dress Joint Board and the association of jobbers and manufacturers, signs of economic recovery had appeared. In the negotiations and final agreements much progress was made in solving the jobber-manufacturer-contractor problems. The jobbers and manufacturers were required to deal only with those contractors who were in contractual relations with the union and who complied with labor standards set forth in the agreements. Jobbers and manufacturers were required to register with the Dress Joint Board the names of the contractors to whom they sent work, and to be responsible for the maintenance of the contractors' wage rates.

In the coat and suit industry, the Joint Cloak Board in its 1933 negotiations demanded the adoption of the recommendations of the Governor's Commission with respect to jobber, manufacturer-contractor and sub-manufacturer relationships. The employers rejected the demands of the union and proposed instead a program that included the establishment of piece work system of production. The union thereupon by referendum to the membership rejected the employers' proposals and began preparations to strike.

## THE NRA AND STABILIZATION

Just before the outbreak of the strike in the coat and suit industry, the NRA was passed by Congress. Representatives of the International, the Cloak Joint Board and the employers' associations were invited to present proposals for a code of fair competition for the industry.[22] The code for the coat and suit industry as approved in August 1933 was a tremendous gain for the workers, because it placed into effect the main principles as suggested by the Governor's Commission of the 1920's. These included: 1) a system of designation of contractors and sub-manufacturers; 2) jobber responsibility for wages and earnings in outside shops; 3) the guarantee of equitable divisions of work among designated contractors; 4) adoption of the

NRA label. The union disliked the legalization of piece work in the code, but it finally agreed to accept this provision because of the inclusion of the four principles mentioned above.[23]

In the dress industry, the NRA Code as approved in October 1933 provided in part: 1) All manufacturers and jobbers who have their garments made by contractors shall adhere to the payment of wages provided in the code and in addition a reasonable payment to the contractors to cover their overhead; 2) Manufacturers and jobbers shall designate the number of contractors to meet their business requirements; 3) The code authority, subject to veto of the administrator, shall have the power to prevent the jobber or manufacturer from unreasonable discrimination in the distribution of work between contractors which might deprive workers of employment unfairly.

The provisions in the dress industry code were not as satisfactory as those in the coat and suit industry, because the jobbers and manufacturers tended to thwart the system of "registration of contractors." They would "set up" secretly a number of contractors in business, or would do business with non-registered contractors, or deal with non-registered contractors on the excuse of delays in deliveries and for other technicalities often without adequate facts to support their claims.

When the NRA was declared unconstitutional in May 1935, many employers began taking advantage of their freedom in both the dress and coat and suit industry by unfair competitive underbidding of contractors in terms of cheaper labor costs. At the expiration of the 1935 collective agreements in the dress industry, the Dress Joint Board demanded that the new collective agreements contain provisions for: price settlement on jobbers' premises, the unit system of price settlements, and a clear-cut system of limitation of contractors similar to that in the coat and suit industry. The price settlement on jobbers' premises was important to the workers because under the system then in effect, known as the "auction block system," the prices to be paid the piece workers were settled by committees of workers in the various contracting shops. The result was that the workers in the different shops were pitted against each other for the privilege of making up dresses for the jobber. The union felt that only when prices are settled on the jobbers' premises could the competition between contractors be stopped and stability promoted on the basis of equal labor costs. The unit system of price settlement was an important corollary to price settlement on the jobbers' premises, because it would eliminate elements of doubt and speculation in the settlement of prices for the product. The unit system as worked out by the union was a method of calculating the exact time it would take a worker to make a given dress. The dress was divided into component parts, and the time to complete the parts was determined. The wage clauses in the collective agreement established the value of time for the worker and the price rate for the dress. Under the unit plan, the workers in all shops would receive the same rates for the same labor.

The employers immediately opposed the Dress Joint Board's program which resulted in the preparation of a strike by the union. The union in a clear-cut statement pointed out how the jobber-contractor system was at the roots of the trouble. It showed that the jobber has more contractors than needed which caused the contractors to bid against each other for work. It revealed that workers on contractor dresses earned over 50 per cent less yearly than those employed in inside shops.[24] After months of negotiation, the employers' association accepted the major demands of the union in February 1936. This was a tremendous accomplishment because it lifted the dress industry out of its past chaos and confusion.[25]

### 1937-1941 PERIOD

In the business recession of 1937-38 the wages of garment workers did not wholly escape the effects of the decline. Competition, always keen in the industry, was intensified. The trend toward lower-priced garments and the pressure of retailers for better "values" led many manufacturers to increase their efforts to lower wages, but the organized strength of the ILGWU made unrestricted wage cutting difficult as indicated in Table XIV, page 114. If the ILGWU became convinced that wage cuts were necessary in order to keep employers in business, occasionally the union would grant such a request.

In 1939 the New York Cloak Joint Board demanded a substantial increase in wage scales and a shorter work-week. These efforts were successful as the new agreement provided an increase of $5 per week to all week workers and a 10 per cent raise to piece workers. The work-week was reduced to 32½ hours conditioned on the establishment of the same in other coat markets and the New York dress industry.[26]

Although 1939 was a year of business recovery for most industries, it did not prove so for the dress industry. Diminished production volume, grave unemployment, and high employer mortality were experienced. The New York Dress Joint Board turned its attention to meeting the slump. On the basis of a survey of the New York dress industry made by Julius Hochman, a comprehensive program was worked out for rehabilitating and modernizing the industry. It centered around two points: efficiency and promotion. To obtain efficiency, the program called for a clause in the collective agreements that would make certain minimum standards of efficient management mandatory upon the employers. As a corollary to more efficiency, the union plan stressed the need for market promotion to increase sales and maintain New York's leadership in the dress industry. At first the employers displayed little enthusiasm for the program, but after several weeks of negotiation, they adopted the plan. The collective agreements of January 1941 included an efficiency clause and a clause for the financing of a promotion campaign.[27]

To implement the promotion clause, the New York Dress Institute was organized in 1941. A combination union and fashion label was adopted for which the manufacturers paid one-third of one per cent of their monthly sales. The ILGWU agreed to contribute $100,000 during the period of the collective agreement. An efficiency engineering department, staffed by industrial engineers, was established in 1941, which visited the dress shop and gave advice on more efficient procedures. It also made investigations upon complaints of the union under the efficiency clause.[28] The success of the union and management in their efficiency and promotion scheme is partly revealed by the fact that the hourly wage earnings stopped their downward trend in 1941 as shown on Table XIV.

It is interesting to observe that the ILGWU began to turn its attention in the latter part of the 1930's to the guarantee of annual wages for its membership. In 1937 the International stressed the need for achieving more regularity of work and gave its approval of the guaranteed annual wage. The International had previously some scattered instances of job security in collective agreements under which a specified number of weeks of work were guaranteed to regular employees in each year. The Cleveland Garment Manufacturers' Association and the ILGWU plan adopted in 1922 was one of the earliest experiments, but it was terminated with the Great Depression in 1931. The plan guaranteed each worker not less than 40 weeks' employment per year at two-thirds his minimum rate. It was later changed to half of the minimum rate.[29] Other less-known plans were tried for a time and then abandoned.

### 1941-1945 WAR PERIOD

With the outbreak of the Second World War average hourly earnings in the various branches of the industry rose substantially as shown on Table XIV, page 114. But with the establishment of the wage stabilization program much unrest was created among the garment workers as was true of workers generally. The General Executive Board urged the government to liberalize the wage stabilization program, including the scrapping of the outdated "Little Steel Formula," in order to meet the urgent need of the American people. It felt that labor had been falling behind in the upward spiral of wages and prices.[30]

Some gains in wages and welfare benefits were made in spite of wage controls. The New York Cloak Makers won an industry retirement fund in May 1943, which was entirely employer-financed. This was the first industry-wide agreement under which industry had assumed the responsibility for old-age pensions for its employees.[31] Under the plan a cloak maker became eligible for old-age benefits at 65 years of age to the extent of $600 per year. A wage escalator clause was obtained by the cloak makers in their 1943 contract in order to protect the worker's wage against the rising cost of living. The tying of wages to the cost of living was not an innovation in the garment industry. It was first introduced in 1921, later to be discontinued. Introduction of it was made again in 1939, and during the postwar period a predominant number of contracts in the trade resorted to its use or provided a wage reopening clause in the contract.

In the New York dress industry the workers won a health-and-vacation fund in 1944. Every jobber and manufacturer in the industry paid 3½ per cent of the weekly payroll into a fund which was to be administered by the union. This marked the first adoption of a health plan through collective bargaining.[32]

### POST WORLD WAR II PERIOD

When wage controls were modified and then finally lifted in 1946, wage rates increased substantially. The greatest gain since the 1944 convention was found in the dress industry which experienced a 28 per cent rise in hourly earnings.

Foreseeing the reconversion problems which would beset the country at the close of hostilities, the General Executive Board recommended that the guaranteed annual wage plans be promoted through collective bargaining and by legislation wherever conditions required it. In 1947 the Kansas City Joint Board of the ILGWU negotiated a contract guaranteeing employment and earnings with the Gernes Garment Co. of Kansas City, Mo.[33] Particularly noteworthy is the Philadelphia Fair Income Fund installed by the Philadelphia Dress Joint Board in 1945. According to this plan, earnings of workers affected by lay-offs are supplemented by payments from the "fair income" fund jointly administered, to which employers contribute 3½ per cent of their payroll. For each three weeks of unemployment, which need not be consecutive, a union member in good standing receives 70 per cent of his average weekly earnings, such payments being limited to five checks a year with a maximum of $40 per check. These payments are in addition to whatever state unemployment benefits the workers may receive.[34] The General Executive Board also urged that the Fair Labor Standards Act be amended to raise the minimum hourly rate from 40 cents to 70 cents together with provisions for further rises to a minimum of $1.00 an hour.[35] The following resolutions adopted by the 26th Convention in 1947 reveal the demands of the membership for strengthening and broadening the social security laws.

1. The old age and survivors program should include coverage of workers excluded under the act, increase benefits to help meet increased cost of living, extend duration of benefits, age eligibility reduced from 65 to 60 with a further reduction in age eligibility for women;
2. Adoption of an adequate health program for entire nation;
3. 75 cents hourly minimum wage;
4. Maximum work week of 35 hours in the ladies' garment industry—wherever conditions make it possible;
5. Further investigation of the problem of the guaranteed annual wage in the light of the studies and experience available and preparation of proposals for action appropriate to the industry.[36]

On October 25, 1945, the Cloak Joint Board requested a health and vacation fund to provide systematic health care and sick benefits for all cloak workers. Although employer opposition was incurred, an arbitration award created such a fund on June 1, 1946. Like the health fund in the dress industry, the money was provided through employer contributions.

A retirement fund for the New York dress industry, similar to the earlier plan created in the New York cloak industry, was won on February 28, 1947. This fund was also financed by employers.[37]

In spite of the general prosperous conditions of the nation following the war, the women's garment industry did not picture a uniform well-being as it did in the war years. Among the conditions which adversely affected the economic status of the workers were: shorter work-hours with corresponding reduction in overtime pay; adjustment to a buyer's market and the increased emphasis on lower priced items; changes in fashion trends; increased number of different styles and the shorter runs on individual styles; greater emphasis on quality of workmanship. On the whole, the wage structure stood up firmly, and casual employer attempts to weaken it were resisted by the union.[38]

A comparison of the average hourly earnings in the women's and men's garment industry during the postwar years reveals some pertinent facts. As shown in Table XIV, page 114, the average hourly earnings in women's coats, suits and skirts declined from $1.95 in 1947 to $1.90 in 1950 or three per cent while men's suits and coats increased from $1.28 to $1.36 or six per cent. In other divisions of women's and men's garments the pattern of wage increases was about the same. A comparison of the average hourly earnings in the garment industry with that of all manufacuring shows that the clothing industry lagged behind in wage gains. This phenomenon may be partly explained by the unusually large demand for durable manufactured products caused by shortages during the war. Wages of garment workers compared favorably with those of other industries. Employment in the women's garment trades continued at higher levels than before World War II, but considerable fluctuation has been experienced. With increased demand for clothing in 1952 and 1953 wage gains were made in almost all divisions. The greatest gains on the whole were found in the lower wage branches.

It was in the field of welfare benefits that the ILGWU made its greatest gains in the postwar period. It expanded its coverage to practically every affiliate of the union. One of the most outstanding features was retirement benefits. Beginning in the cloak and suit and dress trades of New York, the welfare benefits spread rapidly to the garment centers in the Eastern States, New England, and the Midwest.[39]

KOREAN WAR PERIOD

With the outbreak of the Korean War and the resumption of the rise in the cost of living, the ILGWU again pressed for wage increases and more fringe benefits. The New York Cloak Joint Board invoked the escalator clause in its contract in the fall of 1950. Acting in accordance with a resolution adopted by the International's Executive Board, the Joint Board demanded a 15 per cent wage increase from the employers' association. The request was met by a refusal and had to be submitted to the industry's impartial chairman, who awarded the cloakmakers a wage increase of $5 a week. For piecework operators the $5 increase was converted into 6 per cent raises for operators and 7 per cent for finishers.[40]

The Boston Joint Board of the Cloak, Skirt and Dressmakers informed all affiliates in the New England area to begin immediate negotiations for a 15 per cent across the board increase for all workers. The union pointed out that this increase had been the pattern for its members in the New York market and in other centers, and it would be inequitable to withhold a similar increase in the New England market. The union further requested that current contributions to health and retirement funds be increased. An arbitration award requested varying pay increases with additional contributions by employers to the health and retirement funds of one-half of one per cent of their total payroll.[41]

In the renewal of the collective agreements in the spring of 1951, difficulties were again encountered with the New York Cloak and Suit employers' associations. The employers objected to the union proposals for improvements in the contract. A two-day stoppage of the cloakmakers forced the employers to accept the workers' demands. The gains in the new contract included: 1) an increase in minimum wages; 2) increased payments to the health and vacation fund from 3½ to 4½ per cent of payrolls; 3) increased benefits to families of deceased members receiving retirement benefits at the time of death; 4) a uniformity of labor costs to prevent unfair competitive advantages in any part of the industry; section shops operating on a week-work basis were to be converted to piece work; 5) a formula was agreed upon to achieve an equitable distribution of available work among workers in the "inside" and "out of town" shops working for the New York market.[42]

During 1952 the cloakmakers launched a campaign to eliminate the open-shop fringe which might menace work standards and stability in the New York market. Through the use of the strike and unfavorable publicity the open shop members began to sign up with the union, until almost all had become unionized. Following the successful campaign in the coat and suit industry, a similar organizational drive was conducted in the skirt and sportswear field in the spring of 1953.[43] The New York Dress Joint Board obtained new agreements in 1951 which provided wage increases and improvements to the health and welfare fund. All piece workers received 30 per cent on top of their total piece-rate earnings instead of 22 per cent previously received. Week workers' increases ranged from $3 for examiners, cleaners and pinkers to $5 for cutters. Payments to Health and Welfare Fund were raised from 4½ per cent to 6½ per cent. Like the cloak and suit industry, the dress industry found it necessary to conduct an intensive organizational drive in 1952, with aid of strikes, to wipe out non-union jobber firms. As a result, most of the new jobbers agreed to unionize their shops and to confine their work to union contractors.[44]

The General Executive Board of the ILGWU at a wage policy meeting in the spring of 1952 declared that the only fact common to all women's garment markets at present is the justice of seeking wage increases to fill the gap between the full rise in the cost of living and adjustments obtained since the outbreak of war in Korea. But it is interesting to note that the General Executive Board recognized that it was impracticable to attempt to impose a single uniform wage formula on the many garment centers and trades. It recognized that some firms are operating at the margins, and that disregard of a firm's financial condition would prove to do more harm than good. As no one firm is dominant in the garment industry as is true in industries such as steel and automobiles, wage levels and policies cannot be uniform and regional markets have not reached the same level of productivity and profits. Likewise, competition among firms, markets and regions is widespread.[45]

Small increases in wage rates were obtained in the 1952 negotiations for both women's and men's garments, as indicated by Table XIV, page 114. The negligible wage improvement was due to the temporary slow down in the garment industry. Because of the war stimulus in the heavy manufacturing industries, earnings of workers in this area of the economy experienced much sharper advances than for the garment workers.

By 1953 the International was convinced that substantial wage increases were necessary because of a pick-up in garment sales, the lag in the garment workers' wages in comparison to wages of other employees during the past two years, and the need to restore the workers' real income which had been lessened by higher living costs. The New York cloakmakers were among the first to receive a substantial increase of $5 or about 14¢ an hour. The New York dressmakers submitted their demands and obtained a decision from their impartial chairman for a wage increase comparable to the coatmakers.[46]

With the exception of knitted outerwear, knitted underwear and children's outerwear, the year 1954 witnessed a decline in the dollar volume of women's apparel. The recession was not conducive to wage increases and, in coats, suits and skirts, the average hourly wage dropped from $1.97 to $1.96. In line with the union policy of winning an overall 35-hour work-week, it is interesting to note that the small increases in average hourly earnings in 1954 in other branches of the ladies' garment industry were achieved by a reduction in weekly hours without a loss in weekly pay. In 1953 approximately 52 per cent of the workers were on a 35-hour week, 18 per cent were working 37½ hours, and 30 per cent were still on a 40-hour week. By 1954 a further extension of the 35-hour week was made. Employees working 40 hours a week were reduced to 37½ hours, and those previously working 37½ hours now worked only 35 hours. The union feels that the reduced working week will: 1) iron out monthly fluctuations in production and employment, 2) stabilize the industry, 3) improve working conditions. During the period of fifty years the ILGWU has reduced hours in the industry from 70 to 60, to 56, to 48, to 44, to 40, and lastly to 35.

### ILGWU HEALTH, WELFARE, AND RETIREMENT PLANS

One of the most outstanding achievements of the ILGWU has been its pioneering in the field of health and welfare programs. Unquestionably, the union has created a body of experience which other labor organizations have used. The union has felt that the welfare of the worker is the concern and responsibility of the employer and of society, because they both profit from the labor of the employee. This philosophy explains why the union has shifted the financial responsibility of welfare plans to the employer.[47]

Medical and health care was the first objective. This was natural because conditions in the industry were conducive to ill health such as: long hours of work, filthy work shops without proper sanitation, tenement home work, and low wages. Through employer contributions from payrolls the union has established health centers in the principal sectors of its membership. In smaller places where the concentration of memberships could not justify the health centers, automobile units for the diagnostic care of members in their respective shops have been established. In still other areas members are cared for through direct arrangements with physicians.

With the passage of time the health benefits have been expanded, and other welfare benefits have been added to include vacations, pensions and death benefits. By 1953 the ILGWU benefit achievements for its 430,830 members are as follows:[48]

Total Protected by Health and Welfare Benefits—419,000

393,230 members receive benefits from union-administered funds.

25,770 members receive benefits under insurance carried by employers.

Total Receiving Vacation Benefits—388,090

350,541 members receive benefits from union-administered funds.

37,549 members receive payments directly from employers.

Total Protected for Old Age—337,914

199,580 members are covered by funds which are paying benefits.

138,334 members are covered by funds scheduled to start payments in the near future.

Total covered by Death Benefit—429,537

400,672 members are covered by the regular $150 death benefit, and the $350 and $500 supplementary death benefits for a total benefit of $1,000.

21,972 members are covered only by the regular $150 death benefit and the $350 supplementary death benefit for a total benefit of $500.

6,893 members are covered only by the regular $150 death benefit.

Total Eligible for Care at Union Health Centers—350,025

326,025 members receive care at existing centers.

24,000 members are to receive care at centers now under construction.

The wage policies of the ILGWU, like those of the ACWA, have been affected by the nature of the industry and the system of production. During most of its history the industry has experienced keen competition and much irregularity in production and employment. The following wage patterns have been expressed.

## I. Stablilization of Wages and Employment

In order to protect labor standards the International during its earlier years centered its attention on achieving some degree of wage parity between employers. The New York dressmakers and the New York cloakmakers went on prolonged strikes. A "protocol of peace" was effectuated by which the two branches of the union obtained many concessions for protecting working standards. However, the "protocol of peace" did not last long as the "inside" manufacturers evaded their agreement.

In the early years of the 1920's the International was convinced that it must attack the problems at the real source—the jobber and the manufacturer. A program was formulated by the New York Cloak Joint Board which recognized that the jobbers and manufacturers were indirectly the true employers of labor and should accept responsibility for labor conditions in the shops of the contractors and sub-manufacturers. Upon refusal of the employers to acquiesce to this principle with a general strike threatening, Governor Alfred E. Smith appointed a commission to investigate the problems in the industry and to make advisory recommendations. The final report verified the union's position. To accomplish this, the report recommended: 1) limitation of sub-manufacturers, 2) designation of sub-manufacturers by the jobber, 3) equitable distribution of work among sub-manufacturers and contractors. The commission's recommendations were largely rejected by the employers and the Cloak Joint Board whose leadership turned Communistic.

The NRA provided the opportunity to bring order out of chaos. The codes of fair competition in 1933 placed in effect many of the chief principles recommended by the Governor's Commission and long sought for by the International and New York joint boards. The dress codes were not as satisfactory as those in coats and suits, and the jobbers and manufacturers in this branch of the industry dodged their responsibilities. In 1936 stabilization was finally achieved in women's dresses.

As a necessary aid in the stabilization of the dress industry the N.Y. Dress Joint Board demanded and finally attained price settlement on jobbers' premises, the unit system of price settlement and a limitation of contractors.

The following provisions in the collective agreements in the coat and suit industry since 1933 and the dress industry since 1936 have greatly improved the stability of the women's garment industry: 1) designation of contractor; 2) designated contractors and submanufacturers must maintain union shops that employ at least fourteen machine workers and a complement of employees in other branches of work; 3) equitable distribution of work; 4) permission to enlarge or decrease the size of the shop; 5) union approval to add, subtract or discharge contractors; 6) responsibility of jobbers and manufacturers for payment of wages to the workers in the contracting and sub-manufacturing shop; 7) establishment of an umpire in the industry; 8) responsibility of jobbers and manufacturers to pay reasonable amount for overhead to their contractors and sub-manufacturers as a separate item; 9) elimination of contracting or sub-contracting within the shop; 10) protection of workers against new machinery and technological changes.

The International has always been alert to factors in the industry and the economy affecting wages and standards of living for its members. During the rapid and continuous spiraling of prices following World War II it demanded escalator clauses in many of its contracts. A predominant number of contracts have such a clause or include a wage reopening provision. The ILGWU has always striven for complete unionization of the industry as a means not only to solve stabilization but to enhance the workers' well-being.

The latest move on the part of the union to maintain stability of wages and employment is the reduction of the work-week to 35 hours and to obtain amendment of the Fair Labor Standards Act. The union wants to increase the national minimum wage from 75 cents to $1.25 per hour, but to provide an equivalent adjustment in cents per hour in Puerto Rico and the Virgin Islands, the United States has allowed minimum wage rates on the Islands to be set by industry committees below the levels provided by law. With the passage of years the insular minimum and average wages have failed to keep pace with the mainland minimums, which has created an unfair differential. The problem has become acute for the apparel industry on the mainland owing to this competitive disadvantage in labor costs. President Dubinsky has appeared before the Senate Committee on Labor and Public Welfare seeking to make the necessary adjustments on the Islands. Dubinsky believes that this change is necessary not only to protect the industry and workers' standards in the United States but also to raise the economic level of the workers on the Islands.

## II. Union-Management Cooperation

The International and the joint boards have welcomed the opportunity to work with management for the benefit of both parties. In 1939 the New York Dress Joint Board devised a program for rehabilitating and modernizing the dress industry. In 1941 under the impetus of the union the New York Dress Institute was established for promoting the dress industry. In the same year an efficiency engineering department was set up by the New York board for the purpose of working with employers.

In its negotiation with management, the joint boards and the International have recognized that it is impractical to attempt to impose a single wage formula in the trade. It has tried to determine for each market and branch the most advantageous terms. It has acknowledged that some firms are operating at close margins while others are more prosperous.

## III. Welfare Benefits and the Guaranteed Wage

Although the ILGWU began to emphasize fringe benefits in its wage policies in the 1920's, it was not until World War II that the union made welfare benefits an important part of the program. Faced with a wage freeze, the union sought health insurance, retirement benefits, and vacations. During the post war years the ILGWU made its greatest gains in the field of welfare benefits and created a body of experience which other unions have emulated. One of the unique features of the ILGWU benefit programs is the establishment of health centers in localities where there is a concentration of its membership. Benefits now cover practically all of its members in a broad capacity.

Unlike the Amalgamated, the ILGWU has not achieved full reciprocity in the vesting of pension rights in all branches of the industry. Although a worker can move from shop to shop in the same branch of the industry without losing his pension rights, he cannot do so if he transfers to another branch. In 1953 the International adopted a "reciprocity retirement" formula to permit its members to retain their rights to retirement benefits even if their membership is divided among more than one local union of the International, or if they are employed in more than one branch of the industry. The implementation of this principle is still to be achieved by collective bargaining.

The guaranteed annual wage has been given consideration by the ILGWU on several different occasions during the last thirty years. The earliest experience dates back to the early 1920's with the adoption of a limited guarantee by the Cleveland Garment Manufacturers' Association. In the latter part of the 1930's and during World War II the union felt the need for employment guarantees and began to promote such schemes through collective bargaining and legislation. In a few instances the union was successful in obtaining a guarantee of employment and earnings. The ILGWU recognizes that before the guaranteed annual wage can become a reality much study of the subject is required, and it is constantly exploring the principle for application to the women's garment industry. It believes that the winning of the guaranteed annual wage in the basic industries such as steel and automobiles will pave the way for its universal adoption.

## IV. Legislative and Political Demands

The ILGWU has increasingly resorted to legislative and political channels to improve its well-being. This is evidenced by its pioneering work for the adoption of the Fair Labor Standards Act and for its amendment to increase minimum wages. The union is a strong advocate for improvements in the Social Security Act. It desires to increase old age benefits and raise state unemployment insurance payments to more realistic levels. National Health Insurance has been actively sought and, last but not least, the amendment of the Taft-Hartley Act.

## TABLE XIV

### Average Hourly Earnings in Women's Garment Industry Compared with Men's Clothing and Other Industries

| Women's Garments | 1901 | 1919 | 1933 | 1934 | 1935 | 1937 | 1938 | 1939 | 1940 | 1941 | 1942 | 1943 | 1944 | 1945 | 1946 | 1947 | 1948 | 1949 | 1950 | 1951 | 1952 | 1953 | 1954 |
|---|---|---|---|---|---|---|---|---|---|---|---|---|---|---|---|---|---|---|---|---|---|---|---|
| Coats, suits and skirts | .21 | .60 | .83 | 1.065 | 1.086 | 1.13 | 1.13 | 1.02 | .92 | .98 | 1.13 | 1.37 | 1.56 | 1.675 | 1.92 | 1.95 | 2.02 | 1.96 | 1.90 | 1.94 | 1.95 | 1.97 | 1.96 |
| Cotton garments | .11 | .29 | .296 | .39 | * | .37 | .39 | .39 | .42 | .46 | .53 | .60 | .67 | .74 | .83 | .84 | .875 | .88 | .96 | 1.03 | 1.06 | 1.08 | 1.10 |
| Dresses (except cotton) | .12 | .45 | .55 | .73 | .705 | .80 | .75 | .73 | .72 | .73 | .80 | .99 | 1.14 | 1.28 | 1.44 | 1.35 | 1.40 | 1.37 | 1.38 | 1.44 | 1.45 | 1.49 | 1.50 |
| Corsets and allied garments | * | * | * | .47 | .455 | .46 | .46 | .456 | .475 | .51 | .58 | .66 | .73 | .77 | .87 | .94 | 1.00 | * | * | 1.19 | 1.24 | 1.30 | 1.34 |
| Knitted Outerwear x | * | * | .356 | .44 | .46 | .46 | .47 | .46 | .48 | .50 | .57 | .67 | .74 | .80 | .88 | .99 | 1.05 | 1.075 | 1.13 | 1.23 | 1.26 | 1.33 | 1.39 |
| Knitted Underwear x | * | * | .30 | .395 | .40 | .41 | .42 | .415 | .44 | .47 | .54 | .60 | .65 | .70 | .80 | .91 | .99 | 1.00 | 1.06 | 1.15 | 1.18 | 1.20 | 1.22 |
| Women's clothing not elsewhere classified | * | * | * | * | * | .45 | * | .42 | .45 | .49 | .56 | .68 | .78 | .86 | .94 | 1.16 | 1.21 | 1.205 | 1.21 | 1.29 | 1.31 | 1.375 | 1.39 |
| **Men's Clothing** |  |  |  |  |  |  |  |  |  |  |  |  |  |  |  |  |  |  |  |  |  |  |  |
| Suits, coats | * | * | * | * | * | * | * | .67 | * | * | * | * | * | * | * | 1.28 | 1.37 | 1.345 | 1.36 | 1.47 | 1.49 | 1.57 | 1.62 |
| Furnishings, work clothing | * | * | * | * | * | * | * | .42 | * | * | * | * | * | * | * | .87 | .92 | .92 | .99 | 1.06 | 1.08 | 1.11 | 1.14 |
| Shirts, collars, nightwear | * | * | * | * | * | * | * | .398 | .42 | .455 | .527 | .582 | .65 | .694 | .79 | .88 | .93 | .93 | .99 | 1.07 | 1.08 | 1.11 | 1.14 |
| Separate trousers | * | * | * | * | * | * | * | * | * | * | * | * | * | * | * | .94 | .99 | .98 | 1.04 | 1.12 | 1.14 | 1.19 | 1.20 |
| Work shirts | * | * | * | * | * | * | * | .309 | .351 | .394 | .449 | .482 | .533 | .576 | .653 | .74 | .74 | .77 | .87 | .93 | .93 | .93 | .95 |
| All Manufacturing | * | * | .442 | .532 | .550 | .624 | .627 | .633 | .661 | .729 | .853 | .961 | 1.019 | 1.023 | 1.086 | 1.24 | 1.35 | 1.40 | 1.47 | 1.59 | 1.67 | 1.77 | 1.81 |
| Non-durable goods | * | * | .427 | .515 | .530 | .577 | .584 | .582 | .602 | .640 | .723 | .803 | .861 | .904 | 1.015 | 1.17 | 1.28 | 1.33 | 1.38 | 1.48 | 1.54 | 1.61 | 1.66 |
| Durable goods | * | * | .472 | .556 | .577 | .674 | .686 | .698 | .724 | .808 | .947 | 1.059 | 1.117 | 1.111 | 1.156 | 1.29 | 1.41 | 1.47 | 1.54 | 1.67 | 1.77 | 1.87 | 1.92 |
| Automobiles | * | * | .593 | .700 | .739 | .891 | .925 | .845 | .851 | .953 | 1.03 | 1.23 | 1.27 | 1.26 | 1.33 | 1.47 | 1.61 | 1.68 | 1.69 | 1.81 | 2.04 | 2.14 | 2.21 |
| Primary metal industries | * | * | * | * | * | * | * | * | * | 1.042 | 1.124 | 1.167 | 1.118 | 1.118 | 1.291 | 1.44 | 1.58 | 1.65 | 1.69 | 1.91 | 1.90 | 2.06 | 2.09 |
| Millinery | * | * | * | * | * | * | * | * | .666 | .700 | .738 | .849 | .925 | 1.161 | 1.228 | 1.34 | 1.44 | 1.51 | 1.54 | 1.60 | 1.60 | 1.62 | 1.62 |
| Printing, publishing, and allied industries | * | * | * | * | * | * | * | * | .882 | .900 | .952 | 1.00 | 1.08 | 1.14 | 1.283 | 1.52 | 1.70 | 1.82 | 1.88 | 1.96 | 2.10 | 2.20 | 2.27 |
| Rubber products | * | * | * | * | * | * | * | * | .766 | .822 | .92 | 1.02 | 1.095 | 1.125 | 1.254 | 1.39 | 1.46 | 1.51 | 1.58 | 1.69 | 1.83 | 1.93 | 1.97 |
| Cotton, silks, synthetic fibre | * | * | * | * | * | * | * | * | * | * | * | * | * | * | * | 1.01 | 1.126 | 1.153 | 1.20 | 1.28 | 1.29 | 1.30 | 1.29 |
| Woolens and worsteds | * | * | .396 | .493 | .493 | .493 | .545 | .528 | .564 | .634 | .744 | .809 | .841 | .872 | 1.012 | 1.16 | 1.31 | 1.32 | 1.36 | 1.48 | 1.56 | 1.56 | 1.53 |

*Not available

xIncludes both men's and women's garments

Ladies' Garments:

1901 - 1919 — Report and Record, 27th Convention, ILGWU, 1950, p. 60.
1932 - 1935 — Employment, Payrolls, Hours, and Wages in 115 Selected Code Industries, 1933-1935. National Recovery Administration, Division of Review. Washington, 1935. (Bureau of Labor Statistics)
1932 - 1938 — Report to 24th Convention ILGWU, 1940. Based on B. L. S. Statistics and N. R. A. Division of Review.
1939 - 1946 — Compiled from Bureau of Labor Statistics Reports by ILGWU Research Department.
1947 - 1953 — U.S. Dept. of Labor, B. L. S. Employment, Hours, and Earnings, Historical Series: Women's Suits, Coats, Skirts, Feb, 1953, April, 1954.
        Ibid., Corsets and allied garments, Feb., 1954.
        Ibid., Women's dresses, Feb., 1953, April, 1954.
        Ibid., Knit Outerwear, Feb., 1953, April, 1953.
        Ibid., Knit Underwear, Feb., 1953, April, 1953.
        Ibid., Household apparel, Feb., 1953, April, 1954.
        Women's clothing not elsewhere classified — compiled by ILGWU Research Dept. Based on unpublished industry data by B. L. S.
1933 - 1947 — Handbook of Labor Statistics, 1947 edition, U.S. Dept. of Labor, B. L. S., Bulletin No. 916, U.S. Govt. Printing Office.
1947 - 1950 — Ibid, 1950 edition. Bulletin No. 1016, U.S. Dept. of Labor, B. L. S. Monthly Labor Review, Aug., 1954, Vol. 77.

## CHAPTER SIX

# The Amalgamated Clothing Workers of America

### INTRODUCTION: CHARACTERISTICS OF THE INDUSTRY

The wage policies of the Amalgamated Clothing Workers of America, like that of its sister union ILGWA, can best be understood in the light of the background of the industry and its workers. In many respects, the characteristics of the men's clothing industry closely parallel the women's clothing industry.

The industry is concentrated in and about a few large cities. New York City, Philadelphia, and Chicago are the three largest producing centers with Rochester, Baltimore, Cleveland, Cincinnati, Boston, and St. Louis ranking next in importance. A substantial amount of clothing is produced in some lesser cities primarily located in the East and Middle West.

A considerable degree of irregularity of production and employment has characterized the industry. Unquestionably this instability has influenced the union wage policies as will be pointed out shortly. What are the factors and conditions affecting the regularity of production and stability of employment? The first factor is the nature of the demand. The demand is subject to both seasonal and cyclical variations, but the former varies with the latter and is a function of it. Much of the irregularity in production which appears to be due to seasonal factors is in reality accounted for by the business cycle. For the most part the variations in the aggregate demand for the product are closely related to the national income. A rise in the national income expresses itself in an increase in the number of units sold and in the amount spent per unit, and a decline in income will have the reverse effect. However, the percentage of income spent for clothing by various income groups from year to year shows a marked constancy.[1]

The second and third factors which affect regularity of production and employment are the nature of production and distribution. The manufacturers of ready-to-wear clothing may be classified by the type of shop which may be either "inside shop," the "contract shop" or "integrated manufacturer." The "inside shop" establishment carries on all manufacturing under its own independent direction on its own premises and sells the finished product either at wholesale or to retail stores. Under the "contract shop" system, the manufacturing operations are divided among a manufacturer and several contractors who operate "contract shops." The manufacturer sends the cut-up cloth to "contract shops" which perform the tailoring operations for agreed contract. The product is then sold through independently owned and operated retail stores or department stores. In 1939 "contract shops" employed about 35 per cent of wage earners in the industry. The "integrated" manufacturers produce the product in their own shops and sell it in company-owned and operated retail stores. The records reveal that the shops of the "integrated" manufacturers operate for longer periods each season than the other producers, and their seasonal fluctuations are less marked than their competitors.

A fourth influence on regularity is the capacity in relation to the demand for the product. The industry normally experiences much excess capacity. There have been a number of causes for this condition such as: 1) ease of entry into the industry because of low capital requirements; 2) readily accessible supply of raw materials on easy terms; 3) surplus labor force which can be quickly and cheaply trained. The low capital requirements which have permitted entrance into the industry have in turn greatly accentuated the competitive nature of the business. No one company employs as many as 4 per cent of the total workers in the men's clothing industry.

The final factor influencing the industry is the character of the working force. About 62 per cent of the total workers are women. Earlier census figures showed a lower percentage of women workers in relation to men. In earlier years immigrants comprised the bulk of the employees. Since the curtailment of immigration, an increasing proportion of the workers is native-born.

The Amalgamated Clothing Workers Union was founded in 1914, but its antecedents go back to 1891 with the organization of the United Garment Workers of America. In 1933 the Amalgamated joined the AFL but affiliated with the CIO in 1935. During the early years the working conditions of the employees in the men's clothing industry were similar to those in the women's garment industry; namely, long hours of work in crowded, dirty, and dimly lighted shops at deplorably low wages. At the time the union was founded in 1914, the full-time work-week was 51 hours, and the average hourly earnings were 27 cents. Early documents of the union show that the union recognized the need to reduce the working hours to eight per day and forty-four per week, and to raise wages in order to protect the workers' standard of living.[2]

EARLY WAGE POLICY

The constant threat of deterioration in wage standards was evidenced in the union's early wage policy to establish uniform wage scales in all the clothing markets. Lack of uniformity gave advantages to unscrupulous manufacturers. A resolution was passed at the 1920 convention instructing the General Executive Board to inaugurate a policy which would result in securing uniformity in wage scales in all markets,[3] but realized unilateral wage reductions continued to be a complaint of the union membership. It became so acute in New York City that the 1926 convention adopted a resolution authorizing the General Executive Board in conjunction with the New York City administration to start an immediate campaign for a minimum scale of wages.[4] In 1928 the New York locals won a significant victory for minimum wage scales for coatmakers, tailors, pressers and pants makers.[5]

From the beginning the ACWA was opposed to piece-work system of wage payment on the grounds that the increased production per worker was at the expense of the health and safety of the workers, a fear of wage cutting when the workers' production went up, and a fear of unemployment caused by increased productivity. The workers' resentment of the piece-rate system was not based on a fanciful fear but rather was attested by the repeated experiences of many shops.

In 1920 the employers in the New York City market submitted demands which included the right to install piece-work systems and wage scales which prevailed in other clothing centers in order to meet competition. To the union the demands were unacceptable as they would have produced a breakdown in labor standards.[6] The union's policy on a suitable basis of pay prevailed for some time in almost every sector of the industry, and until the latter part of the

1920's, time wages were used extensively. A change in the union's position began to appear in 1928. In that year an agreement between the New York Clothing Manufacturers' Exchange and the New York Joint Board of the ACWA resulted in the introduction of a piece-rate system for the coatmakers' locals but confined to only the inside shops. In order to protect the workers against exploitation, the union insisted that a joint board of union and employers' representatives be responsible for establishing the rates.[7] The piece-work system is now widespread with the exception of a very few highly skilled jobs. According to Kurt Braun, the adoption of the piece-rate system by the union leaders and members is traceable to the development of union-management cooperation. When the unions gained a more secure position and a voice in the industry, the union's objections to the piece-rate system disappeared. The union became convinced that the only way to improve the conditions of the workers was to improve the general health of the industry. The piece-rate system was suited to increase production and returns to both employers and employees. It was also conducive to the maintenance of more uniformity in wage costs and was best fitted to bring about stabilization programs. Without equal wage costs per unit in competing shops, wage standards would always be endangered.[8]

## POST WORLD WAR I PERIOD

Following the First World War employers in the men's clothing industry, as was true elsewhere, began to return to the non-union shop. In New York City the employers proceeded to lock out the members of the Amalgamated in violation of their arbitration agreement. A six months' struggle was finally won by the union. The settlement in June 1921 provided:

1. Establishment of the union shop;
2. 44-hour work-week;
3. Standards of production in each shop to be determined for each operation by representatives of the union and employers;
4. A joint committee of the union and the clothing association to determine the scale of wages;
5. Appointment of a commission of representatives of the union and employers to work out the relations between the union, the association, and the contractors;
6. A 15 per cent reduction of wages except for cutters;

7. Establishment of a board of arbitration to which was vested the administration of the new agreement.[9]

Although the agreement gave every appearance of establishing cooperation between management and the union through which all parties would benefit, it was short-lived. The sick condition of the industry was to a large extent responsible for this. Except for a spurt in 1923 the values of the products declined steadily, and payrolls fell also. The industry was over-expanded during the 1920's and early 1930's because of the constant exploitation of new areas. These untapped regions were developed because of the availability of low-wage labor, freedom from union controls and cheap factory space. Then, too, competition among contractors for tailoring work on a contract basis from manufacturers accounted for much of the instability. The union recognized that it must unionize the contract shops as well as the entire industry if cutthroat competition were to cease. The following resolution adopted by the 1924 convention shows the importance it attached to the control of the contract shop.

"Whereas, the contracting system in our industry is used by the manufacturers as a means of undermining the wages and working conditions, and constitutes a menace to the life and welfare of the workers in the industry, and

Whereas, the contracting system now prevalent in the industry is largely responsible for the reappearance of the sweatshop system; therefore, be it

Resolved, that the incoming General Executive Board bend all its energies for the elimination of the contracting system and the re-establishing of the inside shop throughout the industry."[10]

The Amalgamated turned its attention to the new areas which were being exploited and began organizing drives to unionize the entire industry. Its attempts to realize its objective were unsuccessful because of the threat of unemployment in a declining industry. Between 1920 and 1925 the membership of the union dropped substantially.

In the spring of 1924 the Chicago manufacturers demanded a substantial reduction in wages. The union refused to accept this course of action as a solution to the ills in the industry. However, it turned its attention to cooperation with the employers in order to reduce costs through greater efficiency. As a result, the wage negotiations of 1924 were converted into a survey of the industry, with a view of discovering all possible sources of saving and means of increasing employment. Technically trained union experts worked with management in devising more economical methods of production.[11] Restrictive rules benefiting small groups of highly skilled workers were abolished. On the other hand, the union insisted that management be efficient and that competent supervisors be appointed.

In several instances the union assumed the chief responsibility in organizing a new shop for established firms in order to enable them to compete in a lower price-range. An outstanding example was the introduction of a cheaper line by Hart, Schaffner and Marx after 1924. The union gave the firm a definite labor cost per suit and took the responsibility of setting piece rates so that the cost would fall within the agreed limit. Union officials helped to design the garment and assisted the firm to maintain quality.[12] In the city of Cincinnati the union helped to reorganize the shop of a firm which had been losing money for several years. Many antiquated methods of performing operations were discovered and changed, with resulting benefit to both the firm and the workers.[13] On several occasions the union gave temporary financial aid to union manufacturers who were exposed to the danger of liquidation. In all cases, the financial assistance prevented the firms closing and throwing out of work thousands of employees.[14]

In 1928 the General Executive Board of the union decided to ask for improvement in work standards which included an upward adjustment in wages in both the Chicago and Rochester markets, a 40-hour work-week, and increases in employer contributions in Chicago to an unemployment fund. However, because of depressed conditions in both markets and severe non-union competition, the Amalgamated did not press its demands. Its wage policy was to deal realistically with the problems of the industry. It recognized that it could not insist on more than the industry was capable of paying.[15]

The beginning of the Great Depression in 1929 gave the Amalgamated more trouble. The shrinkage of sales in the men's clothing industry impeded the union from carrying its unionization program to the remaining open shop markets in Buffalo, Cleveland, St. Louis, and Baltimore.[16] Despite adverse conditions, the union was constantly extending and consolidating the boundaries of its organization. A great victory was secured with the organizing of the Philadelphia market in 1929.

A breakdown of pay rates occurred during this period as a result of work scarcity and competition for jobs. In all markets employers pressed for wage reductions. In February 1932 the General Executive Board determined on a systematically organized resistance to the weakening of standards. The Board felt that a continued downward movement of wages would result in a market collapse. In order to bring pressure to bear, a work stoppage was ordered in July 1932 in the eastern territory. The fight for recovery was carried on along three major lines: 1) the sweat shop; 2) collective bargaining; 3) wage increases. The union emerged from the decade of the 1920's recognized by the majority of employers. By keeping the core of the union strong, the work of organizing the non-union markets was greatly facilitated. By 1933 the Amalgamated was in a position to exploit the opportunity provided by the NRA. After extending the area of collective bargaining, Sidney Hillman presented demands for wage increases to the president of the New York Clothing Manufacturers and Exchange. Shortly afterwards, similar demands were made upon other markets so as to stabilize conditions on a nation-wide basis.

THE NRA EXPERIMENT

The enactment of the NRA aided the union in its organizing activities and particularly brought about a stabilization in the industry which was greatly needed. It was the belief of the union that the NRA codes were only a working basis for minimum wages and maximum hours per week and that the union should continue from there for better standards.[17] Through the use of the minimum standards the NRA established for the first time in the history of the Amalgamated a uniformity of labor costs among producers in the various markets. One can, therefore, understand why the Amalgamated was so greatly disturbed with the invalidation of the NRA by the Supreme Court in 1935. It explains why the union redoubled its efforts in the summer of 1935 to strengthen the union markets as well as to organize the non-union ones. The results proved gratifying, because by 1939, 90 per cent of the industry was unionized. No substantial competition from non-union firms remained to threaten union standards. The Amalgamated did not rest on its laurels but campaigned politically for a wage-and-hour bill to protect its workers from chiselers. It also worked for unemployment and old-age insurance on a nationwide basis.[18]

The next step by the Amalgamated in its efforts to establish more uniformity in wage costs was to centralize the administration of wages in the national office under the direction of Mr. Hillman. Local unions were not permitted to deviate from the established standards of labor costs and specifications.[19] The union policy bore fruit in the 1937 national agreement in which the Amalgamated negotiated a 12 per cent wage increase with employers in the industry. This marked the first time in the history of the industry that a national union agreement was signed.[20]

With the coming of the recession in 1937 and 1938 in the men's clothing industry, the union stood firmly against any wage reductions. It felt that past experiences had demonstrated that reductions in wages had not relieved the depressed conditions of the industry, but instead had created worse conditions because of the reduced purchasing power of the workers.[21]

THE STABILIZATION OF GARMENTS

From earliest times the union considered wage stabilization necessary because of the competitive situation among local markets. Employers, for the most part, desired wage stabilization because of the chaotic condition in the industry resulting from price cutting. Stabilization was extremely difficult because of the many different price categories involved in the making of a suit of clothes. The union discovered that the attempt to negotiate identical or similar agreements would not elminate these price differences or prevent competition on wage differentials. It was evident that the workers' standard of living could not be raised until wage costs of competing manufacturers were equalized; and the only way to equalize costs was to effect some standardization of production.[22] It was also recognized that the determination of the contractors' wage costs would be futile unless the contractors' prices could cover such costs.

Beginning in 1933, the union began to formulate its stabilization program. At that time about 80 per cent of the industry was unionized, so that it considered the effort worth the experimentation. The New York and Philadelphia markets were selected to inaugurate the plan. It began with coats. The garments were classified with the cooperation of the manufacturers into a number of grades (1,2,3, and 4), and specifications were drawn up for each grade. Minimum labor costs were agreed upon in the first and second grades which were the most competitive and most difficult to control and enforce.[23] The union did not enforce a rigid policy for the first few years. It recognized that it would not be feasible to enforce standards until the stabilization program became better established.[24] The plan did not meet with much success owing to the neglect of the important details and inadequate provision for enforcement and competition from outside markets.[25]

In 1939 the Amalgamated set up a stabilization department, and a joint union-management committee worked out a plan to place the standardization program on a nationwide basis. The plan included the following steps: 1) classification of production within six grades of garments and the prohibition of changes in the grades without consent of the union; 2) fixing a standard labor-cost for each grade; 3) registration of contracts; 4) fixing of contractors' prices; 5) concentration of authority over general wage adjustments in a stabilization department responsible to Mr. Hillman; 6) Employment of inspectors to police the industry and prevent chiseling.[26]

In reporting on the stabilization program at the 1940 convention, the Executive Board stated that not only have severe competition and inter-market rivalry been abolished, but that the members have realized immediate advantage measured in dollars and cents. The increases in wages in sub-standard shops required to bring them up to established standards resulted in an annual pay increase of over one million dollars for 20,000 workers on no. 1 and no. 2 garments. The majority of workers realized increases of between five and ten per cent. In 1944 the General Executive Board reported that chiseling on wages had now been eliminated, and that manufacturers had improved quality without diminution in workers' earnings. The consumer as well as the worker had benefited from the stabilization program.

### WAGE POLICIES DURING WORLD WAR II

With the entrance of the United States into World World War II, the Amalgamated took the position that wage increases promoted rather than retarded the war effort. The union did not press for wage increases until 1941 when it became apparent that the industry could afford to pay them because of its improved financial condition.[27] During the years 1941-1942 the workers were successful in obtaining more than 15 per cent increases in wages. Again in 1943, the union gave notice of a desire to reopen the wage question because of the increased cost of living. During the early part of the war the union turned its attention to welfare benefits, and in 1941 it took steps to establish an insurance plan to include life insurance, accident, sickness, hospitalization, and surgical (including maternity) benefits. By 1945-1946 the union was successful in the realization of this program in all of the branches of the Amalgamated. The plan was financed by employer contributions to the Amalgamated Insurance Fund.[28]

The 1944 convention gave attention to a retirement plan for its members. A resolution was adopted to instruct the General Executive Board to negotiate with employers for the establishment of an employer fund to permit the retirement of employees at a level of decency and reasonable comfort.[29] In January 1947 the men's and boy's clothing industry became the first branch of the Amalgamated to enjoy a retirement plan.

For some time prior to VJ Day the officers of the Amalgamated were concerned about the need for a general wage increase. As a result, the union served notice to the industry that as soon as stabilization regulations permitted, it would demand an increase in wages to offset high living costs and to assure needed purchasing power to ward off unemployment during the demobilization period. Fringe benefits were demanded also, including six paid holidays and more employer contributions to retirement funds. The union obtained a general wage increase of 15 cents per hour, six paid legal holidays, and a three per cent contribution by employers to a retirement fund. The new benefits became effective in December 1945.[30] In 1944 paid vacations became almost universal in the Amalgamated shop.[31]

The continuing inflation soon began to wipe out the wage increases won in 1945. The union presented the problem to the Clothing Manufacturers' Association, and on October 10, 1946, an agreement was reached on a $5 weekly cost-of-living adjustment to be paid on an hourly basis over and above piece-work earnings or established rates. Many of the employers also agreed to a minimum wage of 65 cents which amounted to $10 a week above the federal minimum.

No sooner had the second postwar increase been granted when President Potofsky warned in May 1947 that unless price controls were re-established or inflation halted, the ACWA would be forced to seek a third postwar increase. By the fall of 1947 the Board unanimously decided that a further cost-of-living wage adjustment must be secured. The employers finally agreed to pay an additional cost-of-living increase of $5 a week, effective December 15, 1947. The Amalgamated also obtained a second week's vacation for those employees with two or more years of continuous employment.[32]

On the legislative front the Amalgamated continued its drive for amendment of the Fair Labor Standards Act to raise the minimum wages from 40 cents to more realistic levels in relation to 1948 prices. It also sought higher minimum wage rates under state laws because many of its workers in laundry, cleaning and dyeing industries were excluded from the federal minimum wage-and-hour law. In the field of social security, the 1948 convention urged the speedy enactment of a comprehensive social security program which would include extension of coverage of old age and survivors insurance, an increase in old age survivors' benefits, a federal system of unemployment insurance with standardized regulations and higher benefits, and a comprehensive national health program.[33]

In the period from 1948 to 1950 the union embarked on a broad program which had the following objectives: 1) defending the wage levels and working conditions; 2) improving social insurance and security standards; 3) protecting and increasing the volume of work for its members.

To accomplish the first goal, the union followed a policy of maintaining the union's power both internally and externally through administrative procedures, development of its educational program, and intensive organizing drives in the remaining non-union segments of the industry. The union achieved the second objective of improvement and extension of its retirement and health program in 1949. Effective January 1, 1950, retired workers of 65 years of age and over received a flat sum of $50 a month with a combined federal and Amalgamated maximum allowable benefits of $116. Life, accident, and health insurance, hospitalization, surgical, and maternity benefits were also liberalized.[34] Health centers received increasing attention with the establishment of the Sidney Hillman Health Center in New York followed by another health center in Philadelphia. The health centers were designed as an extension on a local level of a comprehensive sytem of social insurance paid for by employer contributions and providing many types of medical service in addition to hospitalization, surgical, and sick benefits.[35]

In respect to the promotion of a steady volume of work for the workers, the Amalgamated believed this goal was tied to the union's whole program for legislative and political action aimed toward building a stable prosperity for the entire nation. However, the union was not content to work entirely through the legislative and political channels, for it realized this was a long-range approach. It began immediately a publicity campaign to increase the demand for Amalgamated union-made garments.[36] The union believed that the union label program would not only increase the sale of its products but would also be instrumental in achieving its goal of a 100 per cent unionized shop. On the legislative and political front, the union sought to reinforce the purchasing power of all workers through increased minimum wages, more unemployment and old-age insurance benefits, amending the federal income tax to give relief to those in the lower income levels, repeal of war-imposed excise taxes, and effective price controls.

The amendment of the Fair Labor Standards Act on January 25, 1950, raising the minimum hourly wage from 40 cents to 75 cents was warmly greeted by the Amalgamated, even though most of the members were receiving more than the new minimum wage. At the 1950 convention the union went on record to raise the minimum wage to $1 per hour, to extend the act to all workers engaged in commerce including retail and service trades, and to strengthen all state minimum wage laws.[37]

### WAGE POLICIES DURING KOREAN WAR

With the outbreak of Korean hostilities and the concomitant increase in prices, Mr. Potofsky gave notice to the Clothing Manufacturers' Association that a general increase in wages was paramount.[38] Soon after, the executive committee of the union decided a wage increase of $1 a day or 12½ cents an hour on a 40-hour week or 13.9 cents on a 36-hour week was necessary.[39] Negotiations led to an agreement in October 1950 to encompass the requests.

In July 1952 the General Executive Board again formulated a program to enable its members to maintain and increase living standards with the advancing prices. The program as presented to the Clothing Manufacturers' Association included: 1) wage increases; 2) hospitalization coverage for wives of members and their children up to age 18; 3) full pay for six holidays in each calendar year;

4) two weeks' paid vacation after one year's service; 5) severance pay for members of firms that liquidate; 6) union label on all garments produced by manufacturer under agreement with the union; 7) a master agreement providing the same expiration date in all clothing markets.[40]

Effective May 25, 1953, 150,000 employees in the men's and boy's clothing industries obtained a 12½ cents an hour wage increase. Several months earlier a 3½ cents increase in fringe benefits was obtained as a result of an agreement reached between the union and the association in December 1952. The latter included a one per cent employer contribution to the industry-wide social welfare fund to provide hospitalization to the worker's family. Paid vacations and holiday provisions were also strengthened. The cotton garment industry likewise participated in increased fringe benefits including an extension of elegibility for hospital and surgical benefits to the union member's family.[41]

### SUMMARY OF ACWA WAGE POLICIES

The wage policies of the ACWA have been greatly influenced by the irregulary of production and employment in the industry. From 1920 to 1940 production and employment evidenced a marked decline. The industry became greatly over-expanded due to the exploitation of new areas in an effort to obtain cheaper labor and freedom from union control. This movement ceased in 1929 with the organization of the Philadelphia market, the last great clothing market to hold out against unionization. Competition between contractors in the various markets became severe during the 1930's with resulting deterioration in labor standards.

The union wage policies and techniques employed show the following pattern.

### I. *Union Shop—Industry-wide Collective Bargaining*

The union all through its history has recognized that unless all labor employer shops were unionized, it could not succeed in maintaining or in raising the general level of wages. Although the union met much resistance during the 1920's, it was tireless in its organizing efforts. With the completion of the major phases of organization work in 1929, the union turned to industry-wide bargaining.

Aided by the formation of the Clothing Manufacturers' Association of the United States in 1933 under the NRA, the Amalgamated under the leadership of Sidney Hillman began to negotiate industry-wide agreements in 1937. Since that time all major issues have been agreed to by the Association and the General Executive Board of the union with ratification by the members. The industry-wide understandings are then translated into market and local agreements, there being no overall national collective contract.

## II. The Union Label

The Amalgamated has spent much money and effort in promoting the union label. During 1953 and 1954 the Amalgamated union label drive has developed into one of the most extensive educational and promotional programs ever attempted by a labor union. The efforts of the union have been rewarded through the maintenance and extension of the union's gains and its influence for all workers in unions making consumer products.

## III. Wage Stabilization

The Amalgamated and, for the most part, the employers felt that it was imperative to achieve stabilization of the wage structure in order to bring about competitive parity in labor costs among employers. Without comparable wage parity, severe competition and lowering of wages would result. The union with the aid of the employers therefore turned to the device of standardizing labor costs. The impetus, however, in the wage stabilization movement came primarily from the union. The emphasis was not on the individual worker's earnings or uniform piece rates, but on competitive cost parity per unit of product. A definite total labor cost for the manufactured garment was established for a number of grades of the more popular priced garments. The piece rates for different operations were agreed upon by the union and employer locally, so that the total wage cost of each garment would equal the total that was established.

To enforce standardization of costs and to prevent chiseling among employers and local unions, the Amalgamated established a stabilization department in 1939 which provided for periodic examination of piece rates, labor costs and earnings of workers.

## IV. Union-Management Cooperation

During the 1920's the Amalgamated turned its attention to cooperation with employers to solve the basic problems in the industry. The union has furnished engineering experts to help management devise more economical methods of production. In a number of instances the union assumed entire responsibility for organizing the employers' shops so that they could compete more advantageously. The Amalgamated also has given financial assistance to manufacturers in danger of liquidation. In the large firms where the employers had all the advanced technical services, the Amalgamated has demanded the right to review piece rates and to correct specific rates. The union has also asked for the right to send in their own time-study experts or their own grievance committee to study jobs and to determine normal production and proper rates of pay. Although the Amalgamated opposed piece work for many years, it now accepted the piece-rate system. This change in policy was due to the development of union-management cooperation. After the union obtained a voice in industry, it was in a position to protect the workers from rate cutting. Then, too, the union became convinced that the piece-rate system was best suited to effectuate stabilization programs.

## V. Political and Legislative Efforts

The Amalgamated has consistently worked for the passage of laws to wipe out poverty and eliminate parasitic businesses. Under the NRA codes the union pressed for minimum wage and maximum hours. It has sought both federal and state wage-and-hour laws not only to protect the workers from chiselers, but to raise wages in some of the depressed branches of the industry such as laundry, cleaning and dyeing. The union has worked for higher wages because its members have been convinced that high purchasing power is essential for a prosperous and stable economy. Amendments to the federal wage-and-hour law have been demanded to raise the minimum wage to more realistic levels.

The Amalgamated has actively sought to raise the minimum wage levels in the apparel branches in Puerto Rico in order to protect union standards in the United States and to raise the economic level of the Puerto Rican workers.

Adequate social security legislation has received wholehearted support including old age benefits, unemployment and health insurance.

During recent years the union has demanded effective price control laws and their enforcement as well as an equitable tax system.

## VI. Fringe Benefits—Welfare Programs

Beginning in 1920 the Amalgamated envisioned the time when the clothing workers would enjoy a program of social insurance. In 1923 an unemployment insurance fund for workers in the men's and boy's clothing industry was established in the Chicago area. With the passage of the Social Security Act in 1935, the Chicago Unemployment Insurance Fund was no longer needed. Upon agreement it was converted into a life and health insurance plan. This plan became the forerunner of a widespread program of social insurance for the industry in 1940 with the establishment of the Amalgamated Life and Health Insurance Company. By 1945 the union members in all the branches of the union were obtaining benefits under a social insurance program.

During the Second World War the union gave increasing attention to welfare benefits when deprived of wage increases under the wage stabilization programs. In 1941 it sought employer-financed insurance programs to include life, accident, sickness, hospitalization and maternity. Later pension plans to supplement the inadequate social security benefits were included. The union has been successful in securing all of these.

The Amalgamated is one of the few unions in the United States that has achieved a reciprocity agreement on pension rights for its members between all branches of the industry. A union member may move from shop to shop, or from one industry under the union's jurisdiction to another, without any loss of retirement benefits. The Amalgamated has also developed the health center scheme which is an extension on the local level of a comprehensive system of health insurance paid for by employers.

Vacations and holidays with pay have been demanded by the union and finally were included in all collective bargaining contracts during the Second World War and postwar period.

## VII. Increasing the Volume of Work

Because employment and wage rates in the industry are sensitive to cyclical fluctuation, the union realized that it was necessary to maintain stable prosperity of the whole country, and its political program has been aimed in part toward this end. Not content to rest in this course alone, the union turned to educational channels and has carried on a campaign to increase the demand for union-made garments.

## VIII. Guaranteed Annual Wage

In spite of the irregularity in the workers' annual earnings in the men's clothing industry, the guaranteed annual wage has not been given priority by the union.

During the last twenty years many devices have been worked out by the Amalgamated and the clothing manufacturers to afford a basis for greater stability of employment such as a shorter work-week and union-management cooperation in matters of seasonal fluctuations, production efficiency, planning, business expansion, and the like.

The shops of the integrated manufacturers have tended to operate with greater regularity than the non-integrated. A few large producers with their own retail outlets, such as Howard's and Bond's, have provided continuous employment the year round.

The closest approach to the guaranteed wage policy is found in the laundry branch and journeyman tailors. In the New York laundry industry the Amalgamated has a contract with the employers which provides a guarantee of 40 hours per week to men employees; a dollar and cents guarantee to women workers on somewhat smaller scale; a guarantee of almost a full year's work to journeyman tailors. It is interesting to note that these are not seasonal branches of the industry and therefore are not subject to wide fluctuations in production.

The union has sought to mitigate the effects of employment insecurity by devices such as equal division of work, regulation of hiring and discharge, seniority plans, and dismissal compensation. Mr. Potofsky, upon his return from Europe in June 1955, stated that the Amalgamated board would study the possibility of applying the guaranteed wage to the clothing industry.

# International Brotherhood of Pulp, Sulphite and Paper Mill Workers and the International Brotherhood of Paper Makers

## INTRODUCTION

The two principal unions in the paper industry are the International Brotherhood of Pulp, Sulphite and Paper Mill Workers with a membership of 140,000 and the International Brotherhood of Paper Makers comprising about 70,000 members. The former is a semi-industrial union which generally extends its membership to all production and maintenance workers except those belonging to the latter union. The paper makers' union by tradition is a craft organization with skilled operation. However, in recent years it has not hesitated to organize new plants on either a semi-industrial or industrial basis when it served its purposes. Both unions are affiliated with the AFL. They are considered together here, because they negotiate many joint contracts and are the leaders in the industry in determining wages and working conditions. Both unions have a comparatively long history of collective bargaining going back to the early years of the present century.

The industry is composed of many paper and converting plants scattered over the North American continent. Its products include newsprint, book paper, kraft board and paper, corrugated boxes, paper bags, paper milk cartons, etc. The largest producer is the International Paper Company. The second largest company in terms of total assets is the Crown-Zellerback Corporation. The St. Regis Paper Company with many plants throughout the United States ranks third in the industry. The next largest producer is the Great Northern Paper Company with mills located in Maine and the North East.

The pulp and paper companies are typically large-scale businesses requiring a vast amount of capital, while the converting business is generally smaller in scale, in size and in capital requirements. Price leadership is characteristic of the industry. Since 1939 the tremendous demand for paper has provided an unlimited market for all producers. Capital expansion has been occurring at a rapid pace, and prosperous conditions have been enjoyed by most companies.

The key wage regional bargaining agreements in the United States are:

1. Pacific Coast Association of Pulp and Paper Manufacturers, comprising 35 large producers on the West Coast. Since 1934 the association has been bargaining jointly with the two brotherhoods under the Uniform Labor Agreement;
2. Southern Kraft Agreement comprising nine plants of the International Paper Company. This is known as a multi-plant agreement and dates back to 1938. Unlike the West Coast negotiations, the unions do not bargain jointly;
3. Great Northern and Robert Gair agreements. These are multi-plant agreements principally in the New England region;
4. I.P. Book and Bond and St. Regis agreements. These are multi-plant agreements principally in the State of New York;
5. Consolidated and Marathon agreements. These are company-wide agreements with two outstanding producers in Wisconsin.

The key bargaining agreements in Canada are:
1. British Columbia (Standard Agreement)—a multi-employer agreement;
2. Quebec News Print agreement. In the latter agreement some companies bargain jointly with the unions, but each company signs separate contracts.

#### WAGE POLICIES DURING THE EARLIER YEARS

When the first locals of pulp, sulphite and paper mill workers were organized in New York and New England states in 1901, the hours of labor for a tour worker were 72 a week and for a day worker 60. The weekly earnings were from $7 to $9. The first convention of the pulp and paper mill workers in 1902 went on record to ask for a 2½ ¢ an hour increase in wages, a 65-hour work-week for tour workers and a 59-hour week for day workers.[1] Later demands insisted on the hourly basis of pay instead of a daily wage, 8-hour work-day, time and one-half for overtime, and classification of jobs.[2]

In the early years and through the 1920's the unions were seldom free from strikes. In fact, most of the energy of the officers and practically all of the finances of the unions were consumed in conducting strikes. The five-year strike of the International Paper Company in the early 1920's resulted in the loss of all the international union's locals in the company's mills.

In the latter part of the 1920's the business boom enabled the brotherhoods to obtain many gains in wages and working conditions. In spite of prosperous conditions, the unions were unable to secure a 45 cents minimum wage in all mills in the industry.[3]

With the coming of the Great Depression in 1930, unemployment became acute in the paper business. This coupled with keen competition in the industry put the unions on the defensive in their bargaining conferences. At first they fought to hold wages and working conditions, but beginning in November 1930 a number of non-union firms put into effect a 10 per cent reduction in wages. The international unions protested but could not prevent such action. The unions were successful in stalling further reductions until the spring of 1931. Wage reductions in the unionized mills were moderate, averaging five per cent, with no decrease at all in the base rates of most mills. In a few union mills no reductions were experienced in 1931.[4]

Before the close of 1931 the paper industry went from bad to worse. Some companies were operating only a few of their plants. A sharp drop in the price of paper in the spring of 1932 upset all hope of wage stabilization, and the unions were faced with a demand for wage reductions. After a number of conferences the unions negotiated agreements with the majority of companies for wage reductions averaging 8½ per cent, while accepting for the first time a decrease in the base rate.[5]

By the spring of 1933 the workers had taken an average reduction in wages of about 13½ per cent. Before long the manufacturers insisted that a substantial reduction in wages was necessary. Faced with the third cut in wages since the beginning of the depression, the unions decided to contest every inch of ground. Wage cuts from seven to nine per cent were experienced. In summarizing the policy of the union at the 1935 convention of the pulp, sulphite and paper mill workers, President Burke said: "Because of the organized strength of the small minority of workers in the industry, the union was able to protect the hourly wage rates to a remarkable degree.

Although the union took three reductions in wages, they were moderate, averaging about 20 per cent in the union mills. Most of the union mills experienced a 10 per cent reduction off the base rate. The workers in all the union mills were able to save the union shop agreements, time and one half for overtime, and other union standards. In contrast, the workers in the non-union mills were forced to take many more reductions, and in addition, lost time and one half for overtime."[6]

### STABILIZATION UNDER THE NATIONAL INDUSTRIAL RECOVERY ACT

The passage of the NRA in 1933 proved beneficial to both workers and management in the industry. It marked the stoppage of further wage reduction; it stabilized the price structure; it made for greater parity in labor costs between union and non-union firms; and it gave the workers the protection of the government in their organizing and bargaining activities. The labor codes for the industry provided a maximum of 40 hours a week and a minimum wage of 38 cents for men and 33 cents for women in the northern zone, and 30 cents for both men and women in the southern zone, time and one-third for time workers in excess of eight hours in any one day. After the codes became effective on November 7, 1933, most of the union mills in the North increased the minimum rate of wages from 38 to 40 cents. On the Pacific Coast the unions obtained a 45 cents minimum for men and 37 cents for women.[7]

When the NRA was declared unconstitutional, the unions feared that the workers in the non-union factories would be at the mercy of the employers. A campaign to organize the unorganized was deemed necessary to protect the standards set up by the codes.[8]

### WAGE POLICIES, 1935–1940

With the sharp business recovery and the concomitant rise in the cost of living, the pulp and sulphite workers at their 1935 convention went on record demanding a 7 cents increase in wages per hour and approved the 6-hour day. At the 1937 convention the union passed a resolution approving a 15 cents increase in wage rates or more if exceptional conditions in the different mills or districts seemed to warrant it. The union policy appeared to be opposed to seeking a uniform wage scale throughout the industry. The committee on wages and working conditions on taking this stand said that it was difficult to establish uniform wage schedules in the paper industry because of differing local and financial conditions of the 700 companies in the nation.

During the period from 1937 to 1939 the union was successful not only in obtaining wage increases from 15 to 20 per cent but also in making a substantial improvement in working conditions. Time and one-half for overtime work and vacations with pay were secured in many mills. The recession in business beginning in July 1937, bringing with it sharp reductions in the price of paper, caused some wage decreases. For example, in the Southern Kraft mills there was a five per cent reduction in wage rates, but on the West Coast the workers took no wage decrease. In most cases, the wage cuts were restored in about a year.[9]

At the 1939 convention of the International Brotherhood of Pulp, Sulphite, and Paper Mill Workers, resolutions were adopted favoring pensions and holidays and vacations with pay. The paper makers' union at their 1939 convention also passed a resolution favoring annual vacaions with pay.[10]

### WAGE POLICIES, 1940–1950

Except for the war years, the negotiations between the international brotherhoods and the Pacific Coast Association of Pulp and Paper Manufacturers reveal the demands of the unions and the arguments used in their promotion. (According to President Burke, the basic pattern of demands and the tactics of the two unions would be similar in all parts of the country with minor deviations.) In the three years prior to the entrance of the United States in World War II 1940-1942, the brotherhoods demanded increased wages, vacations with pay and other miscellaneous improvements. In 1940 the unions on the West Coast sought a 17 cents per hour increase in wages but settled for 2½ cents.[11] In the Southern Kraft Mills a three cents per hour increase was obtained. From the Great Northern Paper Company the unions won one-week paid vacations for one year's service.[12] According to the paper mill workers, the big accomplishment of 1940 was the start made in getting vacations with pay.[13] With the opening of agreements in 1941 the brotherhoods obtained wage increases from five to ten cents an hour from most of the mills in the United States. Many of the locals, in addition, obtained one week's vacation with pay, and a substantial number received two weeks' paid vacation.[14]

In the spring of 1942 the unions on the Pacific Coast asked for a 15 cents per hour increase, but the final settlement was a ten cents per hour increase. To strengthen their case for improved wages and other benefits, the brotherhoods in the three years preceding the war stressed the following factors: 1) the rising price of paper and the exceptionally good profits of the paper companies; 2) the upward movement of wages; 3) the increased cost of living; 4) the lag in paper workers' earnings in comparison with other industries; 5) the danger of labor turnover; 6) the higher productivity of the workers in the West Coast paper and pulp industry.[15]

The policy of the brotherhoods during the war period was to turn to "fringe benefits" and the correction of "wage rate irregularities" which would not be in violation of the "Little Steel Formula." The unions sought two weeks' vacation with pay, a pension system, six paid holidays, shift differentials, group insurance including life, hospitalization and accident.[16] In order to adjust wage rate irregularities, the paper makers set up a job analysis service and worked in cooperation with the paper companies in the analysis of operations in the mills.[17]

With the termination of the war and the elimination of wage controls, the unions immediately pressed for substantial concessions. The demands of the unions in their negotiations with the Pacific Coast employers included a wage adjustment of 10 per cent to be applied to present hourly rates, an additional 18 cents per hour across the board increase, and miscellaneous fringe benefits. The unions finally settled for an increase in rates of pay of 10 per cent plus a 7½ cents increase, and three holidays with pay.

At a meeting of the joint executive boards of the two international brotherhoods in January 1948, it was decided that in the spring the two unions would seek wage increases consistent with the rising cost of living and company earnings.[18] In their negotiations with the Pacific Coast Association of Paper Manufacturers, the unions asked for 22½ cents increase on all rates up to $1.50 and 15 cents on all rates above $1.50. The employers' final offer of nine per cent on all rates with a minimum increase of 15 cents on all male rates was agreed upon by all representatives. This settlement gave a base rate for male workers of $1.42½ which amounted to an increase in all male rates from 15 to 25 cents.[19]

In spite of the business recession of 1949, the joint executive boards of the two international brotherhoods in January 1949 went on record for the opening of all joint labor agreements in the spring and for a vigorous pressing for higher wages. The joint boards felt that profits of the paper industry appeared good.[20]

At the joint bargaining session with the West Coast employers in April 1949, the unions asked for a 7½ cents per hour upward revision on all wage rates and improvements in paid holidays and vacations. The employers refused to grant the increase because of the cloudy outlook for business. It was finally agreed to reconvene in September 1949 to reappraise the business situation. Since general wage progress could not be made, the union concentrated on pensions and other fringe items with resulting improvement in fringe benefits equal to five cents per hour for most members.[21]

At the union meeting of the joint boards in January 1950, President Phillips of the International Brotherhood of Paper Makers outlined the pattern of demands of the two unions for 1950. He pointed out that improvements should be achieved in pensions and welfare programs. Since social security was unlikely to be satisfactory for a long time, it should be supplemented. He believed that the employers should assume more, if not all, of these programs and three weeks' vacation for older employees. Because of inflation, there was a need for an increase in wages, and consideration should also be given to matters of severance pay, sick leave, and in some instances to the guaranteed annual wage. President Burke of the pulp and paper mill workers voiced agreement with this program but warned that the details must be decided later on the basis of areas and conditions. It was voted that the international unions go on record as intending to open contracts and wherever practicable to seek wage increases as well as improvement in working conditions and social benefits.[22]

In the bargaining negotiations of the two brotherhoods in the spring of 1950, the unions requested a five per cent upward revision of wages; three weeks' vacation after 15 years' service; two weeks' vacation after three years' service; three additional non-restricted holidays; eight hours pay for all employees and time and one-half for all time worked in excess of eight hours per day; an increase in the night shift differential from four to six cents per hour.

The major changes agreed upon during the 1950 West Coast negotiations were:

1. General wage increase of three per cent to apply to all jobs across the board. This brought the base rate for women's jobs to $1.20 per hour and for men to $1.47;
2. Three weeks' vacation after five years of continuous service;
3. Three non-restricted holidays, New Year's Day, Memorial Day, and Thanksgiving, will be paid holidays.

Considerable progress was made in the 1950 negotiations in overcoming the wage discrepancies between northern and southern pulp and paper mills. Speaking about the good settlement with the Union Bag and Paper Corporation at Savannah, Georgia, the Southern Kraft Division of the International Paper Company, and the West Virginia Pulp and Paper Company at the Charleston mill, Mr. Burke said: "It is not so many years ago that the northern pulp and paper manufacturers used the low rates paid in southern mills as a reason for not giving wage increases. Today, however, we never hear any reference to the low rates paid in southern mills in our negotiations with northern companies, because there are no low rates. Amazing progress has been made in building up wage rates and improving working conditions in the pulp and paper mills in the Southland."[23]

At the 1950 convention of the International Brotherhood of Pulp, Sulphite and Paper Mill Workers the union went on record to gain pension plans by collective bargaining. It recommended that retirement benefits should in no case be less than than $100.00 a month and that the cost of the pension plan should be borne entirely by the companies.[24]

WAGE POLICIES DURING THE KOREAN WAR

Because of the rapid advance in the cost of living with the beginning of the Korean War, the brotherhoods called upon the paper industry to open negotiations for an upward revision of wage rates in September 1950. In most instances wage increases were obtained that equaled or exceeded those negotiated in the spring of 1950.[25]

In 1951 the brotherhoods were prepared to press for an improvement in the conditions of the membership in spite of wage controls over the economy. Stabilization regulations provided a ten per cent increase in wage rates over January 1950 levels. The paper makers felt they were entitled to a larger increase, because their last wage increase in the spring of 1950 was a fourth round advance instead of a fifth round as was the case in many industries. The 1949 recession in the industry accounted for this lag in the paper workers' wages, as many wage increases were omitted in that year. It was the hope of the unions to restore the normal relationship in wage rates with the other unions.[26]

The 1951 negotiations between the brotherhoods and the West Coast manufacturers resulted in a general wage increase of 12½ cents per hour across the board. In view of the wage stabilization ten per cent formula, only 5½ cents of the negotiated increase was made effective without prior approval of the Wage Stabilization authority. The unions and the manufacturers agreed to file a joint application requesting approval of the additional seven cents per hour, retroactive to June 1, 1951, as well as some agreed changes in fringe benefits.[27]

The Wage Stabilization Board approved the request of the unions and companies for the full 12½ cents raise under the uniform agreement, and an eight cents increase in wages as bargained by the unions in the Southern Kraft agreement.[28]

The year 1952 showed continued gains through the negotiations of the two brotherhoods. The major items agreed upon were:

1. General wage increase: 4½ per cent across the board in all hourly job rates;
2. Health and welfare: a health and welfare plan on a 60 per cent employer-40 per cent employee basis;
3. Job analysis: a revision in job analysis program with resulting increases in step value.

At the 1953 spring negotiations, the employers on the West Coast took a determined stand to resist the wage demands of the brotherhoods. They pointed out that it was impossible to grant the unions' wage request primarily on the grounds that further widening of the wage differential between the West Coast paper industry and other regions would jeopardize the jobs and profits of the West Coast plants. The unions, not ready to accept defeat, notified the federal government that a dispute existed and requested the appointment of a conciliator.[29] It is interesting to note that the final settlement for a two and a half per cent increase in wages was preceded by a three per cent increase in the Southern Kraft agreement. These settlements raised the male common rate for the West Coast to $1.76½ an hour against $1.37 for Southern Kraft.

Again in 1954 the West Coast manufacturers refused to grant the union request for wage increases with the same arguments that were used the previous year. As a result Southern Kraft repeated the role of wage leadership. The wage settlement for Southern Kraft amounted to a general increase of seven cents per hour compared to 4½ cents on the Pacific Coast. The new base rate for the South is now $1.44 compared to $1.80 for the West Coast, and represents a narrowing of the wage differential by 3½ ¢ over 1953.[30]

## CONCLUSIONS

In this study of the wage policies of the International Brotherhood of Pulp, Sulphite and Paper Mill Workers and the International Brotherhood of Paper Makers, the following observations are pertinent.

### WAGE STANDARDIZATION

In spite of the large amount of autonomy placed in the hands of the locals, the brotherhoods have sought wage stabilization throughout their history. On the West Coast multi-employer bargaining with the unions has been the accepted procedure since 1934. It has resulted in standardization of wage rates for that area with accompanying advantage to both employers and the unions. For the employers it has eliminated competitive cost advantages in labor costs and has undoubtedly created better morale among the workers as wage grievances have been reduced. To the unions it has given security conducive to responsible and intelligent union leadership. A mutual advantage has been freedom from strikes and lockouts.

In other parts of the country and in Canada the unions have sought to come to terms first with the larger companies, using their agreements as a key pattern for smaller plants. To implement this goal, the unions have devoted much time to intensive organizing work particularly in Canada and in the South until they have now unionized almost all of the larger plants in these strategic regions.

The brotherhoods have not followed a uniform wage scale for the entire nation, because of their desire to take into consideration regional cost differences. However, they have worked to eliminate the wage differentials between northern and southern mills, as revealed in Table XV, page 145. Although the South still possesses a lower base rate, its semi-skilled and skilled rate jobs are now higher than in the North, for the most part. The lower base rate in the South is largely explained by the fact that most unskilled jobs are filled by Negro workers. The brotherhoods have worked to overcome this discrimination as revealed by the fact that the differential between the Southern base rate jobs and those in the New England region has been narrowing. The differential in October 1954 between the Northern New England and Southern base rate jobs was only three cents, while in the New York mills it was six cents.* The West Coast region, which has enjoyed the highest wage structure in the industry, is losing its position to the South, particularly in the skilled rate jobs. While the semi-skilled and unskilled rates are still considerably below the Pacific Coast, percentage-wise they are moving up somewhat faster than the West Coast. The unions feel the South should be the leader in wage rates because of its cost advantages. Its lower costs are due primarily to the longer growing season for timber, which makes for an abundance of cellulose, and to the rapid capital expansion which is reflected in more modern equipment. Recognizing this, the Pacific Coast employers in the last two years have protested the continuance of their role as leader in wages for the paper industry.

In line with the union's policy of wiping out the wage differentials between the North and South in the United States, the brotherhoods have sought to eliminate the lower wage differentials of Canada with that of the United States. Their goal has for the most part been achieved.

RAISING THE LEVEL OF WAGES

One of the main objectives of the unions has been to secure and maintain a living wage for its membership. Although considerable progress was made toward this goal during the 1920's, the Great Depression of the 1930's caused a temporary setback. The NRA assisted the unions in securing wage increases in all work classifications. Although some cutting in wages was experienced in the recession of 1937, in most cases, wage cuts were restored by the following year. During the 14-year period 1939-1952 as shown in Table XVI, page 146, the brotherhoods have been able to keep wages ahead of the rising price level.

* The union policy has also opposed wage discrimination within the confines of the Southern region. Equality of pay between Negroes and white workers on similar jobs has now been achieved.

Average hourly earnings have advanced from .592 cents in 1939 to $1.69 in 1953, or 185 per cent, and average weekly earnings from $23.72 to $72.67, or 206 per cent. The cost of living during the same period rose from 99.4 to 191.3, or approximately 92 per cent. Deflating hourly and weekly earnings by the cost of living, we find that the real average hourly earnings rose from .596 cents in 1939 to .883 cents in 1953, or 48 per cent, while real average weekly earnings increased from $23.86 to $37.98, or 59 per cent. In terms of productivity, the 48 per cent advance in real hourly earnings would indicate that the unions have succeeded in keeping abreast of the 2½ per cent annual increase in output per man hour for the entire nation. However, the unions feel that in some regions productivity has outstripped the national average. The South and West Coast particularly have shown more rapid advances than in other regions.

### FRINGE BENEFITS, GUARANTEED WAGE

The brotherhoods have taken the position that fringe benefits should be confined within definite limits of vacation and holidays with pay, sick leave with pay, group insurance, old age retirements, and shift differentials. In some sections of the country local peculiarities have sometimes altered this policy. Many workers now receive pay for five weeks annually for which they render no service (three weeks vacation, six holidays and six days for sick leave.)

The paper industry has been a leader in fringe benefits. Since 1940 the brotherhoods have bargained for welfare benefits. Almost all of their contracts now have vacation and holiday provisions. More than 75 per cent have some sort of retirement provision. Most of the contracts now have hospitalization, health, life and accident insurance either on a contributory or non-contributory basis. In some cases health and accident benefits cover the entire family. According to President Burke, the cost of fringe benefits to the employers amounts to 25 cents per hour on the average. Hourly wage rates, therefore, do not represent the true cost of labor as was formerly the case.

The guaranteed annual wage has not been pressed by the brotherhoods as have so many of the CIO unions. No plan has yet been devised which will solve the problems necessary for its acceptance. The principal obstacles are: the dispersion of the industry, diversification, the large number of companies (700), and keen competition at times.

The high caliber of union leadership has brought about cooperation with management in solving industry problems. The first formal effort in cooperation was evidenced during the Great Depression when the unions sought to work with management in controlling production. Under the NRA the unions worked with employers in establishing codes of fair labor conditions. During the Second World War the paper makers' union, through its job analysis service, cooperated with management in the establishment of equitable wage rates and wage scales. In the West Coast Association, the employers and the unions have worked together on a revision of company wage scales to correct inter-plant and intra-plant inequities.

It is a widespread practice in the paper industry for both employers and unions to approach each other in the solution of their problems. Labor-management committees are common, and they have been encouraged by the brotherhoods.

In the West Coast region the unions have stressed external factors more than internal factors. Frequent reference has been made to comparable wage rates of the Pacific Coast, with particular stress on the lumber industry. The cost-of-living argument has been in constant play in conjunction with the spiraling of prices since the termination of the Second World War. Ability to pay with reference to profits, increase in net worth, prospects for the future, and increased productivity have been used as talking points when the occasion warranted.

In respect to other sections of the country and in Canada, reference most frequently has been made to the cost of living, ability to pay, wage trends, productivity, general business conditions.

The unions have not advocated the tying of wages to the cost of living and productivity. Only a few contracts have included such provisions. Because of the fluctuating nature of consumer prices the unions believe that the workers will be more certain of their wage earnings without the cost-of-living escalator clause. However, they are given protection against the spiraling of living costs by their in-

TABLE XV

Average Straight-time Hourly Earnings of Workers in Selected Skilled, Semi-skilled and Unskilled Occupations in the Pulp, Paper and Paperboard Mills, by Regions, Oct. 1945 and April 1952 [1]

| Department and Occupation | United States | | New England | | Mid-Atlantic States | | Central States | | South | | Upper Lake States | | Mid West | | Pacific | |
|---|---|---|---|---|---|---|---|---|---|---|---|---|---|---|---|---|
| | Avg. Hourly Earnings 1945 | 1952 | Avg. Hourly Earnings 1945 | 1952 | Avg. Hourly Earnings 1945 | 1952 | Avg. Hourly Earnings 1945 | 1952 | Avg. Hourly Earnings 1945 | 1952 | Avg. Hourly Earnings 1945 | 1952 | Avg. Hourly Earnings 1945 | 1952 | Avg. Hourly Earnings 1945 | 1952 |
| **Woodyard and Wood Preparation** | | | | | | | | | | | | | | | | |
| Crane Operators | - | 1.87 | - | 1.47 | - | 1.64 | - | 1.89 | - | 2.03 | - | 1.67 | - | 1.64 | - | 1.99 |
| Chippermen | .78 | 1.48 | .72 | 1.36 | .81 | 1.42 | .66 | 1.42 | .72 | 1.39 | .73 | 1.46 | - | 1.42 | 1.02 | 1.77 |
| **Pulp Making** | | | | | | | | | | | | | | | | |
| Cooks (Digester operators) | 1.08 | 1.88 | .94 | 1.62 | 1.06 | 1.65 | - | 1.72 | 1.22 | 2.12 | 1.02 | 1.74 | - | 1.59 | 1.21 | 2.19 |
| Screenmen | .79 | 1.56 | .73 | 1.38 | .77 | 1.39 | .68 | 1.54 | .80 | 1.59 | .78 | 1.47 | - | 1.47 | 1.04 | 1.85 |
| Bleachermen | .96 | 1.77 | .79 | 1.48 | .87 | 1.48 | .79 | 1.83 | 1.09 | 2.13 | .84 | 1.59 | - | 1.57 | 1.20 | 2.15 |
| **Recovery, Caustic and Acid Making** | | | | | | | | | | | | | | | | |
| Acid Makers | .97 | 1.66 | .90 | 1.54 | 1.01 | 1.54 | - | - | 1.11 | - | .87 | 1.56 | - | - | 1.15 | 1.99 |
| **Paper and Paper Board** | | | | | | | | | | | | | | | | |
| Beatermen | .82 | 1.47 | .76 | 1.35 | .81 | 1.45 | .76 | 1.27 | .83 | 1.39 | .84 | 1.47 | - | 1.56 | .96 | 1.75 |
| **Machine Room** | | | | | | | | | | | | | | | | |
| Paper-Machine Tenders | 1.07 | 1.97 | 1.10 | 1.75 | .99 | 1.88 | .97 | 1.85 | - | 2.41 | 1.15 | 2.01 | - | 1.97 | - | 2.39 |
| Fourth Hands | .77 | 1.45 | .75 | 1.35 | .76 | 1.38 | .58 | 1.34 | - | 1.62 | .82 | 1.48 | - | 1.47 | .94 | 1.75 |
| **Finishing, Roll** | | | | | | | | | | | | | | | | |
| Rewinder Operators | - | 1.51 | - | 1.41 | - | 1.48 | - | 1.43 | - | 1.56 | - | 1.58 | - | 1.54 | - | 1.78 |
| **Finishing Sheet** | | | | | | | | | | | | | | | | |
| Cutters, guillotine type | .90 | 1.53 | .80 | 1.40 | .98 | 1.55 | .72 | 1.45 | .73 | 1.47 | 1.01 | 1.51 | - | 1.51 | 1.13 | 1.78 |
| Cutters, rotary or sheet | .82 | 1.49 | .75 | 1.46 | .82 | 1.50 | .68 | 1.40 | .93 | 1.36 | .84 | 1.47 | - | 1.50 | 1.02 | 1.83 |
| **Common Labor** | | | | | | | | | | | | | | | | |
| Janitors | .71 | 1.35 | .70 | 1.27 | .69 | 1.30 | .65 | 1.12 | .62 | 1.23 | .75 | 1.37 | - | 1.33 | .91 | 1.67 |
| **Miscellaneous** | | | | | | | | | | | | | | | | |
| Electricians, Maintenance | 1.12 | 1.87 | .96 | 1.61 | 1.07 | 1.71 | 1.04 | 1.86 | 1.25 | 2.07 | 1.07 | 1.77 | - | 1.88 | 1.25 | 2.15 |
| Millwrights, Pulp and Paper | 1.06 | 1.80 | .95 | 1.58 | .99 | 1.63 | .97 | 1.74 | 1.22 | 2.02 | .92 | 1.76 | - | 1.75 | 1.22 | 2.10 |
| Pipe fitters, Maintenance | - | 1.86 | - | 1.61 | - | 1.68 | - | 1.87 | - | 2.05 | - | 1.76 | - | 1.75 | - | 2.11 |
| Over-all Average Hourly Earnings | .83 | 1.52 | .79 | 1.39 | .84 | 1.47 | .75 | 1.46 | .79 | 1.53 | .86 | 1.51 | - | 1.55 | 1.02 | 1.86 |

1. U.S. Department of Labor, Bureau of Labor Statistics, Washington, D.C. Wage Structure Pulp, Paper and Paper Board Oct. 1945 – April 1952. Series No. 34, pp. 17-18, Series No. 91, pp. 10-15.

The above table is intended to show wage trends in various occupations between the regions. Because of some differences in job content between 1945 and 1952 the changes in wage rates do not reflect accurately the extent of changes in all cases.

sistence on reopening clauses in their contracts within 30 days' notice. Their objections to a productivity clause are based on the belief that while benefiting workers in some companies, it would be disadvantageous to others. Under prosperous conditions there is a better opportunity for securing increases than would be permitted under the productivity clause.

On the whole, the brotherhoods have exercised an intelligent and mature wage policy during the last two decades. They realize that there is a limit to the amount they can secure. They expect management and the stockholders to receive a fair return. But they have never hesitated, after an examination of the facts, to demand their rightful share. They have endeavored to comprehend the company's and the industry's problems but in return they have expected that management be willing to understand the point of view of the workers.

## TABLE XVI

Average Hourly and Weekly Money Earnings and Real Hourly and Weekly Earnings in Paper and Allied Products 1939–1953*

| Year | Avg. Hourly Money Earnings | Avg. Weekly Money Earnings | Avg. Hourly Real Earnings 1935–39  100 | Avg. Weekly Real Earnings 1935–39  100 |
|------|------|------|------|------|
| 1939 | .592 | 23.72 | .596 | 23.86 |
| 1940 | .613 | 24.48 | .612 | 24.43 |
| 1941 | .660 | 27.75 | .627 | 26.38 |
| 1942 | .743 | 31.29 | .637 | 26.83 |
| 1943 | .798 | 36.02 | .645 | 29.12 |
| 1944 | .846 | 38.95 | .673 | 30.99 |
| 1945 | .883 | 40.50 | .687 | 31.49 |
| 1946 | 1.001 | 43.47 | .718 | 31.16 |
| 1947 | 1.165 | 50.21 | .730 | 31.46 |
| 1948 | 1.291 | 55.25 | .751 | 32.14 |
| 1949 | 1.342 | 55.96 | .790 | 32.88 |
| 1950 | 1.412 | 61.14 | .821 | 35.57 |
| 1951 | 1.526 | 65.77 | .822 | 35.44 |
| 1952 | 1.61 | 68.91 | .849 | 36.33 |
| 1953 | 1.69 | 72.67 | .883 | 37.98 |

* *Handbook of Basic Economic Statistics,* Economic Statistics Bureau of Washington, D.C., 1948 Annual Edition, Jan., 1948, vol. II, p. 58 and 1953 Annual Edition, Jan., 1953, vol. VII, p. 35. *Monthly Labor Review,* U.S. Dept. of Labor, B.L.S., Washington, D.C., May, June, 1953, vol. 76, p. 671. *Monthly Labor Review,* U.S. Dept. of Labor, B.L.S., August, 1954, vol. 77, p. 939.

The difference in average hourly earnings between Table No. 15 and Table No. 16 for 1954 and 1952 is due to the fact that Table No. 15 is based on straight time hourly earnings while Table No. 16 is based on gross hourly earnings.

## CHAPTER EIGHT

# United Steelworkers of America

## INTRODUCTION

The wage policies of the United Steelworkers of America are of importance because the wages and working conditions of steelworkers set a pattern for the heavy industries in the nation. Steel wages also have a significant influence upon other industrial groups, becuase steel is the core of the American economy, essential to a great variety of industries for which it is the principal raw material.

The steel industry comprises a relatively few large companies. As of January 1, 1954, the ten largest companies account for nearly 80 per cent of the nation's steel ingot capacity. United States Steel and Bethlehem have 46 per cent of the total ingot capacity. Price competition has rarely been evidenced in the industry. Cooperation in one form or another has expressed itself almost continuously since the turn of the century. United States Steel, the largest company, assumes the role of leadership in price making, although there are times when other firms have initiated changes.

The industry has often been termed a "prince or pauper." Although the analogy was true for many years, since 1939 most of the companies have enjoyed prosperity because of the influence of the Second World War, the shortages of consumer durable goods following the war, the price policies which were designed to yield high profits, and the Korean hostilities. The years 1946, 1949 and 1954 temporarily interrupted the high levels of prosperity; in those years occurred postwar readjustments and a decline in general business conditions throughout the United States. In general, the demand for steel is subject to wide fluctuations, and in the past this has resulted in much instability in employment and insecurity for the worker.

Before the unionization of the industry, working conditions were deplorable as was the case with most industries. In the first two decades of the present century the twelve-hour shift and the seven-day week were prevalent. During the 1920's some improvement was made in the length of the work shift, but there was little change in respect to the seven-day week. Under the steel codes of the National Industrial Recovery Act in 1933, a five-day week and eight-hour shift became standard. In respect to wages, in 1929 the average hourly steelworker's wage was 63½ cents versus 51.6 cents in 1933. In 1929 the average annual wage of the steel employee approximated $1,620 compared with $560 in the period preceding the NRA. The average annual earnings were considerably lower than those of other industries during the period of the Great Depression. On the whole, industrial relations were notoriously bad. Workers were often forced to live in company-owned houses, pay excessive rents, and sometimes accept their pay in company script.[1] Bitter struggle and bloodshed between management and the workers occurred intermittently.

Prior to the founding of the United Steelworkers, three independent labor organizations claimed jurisdiction. The largest and oldest was the Amalgamated Association of Iron, Steel and Tin Workers of North America. The second was the International Union of Mine, Mill and Smelter Workers, and the third was the Steel and Metal Workers' Industrial Union. The combined membership of the organizations represented a very small percentage of the total working force in the industry. The Amalgamated, the strongest of the three unions, made little attempt to incorporate the unskilled workers, because it represented the skilled and more highly paid workers. Although the passage of the NRA gave the Amalgamated an opportunity to organize the industry, it did not choose to do so. In the spring of 1936 the Steel Workers Organizing Committee was formed as an affiliate of the newly established Committee for Industrial Organization. With the financial backing of the CIO and the United Mine Workers of America, the SWOC launched an organizing drive that proved remarkably successful. By March 1937 the United States Steel Corporation and several smaller companies announced recognition of the SWOC as the bargaining agent for their employees, and proceeded to sign a contract with the new union. The original demands of the SWOC were $5 minimum daily wage for common labor, an additional 10 cents increase for all other workers, and a basic 40-hour week. All of these requests were incorporated in the contracts mentioned above.

Three months after the signing of the first agreements, the SWOC showed a tremendous expansion in membership. Over 300,000 members were claimed, and 114 agreements were signed. Resistance was still shown by the "Little Steel" group comprising Bethlehem, Inland, Republic and Youngstown.

When the 1937 contracts expired in February 1938, the nation was in a recession. The U.S. Steel Corporation and others tried to press for wage cuts on the grounds that costs were out of line with prices. The union officers took a firm stand against these proposals. They believed that increased productivity due to technological improvements should enable the industry to maintain wage levels.[2] The SWOC was unable to renew its contract for another year, or any specified period, but it did succeed in securing renewal of the old contracts for an indefinite period subject to either party's giving the other ten days' written notice of a desire to begin negotiations for revision, and upon failure to agree within 20 days of such notice the 1937 agreements would be terminated. By the refusal to take wage cuts and thereby strengthening other workers to maintain wages, the SWOC believed it had contributed to the shortening of the recession.[3]

With the improvement in business conditions in the fall of 1938 and 1939, the SWOC gave increasing attention to organization work. Many lodges in steel mills were strengthened, and many new ones established. Spectacular progress was made in organizing the smaller fabricating and steel producing companies. The "Little Steel" companies were the last formidable obstacle to unionization. In the summer of 1941 the SWOC finally won their recognition. Within a span of five years the SWOC was the unchallenged labor organization in the steel industry.[4]

At the 1940 spring meeting of the international wage and policy convention, the Wage Scale Policy Committee formulated the following program which was unanimously adopted by the convention. The officers were to exercise their best judgment in obtaining:

1. A general wage increase;
2. Simplification of classifications of work and rates, together with provisions for uniform minimum rates for comparable work;
3. Improvements in vacation clauses on the basis of economic conditions existing in each branch of the industry;
4. The guaranteed annual wage to be given consideration and study;

5. A forty-eight hour rest period following eight-hour turns on five consecutive days;
6. Simplification of seniority clauses in contracts with the chief emphasis upon length of service;
7. Provisions of the union shop and check off dues wherever possible;
8. Five-day, forty-hour week to be protected, pending changes contemplated by a reduction in the work week from 40 to 30 hours.

Regarding this last recommendation, it is interesting to observe that the Wage Scale Policy Committee was much concerned about the problem of technological unemployment. It was felt that the union should demand a 30-hour week in the steel industry unless steps were taken to evolve a broad national program for the solution of technological unemployment.[5] Their concern with the problem is understandable because of the labor displacement which occurred from August 1936 to September 1939 in the steel industry. During this period 30,000 steel workers were eliminated from their jobs, with an estimated reduction of $14,000,000 from the total monthly wages.[6]

The 1941 negotiations took place at a time when the steel companies were making substantial profits. With a mandate from the union to seek the best possible wage increase, this issue became the chief demand. The first company approached was U.S. Steel. The SWOC demanded a program which included: 1) a 10 cents an hour wage increase and more liberal vacations with pay; 2) the creation of a joint commission of representatives of management and the union in order to establish equalization of rates in various classifications of labor; 3) layoffs and promotions to be governed only by length of service; 4) change in grievance procedures; 5) the recognition of the union as exclusive bargaining agent and the establishment of machinery to permit the union to collect dues from all employees receiving benefits from the basic agreement.

The National Steel Corporation was the first company to announce an increase of 10 cents in wages. The U.S Steel Corporation immediately fell into line. The contract with the latter company became known as the "New Standard Agreement" of 1941 and set the pattern for the industry. The 10 cents an hour increase raised the minimum for common labor to 72½ cents which compares with 62½ cents in 1937 and 52½ cents in 1936; for all workers it raised the average hourly rate to 96½ cents versus .671 in 1936. The vacation clause was changed permitting employees with three to five years' service to receive one week's vacation, and those with 15 or more years obtained two weeks' vacation. Time and a half premium pay was given to workers in non-continuous operations on July 4, Labor Day, and Christmas. A forty-eight hour rest period was granted for each worker in each calendar week. The corporation made few concessions in respect to the demand for adjustment of individual and group rates, and no change in job security and union status. However, some alterations were effected in grievance procedure which were advantageous to both parties.[7]

### STEELWORKERS' WAGE POLICIES DURING WORLD WAR II

In August 1941 the union representatives of four of the "Little Steel" companies adopted a ten-point program for negotiation. The agenda included a wage-rate increase, minimum daily guarantee, the union shop and the check off of dues. Little progress having been made by January 1942, it was decided, among other things, to ask for $1 a day wage increase. The United States became fully involved in World War II and the establishment of the War Labor Board made it mandatory that labor disputes be adjudicated by it as a last resort. Having reached an impasse, the steel dispute was handed to the War Labor Board for settlement. It became popularly known as the "Little Steel" case, because it involved the leading companies in the "Little Steel" group.

### THE "LITTLE STEEL" CASE

Speaking in defense of the $1 a day wage increase and a guaranteed minimum for each day of work, the union predicated its case upon three bodies of data: 1) ability to pay; 2) increasing productive efficiency; 3) increasing living costs.

In respect to the first argument, the union briefs showed that the companies had the ability to pay the wage increase without any rise in prices. The companies earned excessive profits in 1941. The rate of return was even better than it had been in previous years, which was more than adequate for the owners. The introduction of technological improvements during the last four years had so greatly increased efficiency that the small raises had been more than absorbed in rising man-hour output. The $1 a day raise was necessary to effect a more equitable distribution of the earnings.

Finally, the standard of living of the steelworkers had been lowered by the rising costs of the family budget. The output of steel depends upon the productive efficiency of the workers, and unless their living standards are restored by the requested wage increase, the output of steel will be adversely affected.

While the War Labor Board was in deliberation over the steelworkers' case, President Roosevelt issued his seven-point program for economic stabilization. This program included three major lines of action: a taxation program to keep personal and corporate profits down; price and rent control to keep the cost of living down; and the stabilization of wages to keep wages from rising. On the basis of this program, the Board decided the "Little Steel" case on July 16, 1942, according to the following formula: Since the cost of living had gone up 15 per cent between January 1941 and May 1942, wages were entitled to be increased by the same percentage. This principle of wage adjustment became known as "The Little Steel Formula." It was intended to set a limit to the increase in the level of wages arising from across-the-board increases applicable to all employees in a bargaining unit, plant, industry, or other customary area of wage setting. It was intended to permit lagging groups of workers to keep pace with wage increases obtained by the majority of employees.[9] Special considerations, however, were to be given to inequalities and the elimination of substandard conditions of living. The Board granted the steelworkers a 5.5 cents an hour increase but only 3.2 cents was accounted for under the 15 per cent formula. The other 2.3 cents was justified because of the equities in the steelworkers' dispute.[10]

THE UNITED STEELWORKERS AND "THE LITTLE STEEL FORMULA"

In April 1942 President Roosevelt recommended an overall stabilization program in which all groups would equitably share the burdens of the war, but Congress adopted a wage stabilization program which froze wages but did not adequately control profits and prices. The union, believing it was discriminated against, called a union wage and policy conference in the winter of 1943, at which time the following resolution was adopted:

1. That the United Steelworkers submit to the steel employers a request for wage increases to offset the rise in living costs;
2. Request collective bargaining conference;
3. Call upon Congress and the executive agencies of the government to adopt the necessary measures to carry out effective economic stabilization.[11]

In addition to this wage demand, the conference formulated and approved a 22-point program of necessary improvements in working conditions. Two requisitions were subsequently added, making 27 different points altogether. Included in the program were the following fringe benefits: guaranteed weekly wage, an improved vacation plan, severance pay when plants are permanently closed, sick-leave allowances, and shift differentials. Pending negotiations or War Labor Board order it was proposed to each company that a supplemental agreement be made continuing the present contract, with the provision that any wage adjustment be retroactive to the date that the contract would have terminated. Few companies found the supplementary proposal acceptable, whereupon the union petitioned the War Labor Board to issue a directive order incorporating the alternative proposals for extension of the existing contract during settlement of the dispute and the fixing of retroactivity to the date of termination of the contracts. On December 27, 1943, the Board issued an interim order incorporating these proposals.[12] On February 2, 1944, the Board took jurisdiction of the case, and a special panel was established to hear evidence. Because of the importance of the case in reference to a revision of the government's wage policy, AFL representatives were permitted to present evidence to the panel.

The first item on the agenda for the steelworkers was their demand for a general wage adjustment. The union asked for a 17 cents an hour increase or $1.36 for each eight-hour turn. Data submitted on the cost of living showed that prices had advanced 45.3 per cent from January 1941 to March 1944. In order to bolster its case, the union presented the results of a recent survey of the income and expenditures of 589 steel worker's families. It showed the average weekly income was $56.04 per week, while the average weekly expenditures were $58.57. In other words, the steel workers were going into debt.

The union contended that the steel corporations could well afford to pay the requested increase without raising the price of steel.

Evidence showed that the average profits for the industry for the years 1940–1943 were 355.8 per cent higher than in the peacetime period 1936–1939.

The second request by the union was for the establishment of a fund for its members in the armed services. The union asked that each wage earner contribute $20 to be matched by the steel companies. The monies in the fund were to be paid to the workers in the armed services and the merchant marine when honorably discharged.

The third request was the guaranteed minimum weekly wage for each worker during the life of the contract. Having experienced so much instability in former years, the union called for the fulfilment of that part of the Atlantic Charter pertaining to freedom from want and fear.

The fourth demand was a change in vacation procedures. The present elegibility requirements (one week's vacation for three years' service and two weeks after fifteen years) were archaic in comparison to other industries. The union asked for one-week vacation for employees with one to three years of service, and two weeks' for three or more.

The fifth request was for dismissal or severance pay. The union asked for four weeks' pay for all employees having one year and less than three years of continuous service and eight weeks' pay for those having three or more years of service, provided the plant or any portion thereof is permanently closed. The union's position was based on the fear that steel production would be reduced by over six per cent after the war with resulting loss of jobs. It stressed the fact that the principle of severance pay is well established in American industry.

The sixth request dealt with sick leave. Each employee with continuous service of one year and less than three years should be entitled to seven days' sick leave with pay; for three years or more of service, fourteen days of sick leave should be provided. The union in its argument said that it would not increase costs for the steel companies, but instead would reduce costs because of improved health and productivity.

The seventh request involved shift differentials. Here the union asked for five cents an hour for the afternoon shift and ten cents for the night shift. Its demand was based upon the current standard practice in comparable industries.

The eighth demand was concerned with holidays. The union

asked for Thanksgiving, January 1, July 4, Labor Day, Christmas, and Memorial Day. Should an employee be required to work on any of these holidays, he should be paid time and one half.

The ninth, tenth, eleventh, and twelfth demands represented the union's belief that there should be "equal pay for similar work throughout the industry." They included: elimination of geographical wage differentials; provisions to govern wage rates; provisions to govern rates of pay for mechanical and maintenance occupations; learners be paid not less than the rate for common laborers.

The thirteenth demand was for the amendment of the maintenance-of-membership clause to permit for increase in dues.

The fourteenth request was for a group insurance and retirement fund.

The remaining twenty-seven demands were deferred upon the request of the union for further collective bargaining. They comprised the following: seniority; adjustment of grievances; safety and health; military service; in-plant feeding; local conditions; supervisors; salaried employees; checking of tonnage weights; contracting of work in plants; apprenticeship; seniority for local union officials; termination date.[13]

On November 25, 1944, the NWLB issued its directive in the Basic Steel Case. On the wage demand the Board held that it was without authority to grant the wage increase. On the issue of the guaranteed annual wage, the Board, while denying the union's demand, recommended a study of guaranteed wage plans and the "possibility of their future development in American industries as an aid to the stabilization of employment and the regularization of production."[14]

Regarding fringe benefits, the following improvements were made: on vacations, while the old contract provided one-week vacation for three years' service, and two weeks for fifteen years, the Board directive provided one week for one year's service and two weeks for five years'.

On shift differentials there had been none. The Board ordered four cents for the second shift and six cents for the third shift.

On the question of holidays, the request of the union was not actually an improvement over the requirements of Executive Order 9240. The union was merely asking that the provisions of the Order be set forth in the collective bargaining contract. The provisions of

must yield increased earnings commensurate with increased effort and productivity;

7. Improvement in vacation benefits;

8. Double time to be paid for time worked on holidays.[18]

After three months' negotiation between the union and the U.S. Steel Corporation, an agreement was reached on April 22, 1947, to be followed by the other basic steel producing companies and fabricators. The new contract incorporated many improvements including a general wage increase of 12½ cents an hour and other fringe adjustments totaling about 15 cents per hour. From the U.S. Steel Corporation the union secured in the above package, an increase from three and a half cents to four cents in increments between job class rates in order to yield an additional increase to semi-skilled workers and even more to skilled workers; a reduction of three cents in the southern differential affecting the Tennessee Coal, Iron and Railroad Co., an elimination of the two and a half cents differential of the Duluth Works of American Steel and Wire; severance pay for workers in discontinued plants; three weeks' vacation allowance for workers with twenty-five years' service; a joint insurance study to be completed by November 1, 1947.

From most of the other steel companies, the union was successful in achieving the 15 cents package as it had from U.S. Steel.

INTERCOMPANY WAGE EQUALIZATION (WAGE INEQUITY PROGRAM)

On May 8, 1946, the U.S. Steel Co. and the union made an agreement known as the "inequity settlement." The settlement served not only as the basis for a job classification program in the U.S. Steel Co., but also in most of the other steel companies in the industry. Actually, the development of the program involved representatives from many steel companies who banded together in a cooperative wage study from which an industry-wide classification program evolved through negotiation and modification of the findings with the union. The U.S. Steel Co. agreed to spend 3⅝ cents per man-hour for each subsidiary company in the elimination of inequities, but it spent closer to 5.2 cents. The company also provided that the standard hourly wage scale in each plant should start with the existing base common labor rate. The problem of eliminating differences in the base common labor rates between plants was for the most part handled as a separate problem, but in those companies which had the same common labor rate, the classification program resulted in the same job class rates up the rate scale.

The final wage inequity agreement with the U.S. Steel Co. was signed on January 13, 1947, and represented the culmination of the inequity program in rate structure. The 1947 contract did not actually see the completion of the program; all it settled was the establishment of a rate scale system. The agreement on job classifications in most of the plants did not occur for many months after signing of the agreements. At the time the first rate scale was established under the job classification program on February 1, 1947, the rates for U.S. Steel's subsidiary, the Tennessee Coal, Iron and Railroad Company, were uniformly 17½ cents below those of the other steel-producing subsidiaries, while the rates of the Duluth works of American Steel and Wire Company were 2½ cents under the parent company's subsidiaries. An agreement on April 22, 1947, resulted in an extra three cents general increase in the Tennessee Coal, Iron and Railroad Company, thereby reducing the differential to 14½ cents while the Duluth differential disappeared.[19]

### THE UNITED STEELWORKERS AND SOCIAL INSURANCE

On February 18, 1948, the International Policy Committee adopted a new policy which called for the establishment of social insurance plans. The union had given consideration to the question of pensions for its members for some time. It felt that the federal old age insurance program did not provide sufficient benefits to give a decent standard of living for elderly persons. The steel companies had failed miserably to provide for their older employees. Thirty per cent of 2,000 workers retired by the U.S. Steel Corporation in 1947 upon reaching retirement age obtained no pension benefits whatsoever. Few plans in the industry paid any benefits during sickness, and hospitalization and surgical insurance was rare. The insurance plans that existed were almost all employee-paid, with the company serving only as a check off agency to facilitate the functioning of the group insurance arrangement.[20] In the U.S. Steel Co. the only company contribution was for group life insurance which averaged two cents per hour.

In the 1947 negotiations an insurance study to be completed as of November 1, 1947 was agreed upon, although it was not actually completed until March 1, 1948. As a result, the U.S. Steel Co. was unwilling to negotiate on this matter until the question of wages was reopened under its contract. The wage and insurance negotiations were therefore delayed until the spring of 1948.

In the collective bargaining conferences with the U.S. Steel Corporation in 1948 the union's social insurance proposals included: life insurance amounting to 18 months' average wage of the employee; a fully paid life insurance policy of $1,500 for each employee upon attaining the age of 65; hospitalization provided by the employer at eight dollars per worker; sick benefits of $35 per week during period of illness; maternity care for mother and child care for children; surgical care to maximum amount of $225. The combined cost of the social insurance proposal was 9.65 cents per hour. The insurance plan offered by the U.S. Steel Corporation contemplated expenditures just short of five cents per hour. The corporation's contribution would have amounted to about 2½ cents while the union would pay the same. A final settlement omitted the insurance program because the company insisted that it be a contributory program, and that the company's share of the plan be at the expense of the wage proposal. As a result the settlement was in the form of a wage increase amounting to an average of 13 cents per hour. The union had requested Mr. Latimer, social security consultant, to prepare a pension plan for the 1948 negotiations but it was not presented at that time to the steel industry. Nevertheless, President Murray stated that a pension scheme would be requested "in due course."[21]

On May 4, 1949, the International Policy Committee formulated the 1949 bargaining program. The following policy was recommended to cover all contracts which might be opened: a) a general wage increase, b) adequate pensions, c) social insurance benefits, d) guaranteed annual wage, e) improved vacations, etc.[22] Collective bargaining conferences with U.S. Steel began on July 15, 1949. To support its demand for a general wage increase, the union brief showed that a wage increase was needed to meet the higher cost of living. Emphasis was given to the need of raising the purchasing power of consumers to avoid a depression. The union spokesmen were convinced that the corporation could grant the wage increase while at the same time reduce steel prices because of the record high profits of the steel business. To support its demands for pensions, the union pointed to the National Labor Relations Board decision in the Inland Steel Case in which employers were obligated by law to bargain on pensions, and the Supreme Court's refusal of a company to review the decision of the Circuit Court of Appeals upholding the NLRB position. Mr. Latimer, the union's consultant, pointed out the record of the corporation's retirement program. Evidence revealed that the customary pension was around $5.00 per month, while many employees received no pension benefits upon reaching the age of 65. In the field of social insurance, it was shown that the company contributed less than one-fifth of a cent per hour for social insurance.

The corporation, in reply to union demands, turned down a wage increase and said that the subject of pensions was not bargainable. It offered to give two cents per hour for insurance benefits, provided the employees would contribute likewise.

With the breakdown of negotiations on July 7, 1949, the Federal Mediation Service attempted to mediate the issues, but was unable to succeed. The President of the United States, under the authority of the Taft-Hartley Act, appointed a Steel Industry Board to examine the issues in the case. The union, in support of its proposals, presented forty-four exhibits on the many questions involved. Several experts were secured to give added authority to the union's plans. Robert Nathan presented an economic analysis of the steel industry and the national economy which supported the union's claim that a wage increase was necessary to offset rising costs of living and provide a balanced economy. Mr. Latimer spoke about the theoretical and practical aspects of pensions and social insurance and the failure of the steel industry to provide adequate pensions and insurance for its workers.[23] Mr. Brubaker, the steelworkers' economist, presented a series of fact sheets covering each company involved in the dispute. They set forth significant operating and financial data of these companies from 1939 to 1949. They served as a major source of the union's conclusion concerning the companies' ability to grant the proposed wage, insurance, and pension benefits without price increases. President Murray, in summarizing the position of the steelworkers for a wage increase, stated that the workers shared only modestly in the prosperity of the steel industry from 1939-1944, and since 1944 they had scarcely participated in the high earnings of the industry. Secondly, the rising cost of living had to a large extent nullified the increased earnings. Measured in terms of real earnings, the steelmaker's wages were 92 cents per hour in 1944 compared with 84.5 cents in 1939; then declined to 89.8 cents in 1947, and rose to 96.6 cents in the first quarter of 1949. Thus, the steelmaker's real wages rose about eight cents per hour between 1939 and 1944, and only four cents since 1944. Thirdly, the productivity of the steelworker has increased out of proportion to his wages. Finally, the steelworker's percentage increase in wages had been less than that of workers in all manufacturing industries. During the period from 1939–1949 real wages for steel workers increased 14.3 per cent, while real wages for all manufacturing industries rose 27.3 per cent. In contrast, the profits in the steel industry increased 255.3 per cent, while profits for all manufacturing industries rose 120.6 per cent.

In respect to social security benefits, Mr. Murray pointed out that they have always been inadequate and have not even kept up with rising living costs. The workers must look to industry to be protected adequately against illness, accident, old age and death. Decent protection for the workers and their families against the hazards of life is a legitimate cost of production. "The worker is essential, more essential than any other element in production. Particularly in a heavy industry like steel, with its accidents, occupational disease and wearing out process, workers do not last forever. They become worn out physically and occupationally. Finally, the worker is too old to work and too young to die. He must live in destitution or become a public charge. The costs of his care should be placed squarely on the industry which used his labor and exhausted his sinews.

"We will no longer tolerate the double standard whereby machines are preferred over men. Every well-operated company sets aside money for depreciation, repair, and replacement of machinery. Only infrequently, however, does it make similar provisions for the care of its employees. . . .

"Illness means a double loss to workers. When a man is unable to work, his pay check stops coming. . . . The medical, hospital, and surgical treatment of the members of his family is as important to the steelworker as the provisions he must make for shelter, food, and clothing. . . .

"And when the steelworker is gone, his family must turn somewhere to survive. There is no fund set aside by the steel industry for widows and orphans; there are funds for protection against fire, theft, breakdowns, price declines, but not for the death of a steelworker."[24]

Philip Murray emphasized that the additional purchasing power in the hands of the steelworkers would give strength to the economy. It would arrest a business decline and achieve a level of full production and employment.[25]

In the Board's report and recommendation to the President on September 10, 1949, the Board expressed little disagreement with the factual statements of the union, but differed considerably in the interpretation which should be placed on the facts and the conclusions which could be drawn from them. It is significant, however, that the Board accepted, almost without qualification, the union's basic premise of the industries' ability to grant wage, insurance, and pension benefits within their existing price structures. The Presidential Board recommended improvements to the workers costing 10 cents per hour to be granted without a price increase, and that instead of a wage increase, the companies ought to pass additional benefits on to the consumers through a price reduction. The Board further recommended that unless the companies did reduce prices, the union would be justified in reinstating its demand for a wage increase, because the ability to pay such an increase was clearly evident. The Board believed that social insurance and pensions should be considered a part of the normal business costs to take care of temporary and permanent depreciation in the human "machine" in much the same way as provision is made for depreciation of plant and machinery. Although the steel industry had kept pace with other industries in wages, it had lagged behind other basic industries in social insurance and pensions. The Board recommended that a non-contributory social insurance plan costing four cents per hour per worker be established, and a non-contributory pension plan costing six cents per hour per worker also be effectuated.[26]

The union accepted, though somewhat reluctantly, the entire recommendations of the Presidential Board, including the denial of any immediate wage increase. Upon the refusal of the steel industry to accept the Board's recommendations and to bargain further, the union called a strike of over 500,000 workers which lasted 30 to 45 days. The Bethlehem Steel Corporation was the first major steel company to reach a settlement on pensions and insurance, shortly followed by the other major steel companies. Quite a number of the smaller companies reached agreements prior to the two major companies.

The basic principles of the pension and insurance program incorporated in the union agreements were:

1. A non-contributory pension for all employees at age 65 or over with 15 years of continuous service. All workers who become totally and permanently disabled are entitled to pension benefits at any age provided they have 15 years of continuous service.

2. A worker's pension is computed on the following formula: one per cent of average monthly compensation over the last 10 years multiplied by the total years of continuous service. The pension program provided a $100 monthly guarantee for an employee with 25 years' service, ranging down to $60 for 15 years' service.

3. The insurance program, although varying somewhat between companies, was similar to the following U.S. Steel plan: A contributory social insurance plan, providing a 50–50 division of cost between the worker and the employer, fixing a total cost of five cents per hour. Group life insurance averaging $2,600, and after retirement $1,250; National Blue Cross hospital benefit plan paying virtually all expenses of hospitalization in a semi-private room for 70 days per confinement for employees and their dependents; accident and sickness benefit of $26 per week, starting on the first day of an accident and the eighth day of an illness with a maximum of 26 weeks for any single spell.[27]

### WAGE POLICIES SINCE THE KOREAN WAR

With the rising cost of living after the outbreak of the Korean War in the summer of 1950, the Union Wage Policy Committee requested wage adjustments. Ensuing negotiations with the steel companies resulted in, first, a wage agreement effective December 1, 1950, providing for a general wage increase of 12½ cents per hour plus a five cents increase in increments between job classes; secondly, an extra 4½ cents increase in rates in the southern plants, thereby reducing the southern differential in U.S. Steel to 10 cents per hour; third, an agreement to work out a job classification program for the iron ore mining operations of the U.S. Steel Corporation at a cost of 8½ cents per hour over and above the general increase. This was later extended to other iron ore mining companies or steel companies with iron ore mining operations.

With the reopening of the steel contracts in November 1951, the union demanded a 22-point program which included a wage increase averaging 18.5 cents per hour. Upon the steel industry's refusal to bargain and after all efforts were made to resolve the issues, the dispute was certified to the Wage Stabilization Board. In addition to the 18½ cents wage increase, the union asked for: an increase in shift differential; payment for eight unworked holidays per year; premium payment of time and one-half in addition to holiday pay for time worked on holidays; improved vacation plan to provide one week of vacation after one year of service, two weeks after two years, three weeks after five years and four weeks after 15 years; increased reporting allowances; premium pay for Saturday and Sunday work; a minimum guarantee or 32 hours' pay per week based on the employee's average hourly earnings, for any period of unemployment up to one year following employee's lay-off or termination by the employer; severance allowance equal to one week's pay for each year of continuous service with any amounts paid out under the guarantee provision to be deductible from the severance allowance; demotion allowance equal to the difference between the employee's earnings prior to, and subsequent to, the demotion, for a period of one year when the demotion has been caused by technological change or by abandonment of facilities by the employer; an elimination of north and south differentials; and the establishment of the union shop.[28]

To justify these demands, the union dealt with the continuing growth of the steel industry; the ability of the industry to absorb the cost of the demands without resort to price increases; the lag in the steelworkers' wages in comparison with steel prices, profits and dividends; the failure of the workers' real wages to reflect the increased productivity of the industry; the relative decline of labor costs as compared to total costs; the relationship of the union's wage demands to the Wage Stabilization Board's regulations, policies and prior decisions; the consumers' price index in relation to the union's requests; wage movements in major industries since January 1950; and the equities involved in the fringe demands.

Regarding the ability of the steel industry to meet the demands, the union brief pointed to the fact that the industry could no longer masquerade as a "feast and famine" industry, for it had enjoyed almost continuous progress since 1939. Turning to the productivity of the industry, the union indicated that the output per man hour had shown a remarkable increase within recent years, but that its gains were not being reflected in increased wages or in reduction of steel prices. In an examination of steel profits, the union stressed their Gargantuan growth in spite of the use of accelerated amortization allowances. Looking at net worth as a criterion of profitability, the union pointed out that since 1939 the twenty largest companies have almost doubled their net worth, with most of the increase taking place since 1945. The average rate of return on the net worth of the twenty companies increased from 4.2 per cent in 1939 to almost 11 per cent in 1951.

Additional union briefs in the justification of its demands stressed the deterioration in the steelworkers' real wage and the fact that the average steelworker's weekly earnings are insufficient to maintain a modest standard of living. Citing the Bureau of National Affairs budget for mid-November 1951, the union revealed that a $4,132 yearly wage or $79.46 per week was necessary to provide a modest but adequate standard of living. But the average weekly earnings of steelworkers in September 1951 were $78.30. Since more than half (60 per cent) of the steelworkers earn less than $78.30 per week because the weekly earnings average is pulled upward by reason of the high incentive earnings of a few employees, the spread between the average steelworker's weekly wage and the amount required to meet the Bureau's budget is much greater than actually revealed.

An irritant to the union was the inequity of wage rates between the northern and southern steel mills and iron ore companies and the differences in wage rates because of diverse locations of the plants and mines. The union believed there was no excuse for a continuation of inequality in wage payments for equal work.[29]

In support of the guaranteed minimum wage, Mr. Murray stressed that the plan is practical and feasible. On the basis of Mr. Latimer's study he concluded that the security of the steelworkers and the iron ore workers can be obtained under most foreseeable circumstances for a small cost and within the industry's capacity to pay.[30]

The Wage Stabilization Board recommended the following award: a general wage increase of 17½ cents, 12½ cents at expiration of contract on January 1, 1952, and two additional increases of 2½ cents each at successive six-month intervals. The recommended increase took into account the growing productivity, the fact that there had been an 8.8 per cent increase in the cost of living since the last general wage increase, and that employees in other industries had received larger increases than steelworkers during recent years.

In addition, the Board recommended the following changes in fringes in order to make the steel industry more comparable with

other industries: a liberalization of vacation allowances to provide
that eligibility for the third week of vacation be reduced from 25
years to 15 years of service; that the premium pay for Sunday work
be instituted where none previously existed; that double time be paid
for work on holidays to replace the former time and one-half rate;
that there be straight time pay for six unworked holidays which
was an innovation in the industry; that shift differentials be increased
from four cents to six cents on the second and six cents to nine cents
on the third shift. In respect to the guaranteed wage, the Board urged
that the steel companies and the union undertake joint study of the
question. The Board recommended that the companies consider extension of severance pay currently payable only upon termination due to permanent shutdowns. Reasonable notice should be given
in advance of layoffs or severance, and reasonable compensation for
failure to give notice. On the equal pay for equal work question, the
Board believed that the 10 cents difference in pay between southern
and northern plants should be reduced to five cents, and all other differentials should be negotiated between the union and employers. In
regard to demotion penalty, the Board recommended that the union
withdraw its demand for pay guarantees on the grounds that the
proposal would introduce inequities into the wage structure. Finally,
on the question of the union shop, the Board recommended that
the parties include a union shop agreement in their contract, and that
the negotiations should cover only the question of the details and
precise form of such a clause.[31]

The United Steelworkers hailed the Board's findings as representing a constructive attempt at reaching a compromise. Nonetheless,
they felt that the increase fell short of that to which the workers were
entitled. The steel companies greeted the recommendations with a refusal, which was hinged directly to their demand for a price increase,
just as in 1946.

After continued failure to reach a settlement with the steel industry,
the union called a strike which lasted for 53 days. The agreement
which was reached, at the instigation of the President of the United
States, with six steel companies on July 24, 1952, provided an average
hourly wage increase of 16 cents, including a 12½ cents general increase and another one-half cent increase in the job class increment,
bringing it to 5½ cents. The fringe benefits included the Board's recommendations on vacations, shift differentials, and holidays, and a

further general increase of five cents for the southern plants, thereby reducing the remaining southern differential to five cents per hour. A compromise form of the union shop was provided. To compensate the steel companies for the increased wages and other costs, the government granted them a $5.20 increase in the price of a ton of steel.[32]

In 1953 the steelworkers agreement showed continued gains. It provided an 8½ cents general wage increase and a five cents reduction in geographical differentials. The latter provision was sufficient to eliminate the southern differential for the U.S. Steel and Republic Steel companies, the two largest companies with southern subsidiaries.

In the summer of 1955, after long negotiations and a brief strike, the steelworkers signed contracts with the six major producers which provided a substantial gain of 15 cents per hour. The wage increase amounts to slightly more than 7.5 per cent in the straight-time average hourly wage. The new average straight-time rate is $2.13 compared with $1.98. With the addition of overtime and shift differentials the new average hourly wage is $2.44 versus $2.27. Steel wages under the new increase represent the highest wage for any basic industry except coal mining and oil refining.

### UNION MANAGEMENT COOPERATION

An examination of the union literature reveals that union-management cooperation has been interwoven with the steelworkers' policies. During the early years the SWOC realized that increased wages are limited unless costs are reduced. To this end the union was ready to increase productivity through cooperative efforts with management. The SWOC believed that union cooperation would be difficult to accomplish unless the union obtained security through the union shop.

Early in its history the SWOC stated the principles of production efficiency in a manual entitled *Production Problems, A Handbook for Committeemen of Local Lodges of S.W.O.C.* The actual application of the principles was made in about a dozen small concerns.[33] The Empire Sheet and Tin Plate Company (now Empire Steel Corporation) of Mansfield, Ohio, became the pioneering ground for union-management cooperation. In 1938 it appeared that the company must close because of financial difficulties. Advice and assistance were sought from the SWOC by the local lodge. Conferences between management and the local union officials revealed that the only way the company could be saved was through fullest cooperation between the company and workers. After the company granted the necessary union security, the union proceeded to carry out the principles outlined in the manual, *Production Problems*. Tangible savings of between $150,000 to $200,000 were accomplished during the first year. Both the union and management gained. The union was placed on a firm basis. A rate structure was reestablished which compared favorably with competitors.[34] Bonuses and job security were enjoyed. Management ended the year 1941 with a net profit of $500,-000.[35]

Much credit in the achievement of wage standardization in the steel industry was due to union-management cooperation in eradicating wage inequities. A considerable amount of the preliminary work of job description and classification was effected through local union-management committees at the plant level. As a result of the cooperative effort of the union's wage inequity program, order was finally achieved in wage rates.[36]

The National Planning Association has published several pamphlets dealing with union-management cooperation in the steel industry in its series of case studies on the "Causes of Industrial Peace under Collective Bargaining." None of the larger companies was covered in the studies. Of the medium sized companies, the only ones included were Sharon Steel and one plant of Colorado Fuel and Iron Co. The long period of industrial peace in the Sharon Steel Corporation has been due in part to the sincere acceptance of the union by the management, the quick settlement of grievances, simplicity and flexibility in wage decisions and methods of wage payment, and good communication and consultation between management and the union. The benefits of good relationships have accrued to the workers in the form of earnings comparable to the industry and a high degree of job security; to management and the owners has come improvement in the company's competitive position. Net income rose steadily from a loss in 1938 to about seven million dollars in 1947, while dividends have more than quadrupled since 1939. The public has gained by the better quality of the company's products, without a day's interruption.[37]

CONCLUSIONS

The wage policies of the steelworkers of America have been shaped by the strategic importance of steel in the national economy, the wide fluctuations in production, the influence of the late Philip Murray, and the stubborn resistance of the steel industry to seeing fully the needs and problems of the workers.

## I. Wage Stabilization

1. Unionization. The steelworkers realized that unionization of the industry was a requisite for effective standardization of wages. This objective was achieved for the major portion of the industry by 1941, but there are still significant segments of the industry which are either unorganized, or are organized by so-called independent unions. These include major segments of two of the large companies, National Steel (Weirton) and Armco Steel.

2. Equalization of wage rates between various classes of labor and the elimination of inequities. The U.S. Steel Agreement of 1941 was the first attack on the problem. The corporation agreed to make an attempt to adjust individual and group rates. In 1944 the National War Labor Board issued a directive order for the elimination of inequities by all the steel companies. Further attempts were made after the war. Substantial progress was made in the 1947 wage inequity agreement with the U.S. Steel Co. Although the equalization program has been almost completed in the larger steel companies, many smaller companies have never solved their problems relating to inequities.

3. Elimination of geographical wage differentials. The union has stood firmly on the principle of equal pay for equal work. During World War II the union tried to use the National War Labor Board to achieve this goal, but it was not until after the war that any progress was made. The 17½ cents southern differential that existed in the operations of the major steel companies in 1937 was eliminated from 1947 through 1953. It included the following steps: 1947—three cents; 1950—four and a half cents; 1952—five cents; 1953—five cents.

4. Key company or pattern bargaining. The steelworkers have used their agreements with the U.S. Steel Corporation as a pattern for all the other companies in the industry. Actually, this parallel movement of wages predated the existence of collective bargaining in the industry. It represented an attempt on the part of the companies to

keep their wage costs at least roughly similar to each other. The union has never formally requested industry-wide bargaining. In 1942 it indicated that industry-wide bargaining was appropriate under the existing circumstances, but it did not make a direct demand on the companies. For many years the union has not indicated any interest in industry-wide bargaining.

## II. Improvement in Economic Standards of Members

The union has been alert in obtaining wage increases and better working conditions for its members. Immediately after winning recognition by the U.S. Steel Company in 1937, the union demanded and obtained a $5.00 minimum daily wage for common labor and a 10 cents increase for all other workers, along with a 40-hour week. During the recession of 1937-38 the union was successful in preventing wage cuts, and with the improvement of business in 1941 they obtained a 10 cents an hour increase. This gain in wages raised the minimum rate for common labor from 62½ cents in 1937 to 72½ cents in 1941 and for all workers it raised the average hourly rate from 82½ cents to 96½ cents.

During the Second World War the union was constantly attempting to obtain benefits within the wage stabilization rules. Soon after the entrance of the United States into the war, the union asked for $1.00 a day wage increase and a guaranteed minimum for each day of work. The National War Labor Board, following the government stabilization policy, formulated the "Little Steel Formula" which became a criterion in all wage disputes, namely, that workers are entitled to a 15 per cent raise in wages from January 1941 to May 1942 to correspond to the rise in the cost of living.

The steelworkers, like other unions, soon found that although wages were frozen, the cost of living was not, and accordingly demanded wage increases to offset the spiraling of prices. Although the steelworkers were unable to obtain further advances in wages during the war, they were successful in obtaining many improvements in working conditions such as adoption of shift differentials, the formalization in their contracts of holidays with pay in accordance with the government policy, improvements in vacations with pay, and the like.

On the return to peace, the union demanded a $2.00 a day wage increase to make up for the reduced share of the workers in company earnings during the war and the shrinkage in weekly earnings due to the shorter work hours and downgrading of the employees. After a strike the union obtained an 18½ cents an hour increase which became the pattern wage adjustment for many workers throughout the United States. In 1947 the union won a 12½ cents per hour general wage increase together with fringe benefits which totaled 15 cents an hour. Again in 1948 the union achieved a 13 cents hourly wage increase but failed to gain its goal of social insurance and pensions. After the union pressed in vain for more wage gains and social insurance and pensions in 1949, a fact-finding board recommended noncontributory social insurance and pension plans. After a strike that lasted from 30 to 45 days, Bethlehem Steel became the first major company to effect a settlement and was followed shortly by the other steel companies.

The rising cost of living after the outbreak of the Korean War occasioned the steelworkers' demand for another general wage increase in 1950. It resulted in a wage advance of 12½ cents per hour plus a five cents increase in increments between job classes, a 4½ cents increase in rates for southern plants, and a job classification program for iron ore companies of the U.S. Steel Co. amounting to 8½ cents per hour over the general wage increase. Again in 1951 the union sought wage advances as well as other adjustments in working conditions. The steel industry, after a refusal to abide by a recommendation of the Wage Stabilization Board, was tied up for a period of 53 days. With permission granted to increase the price of steel, a settlement was reached simultaneously in 1952 at the White House with six companies. The agreement provided an average hourly wage increase of 16 cents and the inclusion of many fringe benefits recommended by the Stabilization Board. In 1953, the union obtained further gains. These included an 8½ cents general wage increase and another five cents reduction in geographical differentials which was sufficient to eliminate by January 1, 1954, the southern differential for the two largest steel companies with southern operations, namely, U.S. Steel and Republic Steel. In 1955 the union won a substantial wage increase of 15 cents per hour, which brought the average straight-time hourly rate to $2.13. With the inclusion of overtime and shift differentials the new average hourly rate is $2.44.

The arguments of the union to bolster its case for wage demands hinged around the following: cost-of-living increases, ability to pay based on profits and growth of the industry, the trend of wages in the basic industries, increased productivity, and the purchasing power theory. Regarding the last factor, the steelworkers in common with other unions felt that substantial increases in wages were needed to enable the workers to buy goods in sufficient quantity to maintain full employment.

The steelworkers have been opposed to the use of escalator clauses in their contracts which pin wages to the cost of living or the provision of annual productivity increases. They have preferred to bargain early for substantial gains to cover both the changes in prices and advancing productivity.

### III. Social Insurance and Pensions

In 1948 the union adopted its policy calling for the establishment of pensions and social insurance. The steel industry had lagged in this area as shown by the fact that pensions averaging $5 monthly were the characteristic pattern. There were only a few health plans which paid any sick benefits. The union felt that protection for its workers and its families against the hazards of life was a legitimate cost of production. In 1949 the union's demands became reality in the form of non-contributory pensions and a contributory social insurance plan on a 50–50 division of cost between the workers and the employer.

### IV. Guaranteed Annual Wage

Having experienced insecurity in employment in past years and concerned with the instability of employment which has characterized their industry, the steelworkers during the last war turned their attention to the guaranteed minimum weekly wage. While the War Labor Board denied the union's request, it recommended that the President of the United States inaugurate an over-all study of the problem. This study has opened up possibilities for the eventual adoption of such a program. During the postwar years the union has again reiterated its demand for the adoption of the guaranteed annual wage. On March 24, 1953, the union served notice that the guaranteed annual wage would be its next big objective. The guaranteed wage was not pressed by the union in the 1955 negotiations owing to general agreement within the industry that only wages would be subject to bargaining. However, the union has stated that the guaranteed wage will be sought in the 1956 contracts.

## V. Union-Management Cooperation

During the earlier years, 1937–1940, the steelworkers welcomed the opportunity to cooperate with management in reducing costs and increasing productivity. The union was a pioneer among the CIO unions in union-management cooperation. It has given not only advice and technical assistance to management, but also in one case financial aid in the form of a percentage of employees' wages loaned to keep the company in operation. The union has assisted management in effecting wage standardization through job description and classification. It has been known to modifiy its wage rates to help companies in financial distress. It tries to insist that any deviations from key bargaining patterns must be justified by individual concerns.

# International Union, United Automobile, Aircraft and Agricultural Implement Workers of America (UAW-CIO)

## INTRODUCTION

Only the wage policies of the automobile workers will be considered in this chapter, because here the UAW has made its greatest impact on wages owing to its complete organization of the industry. Although the aircraft and farm equipment industries are almost as well organized, they are split between the UAW, the IUE, UE, and the International Association of Machinists.

The production of automobiles is concentrated in about six corporations, three of which produce nine-tenths of the total units sold. The industry is an outstanding example of mass production. Most of the work is highly specialized and the jobs are semi-skilled, for the most part.

Employment in the industry before World War II had been subject to sharp seasonal and cyclical fluctuations. The seasonal changes in employment were attributed to the introduction of new models in the winter period, but by pushing ahead the date from winter to fall in 1935 some reduction in seasonal unemployment was experienced. Regarding cyclical fluctuations, sales of automobiles dropped quite sharply in the early stages of the depression and rose rapidly with the improvement in business conditions. Fluctuations in automobile sales are estimated to be about twice as great as the general level of industrial production.

The auto industry, like steel, is subject to little price competition. Competition occurs largely in the form of quality, styling and advertising. One of the principal reasons for the reduction in wages is eliminated by the rare occurence of cutthroat competition.[1]

The General Motors Corporation is the leader in the automobile industry. It makes nearly half of the cars and trucks produced in the United States. Its financial resources rank it as one of the largest corporations in the world. It affects directly the lives of over 400,000 workers in the United States and indirectly thousands of other workers through the many products it purchases. General Motors and Ford tend to set the pattern of wages as well as prices in the automobile industry. Chrysler and the independents usually trail along with the leaders.

Before the genesis of the CIO, the AFL made some feeble attempts to organize the automobile industry, first on a craft basis and later on an industrial basis. The Automobile, Aircraft, and Vehicle Workers of the AFL had a membership of about 20,000 in 1920. Organizational drives by the AFL during the 1920's resulted in little progress in unionization. The passage of the NRA in 1933 stimulated the AFL to further organizational work. Many new locals of the federal type were established, but they had no international union to tie them together, which meant they were unable to do an effective job in bargaining or striking against the giant corporations. In August 1935 the AFL combined its federal labor unions in the industry into a new national and called it the United Automobile Workers of America. In 1936 the union was granted complete autonomy by the AFL, and Homer Martin became its first president.

The UAW grew rapidly through mergers of several independent unions, membership drives, and the stimulus of returning prosperity and the National Labor Relations Act. Much discontent was expressed over the policies of union jurisdiction of the AFL. Because many workers wanted an industrial union, their interests lay more closely with the newly formed Committee for Industrial Organization. In July 1936 the UAW joined the CIO and claimed jurisdiction not only over automobile workers but also over those employees associated with the aircraft and farm equipment industries. In August 1941 the UAW-CIO changed its name to the International Union, United Automobile, Aircraft and Agricultural Implement Workers of America, but it retains its old initials of UAW.[2] In May 1954 the UAW-CIO reached a membership of about one and a quarter million workers and is the country's largest union.[3] It is now recognized as a pacesetter in shaping union demands.

During the first three decades of the twentieth century the automobile industry was notoriously anti-union. Discharge and discriminatory layoffs were meted out to employees suspected of union activity. The use of blacklisting and spies was a common procedure to prevent union influence. Working conditions were generally bad. As usual during the earlier period, large profits went into the hands of the owners and a small trickle into the pay envelopes. During the first decade the average weekly wage was under $12.00, and the average yearly earnings were about $500 to $600. The average yearly earnings for a selected number of years follow: 1914, $802; 1919, $1,431; 1921, $1,498; 1923, $1,630; 1925, $1,675; 1933–34, $749; 1934–35, $1,014; 1935–36, $1,294; 1937–38, $906; 1938–39, $1,328. The Ford Motor Company adopted a $5 minimum wage per day policy in 1914, but when the total annual hours worked are considered, the annual earnings were still small. In a study by Reinhold Niebuhr in 1926 it was revealed that with the exception of a few thousand highly skilled workers it was almost impossible to find a Ford worker earning more than $1,500 a year.[4]

The speed-up has been characteristic of the automobile industry during most of its history. After a man spent fifteen or twenty years in the auto factories, he was no longer fit for work. Lay-offs lasting between three or four months or longer in each year were an accepted pattern. There was no job security. The hours of work during the business season were long. In 1925 the 50-hour week was common in the industry with the exception of the Ford Motor Company. Sunday and holiday work was widespread during rush periods, often making a work-week of 70 hours.

### EARLY WAGE POLICIES

Following the UAW affiliation with the CIO in 1936, the union policy became aggressive in character. The union realized that it must fight for union recognition, before it would be able to obtain improved economic conditions for the workers. Over the next years many local strikes occurred, culminating in the sitdown strikes. General Motors was the first automobile company to grant union recognition in February 1937. In less than a year the UAW had won contracts with every automobile company but Ford. Wage increases generally accompanied union acceptance.

The 1937 contracts won by the UAW provided minimum wages of 75 cents per hour for men and 65 cents for women; time and a half, and, in some cases, double time for Saturday, Sunday, and holiday work; seniority rules; shop committees; grievance machinery; elimination of speed-up system and company spies; and finally a wage increase.[5] During the depression of 1937–38 the union policy of preventing wage reductions proved highly successful, as wage reductions were the exception rather than the rule.[6]

Following the great victories in unionization in 1937, there was much dissension within the UAW with a subsequent decline in membership and refusal of the manufacturers to recognize the union. The union had not yet achieved stable leadership or developed a long-range program. Homer Martin was a demagogue and lacked integrity. The UAW was also beset by efforts of political groups to use the union for selfish purposes. After the election of R. J. Thomas as president, the newly reorganized UAW outlined a program for rehabilitating the union. To accomplish this goal, it was necessary to compel the employers to once again recognize the UAW as spokesman for the employees. A strike of the General Motors tool and die makers in 1939 under the leadership of Walter Reuther, director of the union's General Motors Department, forced the company to recognize the UAW. Similar demonstrations occurred with other manufacturers. In 1940 a contract with the General Motors Corporation included the principle of vacation with pay for the first time in the automobile industry. In the following year the UAW won 10 cents an hour wage increase for the General Motors workers and a $5,000,000 fund for correcting inequities in wage rates for individual jobs. Similar gains were obtained from other major companies. The last remaining fortress of anti-unionism to capitulate was the Ford Motor Company. In 1941 after a ten-day strike, the company recognized the union. An agreement which followed brought the UAW its first union shop and the check off of dues.[7] As in the case of General Motors, the company also provided job classification increases so that pay rates would be at least as high as those of the major competitor.

### WAGE DIFFERENTIALS

The provisions for wage equalization in the 1941 contracts of the UAW arose from the insistence of the union that variations in wage rates between different plants in a company be equalized. At the 1941 convention a resolution was adopted requesting that the international union and its officers use their efforts to have low wage rates increased throughout the industry, thus eliminating the extreme wage differentials.[8] Not only variations in wage rates between plants but variations between regions in the country were opposed by the UAW. In 1937 the average hourly earnings in the automobile factories were 91.3 cents in the North, 85.7 cents in the West and 83.3 cents in the South. Variations in wage rates were also noticeable in the manufacture of automobile bodies and parts. The union claimed that the price of an automobile was the same for all regions and sections of the country, that work done in any area was worth as much as that done in Detroit, and that the policy of equal pay for equal work was sound.[9]

The UAW as early as 1937–1938 began to consider with management the feasibility of a guaranteed minimum employment because of the instability of employment in the industry. At the 1940 convention a resolution was adopted favoring the annual wage and the thirty-hour week with forty hours of pay. It was felt that a guaranteed minimum of employment combined with a reduction in the number of hours of work would help in providing more stable employment as well as giving the workers a decent standard of living.[10]

In 1939 the General Motors Corporation suggested a two-fold plan for income regularization. The plan covered "income security" and "layoff benefit" payments. Under the provision of the plan the employees would receive during periods of slack work or lay-offs advance pay for work they did not perform. During the busier season they would work longer hours to repay the company for benefits received during the dull or idle period. The UAW officials were critical of the plan considering it paternalistic since they had no part in its formulation and announcement.[11]

### WORLD WAR II AND UAW WAGE POLICIES

The wage policies of UAW during the war period did not differ greatly from that of other labor unions. When the President of the United States froze wages on October 3, 1942, the UAW believed that labor was being treated unfairly in view of the upward swing of the cost of living. It was felt that wage rates should have been raised sufficiently to restore the purchasing power at the time of the wage freeze. A correction was made later under the "Little Steel Formula" which pacified the UAW for a time. Soon, the UAW, angered by the mounting cost of living, petitioned the President of the United States, the Office of Economic Stabilization, and the War Labor Board to terminate the wage freeze and scrap the "Little Steel

Formula." It urged the union officers to take the following steps in order to enact a sound and just wage policy:

1. A rollback of prices, or a wage increase which shall restore the purchasing power of wages where it existed in May 1942;
2. Industry-wide agreements in the automotive, aircraft and parts industry based on the principle of equal pay for equal work;
3. A guaranteed 48-hour week or 48 hours of guaranteed pay per week if the work-week is less than 48 hours because of material shortages.

During the early part of the war a communistic group in the UAW tried to induce the locals and the international union to change their traditional opposition to incentive wages. Their desire for incentive wages, according to their opponents, was based on the pretext that this method of compensation by stimulating greater production would be of assistance to Russia. At the 1943 convention of the UAW Victor Reuther made the following motion on incentive wages which was overwhelmingly approved. ". . . The International Union of the UAW-CIO reiterates emphatically its traditional opposition to the introduction of incentive or piece-work plans in the plants within our jurisdiction where such plans do not exist. The International Union will continue to leave to the autonomy of local unions the continuance of piece-work systems in keeping with the minimum standards set forth by the Columbus Board meeting.

"The convention of the UAW takes a firm position against extension of incentive pay plans because we believe that piece-work will neither bring our nation maximum war production nor provide workers an adequate annual wage.

"Piece-work will result only in further aggravating the dislocation and unbalancing of production schedules, resulting in layoffs, unemployment and dissipation of our manpower. Piece-work systems would have the result of further intensifying the problem of wage inequalities and differentials, will block the union's effort to establish an industry-wide wage agreement based upon equal pay for equal work, and will further demoralize workers who are, at present, getting less money for doing the same work. Piece-work systems would reintroduce the old system of speed-up, in which the worker is robbed of higher earnings through management's using every insignificant engineering change or pretext to cut rates. . . Be it finally resolved: That this eighth annual convention of the UAW-CIO direct all of its officers, board members, international representatives . . . to conform strictly to this policy on piece-work, and to do everything within their power to advance sound wage and production programs in conformity with policies set forth by this convention."[12]

The present policy (1955) of the UAW in respect to local unions or plant units operating under a wage incentive plan is as follows: they retain the right at any time to eliminate such plan when it becomes apparent that the plan is not securing the objectives for which it was established.[13] The Studebaker Company and the Kaiser-Willys Motors Company are two independents that have eliminated their wage incentive systems within recent months. There are still a few cases in individual plants in the automobile industry where incentive systems are being used, but on the whole the industry is operating on the day rate basis and has been for many years. In order to protect piece workers as well as day workers against exploitation, the UAW established many years ago a time study and engineering department. Its primary concern is with production standards. If workers believe the standards are too high, they can file grievances. The local union then calls on the UAW time study and engineering department to make a study to determine whether the standard is reasonable.

Wage changes and related benefits in 1942 were influenced largely by the National War Labor Board. A directive of the Board granted the General Motors and Chrysler workers a four cents an hour increase and provided for additional increases to skilled tool and die makers and skilled maintenance workers. To the Ford Motor Company the board's directive increased the maximum rates five cents per hour for the skilled and semi-skilled maintenance, power house, and construction workers; 10 cents an hour increase for the skilled tool and die makers and pattern makers. New maximum rates were also established at 20 cents an hour above the minimum rates for skilled tool, die, and pattern makers. Increased pay in lieu of vacations for employees of five years or more seniority, an increase in reporting time, and equal pay for women were decreed by the Board for General Motors, Ford, and Chrysler.[14]

In April 1943 the National General Motors Council met to formulate wage and vacation demands. The following basic demands for wage structure changes were adopted for General Motors plants:

1. Organization of production and material scheduling so as to provide each employee with a minimum of 48 hours per week;

2. Initiation by government of a national wage policy which will guarantee 40 hours pay per week to employees who work less than 40 hours a week through no fault of their own; the cost to be borne by government when the short work-week is due to material shortages, change of schedules and specifications, etc., and by management when it is responsible;

3. Institution by the War Labor Board of an industry-wide wage stabilization policy and the creation of tripartite (government-management-labor) wage commissions in the automotive and allied industries to work out and administer a master wage agreement based on the principle of equal pay for equal work;

4. Establishment by General Motors Corporation of a workers' postwar security fund equal to the fund set aside by the company for postwar contingencies.[15]

The General Motors Corporation refused to consider the new demands. The case was thereupon certified to the War Labor Board, which ruled that the demands could not be considered until the entire General Motors agreement was opened for renegotiation. Following the ruling the National General Motors Council of the UAW asked for a renegotiation of the whole General Motors contract in August 1943. In addition to the original requests, the Council demanded a $1.00 per hour minimum wage and an escalator clause for the adjustment of wages to the cost of living.[16]

The 1943 demands of the UAW on the Ford Motor Company included: elimination of inequalities in wage and a joint endeavor with all the automobile manufacturers to work out an industry-wide plan for wage stabilization based on equal pay for equal work; the establishment of a postwar security fund to aid unemployed workers; establishment of labor-management production committees; establishment of a fair and effective upgrading program.

The demands on the Chrysler Corporation were: increase in bonus in lieu of vacation; elimination of inter-plant and intra-plant inequalities and differentials; guaranteed 40-hour work week for all employees with seniority status; unemployment contingent fund; company-paid insurance premiums for all employees with seniority rights.[17]

The attempts of the UAW to broaden the scope of collective bargaining through the War Labor Board met with failure. The board denied the union's request for employment guarantees, industry-wide wage stabilization, etc., on the grounds that it did not have the authority to consider such measures.[18]

The UAW was not content with the limited scope of collective bargaining. At the 1944 convention of the union it was determined to plan ahead for the conversion to a peacetime economy. Resolutions adopted called for the support of the following policies:

1. A postwar labor security fund established by corporations and equal to the funds set aside for postwar rehabilitation and protection of stockholders. The funds would be used to supplement the wages of unemployed workers and discharged servicemen who hold seniority rights;
2. A permanent national planning board such as sponsored by the CIO in each industry to plan for postwar prosperity;
3. A public policy of higher wages to assure postwar prosperity;
4. After the defeat of Germany, abandonment of manpower controls which restrict wage increases;
5. Continuation of price controls, priorities and allocations;
6. Shortening of hours and adequate take-home pay, as reconversion and unemployment develop;
7. Adequate severance pay;
8. Equal pay for equal work and the guaranteed annual wage.[19]

POST WORLD WAR II AND UAW

The 1945 wage policy of the UAW reflects the policies of Walter Reuther and his forces in planning for peace. Reuther was interested in maintaining a healthy economy with the termination of the war. He wanted to provide full employment and a decent standard of living for all people. To achieve this goal, he thought it was necessary to have over-all planning which would include the reconversion of aircraft factories to build prefabricated houses, the payment of higher wages to workers to compensate for a decrease in take-home pay, and the absorption of increased costs by the employers. When President Truman lifted the government restrictions on wage increases after VJ Day, Mr. Reuther wrote to Charles E. Wilson, President of General Motors Corporation, asking for a 30 per cent increase in hourly wage rates with no increase in the prices of General Motors products. A part of the wage increase was requested to be used to achieve uniform wage rates throughout the company, a part for the creation of a social security fund, and the balance to increase wage rates. In several publications entitled *Purchasing Power for Prosperity* and *How to Raise Wages Without Increasing Prices* Reuther presented the case for maintaining take-home pay without increasing prices. He outlined his thesis as follows: In the first place, the wage increase without price increase is necessary in order to prevent a depression. Secondly, General Motors has the ability to pay the requested increase without raising prices, because of the many years of high profits and the favorable outlook in the postwar period. Finally, the corporation is in most excellent condition and cannot possibly lose, because of large cash reserves, new equipment furnished at public expense, and favorable tax laws.

After many months of negotiation the best offer of the corporation was a 10 per cent wage increase with the stipulation that it must have higher prices to compensate for the increased labor costs. Rejecting the offer, Reuther suggested that the dispute be arbitrated with an examination of the company's books. Upon the corporation's refusal, the UAW called a strike which lasted 113 days. In an effort to resolve the conflict, President Truman appointed a fact-finding board on December 14, 1945. In a brief presented to the board, Reuther reiterated the case for maintaining take-home pay without price increases. He said: "This dispute is labeled the case of UAW-CIO versus General Motors Corporation, and in a narrow sense this is correct. But in a larger sense the case is really the case of the United States versus General Motors Corporation. The union is acting as the protagonist of the interests of the whole American people. It is defending the national policy which calls for sustaining mass purchasing power, holding the line against inflation, and restoring free collective bargaining. . . ."[20]

The following computations were submitted in the union brief in support of the basic demands of the union. On the assumption that work hours will be reduced from 46.1 to 38, a reduction of 22.5 per cent in weekly take-home pay will occur. To restore this cut, an increase of 29 per cent in present wage rates will be required. The downgrading of employees from higher-paying to lower-paying jobs has resulted in a further four per cent cut in wages. The union proceeded to show that the company was able to pay the union's demand. It was indicated that the automobile industry stands among the highest of American industries in profitability, while the General Motors Company is at the top of all corporations in sustained profit-making.

Regarding productivity, the union assumed that after the reconversion period productivity would regain its historic trend and surpass previous years because of the accelerated rate of technology in the automobile industry and the purchase of many improved machines.[21]

Harbison and Dubin believe that the real controversy between the UAW and General Motors centered over the question of whether prices were a proper subject of bargaining. The union thought that prices and profits were of vital concern to the wage question and that the union had a right to bargain about them. General Motors contended that they were the corporation's own private business.[22]

The fact-finding board's recommended settlement favored a wage increase of 19½ cents an hour without the necessity for price increases. In the meantime, the steel industry had set the pattern of 18½ cents increase. The UAW was then compelled to accept the same wage settlement with no assurance as to prices. This wage pattern became general throughout the industry. General Motors had won a decisive victory in management's authority in the determination of prices and profits.

### THE SECOND ROUND WAGE INCREASE

With the ending of the OPA in the summer of 1946, prices and profits continued to climb. The wage increase of the previous year was soon wiped out, and the UAW insisted on further wage advances. On December 12, 1946, Reuther announced his demand for a general wage increase of 23½ cents an hour. Once more the union publicized the high profits in the automobile industry and the skyrocketing living costs. In a publication entitled *Wages, Prices, Profits—The Automobile Workers Case for a 23½¢ Wage Increase*, Reuther linked the autoworkers' wage demands to the welfare of the whole society. "High prices coupled with the present low buying power of the American people spell serious trouble ahead. A business recession is inevitable unless purchasing power is increased. Price reductions would enable people to buy more and thus avoid disaster, but business shows no signs of acting on this simple truth. . . . Wage increases, therefore, offer the only real hope of increasing purchasing power before the downward spiral to depression starts. . . . The wage demand of the auto workers is but part of the larger battle for purchasing power which must be fought and won in all sectors of our economy. Making autoworkers and other workers better customers by giving them higher wages will help to protect the jobs of all who are engaged in making and selling goods and services."[23]

In its negotiations with the General Motors Corporation the UAW, in addition to the 23½ cents wage increase, sought a jointly administered company-paid social security and pension system and a 40-hour pay guarantee for all workers for each week they are called for work. In its request for the last provision, the UAW hoped to take the beginning step toward the guaranteed annual wage.[24]

During the negotiations General Motors made a settlement with the United Electrical, Radio and Machine Workers providing for an 11½ cents wage increase, plus 3½ cents in the form of six paid holidays and some other miscellaneous items, making a total package of 15 cents. The UE's social security demands were placed aside for further study. The UE, by assuming the role of a pattern-setter in the auto industry for the first time, necessitated the UAW's acceptance of a settlement much less than anticipated. Soon afterward, the United Steelworkers reached a settlement with the United States Steel Corporation for an increase of 15 cents in benefits. The UAW obtained a two-year agreement with General Motors Corporation embodying a general wage increase of 11½ cents, additional increases for certain skilled workers, six paid holidays, and improvements in the vacation plan. The social security, pension, and pay guarantee demands were excluded, but the corporation agreed to continue discussion and negotiation on these questions. Similar agreements were secured from the other members of the big three.

#### UAW'S FIGHT FOR SOCIAL SECURITY AND PENSIONS

In Reuther's report to the 1947 convention of the UAW in November of that year, he pointed out that the union's General Motors department would soon begin negotiations for a new contract. The economic demands, in addition to a wage increase, would include a pension plan with at least 60 per cent of the cost borne by management.[25]

At the 1947 convention the guaranteed weekly wage reappeared as an important question for the autoworkers because of the decline in work hours. A resolution was adopted declaring the immediate winning of a guaranteed week's pay a major demand in the UAW program.[26]

In February 1948 the UAW formally notified the General Motors Corporation of its desire to modify and change the national agreement which was due to expire on April 28, 1948. By this time the economic demands called for:

1. A 25 cents an hour wage increase, 10 cents of which may be allocated to the establishment of an adequate old age retirement plan;
2. Five cents an hour for a comprehensive social security—a group insurance program;
3. Equalization of rates by job classification on a corporation-wide basis;
4. A guaranteed work-week of 40 hours;
5. Revision of vacation allowances;
6. Time and a half for Saturday work, double time for Sunday and triple time for holiday employment;
7. Increase in night shift premiums, elimination of merit spreads, time off for voting on primary and general election days.[27]

Reuther's position on the need for wage increases had not changed from that of two years earlier. In a speech at the Philadelphia Evening Bulletin Forum on March 9, 1948, he said: "A full production, full employment economy cannot be sustained unless full employment and full production are balanced by full distribution of the goods produced. There is too much simple-minded faith in production as a panacea. We ought to remember that American industry does not produce because people need its products. American industry will produce only as long as people can afford to buy its products. That is why a mass-production economy must rest on a base of mass purchasing power. . . . Getting this mass purchasing power into the hands of the people is the key to our economic future and it is the point of greatest conflict in the field of labor-management relations."[28]

The general reaction of General Motors Company and the automobile industry was for the most part unfavorable. General Motors showed its resistance by refusing to bargain on the question of group insurance. For two months the Chrysler Corporation stalled in its negotiations and blocked efforts by the union to reach an agreement. Finally, the union called a strike against the company.[29]

On May 25, 1948, the UAW announced a new wage agreement between the General Motors company and the union. There were three main provisions of the settlement:

1. An immediate wage increase of 11 cents per hour, eight cents out of the 11 to offset the increased cost of living since 1940;
2. Interim wage adjustments at quarterly intervals during the

two-year contract period. For each change of 1.14 points in the Bureau of Labor Statistics consumers' price index wages will change one cent an hour. However, cost-of-living wage decreases are limited to a total of five cents per hour, whereas there is no limit to the upper limit increases;

3. An annual improvement factor of three cents per hour will be added to all base rates on May 29, 1949. The three cents an hour was supposed to approximate the increased productivity in the economy as a whole.[30]

The General Motors—UAW contract was not greeted enthusiastically by the autoworkers' union. John W. Livingston, vice-president of the UAW, commenting on the agreement said: "Substantially as it is, the UAW-CIO regards this victory as essentially a holding operation. It can be termed a victory only in the context of today's economic and political reaction. Nevertheless, we are recommending its acceptance by General Motors workers as their contribution to industrial peace, even though it does not represent all they are entitled to and is far short of the contribution which General Motors could and should make to a sturdy, healthy and equitable, national economy.

"In the first place, the base date for measuring wages in terms of buying power is 1940, when an army of eight million unemployed provided striking testimony that wages were far too low to sustain full employment.

"In the second place, instead of sharing its dangerously inflated profits beyond a cost-of-living adjustment based on a depressed 1940 wage, General Motors offered an annual increase of two per cent or three cents an hour as a gesture toward keeping the workers' purchasing power abreast of the increased output resulting from technological advance in the national economy. The figure itself shortchanges the principle involved. . . .

"Third, the UAW-CIO accepts the provison for quarterly wage adjustments to correspond with changes in the B.L.S. cost-of-living index only because most of those in control in government and in industry show no signs of acting at the public interest. . . .

"Fourth, the assumption that workers can expect no more than to remain on the economic treadmill, inching up three cents an hour per year while management and stockholders reap profits proportionately far in excess of that amount is unsound and unwise. This is still the trickle-down theory of prosperity, slightly modified. The modification is extremely important, however, because, in making it,

General Motors has accepted the principle that prices and profits are a concern of labor. This is progress.

"In spite of these criticisms of the settlement, we believe that in accepting it the General Motors workers will be making a substantial contribution to the economic health of the nation and to the welfare of their fellow Americans."[31]

On May 28, 1948, the Chrysler Corporation came to terms with the UAW, ending its strike. The agreement provided a 13 cents an hour wage increase and adjustments in vacation pay and wage inequities.[32]

On July 12, 1948, the Ford Motor Company and the UAW concluded their bargaining agreement which provided a 13 cents wage increase, an advance in premium pay for afternoon and night shifts, improved vacations, improved group insurance plan, agreement that each party would set up a committee for the study of insurance plans, agreement by the company to complete a study of job classification structure, and upon completion to negotiate with the union concerning inequities in wages.[33]

THE UAW VICTORY FOR PENSIONS AND SOCIAL SECURITY

In January 1949 the International Executive Board announced the basic economic demands for the year. The chief emphasis was on pensions and social security plans. A wage increase was also requested to restore the buying power of wages to the level of June 1946. In a letter to the locals Reuther said: "We in the UAW-CIO are no longer willing to tolerate a continuation of double standards in our industry. Under these double standards top corporate executives provide generous pensions for themselves while denying them to the workers who cannot possibly save for their old age out of current earnings. . . .We are taking pension and social security plans out of the category of fringe demands and putting them at the top of the agenda."[34]

At the 1949 convention of the UAW the delegates adopted a resolution supporting the 1949 demands and called upon the officers and executive board to devote the full resources of the union to win the outlined objectives.[35]

The wage pattern for 1949 was set by the presidential fact-finding board for the steel industry when it recommended on September 10, 1949, that the steel companies establish social insurance and pensions costing 10 cents per hour. On September 28, 1949, the Ford

Motor Company agreed with the UAW to a non-contributory retirement plan, which preceded the Bethlehem agreement of October 31, 1949. The Ford pension plan which became effective November 1, 1950, provided pensions of $100 a month including old age benefits under the Federal Social Security Act to employees retiring at 65 or older with 30 years of service, and those workers aged 60 and under 65 with 30 years of service, including 10 years after November 1, 1950, would receive proportionately fewer benefits. Disability retirement of $50 a month less federal social security benefits was to be given those disabled employees after 30 years of service at age 55 or older.[36]

The Chrysler Corporation, after six months of negotiation, continued to reject every reasonable offer. Whereupon, the UAW called a strike on January 25, 1950, which proved to be one of the longest and costliest strikes in the union's history. The Chrysler Corporation was willing to give pensions but refused to agree to funding and the joint administration of pensions. The three basic principles required by the UAW for all pension plans are: 1) non-contributory, 2) funding of benefits on an actuarially sound basis, 3) joint administration. The Ford agreement embodied all of these, but Chrysler would concede only the first principle.[37]

On May 1, 1950, the hundredth day of the strike, the company agreed to meet the UAW's pension proposals and also included an economic package consisting of hospital-medical and insurance programs and additional benefits, including the elimination of wage inequities in 45 job classifications covering thousands of workers, reduction of area wage differentials, wage increases in several Chrysler parts plants, and increased vacation pay. The hospital-medical and insurance package included:

1. The company agreed to pay one-half of the cost of Blue Cross and Blue Shield coverage and one-half of the cost of in-hospital medical care benefits;

2. The company agreed to pay 50 per cent of the cost of sickness and accident insurance;

3. A group life insurance policy of $3,600, 45¢ per thousand borne by the workers and the balance by the company;

4. A $1,000 paid-up life insurance policy for retired employees with 25 years of service paid for by the company;

5. Permanent and total disability benefits provided by the company.[38]

In a letter addressed to all the Chrysler workers Reuther and Matthews commented on the union victory: "The Chrysler strike was more than a fight for pension, hospital-medical, and insurance benefits and a better contract. The Chrysler strike was a part of a great human crusade to build a better tomorrow and a better world—a world in which we and our children can have a little more of the good things in life, a little more security and a little more happiness. In their strike victory, Chrysler workers have made an important contribution to the building of a better and more secure tomorrow."[39]

On March 3, 1950, the UAW-CIO General Motors Department announced its 1950 demands on the company. It included a $125 month pension plan, comprehensive hospital and medical coverage, severance allowance, wage increases and other economic demands. The total cost of the economic package was 31 cents an hour. Surprisingly, on May 23, 1950, the UAW and General Motors signed a five-year contract providing a 19 cents an hour package. It set a new industrial pattern for pensions and hospital-medical and insurance program. The wage-adjustment arrangements contained in the 1948 agreement were extended for another five years. The annual improvement adjustment was raised from three cents to four cents while the quarterly adjustments for the cost-of-living allowance were carried forward without change. A new pension plan financed by the company provided a maximum of $1.50 a month for each year of service up to 30 years, to be supplemented by federal social security benefits, and a minimum pension of $4 a month for each year of service up to 25 years, to be supplemented by federal social security benefits. Disability retirement benefits were also included in the pension plan. A contributory group insurance plan provided, at no extra cost to employees, additional $500 of life insurance, $250 in accidental death insurance, $14 a week in sickness and accident benefits, $10 a month in total disability benefits, and establishment of in-hospital doctor attendance benefits up to $5 a day for a maximum of 70 days. Hospital and surgical benefits were also added with the company paying one half of Blue Cross and Blue Shield. The provision for a modified union shop was among the non-economic gains.[40]

In a press statement announcing the UAW-General Motors agreement Reuther said: "The UAW-CIO today reached a historic agreement with General Motors Corporation which the union regards as the most significant development in labor relations since the mass production industries were organized in 1936-37.

"The General Motors workers have made tremendous gains in this new agreement, both economic and non-economic. The annual automatic wage increase assures a constant improvement in the living standards of General Motors workers. The agreement provides safeguards that guarantee that all the economic gains that go into effect immediately and in the next four years will be translated into real purchasing power that cannot be diminished or wiped out by increased living costs.

"The economic gains won in this new contract when applied to the total General Motors payroll will give General Motors workers a total gain of $144,000,000 during the first year and will increase by $32,000,000 a year, making the total gains for the duration of contract substantially in excess of $1,000,000,000. The economic package will add $700 a year to the income of the average General Motors worker's family in 1955. These figures, it should be noted, represent actual gains in purchasing power, not merely gains in money wages. We believe that this new agreement is not only a tremendous step forward in improving the economic conditions of General Motors workers and in stabilizing labor relations in General Motors, but that it points the way for the same improvements and stabilization throughout American industry.

"The new agreement translates into reality the basic economic and social principles which have been the foundation of the UAW-CIO program during the last five years. It recognizes that increased purchasing power—not just increased money wages—is the only basis of a higher standard of living. It recognizes that workers have a right to a constantly improved standard of living and that they have a right to share in the benefits of greater production made possible through technological progress without additional human effort."[41]

Frederick Harbison believes the General Motors UAW agreement of 1950 is the most significant development in collective bargaining since the Taylor-Lewis steel pact of 1937. It indicates the probable course of collective bargaining and the importance of key bargain patterns as reference points in collective relationships in the mass production industries.[42]

The Chrysler Corporation on August 25, 1950, without a formal wage reopening and without modifying the terms of its contract, agreed to a general wage increase of 10 cents an hour with additional increases of five cents an hour for skilled workers. On December 11, 1950, the Chrysler Corporation and the UAW set aside the agreement and negotiated a five-year contract without reopening provisions. The new contract was similar to the General Motors agreement in respect to the pension plan and the escalator clauses. To bring the Chrysler workers up to the level of General Motors employees, a one cent an hour wage increase plus a cost-of-living wage increment were included in the new contract.[43]

On September 4, 1950, the Ford Motor Company signed a five year contract with the UAW providing economic gains equivalent to 19.4 cents an hour. Included were: a guaranteed $125 a month pension, a cost-of-living wage increase of eight cents per hour, an escalator cost-of-living and annual improvement clause, Blue Cross and Blue Shield insurance for the worker and eligible dependents with the company paying one-half the cost, and many other benefits at no cost to the worker.[44]

### THE KOREAN WAR AND UAW WAGE POLICY

The outbreak of the Korean War found the UAW protected against spiraling costs by their cost-of-living escalator clauses. The workers were also assured of continuing pay increases through the annual improvement clauses. However, the UAW was not satisfied to sit back and enjoy its fruits. It began to press on the political and legislative fronts for many needed legislative enactments to provide the basis for a sound economy. To achieve this goal, they sought: over-all price controls, a more equitable tax system, expansion of strategic metals by government action, provision of legislative funds to supplement unemployment compensation for workers laid off because of conversion from civilian to defense production, expansion of social security program, a national health program, a civil rights platform, adequate housing, aid to federal education, repeal of the Taft-Hartley Law, etc.[45]

In a report to the UAW-CIO membership in May 1952, Reuther expressed dissatisfaction with the union social security plans in spite of the progress already achieved. Temporary disability benefits do not provide adequate levels of income maintenance, he said. There should be a larger coverage of surgical and medical care in the hospitals. Hospital-medical programs for retired workers are badly needed as well as health rehabilitation. Finally, the complete cost of the hospital and medical program should be borne by the employer rather than one half as at present.[46] In the 1952 negotiations the UAW made substantial progress in carrying to fruition these social security demands.

UAW DEMANDS CHANGES IN GENERAL MOTORS FIVE YEAR CONTRACT

In September 1952 the UAW National General Motors Council adopted a resolution demanding a five-cent limit on the cost-of-living allowance with the amounts above this allowance to be included in the basic rates; an increase in the annual improvement adjustment from four cents to five cents; increase in pension benefits; elimination of compulsory retirement; and wage increases for skilled employees. Similar action was taken by the presidents of the Chrysler local unions and the National Ford Council.[47] The UAW announced that it was seeking these changes in its long-term contract with General Motors in order to meet the problems which had arisen since the five-year contract was signed on May 23, 1950. According to the union officials, it had been the established policy of the union to view long-term contracts as living documents. The contracts must not foreclose the working out of difficulties which arise in the interim and which could not be anticipated when the agreements were negotiated. The union was fearful that wage increases won under the cost-of-living escalator clauses would be lost in the event of deflation. The annual improvement factor should be increased, because at the time of negotiation of the old contract the four cents annual increment represented a 2½ per cent increase, but, by the application of the 2½ per cent formula to present day rates of pay, an improvement factor of five cents an hour would be required. The union complained about the shrinkage of the pension due to rising prices, the arbitrary compulsory retirement provisions, and inadequate wages for skilled workers.

Realizing the problems which had arisen since the 1950 contracts, the General Motors Corporation offered to add 14 cents to the permanent base pay out of the 25 cents an hour gained in the cost-of-living adjustments. The union wanted 20 cents out of the 25 cents in order to enable the workers to retain most of their gains, if living costs dropped. General Motors refused to increase the annual improvement factor from four cents to five cents and also gave a negative answer to the request for adjustments in pension benefits and compulsory retirement provisions. The wage increase of five cents offered by General Motors to correct wage inequities for skilled workers was considered inadequate by the union.[48]

At the convention of the UAW in February 1953 the UAW adopted the five demands, four of which comprised the original National General Motors Council's resolutions. The fifth demand related to the protection of the workers' "full equity" in the conversion of the "old series" consumers' price index to the "new series" consumers' price index.

On May 22, 1953, an agreement was reached between the General Motors Corporation and the UAW which included practically all the demands of the union. It provided:

1. Incorporation of all but five cents of the cost-of-living allowance into the basic wage rates;
2. The annual improvement adjustment was increased to five cents;
3. Conversion from the "old series" consumers' price index to the "new series" consumers' price index in determining cost-of-living adjustments;
4. Additional wage increases to workers in specified skilled occupations;
5. Pensions increased to $1.75 a month for each year of service up to 30 years. A maximum pension of $137.50 a month including federal benefits was established. Minimum pension, including federal benefits, to remain at $4 for each year to a maximum of 25 years. The pension increases are to apply to workers already retired. Blue Cross and Blue Shield insurance were made available to retired workers at group rates.[49]

Shortly after the culmination of the General Motors agreement the UAW signed similar agreements with Ford and Chrysler.[50]

### THE NEW DRIVE FOR THE GUARANTEED ANNUAL WAGE

At the UAW Education Conference in Cleveland in March 1952 Reuther placed the guaranteed annual wage at the head of the list of future goals of the union. He declared: "This is the first time in world history that men have the problem of eating and living by the year, but only getting paid by the hour or the piece. We will not solve this basic problem until the cost of unemployment is transferred from the backs of workers onto the backs of industry, where it belongs."[51] In Mr. Reuther's report to the 1953 UAW-CIO convention he reiterated that the guaranteed annual wage would be the new major advance of the union. To achieve it, he called for a sound program based on thorough preparation and a militant membership ready to struggle and sacrifice.[52]

At the 1953 convention of the UAW-CIO the delegates unanimously approved a resolution that the guaranteed annual wage should be the next basic demand of the union. The general principles endorsed by the convention were:

"1. The primary goal of a guaranteed annual wage plan should be to stimulate management to provide steady full-time employment, week by week, the year round.

"2. Guaranteed annual wage payments should be made to workers for whom management fails to provide work in amounts sufficient to insure take-home pay adequate to maintain the living standards which the worker and his family enjoyed while fully employed.

"3. All workers should be guaranteed employment or guarantee payments from the time they acquire seniority. The guarantee should assure protection against a full year of layoff for all eligible workers and for shorter periods on a graduated basis for those who have not worked the minimum qualifying period.

"4. Guarantee payments should be integrated with state unemployment compensation benefits so that employers can reduce their liabilities by effectively working toward the improvement of the state laws.

"5. The plan should be administered by a Joint Board of Administration having equal representation from the union and from management, with an impartial chairman to break deadlocks. Decisions of the Joint Board with respect to eligibility and disqualification should be made independently of decisions made by state agencies with regard to unemployment compensation.

"6. Financing should combine pay-as-you-go, to provide employers with incentives to stabilize employment, with a reserve trust fund to meet abnormal costs. Provision should be made for reinsurance to reduce the size of the required reserves and to spread the risks of abnormal unemployment over the widest possible area of the economy."[53]

An analysis of the UAW guaranteed wage plan reveals the following points. 1) The guarantee and coverage includes the following: a) all workers will be covered by 40 hours of work every week, unless notified in advance that they are to be laid off for the entire week; b) all workers who have seniority status will be covered by the guarantee against fullweek layoffs. 2) The duration of guaranteed payments shows that a) the 40-hour guarantee will be effective for every week the worker is called in, or if no prior notice of full week layoff has been given; b) the guarantee against full-week layoffs will be at a maximum of 52 consecutive weeks of such layoffs. The duration of guarantee payments for full week layoffs will be determined on the basis of a ratio of the number of weeks after the date the worker acquired seniority to the effective date of the plan, plus the number of weeks for which the worker receives compensation (except guarantee payments for full-week lay offs). The graduation guarantee principle for low seniority workers was included in the UAW plan, because the union did not want to prevent employers from hiring new workers, and to avoid discouraging employers from recalling laid off workers. 3) By requiring that laid-off workers register with the State Employment Service and accept suitable employment, the cost of the guarantee to the employer should be reduced. However, in order to protect workers against the pressure to accept substandard jobs, the UAW will reserve the right to define standards of suitability under the guaranteed agreement. 4) The method of financing the plan should reduce the employer costs and provide employer incentives. The union feels that by making the employer bear the full cost of short work-weeks on a pay-as-you-go basis management will tend to plan more effectively a week ahead, thereby avoiding the short work-week. In doing so, this part of the guarantee will cost practically nothing. Requiring the cost of full-week layoffs to be met by the employer on a pay-as-you-go basis up to a specified maximum percentage of the payroll will also provide a real incentive for the employer to avoid layoffs, for in doing so, it will reduce his costs. As the maximum percentage to calculate the employer's contribution is based on the current payroll, the amount of money in the fund will be reduced, should the payroll decline. This should relieve the employer of a heavy fixed liability at a time when his business is slack. In respect to the reserve trust fund, its size will be determined by a specified percentage of the employer's base payroll. The base payroll is defined as the number of man-hours worked in the bargaining unit during a specified number of years multiplied by the average straight-time hourly wage. According to the union, the relating of the size of the reserve trust fund to the base payroll should minimize the possibility that the employer may be discouraged from hiring additional workers when his business improves.[54]

### UAW WINS MODIFIED GUARANTEED ANNUAL WAGE

On June 6, 1955, the UAW after eight weeks of negotiations, won a three-year contract with the Ford Motor Company, providing a modified guaranteed annual wage, or a supplemental unemployment benefit plan which became the pattern for the automobile industry. A week later, on June 13, General Motors reached a similar agreement with the UAW. Although these historic agreements did not fully meet the demands of the UAW, they achieved a new principle in industrial relations, company responsibility to mitigate the vicissitudes of unemployment for the workers. Other changes in the settlement included: liberalized pensions, increases in the annual improvement factor and cost-of-living adjustments, improved vacations, wage inequity adjustments, additional paid holidays, increase in group life and health insurance, a raise for skilled trades, and other miscellaneous changes. An additional gain in the General Motors agreement was a union shop in place of the modified union shop.

In commenting on the Ford settlement, Mr. Reuther said: "This is one of the most historical agreements that we have written in the twenty years of our union. It is the largest economic package that we have ever negotiated. It is in excess of 20 cents an hour . . . It provides for the highest level of pensions that we have ever had . . . It provides for better hospital-medical care, greater insurance coverage, and, of course, it provides the principle upon which we are going to build the guaranteed annual wage."[55]

Mr. Bugas, vice-president of the Ford Motor Company, said: "We think that it offers additional security to our employees and particularly in the automobile industry where historically you have layoffs . . . We recognize that in the Ford Motor Company . . . that we have special responsibility to our employees."[56]

### THE MECHANICS OF THE FORD AND GENERAL MOTORS GUARANTEED WAGE PLAN

The guaranteed wage benefits under the Ford and General Motors contracts cover all hourly rated employees with seniority of one year. A worker after a layoff of one week is assured of 65 per cent of his take-home pay for four weeks to be followed by 60 per cent of take-home pay for the rest of the eligibility period up to a total of 26 weeks. The plan integrates company payments with state unemployment benefits. In case a state benefit level rises, the employers' obligation would be reduced. The maximum amount an employee can draw from the company is $25; the minimum is $2.

Both companies will make a contribution of five cents an hour into a trust fund, based on current levels of employment. At present employment levels, the Ford fund could ultimately reach $55 million and General Motors $150 million. The exact amount to be funded will vary with fluctuations in employment and will be determined monthly. When the funds reach the maximum level, the company contributions will cease and will be resumed only as it is necessary to restore the assets to the 100 per cent level. To enable the funds to be accumulated in the initial stages of the plan, no benefits will be paid until June 1, 1956.

The Ford and General Motors workers will become eligible to participate in benefits through a system of acquiring "credit units" for weeks actually worked. The credit unit is a week of 32 hours or more. The amount of benefit to be paid to a laid-off worker will depend on the "credit units" acquired and the size of the trust fund. A worker with ten or more years seniority receives one credit unit for each two weeks worked, and those with less than ten years of service receive one credit unit for four weeks of employment.

As long as the size of the trust fund is 85 per cent or more of its maximum reserve, a laid-off worker will receive a full week's benefit for each credit unit he possesses up to a maximum of 26 weeks. In the event the fund drops below 85 per cent, a worker with ten or more years of seniority must pay or surrender more credits to receive full weekly benefits, and those with less than ten years service must surrender even more credits. If the trust fund drops below 13 per cent of its maximum level, benefits are reduced to all laid-off workers by 20 per cent. No benefits will be paid if the trust fund drops below a level of four per cent.

### AN EXAMPLE OF HOW THE GUARANTEED WAGE PLAN WILL WORK

Assume a laid-off Ford worker has a wife and one child and earns $85 a week before taxes and $74.98 after taxes. If the state unemployment compensation is $30 a week, he would receive $18.74 from the trust fund for the first four weeks (subject to the waiting week provision), making his total weekly income $48.74 or 65 per cent of his take-home pay. In the next 22 weeks his weekly benefits would be $44.99, or 60 per cent of his take-home pay ($30 unemployment compensation and $14.99 from the trust fund).

OTHER ECONOMIC PROVISIONS IN FORD AND GENERAL MOTORS CONTRACTS

Pensions:— Both companies will liberalize pensions for already-retired workers and those who will retire in the future. The monthly pension payments are raised from $1.75 per month per year of service to $2.25, and the former 30 years maximum service credits are eliminated. Employees will now receive pension credits for service beyond 30 years regardless of whether they retire at age 65 or older. Under the new pension program, an employee who has 40 years of service upon retirement at 65 or over, can expect his company pension benefits to be increased from $52.50 per month to $90.00. If the employee has a wife at age 65, they can receive total pension benefits of $237.80, including both company payments and social security as compared to $200.30 under the old program. After mid-1956 when social security benefits are increased, the same couple would receive $252.80. Permanent and total disability retirement provisions have also been liberalized under the new contracts.

An attractive new feature of the pension program is the vesting of pension rights. This principle may well rank next to the guaranteed wage in its impact on industrial relations. One criticism of industry retirement programs has been that if a worker changes his employer, he relinquishes his company pension credits. Under the Ford and General Motors plan, any worker who is 40 years of age or older and who has acquired 10 years of pension rights, will, upon leaving the company before reaching the age of 60, receive vested pension rights for the years of service after age 30. For example, assume a worker at age 55 having 25 years of service with the Ford Company decides to leave and take a job elsewhere, or become self-employed. He will receive $56.25 (25x$2.25) per month in Ford pension benefits when he reaches the age of 65, in addition to his regular social security benefits.

Escalator Clauses:—The annual improvement and cost-of-living escalator clauses were continued in the new contracts on an improved basis. The annual improvement factor was increased from five cents to six cents per hour or 2½ per cent of each wage classification, whichever is higher.

The cost-of-living adjustments will be revised to reflect the relationship of current wage levels to the government BLS consumer price index. Escalator adjustments will be on the basis of a one cent change in cost-of-living allowance for each ½ per cent increase or decrease in the consumer price index instead of the former .6 per cent change.

Wage Inequity Fund:—A fund of approximately two cents an hour for all hourly workers in General Motors and about 1.3 cents in the Ford Company will be established to provide for adjustments of inequities in wage rate classifications.

Skilled Trades Increases:—Skilled trade workers in General Motors will receive an increase of eight cents in addition to the improvement factor increase, while in the Ford Company the range is from five to ten cents an hour.

Improved Group Insurance Program:—In the General Motors contract the new schedule for group life insurance varies from $3,500 to $7,500 as compared with the previous schedule of $2,500 to $5,000. Retired workers will also enjoy an increase in life insurance. Ford workers will receive a new life insurance coverage from $3,200 to $6,400 versus $2,400 to $4,400.

Weekly sickness and accident benefits have been increased in both companies. In General Motors the range is from $35 to $85 per week for a period of 26 weeks, and in Ford from $38.40 to $76.80 for the same duration. Accidental death and dismemberment insurance benefits are substantially increased in both General Motors and Ford contracts.

Improved Medical Expense Insurance:—Both companies have included the worker's family for coverage under Blue Cross and Blue Shield, or some other local plan, on a 50-50 contributory basis. In the General Motors plan, hospital-medical benefits are extended to 120 days in Michigan (and other states, if possible), while with Ford, the benefits have been increased to five dollars a day up to 70 days or $350. Both Ford and General Motors will arrange with the Blue Shield, or other similar plan, in Michigan or other states, to provide for full payment of surgical expenses for a married worker earning less than $6000 and a single employee earning less than $4,500 yearly.

New Vacation Schedule:—A new category has been added to the vacation pay schedule. Employees with 10 to 15 years of service will receive two and one-half weeks' (100 hours) vacation pay instead of two weeks' pay.

Seventh Paid Holiday:—An additional holiday with pay has been added in the agreements, consisting of a half-day on Christmas Eve and a half-day on New Year's Eve.

Improved Overtime for Saturdays and Holidays:—General Motors will pay its workers time and one-half for all Saturday work, regardless of whether it involves a sixth day of work. Ford will pay time and one-half for Saturday work only when it is the sixth day worked. Both companies will pay double time for holiday work in addition to compensation for the holiday.

Premium for Midnight Shift:—In General Motors the premium pay for the midnight shift is increased from 7½ per cent to 10 per cent, while at Ford it remains 7½ per cent.

Union Shop:—In the General Motors agreement the modified union shop has been changed to the union shop which is now prevalent in the automobile industry.[57]

CONCLUSIONS

The following wage policies appear discernible throughout the history of the UAW-CIO:

I. Wage Stabilization

In order to achieve wage stabilization, the union has striven for:

1. Unionization of the industry. Although thwarted at the beginning, this goal was achieved by 1941.

2. Correction of wage inequities. Beginning in 1939, the UAW demanded company wage stabilization funds for the purpose of ironing out inequities in wage rates of various classes of jobs. Although this objective has been attained with all the employers, constant attention is required because of the changing nature of jobs.

3. Equalization of wage rates. The union has tried to eliminate variations in wage rates by job classes on a corporation-wide basis. During World War II it sought the help of the National War Labor Board in the achievement of this objective, but the Board refused to change the existing patterns in the industry. In 1948 the union asked General Motors to equalize wage rates by jobs on a corporation-wide basis, and the demand was later carried to Ford and Chrysler. Although this goal has not yet been fully achieved, much progress has been made in its fulfilment.

4. Opposition to wage incentive plans. The UAW has been traditionally opposed to bonus or piece rate plans, because they intensify wage inequalities and differentials, aggravate dislocaton and unbalance production schedules, and result in the speed-up robbing the workers of their earnings. The industry is largely operating on a day basis and has been for many years. The present policy of the

UAW is to allow local unions or plant units operating under a wage incentive plan to eliminate the plan when the plan is not securing the objectives for which it was established.

5. Key company bargaining. Because of the keen competition in the industry, the union has adopted a one-at-a-time bargaining strategy, believing that it will make for more effective results than industry-wide bargaining. The company selected is generally one of the big three. General Motors, because of its size, is most often the key company. The terms obtained are then used to get similar concessions from the other producers.

II. Social Objectives and Needs of the Workers

The UAW believes the interests of its members are tied in with the interests of the whole society. It has a deep desire, almost an obsession, to achieve an economy of full employment and decent standards of living for all people. The UAW has an historic role to play in the achievement of a better America because of the size and strength of the union and its influence in one of the major sectors of the economy. The union feels there must be a better distribution of income to provide higher living standards commensurate with the productivity of the economy and to enable the workers to consume proportionately to their production. In an effort to correct the maldistribution of income after World War II, the union tried to enlarge the area of bargaining to encompass not only wages but also prices and profits. In 1945-1946 the General Motors workers struck for 113 days for wage increases without price increases. The winning of substantial wage increases is no solution if prices swallow up all the gain. The union's struggle for pensions and social insurance benefits was another example of its desire to achieve not only for the autoworker, but for all labor, a higher standard of living and a degree of security against the major hazards of life.

III. Escalator Clauses in Collective Bargaining Contracts

To protect the members from advancing prices and to improve their economic position, the union resorted to the escalator device in 1948. The pinning of wages to prices protected the worker against further inflation, and the annual improvement increases assured the employee a share in the gains of technology. The 1948 three-year agreement with General Motors Corporation provided for a three cents per hour annual productivity increase. At the expiration of the

1948 contract the UAW signed a five-year agreement with General Motors and the other major automobile companies which embodied the same cost-of-living adjustments but changed the annual improvement factor from three cents to four cents an hour. The threatened downturn in the price level in 1953 made the UAW fearful that much of the wage increases obtained under the cost-of-living escalator clause would be lost. It demanded that at least 20 cents of the 25 cents be retained as part of the permanent base pay. It also sought a one cent increase in its annual productivity adjustment. The union regarded its long term contracts as living documents which must permit correction for difficulties that may arise in the future.

In the 1955 General Motors and Ford contracts, the UAW obtained improvement in its annual productivity and cost-of-living formulas. The improvement factor was raised to six cents an hour or 2½ per cent of base rate, whichever is higher. The one cent an hour cost-of-living escalator adjustment will move up or down with each .5 of a point on the BLS consumers' price index instead of .6 of a point.

From the standpoint of the union, the major significance of the cost-of-living and annual improvement formula is that it would avoid the necessity for the workers to dissipate their energy repeatedly in a struggle to restore their living standards shrunken by inflation, and to keep pace in the growth of the total national product resulting from technology. The formula gave the union the opportunity to concentrate on its main objective: advancing the economic position of the membership. The UAW never thought that the annual improvement factor was large enough, but it considered it a holding operation in its effort to obtain large fruits.

### IV. Pensions and Social Security

An integral part of the wage policy of the UAW has been its demands for pensions and group insurance. Beginning in 1946, the union demanded protection against the vicissitudes of life. The UAW in 1949 took pensions and social security out of the category of fringe demands and put them at the top of its requests. Non-contributory maximum pensions of $125 per month, hospital-medical insurance programs, paid-up life insurance policy for retired employees, sickness and accident insurance, and substantially improved vacations became realities for automobile workers by the middle of the century. In fact, the UAW-CIO contracts of 1950 established a new industrial pattern for pensions, hospital, medical and insurance programs. By 1953 in keeping with the UAW policy of achieving advances for its workers, maximum pensions including federal social security benefits were increased to $137.50 a month, and the pension increases were made applicable to the already retired workers.

The 1955 contracts with Ford and General Motors witnessed a further liberalization of pensions, group life insurance, accidental death and dismemberment insurance, medical and hospital insurance, weekly sickness and accident benefits, and other miscellaneous gains. Maximum pensions for a married worker and his spouse at age 65 have been increased to $237.80. For the union one of the most rewarding aspects of the new pension program is the vesting of pension rights, a principle in industrial pension rights which is almost certain to spread to other basic industries.

### V. Guaranteed Annual Wage

As early as 1937–1938, because of job insecurity, the UAW began to consider the feasibility of guaranteed minimum employment. During the Second World War the union tried to persuade the National War Labor Board to initiate a 40-hour week guarantee for the industry. At the 1953 UAW convention the delegates unanimously approved a resolution that the guaranteed annual wage should be the next demand of the union. The UAW had been studying the guaranteed wage for a suitable adaptation to the automobile industry. After many weeks of negotiation with the Ford Motor Company, a modified guaranteed wage plan was won in June 1955 and was followed by a similar agreement with General Motors. Although the guarantee is for only 60 to 65 per cent of the workers' take-home pay for a maximum duration of 26 weeks, the union believes that the principle of the guaranteed annual wage has been established. It is a basis upon which a full yearly guarantee of wages can ultimately be achieved. The objectives of the UAW guaranteed wage plan and of the recently adopted Ford and General Motors modified guaranteed wage plan are: 1) provision of practical incentives for management to plan for full-time, year-around employment for the workers, 2) slowing down of the rate of automation in periods of business decline, 3) provision for regular incomes for seniority workers in the event their employers fail to provide work for them, 4) assistance in the stabilization of employment and production throughout the country.

## CHAPTER TEN

# The Textile Workers Union of America

### INTRODUCTION

The workers in the textile industry before the entry of the CIO in 1937 were largely unorganized. The principal union was the United Textile Workers affiliated with the AFL. No attempt was made to organize the heterogeneous mass of unskilled workers, and the union remained structurally a conglomeration of craft locals.

The Textile Workers Union of America was the outgrowth of the Textile Workers Organizing Committee formed in March 1937. The TWUA was officially founded in May 1939 wth Emil Rieve as its president. It continued the aggressive organizing work of its predecessor and after a few years succeeded in organizing the majority of the workers in the various branches of the industry in the North. In the South most of the employees remain non-unionized because of the opposition of the employers and the social milieu of the South (particularly in the non-urban areas where most textile mills are located). The conservatism of the region reinforces the employers' attack against unions so effectively that the workers are either intimidated or so confused by employer propaganda that they do not appreciate the protection which unions afford.

Wages in the textile industry have been considered the lowest in the mass-production industries in the United States. This has been particularly true in the cotton textile field. Since until recent times the family has been considered the working unit, the pattern of wages has not been based on the adequacy of a man's earnings to support his family but on the combined earnings of the family.

The textile mill industry employs over one million workers and is one of the largest industries in terms of dollar value of output. The following are the principal branches, the number of workers employed, and the extent of unionization.

| Industry | Area | Number of Employees | Percentage Union Members |
|---|---|---|---|
| I. Cotton, silk, rayon (Spinning and Weaving) | U.S. | 500,000 | 15% |
| New England and | | | 50% in Middle Atlantic |
| Middle Atlantic States | | 90,000 | 75% in New England |
| South | | 410,000 | 15% |
| II. Woolen and Worsted (Spinning and Weaving) | U.S. | 90,000 | 65% |
| New England and Middle Atlantic States | | 70,000 | 80% |
| South | | 15,000 | less than 10% |
| III. Dyeing and Finishing | U.S. | 75,000 | 50% |
| New England and | | 22,000 | 80% |
| Middle Atlantic States | | 20,000 | 90% |
| South | | 33,000 | less than 10% |
| IV. Carpets and Rugs (wool) | U.S. | 30,000 | 80% |
| V. Synthetic Fibers | U.S. | 30,000 | 80% |
| VI. Full-fashioned Hosiery | U.S. | 60,000 | 20–25% |
| VII. Seamless Hosiery | U.S. | 55,000 | less than 10% |
| VIII. Knit Outerwear and Underwear | U.S. | 80,000 | 10–15% |
| IX. Cordage and Twine (hard-fiber) | U.S. | 12,000 | 25–30% |
| X. Soft-Fiber Products (Linen, jute, yarns, etc.) | U.S. | 5,000 | 40–50% |
| XI. Textile Bags | U.S. | 20,000 | 40% |
| XII. Curtains and Draperies | U.S. | 20,000 | 20% |

The textile industry which was once a classic example of competitive enterprise is rapidly becoming concentrated in the hands of a relatively few large companies. The last twelve years have transformed many branches from decentralized, small, individually owned plants into integrated industrial giants. In the cotton textile field the integration movement has combined the manufacture and sale of yarn and fabric into their use for industrial, household or apparel purposes.[1] The latest significant movement is that of product diversification. In the woolen and worsted branch, the American Woolen Company because of its size and influence has exercised leadership until recently. However, it has suffered financial reverses and liquidations and is now being merged into other large companies. J. P. Stevens and Burlington Mills are now assuming leadership in this industry, but as yet it is quite competitive. The carpet and rug industry is dominated by four major producers which makes for uniformity of prices. Competition expresses itself primarily in other types of floor covering. In synthetic fibers there are about ten major producers with a high degree of uniformity in price. On the whole, in most of the branches of the textile industry prices are now "administered." Price patterns are set by the dominant producers and what competition is left is largely of the non-price variety. The significance of this development is important, because it means that prices are more stabilized and the levels of production are more quickly adjusted to changes in the volume of sales.

In this study of the wage policies of the TWUA the writer will limit his analysis for the most part to cotton and rayon, woolen and worsted, dyeing and finishing, carpets and rugs and synthetic fibers. It is in these sectors of the industry that the bulk of the membership in the TWUA is located. In the hosiery industry the American Federation of Hosiery Workers (AFL) is now exercising jurisdiction.

WAGE POLICIES DURING THE EARLIER YEARS (1937–1940)

Just as the campaign of the Textile Workers Organizing Committee for unionization was getting into swing, the economic recession of 1937 put a damper on the union's organizing plans. The union's energies were diverted to resisting wage cuts which had been customary in the industry at the first signs of a business slump. Although successful at first, before long wage reductions began to appear and spread throughout the country. The union's struggle against wage cutting was believed to be greatly hampered by the lack of unionization, particularly in the South.[2]

As the recession of 1937–38 lifted, the union moved to recover the wage losses. In cotton textiles the fight was waged on two fronts, the economic and legislative. In Washington the union fought for increased minimum rates under the Fair Labor Standards Act. The employers pressed for a general minimum of 25 cents per hour, but TWUA persuaded the Industry Committee appointed under the Wage and Hour Law to establish the first federal industry minimum wage in excess of the 25 cents per hour required by law. On October

24, 1939, a minimum of 32½ cents was set for cotton textiles. The union felt that this was a victory despite the fact that it demanded a 40-cent minimum. The 32½ cent rate represented a substantial increase for the cotton workers in the South and helped to restore wage reductions. Coincidental with its battle for the minimum wage, the TWUA entered into negotiations with the northern cotton and rayon employers for the restoration of wage cuts through its key locals in Fall River, Massachusetts. The companies agreed to a seven per cent increase effective November 1939. The same increase became the pattern for the North even in the unorganized mills.

In the woolen and worsted branch, President Rieve addressed all the organized mills, demanding the restoration of the 12 per cent cut experienced in 1938. Negotiations began with the American Woolen Company and after two months a compromise was reached increasing wages by 10 per cent effective in February 1940, which became uniform in the industry.

In carpets and rugs, the union negotiated a wage increase of five per cent with the Bigelow-Sanford Company in August of 1939 which completely restored the wage reduction of 1938. Alexander Smith, Mohawk Carpets and A. M. Karagheusian, the other members of the big four, followed suit. Another interesting feature of the 1939 agreement was the provision for one week's vacation after one year's service on an unqualified basis, this being the first industry-wide vacation plan in the textile field.

The dyeing and finishing industry participated in a seven to nine cent per hour increase in the area outside of New England and about a five cent average in New England effective in 1941. Employers in the New England region also obtained one week's vacation with pay. In synthetic fibers, a successful strike in the Celanese Corporation set off wage increases of about five cents for the entire industry. The agreement with American Viscose Company yielded in addition a paid vacation plan and dismissal wage for displaced workers.[3]

The policy of the TWUA to restore wage cuts in 1939 was considered historic. In the first place, the textile industry had never before led in an upward wage movement; usually it had lagged far behind. In the second place, it was the first time in the history of the industry that extensive wage increases had been negotiated. Finally, the union wage standards established the pattern for unorganized industry.[4]

NEW DRIVE FOR WAGE INCREASES AND UNION ORGANIZATION

Toward the middle of 1940 business optimism became widespread chiefly because of defense preparation. The TWUA recognized an opportune time for demanding a general increase in wages. Cognizant that progress would be slow because the industry was inadequately organized, the union's strategy was to work along several fronts. First, to raise minimum wages by legislative action, President Rieve petitioned the administrators of the Wage and Hour Law to appoint a new industry committee for textiles with a view to establishing the 40 cents minimum for the nation's textile workers. On July 25, 1940, he wrote that the "experience during the last nine months justifies an increase in the minimum wage . . . Many plants have expanded their facilities . . .; cotton consumption and spinning activity have been maintained at high operating levels."[5] The second effort towards wage increases was the drive for increased unionization. The union's effort to build up its membership grew in militancy and scope. Employers in the North became reconciled to the permanence of the union and the futility of hoping for its collapse. Cotton posed the greatest difficulties in organization, particularly in the southern mills where unionization was severely resisted. The third course of action for the union was direct negotiation with the major mills in each branch of the industry with the hope that success there would spread to the lesser ones.

The wage drive started in the carpet industry. Alexander Smith and Company first granted a three percent increase which was followed by a two per cent increase for Bigelow-Sanford. In the synthetic yarn field, increases were won by the Celanese Company workers, Delaware Rayon Company, New Bedford Rayon, and American Viscose. The American Woolen Company granted a 10 per cent increase effective in February 1940 which became general in the woolen and worsted field. In the cotton branch, it was believed that the increases in woolens and worsteds were the motivating force for increases in cotton. Increases in wages of 10 per cent among the organized Fall River plants soon spread to the unorganized companies elsewhere.

The TWUA prided itself on the fact that the textile workers as a whole were earning more per hour than they had ever earned and that textile wages more nearly approximated the prevailing wage levels in American industry than ever before. The union pointed out that it had also improved the lot of textile workers in other ways. Before TWUA there were few textile concerns which granted vacations with pay. Now it was becoming a common practice for workers to receive one week's vacation for one year's service. A number of contracts also provided for holiday pay or an additional week's bonus in addition to vacations with pay.[6]

Before the end of 1941 another round of wage increases took place in many branches of the textile industry. In cotton and rayon the northern workers repeated a wage increase of 10 per cent while the southern employees again secured a 2½ cents gain. In woolen and worsteds a 10 per cent increase was obtained in May 1941 averaging seven cents per hour. In rugs and carpets the pattern increase was 3½ cents.

The TWUA wage policy appeared to be a flexible one in that it did not attempt to standardize wages among all the companies in its respective branches or to effect identical rates, but it had attempted to establish similar wage trends. The union succeeded in establishing uniform minimum wage rates in many divisions. It recognized that there was no better safeguard to the wage structure in the textile field than a realistic wage minimum. The union in carrying out its wage policy used the strike very infrequently because it was able to win adequate wage increases through negotiation. Wage demands were based upon a comprehension of the economic forces in the industry. When management was making money and market trends were on the advance, TWUA endeavored to capitalize on the favorable situation.[7]

#### UNION WAGE POLICY DURING WORLD WAR II

Before the freezing of wages in 1942, the TWUA sought to obtain wage gains in all sectors of the industry. Of particular concern were the substandard wages of its members in the cotton and rayon industry. To raise the wages of its members in their branch of textiles, the union demanded a 60 cents minimum wage, 10 cents across the board increases, uniform occupational rates, a week's vacation with pay, shift differentials, and a guaranteed daily pay. Unable to win its demands through negotiations, the union's case was carried to the National War Labor Board. A perusal of the brief presented by the TWUA before the War Labor Board for wage increases of the northern cotton and rayon workers reveals the persistence and strategy applied.

The union brief stated: "The New England cotton and rayon textile workers are a group whose present earnings preclude for them an American standard of living. They are denied even a minimum subsistence level . . . Excessive and disproportionate economic burdens are being placed upon them as well as on other low income groups. To cope with these burdens and because the industry they serve can pay them higher wages without distress to the consumer, dislocation of our economic system or undue burden upon our war effort, they are entitled to these increases . . . It is desirable to place them more nearly on par with the wage levels of other workers. This objective has been basic to our entire New Deal effort and has been progressively advanced through wage legislation . . . Low wages and absence of conditions generally shared by American workers have been the seeds of dissatisfaction among this group of workers. It has kept them continuously depressed, unprivileged and disgruntled."[8]

The union spokesmen pointed out that the average hourly earnings of the cotton and rayon textile workers of New England and New York in January 1942 was 58.4 cents per hour. This compared with $1.168 in the automobile industry, .986 cents in steel, .791 cents in meat packing, .956 cents in aircraft, .758 cents in paper and pulp, .702 cents in woolen and worsted, .661 cents in men's clothing, .635 cents in women's clothing.

The union for the first time submitted budgetary studies from the United States Department of Labor of the estimated cost of living for a four person manual worker's family at a maintenance level for three New England cities. The studies revealed that the weekly income of the textile workers in this area was from six to eight dollars short of the income necessary for a maintenance level.

The union next pointed out that the cotton and rayon textile industry was losing workers to other fields of work and that it must increase wages to maintain its personnel.

Finally, the ability to pay argument was introduced. The union claimed that the year 1941 was one of the most prosperous for the industry since the early 1920's. Company reserves and dividend payments were impressive. The union believed that the industry could absorb a good portion of the requested wage increase not only because of its financial ability, but also because the rising man-hour productivity had lowered labor costs. While hourly earnings had risen by 34 per cent between 1929 and 1941, the actual unit labor costs had declined 28 per cent.

The majority of the Board found that a general wage increase should be provided in order to eliminate substandards of living. It was felt that current average wages of .496 cents per hour in the South and .575 cents in the North were substandard in terms of minimum budgets of health and decency. But its decision granting a 7.5 cents per hour increase was awarded not in terms of the substandard condition of the workers but to correct wage inequalities and to align the wages of the plants under discussion with the rates existing in plants which had granted voluntary wage increases during the course of the War Labor Board proceedings. However, the National War Labor Board did not rule upon the question of possible substandard wages in the cotton textile field. In accordance with the Board's decision, the 7.5 cents increase became standard throughout both the northern and southern cotton-rayon mills as of June 1942.

Other important gains during the year 1942 in the textile industry were as follows: in woolen and worsteds, a 6½ cents average increase in wages, vacations and holidays with pay and premium pay for Saturday and Sunday work; in carpets and rugs, 3½ cents increase in wages per hour, vacations with pay and shift premium pay; in dyeing and finishing a five cents to ten cents per hour wage increase with vacations with pay in the metropolitan region; in synthetic yarn, a three cents increase was won with comparable increases in other textile divisions.

The TWUA, like all unions, objected strenuously to the wage freeze. The textile workers in attacking the "Little Steel Formula" chose to do its share by emphasizing the substandard wages of its membership, particularly those connected with the cotton and rayon industry. Its technique was to force a change in the definition of substandard wage rates by the National War Labor Board. In this role it contributed a significant chapter in American labor history by becoming the spokesman for substandard workers everywhere.[9] In order to force the Board to define substandard wages and to support its request for a 60 cents minimum wage and a uniform occupational rate structure for the cotton and rayon textile industry, the TWUA furnished the NWLB with authoritative materials on the minimum income necessary to eliminate substandards of living. Five textile communities were studied to determine the cost of the emergency budget developed by the WPA for relief purposes in 1935 for a family of four. The study revealed that the emergency budget in January and February 1944 was $1,752.18. It also indicated that the income of textile workers in these cities fell far short of meeting this emergency standard.[10]

An outstanding case involving the problems of substandard wages was that of 23 Southern cotton textile mills, 25 New England cotton-rayon companies, and six New York and Pennsylvania rayon companies before the National War Labor Board in October 1944. Mr. Rieve and Mr. Barkin of the TWUA spoke about the economic disenfranchisement of 600,000 workers in the industry. They pointed out that to lead the world in the realization of the Four Freedoms, particularly the freedom from want, it is our responsibility to remove poverty from the doors of the cotton textile workers. Mr. Rieve demonstrated the importance of the textile industry in the war effort and indicated that the American war effort was being impeded for lack of essential textile fabrics. In order to accelerate production, higher wages were needed to attract personnel. Family budgetary studies were presented to convince the Board of the need of wage increases. It was revealed that cotton textile workers were living below the WPA Emergency Relief Budget. A rate of 72.7 cents an hour was needed to maintain a worker and his family on this emergency budget, but the majority of cotton and rayon workers earn less than 72.7 cents an hour. The union claimed that cotton and rayon textile wages were practically the lowest in the country. Out of 135 manufacturing industries surveyed in 1943 the wages of cotton and rayon workers ranked 133rd. Finally the union spokesmen believed that the cotton-rayon industry was able to pay additional labor costs without price relief. This was shown by the fact that the industry made more money during 1942 and 1943 than in any of the past twenty years.[11]

The NWLB decision in the cotton-rayon cases in 1945 provided for a 55 cents minimum and a five cents general increase effective as of October 4, 1944. In addition, the Board ordered a balanced wage scale, shift differentials, vacations with pay, and a daily wage guarantee. By this decision a 55 cents minimum wage became the test of a substandard wage, and the NWLB allowed all American industry to come up to this level.

TWUA never considered 55 cents an hour an adequate minimum. Even its demand for 60 cents was considered a steppingstone to complete elimination of substandard wages. The union believed that it had proved through its budgetary surveys that a family of four required 77 cents an hour in January 1944.

In the fight for higher minima TWUA took the leadership for a 65 cents level. Negotiations for a 65 cents minimum began with the New England cotton-rayon employers. The industry agreed in the fall of 1945 to a 65 cents minimum and a general increase of eight cents across the board. The southern cotton and rayon mills were approached next, and most of them followed the pattern as set in the North.[12] In 1946 the War Labor Board's successor, the Wage Stabilization Board, was persuaded to set the new "substandards" minimum at 65 cents and approved this rate for all southern cotton mills.[13]

The wage policies of TWUA in the other major sectors of the textile industry during World War II followed a somewhat different pattern than in cotton and rayon. The emphasis was not so much on substandard wages as the wage structure was somewhat higher due to greater unionization. The union tactics were: 1) to raise wages commensurate to the advancing cost of living, 2) to raise minimum plant rates, 3) to seek fringe benefits. In the woolen and worsted industry the union through its negotiation with the American Woolen Company established a 54½ cents minimum wage in 1942 which became quite general throughout the industry. In 1944 the union demanded a 10 cents general increase in wages and a 65 cents minimum wage. As the wage freeze was in effect, the union case was heard by the National War Labor Board. The Board found that the wage increase would violate the "Little Steel Formula," but they recommended a renegotiation of occupational rates in accordance with the Board's bracket minima and a daily guarantee.[14] After negotiations with the American Woolen Company an agreement was reached, effective June 1945, providing a 60 cents minimum and NWLB bracket adjustments which brought varying increases averaging 3½ cents per hour. In addition, the workers won a guaranteed daily wage and some equalization of wage rates for specific jobs.[15]

In the synthetic fibers division, the union was able to obtain individual wage increases of about 2½ cents per hour. In the dyeing and finishing branch, the wage movement in the metropolitan area of New York was limited to occupational wage rate adjustments. One of the outstanding achievements was the recognition of the union wage schedule by the NWLB as the bracket minima for the area. This made it possible to bring many individual plants into line. In the New England dyeing and finishing plants, wages tended to follow the northern cotton-rayon pattern. In the South the plants followed more closely the southern cotton and rayon pattern.

The carpet and rug negotiations in 1944 resulted in the establishment of a 55 cents minimum wage. Wage rationalization in January 1945 brought forth varying amounts of increase, and later in the year the workers won improved down-time allowance and a 10 cents general wage increase.

In respect to fringe benefits, the war period produced the following changes.[16] 1) Second week vacation. The NWLB uniformly ordered this practice for employees with five years' service or more with the exception of the South. 2) Holidays with pay. These benefits spread to almost all textile industries but not on a uniform area basis due to variation in regional war labor board practice. 3) Reporting time pay guarantees. Employers in general throughout the industry were required to guarantee four hours reporting time pay for the first and second shift workers and eight hours for the third shift. 4) Guaranteed base rate for piece workers. In the northern cotton-rayon mills the union secured a weekly guarantee of the base rate which is also a day rate for the job. In southern cotton-rayon, the NWLB requested a daily guarantee, but the amount had to be set by the Southern Textile Commission. In the woolen and worsted industry the workers won a guarantee of 80 per cent of their occupational earnings, but no less than the industry day rate for the job. In carpets and rugs the workers were protected by guaranteed rates. In synthetic yarn a weekly guarantee of piece-rate earnings became the pattern. As a corollary to the development of the daily guarantee, the union developed tests of the adequacy of piece-rate earnings in the various branches of the industry. 5) Shift Premiums. With the aid of the NWLB, shift premiums became general in the industry. The Board favored the practice in order to encourage people to work on the second and third shifts. The progress of TWUA in lifting the wage levels of textile industry during World War II is shown on Table XVIII, page 234. From January 1941 to VJ Day the average hourly earnings for the entire textile industry rose from 49 cents to .738 cents or about 51 per cent; in the cotton and rayon industry the increase was from .424 cents to .691 cents or 63 per cent; in woolen and worsted from .567 cents to .832 cents or 47 per cent; in the dyeing and finishing industry from .539 cents to .753 cents or 40 per cent; in carpets and rugs from .666 cents to .907 cents or 36 per cent; in synthetic fibers from .681 cents to .892 cents or 31 per cent.

### TWUA WAGE POLICIES IN POST WORLD WAR II PERIOD

After VJ Day the removal of wage controls changed the wage picture immediately, as wages once more came under collective bargaining. The union felt that the wage stabilization policy had interrupted the worker's increase in wage rates and his participation in the large profits of management. As a result of reconverson, the actual take-home pay of the workers had been cut, and many had been forced to take lower rated jobs. Real wages had suffered because of the rising cost-of-living, and wage rates and earnings were still substandard in some branches of the industry. Finally, labor had failed to participate in the financial gains resulting from technological advances during recent years.

In the cotton and rayon industry the TWUA moved to obtain substantial increases for the workers and to bring the southern cotton textile workers in line with those in the North. As previously mentioned, the union in 1946 won an eight cents per hour increase for its workers in the New England mills and a 73 cents minimum wage. The southern mills in general gave the same wage increase. In January 1947 TWUA won a 10 cents increase in the North while the South followed shortly with an average increase of nine cents.

It is of interest to note that before demanding the 1947 increase the union made an offer to the industry that it would forego an increase if management would cut prices. Mr. Rieve pointed out that although textile profits continued to be extremely high in the first quarter of 1947, there were signs of deterioration as expressed in lay-offs and a shorter work-week. He believed that the ommission of a wage increase would make it possible for the manufacturers to reduce the price of textiles to consumers thereby stimulating demand and employment.[17] The industry did not choose to reduce prices, but rather raised them even before the negotiations.

In August 1947 the union pressed for another wage increase and secured five cents an hour in the North while in the southern mills an 8½ cents average increase was negotiated. In January 1948 the TWUA obtained a 10 per cent increase which averaged 11 cents an hour for the northern cotton-rayon workers. Since no increase was won for the southern mills, the southern minimum wage remained at 87 cents versus 97 cents in the North, which created a 10 cents differential.[18] In the latter part of 1948 negotiations were again re-opened in the cotton-rayon industry. In the meantime a softening in all textile markets had become apparent, but the mills, on the whole, had enjoyed a very profitable year. Living costs were continuing to rise, and cotton-rayon wages were still substandard in comparison to the heavy industries. The union delegates set a 10 cents hourly increase as their goal, but it was met by a refusal from the industry. The union then decided to submit key cases to arbitration. In cotton and rayon, the Fall River and New Bedford Cotton Textile Manufacturers' Association, the leaders in northern cotton, was selected.[19] The union's major contentions in support of its position are summarized:

1. Cost of living—An increase in wages is necessary in order to enable the employees to meet the increase in the cost of living since the agreement of January 1, 1948. The present wage scale is inadequate to meet the city worker's family budget of the Bureau of Labor Statistics and the WPA emergency sustenance budget. The average earnings of the employees (on the basis of 2,000 hours of employment per year) fall short of meeting the city worker's budget by 49 or 55 cents an hour, and the minimum hourly rate of 97 cents falls short of meeting the emergency budget by 12 cents an hour.
2. Bolstering purchasing power—A wage increase is necessary to bolster the purchasing power of the workers in the lower income groups. The cotton-rayon industry has increased prices so greatly that the pattern of income distribution has been greatly destroyed. Consumer income must be increased if markets for production are maintained; otherwise a collapse in the economy cannot be avoided.
3. Area wages—Wages in the cotton textile industry are lower than those paid in most other industries in New England.
4. Increased productivity—A wage increase is required to provide the employees with a share in the benefits from increased productivity in the industry. Technological changes have been made and are being translated into higher output per man-hour.
5. Industry profits—During recent years the textile industry has reaped extraordinary profits. Since liberal dividends have been paid and reserves have been augmented substantially, the companies are financially able to pay increased wages.
6. Demand for textile products—All signs point to a period of high and steady demand for textile products in the months ahead.
7. Removal of competitive handicaps—The union has removed competitive handicaps which formerly have confronted the northern employers. Any wage increases awarded will be applied elsewhere to bring about competitive parity.

In the award the arbitrator refused to grant the union request, although recognizing the justice of an increase due to the rise in living costs and the general increase in man-hour output. His refusal to grant the requested increase was based on the new decline for textiles and the substantial increase in inventories and falling prices.[20]

The wage pattern in the woolen and worsted textiles during the postwar period was as follows: In February 1946 an average increase of 15 cents per hour and a 75 cents minimum were won from American Woolen Company, Botany Worsted and Forstmann Woolen Company which set the pattern for the industry. The same was added in 1947 and 1948 bringing the minimum wage to $1.05 and the average hourly wage to $1.31. The recession which hit the textile market in 1948 affected the woolen and worsted division the hardest. Many reasons are mentioned for this phenomenon such as: increased productivity, high cost of wool and changes in the clothing habits stimulated by the appearance of competitive synthetic fabrics, etc. As in the cotton-rayon industry the union decided to press for wage increases in 1949. Unable to make any progress with the employers, the union selected the American Woolen Company for an arbitration test case. The union arguments for wage increases were:

1. Cost of living—Wage increases were necessary to offset rising cost of living and to enable workers to raise their standard of living closer to the levels of required "budgetary minimum" of the U.S. Bureau of Labor Statistics;
2. Share in gains of increased productivity;
3. Company ability to pay;
4. Company's business prospects;
5. Need for expanding purchasing power for lower income groups.

The union believed that an increasing purchasing power in the hands of the wage-earning class was necessary to assure economic balance for continued prosperity. In respect to the American standard of living, the union pointed out that as of November 1948 the average cost of a "necessary minimum" American standard of living amounted to $3,365 per year in the eighteen cities and $3,483 in Boston. Assuming 52 weeks' pay per annum, $64.71 per week would be required on the average and $66.98 per week in Boston in order to meet the cost of the budget. But the average weekly earnings of the woolen and worsted workers of Massachusetts in November 1948 were $50.02 which is a probable typical wage of the workers in the

American Woolen Company. Therefore, the average deficit was $14.69 per week (using the over-all U.S. budget) and $16.96 per week (using the budget for Boston). Much emphasis was placed on recent price movements to substantiate the wage request. It was also claimed that the consumers' price index understated the rise in living costs, as it failed to measure actual increases in contract rents and cost of home purchases since prewar days. Retail pricing of clothing was too vague to differentiate grades and made no provision for testing quality. Price increases which are not reflected in the index result from a shift by manufacturers from lower to higher price lines. The weights used to combine the various items in the index are based on consumption in the depression period, 1934–1936, and are clearly obsolete.[21]

The arbitrator denied the union's request on the grounds that the market was flooded with men's and women's garments, and because unemployment was gaining. An increase of 10 cents an hour would mean an additional cost of millions of dollars to the company and place it at a competitive disadvantage with other woolen and worsted manufacturers. After this decision no requests were made for general wage increases at times available for reopening of wages.

In the carpet and rug industry the first wage advance since the wage freeze took place in November 1945 with a 10 cents wage gain, followed by an 11 cents increase in September 1946 to hourly workers, six cents to piece workers, and the establishment of a 96½ cents minimum wage. In June 1948 a third increase of 11½ cents was won. Through these advances the straight-time average hourly earnings rose from .907 cents at the close of the war to $1.279 in April 1948.

In the dyeing and finishing industry, the wage increases were as follows: After VJ Day a 10 cents increase was won for men and five cents for women in the metropolitan mills while the New England mills secured an average increase for all workers of five cents. In 1946 the metropolitan mills gave both men and women workers a 15 cents wage boost versus eight cents for the employees in the New England shops. During 1947 two increases were obtained. For the metropolitan area, the first was in April for three cents an hour and the second in September for five cents covering all employees alike. In New England a 10 cents average in April was followed by five cents average hourly increase in August. In 1948 the metropolitan area gave 12 cents per hour increase while the New England mills agreed to a 10½ cents average.

In the synthetic fabrics industry the wage movements during the postwar years were more attuned to the trends in the heavy industries than to textiles. The reasons given for this divergence are that synthetics represent the latest development in the textile industry and that they use the most modern productive processes. Wage increases obtained were: December 1945, 10 cents per hour; April 1946, eight cents; December 1946, 12 cents; June 1948, 15 cents.

### FRINGE BENEFITS DURING THE POSTWAR YEARS

The TWUA was aware that supplementary benefits were vital in protecting the workers from economic hazards and assuring them of a decent standard of living. The supplementary benefits of most interest at this time were company-paid insurance covering illness, accident and death. The woolen and worsted branch of the textile industry was the first to provide employer-paid group insurance. This was won in 1945. During the postwar years the union was able to extend similar plans to the majority of the members in the other sectors of the industry. The only area where insurance was not general was in the South. In its negotiations TWUA constantly broadened the scope of insurance protection and raised the dollar value of benefits. A typical TWUA insurance program now covers life insurance, dismemberment benefits, hospitalization, weekly sickness and accident payments, surgical costs, maternity allowances and doctor bills. Some contracts extend hospitalization and surgical benefits to the workers' dependents. In the area of group insurance TWUA has evidenced leadership among American unions.[22]

To secure more vacation pay for its membership the union negotiated many escalator clauses in its contracts. Additional holidays with pay were obtained in most branches. Six paid holidays were provided in approximately 65 per cent of its contracts. As usual the South lagged behind the North, and many mills gave no paid holidays.[23]

Severance pay was widely demanded by the unions following the war, particularly in the synthetic yarn industry where technology is most rapid. The synthetic workers were successful in this goal.[24]

In 1948 the TWUA turned its attention to providing for its aged members. A resolution unanimously adopted at the 1948 convention states: "Technological advances in the textile industry are proceeding at an accelerated rate. It is becoming increasingly apparent that the aged worker has less and less chance of holding his job. The technological changes and efficiency demands of management upon the employees are of such a nature that the aged worker cannot keep pace with the machines. On the other hand, the textile industry is reaping a fabulous harvest of profits.

"It is our conviction that pensions for the retirement of textile workers are a proper charge upon the industry . . . Be it resolved: That the possibilities of negotiation and securing pensions for textile workers be studied by the national executive council, the joint boards and local unions, that standards for pensions be developed and wherever possible pension plans be made a subject for collective bargaining with textile employers."[25]

In August 1948 negotiations were concluded in the dyeing and finishing industry in the metropolitan area of New York for an area-wide pension system. In the spring of 1950 the TWUA bargained its first complete pension agreement in four of the largest carpet and rug companies whereby a worker received $100 a month on retirement. Pensions were set as the primary goal of the union for 1950. A resolution on pensions adopted by the 1950 convention follows: "There shall be a general demand by our union on all sections of the textile industry for non-contributory pensions of at least $100 a month. Such private pension plans should be non-contributory; their cost should be regarded as a deferred wage, earned by the worker and payable upon his retirement. The union should be full partner in the administration of pensions. These principles have been established by steelworkers, autoworkers and miners; they have been followed by our union in the pension plans we have negotiated to date and will be a part of the program we establish in the future."[26]

### TUWA POLICY ON INCENTIVE AND JOB EVALUATION PLANS

In an industry where incentive wages are widespread, the union since World War II has sought to protect the worker against exploitation. The union has won guaranteed rates in all branches. In northern cotton and rayon it established the base rate on a weekly guarantee. The South has given a daily guarantee of 90 per cent of the average hourly rate. In woolens and worsteds the guarantee was established at 80 per cent of the average hourly rate. In carpets and rugs and synthetic yarn 25 per cent more than the hourly rate was secured. Safeguards were also developed against downtime or machine waiting-time, subnormal working conditions, special work, etc. The union has won the right to participate with management in setting proper piece-rate standards when new equipment was introduced, or changes made in older processes. TWUA has always looked askance on time study and job evaluation techniques. It feels that these tools are not scientific and that their assumptions are false. It has sought to resolve the problem of rate setting and pricing of jobs through the channels of collective bargaining. It has succeeded in doing this in many instances.[27]

TWUA is now actively seeking to establish quality control techniques in the determination of work assignments and standards. The union believes that because of the many variables in the production of textiles it is essential to describe job assignments in terms of actual rather than supposed job requirements. Such control would automatically carry with it the responsibility for maintaining these conditons.[28]

### WAGE POLICIES DURING KOREAN WAR

The outbreak of hostilities in Korea was the signal for another period of inflation and high profits. A wave of buying by consumers in July and August of 1950 absorbed all textile inventories. The industry responded by a frenzied drive to rebuild stocks. The rate of textile-price increases was even steeper than in the period following 1946.[29] The TWUA gave notice that wage increases were imperative. The first division of the industry to receive major wage gains was synthetic yarn. The American Viscose Company set the pattern for this branch of textiles with about an 11 cents wage increase across the board and improvement in pensions.[30] In the cotton and rayon industry, the agreement with the Textron Company for a 10 per cent wage increase, averaging 12 cents an hour, set the pattern in the northern region. In the South an eight per cent increase averaging about nine cents per hour was obtained. The Textron Company, in addition to the 12 cents wage increase, provided for a cost-of-living escalator clause and an annual improvement increase of five per cent in 1951 and 1952. The Textron agreement became popularly known as the "Textron formula," and many companies followed it wholly or in part.[31] Negotiations with the American Woolen Company resulted in a 12 cents average increase which set the pattern in woolens and worsteds. In the dyeing and finishing industry, the New England and Middle Atlantic shops agreed to a 12 cents increase. The gains spread to other finishing centers and helped the union wipe out, in a number of instances, the wage differentials between outlying plants and those in the metropolitan area. In many of the New England dye shops a modified Textron provision was included providing cost-of-living quarterly adjustments and an annual improvement of six cents.[32] In the carpet and rug industry the pattern increase was 10 cents.

Before the expiration of contracts in 1951, the TWUA decided to press again for wage increases and other improvements. In the cotton and rayon industry it was agreed that a major attempt should be made to equalize conditions throughout the industry. The union realized that negotiations would be handicapped because the government wage freeze would give employers an excuse to avoid wage increases. The union contention proved correct. In the woolen and worsted industry a four-week strike was necessary to bring an agreement of a 12 cent wage increase, a cost-of-living clause, improvements in insurance benefits, and the inclusion of retirement severance pay. The War Stabilization Board later reduced the wage increase to 9½ cents, but retained the cost-of-living escalation, retirement separation pay, technological separation pay and improvements in insurance benefits.

In the cotton and rayon industry an agreement with the Fall River-New Bedford associations provided for a 7½ per cent wage increase, averaging 10 cents per hour, a cost-of-living escalator clause, improvements in insurance benefits and retirement severance pay. Threatened strikes in other northern mills soon brought a general agreement. The South, however, resisted, and the union decided to strike at the five largest mills under its control. The Dan River mills and the Cone mills proved to be weak spots in the union strength. This factor together with the softening in the textile industry convinced the union to accept an offer by the Federal Mediation and Conciliation Service to appoint a tripartite mediation panel. A two per cent increase went into effect in April–June 1951. A. D. Juilliard Company stood out as an exception to this wage pattern when it agreed in December 1951 to a 6½ per cent increase and a cost-of-living escalator clause. On the whole, the failure of the South to meet the northern wage increase widened the wage discrepancy between the North and the South. The differential was represented by the 6½ per cent increase approved by the War Stabilization Board and the three cents an hour resulting from cost-of-living escalation.[33]

In the synthetic yarn branch, a 10 to 12 cents an hour increase was obtained in July 1951. The New England dye and finishing industry agreed to a seven cents average increase in April, and the New York area gave a six cents raise, a cost-of-living escalator clause, and improvements in insurance and pensions.

Some progress has been made since 1950 in carrying out the union's goal for pensions as evidenced in the negotiations of pension programs covering 60,000 members. The union believes that the groundwork for extension of pensions has been laid in the winning of severance pay on the basis of age in most of its contracts in the woolen and worsted and the northern cotton-rayon industries.[34]

### DUAL UNIONISM AND THE TEXTILE DEPRESSION

The wage policies of the TWUA beginning in 1951 and continuing to the present time have been influenced by two unfortunate developments. The first was the secession attempt led by George Baldanzi, the second-ranking officer in TWUA; the second was the severe depression in the textile industry.

After Baldanzi's defeat at the 1952 convention of TWUA, he and a group of union staff-members withdrew to the AFL United Textile Workers. Although the actual loss in membership of Baldanzi's group was not large (about 27,000), the cost to TWUA was considerable. The union was diverted from its normal trade-union activity to defending its membership. Employers in some cases used the inferior contract terms of the AFL-UTW to demand a weakening of TWUA standards, while the slanders of Baldanzi against TWUA were used by employers against TWUA in its organizing work.[35]

In respect to the textile depression, production was unable to sustain the level of output reached in 1951. Production declined in the second quarter of 1952 to 78 per cent of the first quarter's volume. There was a pick-up at the end of 1952, and production continued to reach a peak of 90 per cent of the 1951 level but dropped through the last half of 1953 to 80 per cent of the first quarter of 1951. As in the 1920's, the textile industry was sick while the rest of the economy was prosperous. The contraction in production was accompanied by many mill closings with resulting loss of employment for thousands of textile workers.[36] Employment in the industry during this period was the lowest since the founding of TWUA. Because of the combination of adverse circumstances it was not surprising that employers would demand wage cuts. The cotton-rayon firms in the North, headed by Fall River and New Bedford Cotton Manufacturers'

Association, served notice for wage reductions. The TWUA decided that instead of accepting wage reductions, it would freeze wage reopenings in its northern cotton-rayon agreements and the woolen and worsted contracts to be renewed automatically for another year. The American Woolen Company declared its intention of cancelling the present agreement March 15, 1952. It also demanded elimination of paid holidays, its escalator clause and a reduction in vacation and other fringe benefits.[37] However, the American Woolen agreement was finally renewed for two years without substantial change.

In the cotton-rayon textile field, the Bates Manufacturing Company and several smaller employers followed the New Bedford–Fall River group in New England by demanding a cut of 11½ cents an hour and the elimination of future cost-of-living raises.[38] No settlement was agreed upon by the companies and the union, so under the terms of existing contracts, the case was carried to arbitration. During the proceedings Bates extended its demands for a 30 cents pay cut on the grounds that it wished to eliminate the wage and fringe cost differential between the North and the South. The union argued in return that negotiations for wage increases were in progress with the southern mills, which, when completed, would restore the Bates Company and other northern employers to a more competitive level. It also pointed out that the cotton-rayon business was now recovering and that the company losses for the past three months were misleading. Despite the arguments of the union, the majority decision granted the company a 6½ per cent cut in wages and stripped the cost-of-living escalator clause from the contract.[39] The union's executive council in commenting on the decision said: "It places the corporation balance sheet above the basic needs of human beings . . . It imposes the whole burden of inflation on the workers, robbing them of their ability to keep pace with rising prices . . . It rolls back wages while prices are rolling ahead."[40] To correct the injustice to the workers, the council pledged that the union would increase its efforts to wipe out the southern wage differential by more intensive organizing work.

In the Fall River–New Bedford cotton-rayon arbitration case, the union again sustained losses when the companies were granted the right to reduce wages 6½ per cent which averaged 8½ cents an hour. It is of interest to note that the 8½ cents wage reduction was equivalent to the March 1951 wage increase. President Rieve said that the decision reflected the theory that lower wages can somehow result in better business. In the arbitration proceedings the union had argued that the ills of the textile industry in New England were due not to high wages but rather to poor sales, and that wage cuts cannot sell more cloth.[41] In those companies which had Textron formula agreements the union consented to take the same wage reductions believing that it would be unrealistic to force these mills to pay wages which were out of line with their competitors in the same area.[42]

During 1953 the woolen and worsted contracts were subject to reopening and arbitration. American Woolen Company and Botany Mills demanded wage reductions of 30 cents per hour. The union voted to resist any wage reductions. In the arbitration hearings TWUA convinced the arbitrators that wage cuts were no solution to the woolen and worsted industry's problem which was an inadequate demand for goods.[43]

The carpet and rug employers offered the union a five cents an hour increase in their 1952 negotiations. The union believed this was insufficient because the last wage increase was in 1950. Coupled with this small gesture, the employers demanded other concessions which would greatly weaken the workers' contract. After a nine-week strike of the big four, the industry settled for a 10 cents an hour increase for day workers, a nine cents raise for piece workers and improvements in insurance benefits.[44]

In the dyeing and finishing industry the union negotiated a six cents increase in October 1952, but the Wage Stabilization Board allowed only three cents. The remaining three cents was finally won over employer opposition in February 1953. In the synthetic yarn industry the union agreed to a five cents increase in 1953.[45]

The union's northern cotton conference in January 1953 voted to seek the restoration of the pay cut imposed by arbitration during the previous year. The employers demanded reductions in fringe benefits. After the union workers in the New Bedford area demonstrated a strong solidarity for the union's proposals, the employers consented to withdraw their demands if the union would forego its requests. The union decided to accept the offer which seemed at the time to be the soundest course.[46]

Although the TWUA suffered reverses during the years 1952–1954, many contracts were improved. Considerable progress was made in correcting inequities and substandard rates. Many mills were induced to give improvements in fringe benefits; one outstanding achievement was the winning of pensions for the piece dye workers in the New York metropolitan area.[47]

The following wage policies have been discernble throughout the history of the TWUA:

### 1. Wage Stabilization

The union has sought to achieve stabilization of its wage structure. It believes that competitive parity in labor costs among employers will prevent wage-cutting and the destruction of union standards, and will provide for greater stability in the industry. To accomplish this goal, the TWUA has attempted to: 1) extend its union organization to all employers; 2) establish uniform wage scales; 3) achieve minimum wage rates so as to equalize competition between the organized and non-unionized mills; 4) inaugurate industry-wide bargaining; 5) set up key company bargaining; 6) guarantee base rates for piece workers; 7) establish minimum plant rates.

Although much progress has been achieved in organizational efforts in the North, the South remains basically outside the union. This has been largely owing to the opposition of employers and the social milieu of the South. As a result, a substantial differential exists between the two sections in respect to wage rates and fringe benefits which has held off the competitive parity in labor costs, so much desired by both the union and northern employers. In order to escape the higher wage costs of the North and to obtain lower taxes and subsidized credit, many northern textile mills have relocated in the South. This trend has greatly accentuated the problem of the union and the remaining northern employers. Table XVII, page 233, shows the trend to the South in respect to the number of firms and workers in the cotton and rayon and woolen and worsted industries. It points to the imperative need for organization of the southern mills and the prevention of unfair methods to encourage businesses if the objectives of the union are to be achieved.

The union has attained considerable success in key company bargaining. Although there is yet no industry-wide bargaining, the bargaining with key companies seems to have accomplished the same objective in several of the textile divisions as the terms agreed upon have been extended to other employers in the industry. As the key companies are generally unionized, this has meant that even the non-organized plants are brought more evenly to the union standards.

## II. The General Level of Wages

From its inception the TWUA fought to improve the economic well-being of the workers in the textile industry. During the economic recession in 1937–1938 the union prevented wage cuts for an extended period. As the recession lifted, the TWUA initiated conferences for the restoration and increase of wages. The movement spread until every sector of the textile industry participated in wage recovery. The policy of the union to restore wage cuts in 1939 was considered historic.

The movement for better standards of living for the textile workers did not stop with the gains of 1939. With continuing business optimism owing to defense activity, the union in the 1940's demanded a general increase in wages. To achieve its goal, the union worked along a number of paths. These included efforts to raise minimum wages by legislation; an increase in unionization; direct negotiation with major companies so as to set the wage pattern for the industry. The union's efforts proved successful in every part of the industry so that the workers were, on the whole, earning more per hour than they had ever earned. For the first time in the history of textiles, wages more nearly approximated the prevailing wage levels in American industry.

After the termination of the Second World War with its concomitant removal of wage controls, the TWUA immediately began to press for wage increases and fringe benefits, to compensate for the increased cost of living and inequities in textile wages with prevailing wage rates in other industries. The success of the union's effort is revealed by the fact that from December 1943 to February 1946 the straight-time average hourly earnings in the textile industry increased from 65.4 cents to 87.6 cents. Other benefits secured were in the form of two weeks' vacation for five years' service and a tremendous expansion in group insurance which covered more workers and whole branches of the industry. By 1948 the TWUA claimed that the textile workers had gained proportionately more than any other American industrial group with the result that they were now on a comparatively more equal wage basis with those in other mass-production industries.

The power of the union to protect work standards was revealed in the business recession of 1949. Textile wages were not cut, and many contracts were improved in terms of group insurance, vacations with pay and holidays, and many job rates were raised through plant-by-plant negotiations.

In the inflationary postwar period and during the Korean War, the TWUA was successful in obtaining escalator clauses in many of its contracts. In order to raise and improve continuously the worker's standard of living, the union was able to incorporate annual improvement or productivity clauses in a few agreements. During the years 1951–1954 the textile industry was caught in a severe recession. The union fought against wage reductions and was unsuccessful only in the New England cotton-rayon industry. In the woolen and worsted industry, the cordage industry, and in the Middle Atlantic rayon textile industry, the union repulsed employer efforts to cut wages in 1952 and 1953. There were no moves for wage reductions during these years in other branches of the industry.

In 1955 a large segment of the northern cotton and rayon industry was strike-bound for nearly three months. The employers asked for a 10-cent reduction in wages and fringes in order to achieve wage costs comparable to those of the South. The union opposed this demand, because its members had taken wage cuts in 1952 and textile wages were already depressed in comparison to other major industries in the United States. The union feels that the north and south wage differential is not particularly relevant inasmuch as the North is primarily a producer of fine cotton textiles while the South specializes in coarser types. The coarser variety of textiles requires less skilled labor and should be compensated at lower rates. In the settlement of July 1955 between the union and Berkshire, Hathaway, Inc., Pepperell Manufacturing Co., and Luther Manufacturing Co., the employers' demands for wage reductions were defeated. The cost-of-living escalator clause was eliminated, but the previous 3-cent cost-of-living adjustment was incorporated in the base rates. The employers won the right to institute unilaterally work load revisions. Previously, such adjustments had to be agreed upon by both management and the union, or through arbitration channels. Under the new arrangement the union has the right to challenge work load changes, and if not settled, the matter can be arbitrated. Although the work load revision gives the industry much more flexibility than formerly, it may not be of great significance, because the union had in many local situations been granting the employers the right to adjust work loads to meet competitive pressures. The elimination of the cost-of-living escalator clause may not be much loss or gain to either party, because the cost of living has remained relatively stable for over a year.

In the woolen and worsted branch, the severe decline in sales in 1954–55 forced many companies to close while others merged in order to protect themselves. During 1954 the 9½ cent reduction in wages wiped out the gains experienced in 1951. The cost-of-living escalator clause was eliminated, but most of the former adjustments were incorporated in the base rates. In the South the woolen and worsted industry witnessed no change in wages during 1954–55.

In knitted outerwear and underwear and carpets, there has been no change in wage rates during 1954 and 1955, except a few individual adjustments. Like most of the other branches in the textile industry, the cost-of-living adjustment clause was removed.

In cordage and twine (hard), no pattern of wage increase was established in 1954, but in 1955 wage increases from seven to eight cents, plus some gains in fringe benefits were achieved. In dyeing and finishing in the South in 1955, small wage increases of about five cents an hour in both union and non-union plants were gained. This is an interesting phenomenon, because it is the first time there has been an independent movement of wage advances in the southern region of the textile business. Conforming to the other textile branches, synthetic yarns in 1954 showed no wage increases, but in 1955 the industry has reversed the trend with a wage gain of approximately 5 cents.

III. Raising Substandard Wages

One of the chief wage policies of the TWUA during World War II and the postwar years was to eliminate substandard wage levels not only in the textile industry but everywhere. Prior to 1945 the textile industry had often been referred to as the number one low wage industry. To overcome this stigma, TWUA worked along several fronts: 1) extending union organization; 2) continuously pressing for higher minimum wages under the Fair Labor Standards Act and the Walsh-Healey Act; 3) establishing higher minimum plant rates through employer-union negotiation; 4) appealing to the War Labor Board to define substandard wages. As a result of TWUA's efforts, the textile industry was the first industry to emerge from a substandard status. In 1939 textile wages averaged 46 cents an hour, 37 per cent below the 63 cents an hour average for all manufacturing industries. In 1950 textile wages averaged $1.33 an hour versus $1.59 for all manufacturing which was only 19½ per cent below $1.59. The textile recession of 1952–1954 temporarily reversed the upward trend of textile wages as shown by the fact that during 1953 textile wages averaged $1.37 an hour versus $1.77 for all manufacturing industries or 22 per cent below $1.77

## IV. Fringe Benefits—Welfare Programs—Guaranteed Annual Wage

In line with wage increases, TWUA has been a leader in pushing for welfare benefits. Before the founding of the union, vacations and group insurance were rare. Rapid progress was made: first, in securing one week's vacation with pay; next, the second week's vacation after five years' of service; and then the common practice of holidays with pay. These social gains were followed by group insurance for accidents, death, hospital and surgical benefits, and more recently medical care, all costs borne by the employers. Finally, the union turned to pensions for its aged members and severance wages for those laid off because of technological advances, believing that such security is a proper charge upon industry. In the cotton and rayon and wool and worsted branches, the union has a retirement plan termed "retirement separation pay," but in other textile branches a regular pension plan has been won for its members. In the South pension plans in any form are virtually nonexistent.

The guaranteed annual wage became a demand of TWUA during the war years. Although this goal has never been realized in the industry to date, the instability of demand and the lack of complete unionization unquestionably work in its disfavor. Priority must be placed on efforts to organize the textile industry and to obtain higher wages.

## V. Wage Patterns

TWUA wage policy on the whole has been a flexible one in that it has not attempted to force uniform wages among its various branches or among all the companies within each branch. It realizes that some divisions and some companies in the industry have different economic problems. It has, however, sought to establish the highest wage structure in each case. It believes that wage rates should provide

## TABLE XVII

### I. Cotton Textile, Rayon and Silk

(Number of Firms and Workers by Principal Regions 1939 - 1952)

|  | 1939 No. of Establishments | 1939 Workers | 1952 No. of Establishments | 1952 Workers |
|---|---|---|---|---|
| United States | 1370 | 445,418 | 1145 | 520,488 |
| New England | 371 | 103,721 | 146 | 61,724 |
| Middle Atlantic | 730 | 65,313 | 272 | 32,623 |
| South | 814 | 351,660 | 716 | 421,671 |

### II. Woolen and Worsted Manufactures

(Number of Firms and Workers by Principal Regions 1939 - 1952)

|  | 1939 No. of Establishments | 1939 Workers | 1952 No. of Establishments | 1952 Workers |
|---|---|---|---|---|
| United States | 722 | 160,910 | 462 | 111,436 |
| New England | 369 | 97,204 | 290 | 68,586 |
| Middle Atlantic | 168 | 23,536 | 90 | 21,019 |
| South | 30 | 9,783 | 40 | 14,765 |

Source: Sixteenth Census of the U. S. 1940.
Manufactures 1939, vol. 11, Part 1.
U. S. Department of Commerce, Bureau of the Census, U. S. Govt. Printing Office 1942, pp. 288-290, 310-313, 323-324.

Wage Structure Cotton and Synthetic Textiles, March 1952, Series 2, No. 89.
U. S. Dept. of Labor, Bureau of Labor Statistics, pp. 5, 45.
Wage Structure Woolen and Worsted Textiles, April-May 1952, Series 2, No. 90, U. S. Dept. of Labor, Bureau of Labor Statistics, p. 6.

## TABLE XVIII

### Straight-Time Average Hourly Earnings in Textile Industries

#### January 1937 – March 1954

| Industry | Pre-TWOC | 1st TWOC Gain | Low Point | Little Steel | Wage Freeze | V-J Rates | '48 Convention | '50 Convention | '52 Convention | '54 Convention |
|---|---|---|---|---|---|---|---|---|---|---|
| | Jan. 1937 | July 1937 | Jan. 1939 | Jan. 1941 | Dec. 1942 | July 1945 | April 1948 | April 1950 | April 1952 | March 1954 |
| Entire Textile Industry | .471 | .487 | .460 | .490 | .620 | .738 | 1.111 | 1.187 | 1.320 | 1.37 |
| Cotton, Silk, Rayon Goods* | .391 | .431 | .389 | .424 | .564 | .691 | 1.073 | 1.142 | 1.264 | 1.27 |
| North** | — | — | .437 | .467 | .646 | .749 | 1.160 | 1.201 | 1.432 | 1.39 |
| South** | — | — | .362 | .398 | .534 | .660 | 1.022 | 1.124 | 1.227 | 1.24 |
| Woolen and Worsted | .524 | .579 | .519 | .567 | .758 | .832 | 1.275 | 1.288 | 1.503 | 1.54 |
| Full-fashioned Hosiery | — | — | — | — | .747 | .927 | 1.302 | 1.377 | 1.512 | 1.48 |
| Seamless Hosiery | — | — | — | — | .500 | .624 | .850 | .969 | 1.064 | 1.09 |
| Knitted Outerwear | .449 | .462 | .475 | .489 | .600 | .764 | 1.018 | 1.108 | 1.229 | 1.36 |
| Knitted Underwear | .384 | .420 | .418 | .442 | .542 | .680 | .968 | 1.035 | 1.153 | 1.21 |
| Dyeing and Finishing | .520 | .566 | .532 | .539 | .662 | .753 | 1.179 | 1.255 | 1.428 | 1.46 |
| Carpets and Rugs (Wool) | .563 | .640 | .627 | .666 | .785 | .907 | 1.279 | 1.451 | 1.593 | 1.70 |
| Cordage and Twine (Hard-fiber) | — | — | — | — | — | — | — | — | 1.34 | — |
| Soft-fiber Products | — | — | — | — | — | — | — | — | — | — |
| Textile Bags | — | — | — | — | .571 | .704 | .963 | 1.089 | 1.192 | 1.30 |
| Synthetic Fibers | .569 | .615 | .627 | .681 | .813 | .892 | 1.254 | 1.424 | 1.637 | 1.74 |
| Curtains and Draperies | — | — | — | — | .515 | .715 | .891 | 1.007 | 1.053 | 1.12 |

*January 1937 — March 1946 data are for cotton manufactures (including small wares) and silk and rayon goods industries. April 1948 — March 1954 data are for cotton, silk and synthetic broad woven fabrics industries.

**January 1939 — April 1948 data are for cotton manufactures (except small wares) industry. April 1948 — March 1954 data are for cotton, silk and synthetic fibers broad woven fabrics industries.

Source: Executive Council Report, Eighth Biennial Convention, TWUA, 1954, p. 60.

## TABLE XIX

### Wage Trends in Cotton, Silk, Rayon Goods
### General Wage Changes November 1939 – October 1953

#### NORTH

| Date | Provision | Minimum Plant Rate |
|---|---|---|
| Nov. 1939 | + 7% | 36.8¢ per hour |
| March 1941 | + 10% | 40.48¢ per hour |
| Sept. 1941 | + 10% | 44.53¢ per hour |
| *June 1942 | +7.5¢ per Hour | 52.03¢ per hour |
| **Oct. 1944 | + 5¢ per hour | 57¢ per hour |
| Nov. 1945 | + 8¢ per hour | 65¢ per hour |
| Aug. 1946 | + 8¢ per hour | 73¢ per hour |
| Jan. 1947 | + 10¢ per hour | 83¢ per hour |
| Aug. 1947 | + 5¢ per hour | 88¢ per hour |
| Jan. 1948 | + 10% | 97¢ per hour |
| Sept. 1950 | Average + 11¢ per hour; + 10% | 1.065¢ per hour |
| ***March 1951 | Average + 12¢ per hour; + 6½% | 1.135¢ per hour |
| ****Oct. 1951 | Average + 8½¢ per hour; + 1¢ per hour | 1.145¢ per hour |
| *****Jan. 1952 | + 2¢ per hour | 1.165¢ per hour |
| *****July 1, 1952 | + 1¢ per hour | 1.175¢ per hour |
| ******July 19, 1952 | Average − 8½¢ per hour | 1.105¢ per hour |
| *****Sept. 1952 | + 2¢ per hour | 1.125¢ per hour |
| ****Jan. 1953 | − 1¢ per hour | 1.115¢ per hour |
| ****April 1953 | − 2¢ per hour | 1.095¢ per hour |
| ****Oct. 1953 | + 1¢ per hour | 1.105¢ per hour |

#### SOUTH

| Date | Provision | Minimum Plant Rate |
|---|---|---|
| Oct. 1939 | 32.5¢ minimum (Wage and Hour Law) | 32.5¢ per hour |
| March 1941 | + 2.5¢ per hour | 35.0¢ per hour |
| July 1941 | + 2.5¢ per hour | 37.0¢ per hour |
| Oct. 1941 | + 2.5¢ per hour | 40.0¢ per hour |
| July 1942 | + 7.5¢ per hour | 47.5¢ per hour |
| April 1944 | + 2.5¢ per hour | 50.0¢ per hour |
| Feb. 1945 | + 5.0¢ per hour | 55.0¢ per hour |
| Retroactive to Oct. 1944 | + 4.0¢ per hour | |
| May 1945 | + 10.0¢ per hour | 65.0¢ per hour |
| Feb. 1946 | + 8.0¢ per hour | 73.0¢ per hour |
| Aug. 1946 | + 10% | 80.0¢ per hour |
| Feb. 1947 | Average 9¢ per hour; + 9% | 87.0¢ per hour |
| Nov. 1947 | Average 8½¢ per hour; + 8% | |
| Sept. 1950 | Average 8.8¢ per hour | 95.8¢ per hour |
| April 1951 | + 2% (of Jan. 1950); Average 2.2¢ per hour | 98.0¢ per hour |

*In accordance with National War Labor Board Directive of Aug. 20, 1942.

**In accordance with National War Labor Board Directive of Feb. 20, 1945.

***Agreement as modified by Wage Stabilization Board Order of Aug. 3, 1951. The Board also approved an escalator clause providing quarterly adjustments of 1¢ an hour for every 1.32-point change in the BLS-CPI (old series) over the Feb. 15, 1951, Index. Wage rates were not to be reduced below the level of March 19, 1951.

****Quarterly adjustment of cost of living.

*****In accordance with decision of the arbitrator, July 15, 1952, basic hourly rates were to be decreased to those in existence on Sept. 18, 1950; Piece rates were to be adjusted accordingly.

Source: The Wage Chronology Series, Northern Cotton Textile Associations, 1943, Series 4, No. 2, U. S. Department of Labor, B.L.S. Cotton and Synthetic Textiles, Wage Trends, 1950-1953, B.L.S. Report No. 50, U. S. Department of Labor, B.L.S. TWUA Research Dept. Southern Cotton-Rayon General Wage Increases.

## TABLE XX
### Wage Trends in Woolen and Worsted Industry
### General Wage Changes April 1937 – October 1953

| DATE | PROVISION |
|---|---|
| April 1937 | +10% |
| May 1938 | Average +5.3¢ per hour<br>–12% |
| Feb. 1940 | Average –6.0¢ per hour<br>+10% |
| May 1941 | Average +5.0¢ per hour<br>+10% |
| Sept. 1941 | Average +5.7¢ per hour<br>+7% |
| June 1942 | Average +7.0¢ per hour<br>+7.5¢ for jobs paying under 75¢;+5.0¢ for jobs paying 75¢ and over<br>Average +6.5¢ |
| July 1945 | Peg point adjustments<br>Average +3.5¢ |
| Feb. 1946 | +15¢ |
| Feb. 1947 | Average +15¢ per hour<br>+15%<br>Average +15¢ per hour |

| DATE | PROVISION |
|---|---|
| Feb. 1948 | +15¢<br>Average +15¢ per hour |
| Oct. 1950 | +12¢<br>Average +12¢ per hour |
| *March 1951 | Average +12¢ per hour<br>+9.5¢ |
| **July 1951 | Average +9.5¢ per hour<br>+1¢ |
| **Jan. 1952 | Average +1¢ per hour<br>+3¢ |
| **April 1952 | Average +3¢ per hour<br>–1¢ |
| **July 1952 | Average –1¢ per hour<br>+2¢ |
| Oct. 1952 | Average +2¢ per hour<br>+1¢ |
| April 1953 | Average +1¢ per hour<br>+3¢ |
| Oct. 1953 | Average –3¢ per hour<br>+2¢<br>Average +2¢ per hour |

*Agreement as modified by the Wage Stabilization Board order of Sept. 12, 1951. Board also approved an escalator clause providing quarterly wage-rate adjustments of 1¢ an hour for every 1.18-point change in the CPI over the Feb. 15, 1951, index (old series). Wage rates were not to be reduced below March 15, 1951, levels.

**Cost of Living Adjustment.

Source:  The Wage Chronology Series. American Woolen Co., 1939, Series 4, No. 1, U. S. Department of Labor B.L.S. TWUA, Research Dept. Wage Changes in TWUA Mills, by Industry Branch, 1952-1953.

the worker with at least a minimum standard of health and decency. After that provision has been achieved, wages should be based on ability to pay, cost of living, improvements in technology and comparable wages with the other mass-production industries.

### TABLE XXI

#### Wage Trends in Carpet and Rug Industry

#### General Wage and Fringe Changes 1937 – 1952 (Bigelow-Sanford Co.*)

| Date | Wage Provisions |
|---|---|
| April 1937 | 10% to piece work and hourly workers |
| June 1938 | – 5% |
| Aug. 1939 | + 5% |
| Oct. 1940 | + 2% |
| May 1941 | + 3.5¢ per hour |
| Aug. 1941 | + 3.5¢ per hour |
| Oct. 1942 | + 3.5¢ per hour |
| Nov. 1944 | |
| Jan. 1945 | Wage rationalization (varying amounts of increase) |
| Aug. 1945 | |
| Nov. 1945 | +10¢ per hour |
| March 1946 | |
| July 1946 | |
| Sept. 1946 | +11¢ to hourly workers; +6¢ to piece workers |
| June 1946 | |
| June 1948 | +11.5¢ |
| June 1950 | |
| Oct. 1950 | +10¢ (+8¢ on base rates for piece work) |
| | + 5-5½¢ additional for maintenance department |
| Aug. 1952 | + 9¢ to piece work jobs; +10¢ to day work jobs |

*Slight differences exist in pattern for individual companies.

Source: TWUA Research Department Wage and Fringe Benefits Carpet and Rug Industry, 1939-1952.

Each branch of the textile industry in the North appears to follow its own wage pattern more or less, although there is some degree of relationship between them as the union has tried to establish similar wage trends. In the South, southern cotton and rayon set the pattern for southern woolen and worsted and dyeing and finishing. The northern dyeing and finishing industry used to follow the northern cotton and rayon wages, but in late years it has set its own wage structure. Since synthetic fibers is the newest branch of the industry and is enjoying the most rapid technological changes, it has tended to follow mass-production industries outside of the textile field.

## TABLE XXII

### Wage Trends in Dyeing and Finishing Industry

### General Wage Changes 1941 – 1953

#### OUTSIDE OF NEW ENGLAND

| DATE | PROVISION |
| --- | --- |
| June-Aug. 1941 | + 9¢ per hour for men |
|  | + 7¢ per hour for women |
| April 1942 | + 10¢ per hour for men |
|  | + 7¢ per hour for women |
| Oct. 1945 | + 10¢ per hour for men |
|  | + 5¢ per hour for women |
| Nov. 1946 | + 15¢ per hour for men and women |
| April 1947 | + 3¢ per hour for men and women |
| Sept. 1947 | + 5¢ per hour for men and women |
| Aug. 1948 | + 12¢ per hour for men and women |
| Oct. 1950 | + 6¢ per hour for men and women |
| Oct. 1951 | + 2¢ per hour for men and women |
| *March 1952 | − 1¢ per hour for men and women |
| *June 1952 | + 2¢ per hour for men and women |
| *Sept. 1952 | + 3¢ per hour for men and women |
| *Oct. 1952 | + 3¢ per hour for men and women |
| *Feb. 1953 | − 1¢ per hour for men and women |
| *April 1953 | + 1¢ per hour for men and women |
| *Sept. 1953 | + 1¢ per hour for men and women |
| *Dec. 1953 | + 1¢ per hour for men and women |

#### NEW ENGLAND

| DATE | PROVISION |
| --- | --- |
| April 1941 | + 6½-10%, average per hour +5¢ |
| Sept. 1941 | + 5¢ for women and men earning more than 63¢ per hour; +7¢ for others; average per hour +6¢ |
| May 1942 | + 5¢ for employees earning more than 65¢; +6¢ for employees earning 65¢; +7¢ for others; average, +6¢ |
| April 1945 | + 5¢; average per hour +5¢ |
| Dec. 1945 | + 10¢ and adjustments for certain occupations; +10¢ average per hour |
| Sept. 1946 | + 8¢; average per hour +8¢ |
| April 1947 | + 10¢; average per hour + 10¢ |
| Aug. 1947 | + 5¢ general increase; + 10¢ maintenance increase; average per hour +5¢ plus |
| Jan. 1948 | +10.5¢; average per hour + 10.5¢ |
| March 1950 | Occupational adjustments, average per hour +3¢ |
| **Oct. 1950 | +12¢; average per hour +12¢ |
| ***Jan. 1951 | + 2¢; average per hour + 2¢ |
| ***April 1951 | + 7¢; average per hour + 7¢ |
| ***July 1951 | + 1¢; average per hour + 1¢ |
| ***Oct. 1951 | + 7¢; average per hour + 7¢ |
| ***Jan. 1952 | + 3¢; average per hour + 3¢ |
| ***April 1952 | − 1¢; average per hour − 1¢ |
| ***July 1952 | + 2¢; average per hour + 2¢ |
| ***Oct. 1952 | + 1¢; average per hour + 1¢ |
| ***April 1953 | − 3¢; average per hour − 3¢ |
| ***Oct. 1953 | + 3¢; average per hour + 3¢ |

*Wage Changes under cost of living escalator clause.
**Quarterly cost-of-living wage adjustment and annual improvement factor of .06¢ (to be added to wages Oct. 1, 1951 & Sept. 29, 1952)
***Quarterly cost-of-living escalator clause.

Source: TWUA Research Dept. General Wage Increases in the Metropolitan Rayon Dyeing, Finishing and Printing Industry, 1933 to Aug., 1948.
TWUA Research Dept. General Wage Increases in the New England Dyeing and Finishing Industry, 1941 to Oct., 1951.
TWUA Research Dept. Economic Gains by TWUA, 1950.
TWUA Research Dept. Economic Gains by TWUA, by Industry Branch, Jan., 1951 – Jan., 1952.
TWUA Research Dept. Wage Changes in TWUA Mills, by Industry Branch, 1952 – 1953.

## TABLE XXIII

### Wage Trends in Synthetic Fibers

#### General Wage and Fringe Changes 1945-1952 (American Viscose Corp.)*

| Date | Wage Provisions | Fringe Provisions |
|---|---|---|
| Dec. 1945 | + 10¢ per hour | |
| April 1946 | + 08¢ per hour | |
| Dec. 1946 | + 12¢ per hour | |
| June 1948 | + 15¢ per hour | |
| July 1950 | + 10.2¢ per hour | Additional adjustments in certain job classifications for correction of intraplant inequities. |
| March 1951 | +03.3¢ per hour | |
| July 1951 | +03.3¢ per hour | |
| Dec. 1951 | + 05.5¢ per hour | |
| Nov. 1952 | + 05¢ per hour | |

* Slight differences exist in pattern for individual companies.

Source:  The Wage Chronology Series, American Viscose Corp., 1945, Series 4, No. 32, U.S. Dept. of Labor, B.L.S.
TWUA Research Dept. Wage Benefits Synthetic Yarn, 1950-1952.

# United Electrical, Radio and Machine Workers of America (UE). International Union of Electrical, Radio and Machine Workers (IUE-CIO)

## INTRODUCTION

From 1936 to 1949 the United Electrical, Radio and Machine Workers of America had a majority control over the workers in the electrical manufacturing industry, but since the expulsion of the communistic faction by the CIO in 1949, there have been two separate unions. The expelled group continued under the old title of the United Electrical, Radio and Machine Workers of America and assumed an independent entity, while the non-communistic unit adopted a new name, the International Union of Electrical, Radio and Machine Workers and became an affiliate of the CIO. The writer will consider the wage policies of the old UE until the revocation of its charter in 1949. From 1949 through 1954 the IUE wage policies will be analyzed. Some reference will be made to the UE during this later period because its policies have impeded the IUE in collective bargaining. The International Brotherhood of Electrical Workers also exercises some jurisdiction in the electrical manufacturing industry but is relatively insignificant in comparison with the IUE. It should be kept in mind that the wage policies discussed from 1936 to 1949 are those of one union, the UE, which was an affiliate of the CIO.

The United Electrical, Radio and Machine Workers of America emerged out of an amalgamation of AFL federal labor unions and independent local unions. Aggressive union leadership combined with favorable labor legislation and improved business conditions enabled the UE to grow rapidly. By September 1940 it had won contracts in 387 companies covering 154,744 workers.[1]

The electrical manufacturing industry is dominated by the General Electric Company and the Westinghouse Manufacturing Company. Labor agreements with these companies tend to set the pattern for the entire industry. Other major companies which affect labor patterns include: General Motors, Sylvania Electric, Allis Chalmers, General Cable, Sperry Gyroscope and Phelps-Dodge Copper Products Company. In the radio and television branch, Radio Corporation of America, Philco, Zenith, Emerson and Crosley appear to be outstanding.

The General Electric Company was the first large concern to feel the effects of union organization. Local No. 301 at the Schenectady works won exclusive bargaining rights in 1936. This was an important victory for the UE, because of the significance of this unit in the electrical manufacturing industry. It greatly assisted the union in further unionization efforts. The union wage policies in the General Electric Company at this early stage dealt with increasing the wage rates for common labor, diminishing the wage differential between skilled and unskilled rates of pay, and reducing the day rate job classifications. At Westinghouse the management refused to recognize the union until 1940. After the National Labor Relations Board found the company guilty of exercising unfair labor practices, the company finally signed a contract with the UE covering its employees in 24 plants.[2]

Organization was slower in the radio segment of the industry than in other areas of the electrical business, attributable undoubtedly to the preponderance of relatively small plants.

### EARLY WAGE POLICIES

During the depression of 1937–38 the UE was successful in preventing wage cuts among the larger companies and quite generally throughout the industry. However, wage cutting was felt among the less fortunate, unorganized, salaried workers.[3]

At the 1939 convention of the UE the officers outlined the union's program for contract negotiations for the ensuing year. Some of the important goals were: 1) the achievement of the 40 cents per hour minimum wage and the 35-hour work week, 2) uniform wage rates. Although the average hourly earnings in the industry were more than 40 cents per hour, many unskilled employees had not attained this level. At Congressional hearings on minimum pay under the Walsh-Healey Act, the UE presented data in an effort to establish a minimum wage of 60 cents an hour for work performed under government contracts to purchase electrical equipment and supplies. The union believed that if a 60 cents minimum wage were established under the Act, it would be a strong inducement for immediate application of the 40 cents per hour minimum fixed by the Fair Labor Standards Act. Also, an increase in the lower bracket would be reflected ultimately among higher paid groups in the industry.[4]

The 35-hour week was deemed desirable because of the displacement of workers resulting from technological changes. In the reduction of hours there was to be no drop in weekly earnings. A resolution was approved by the convention favoring the attainment of this policy.[5]

The union regarded uniform wage rates as important, because of the disparity in wage rates in the agreements of many of its locals in the same territory and in similar businesses. A resolution was adopted instructing the General Electric Board to work out a program to bring rates of pay in similar shops closer together.[6] At the national convention of the UE in 1940 the union bent its efforts to attain uniformity in wage rates. At this time a resolution was passed empowering the national officers to meet with committees in the electrical industry to set up minimum wages for the various trades, classifications and operations.[7] The policy of establishing minimum uniform rates for all plants appeared to be successful. President James Carey of the UE in an article in the *Labor Information Bulletin*, May 1940 stated that in order to assure the workers at least a definite amount per hour the union had succeeded in establishing minimum uniform rates.[8]

In 1940 the union took a definite stand against tying wages to the cost of living. Although the consumers' price index should be taken into consideration in negotiating wages, the national officers cautioned the locals against binding themselves to price-level clauses. They reasoned that cost-of-living escalator clauses leave out of consideration the question of fair wages and accept the principle that wage levels should be frozen.[9]

In October 1940 the union inaugurated a campaign to increase the wages of its members on an industry-wide basis rather than by individual companies. Demands were first formulated by the national UE conference boards of the General Electric Company, Westinghouse Electric Company, and the electrical division of the General Motors Company. Locals in 350 independent companies soon followed suit with parallel requests. The industry-wide wage policy program met with success. During the months of April and May 1941 many important contracts were signed, bringing the total of annual wage increases in 397 plants in the industry to $63,500,000.

Many company-wide contracts were achieved at this time including that of the General Electric Company, the first contract with the Westinghouse Electric Company covering 55,000 workers, and one with the electrical division of the General Motors Company covering 26,000 employees.[10]

The advancing price level concomitant with the defense boom caused the 1941 convention to enunciate its policy on wages and the cost of living. Locals were urged to insist on increases in wages whenever justified by advancing prices, but they were cautioned not to limit themselves to this sole criterion but to constantly aim for additional increases to enlarge their share in the economic wealth of the society.[11]

Cognizant of the difficulty of protecting economic gains and establishing union standards as long as unorganized shops prevailed with their lower wage levels, the union urged intensive organization to encompass these plants within its jurisdiction. It also instructed its national officers to take steps to increase the present minimum rates established by the Wages and Hours Law to at least 50 cents per hour.[12]

The year 1941 represented a tragic turning point in the history of the UE. James B. Carey was ousted as president of the union by a communistic group led by Albert J. Fitzgerald, Julius Emspak, and James Matles.* Fitzgerald thereupon assumed the presidency of the union. The UE from that time until its expulsion from the CIO in 1949 became a divided and weakened organization. Its leaders became more interested in advancing communism than in fighting for principles of trade unionism. In spite of pleadings from the CIO, the communist officers of the UE refused to be diverted from their purposes. As a result the UE from 1941 to 1949 did not exercise

* The term communistic group and communistic officers as used in this chapter is a charge by the CIO and IUE.

a strong wage policy for its members. Although on the surface the union statements appeared to be in the interests of the workers, they were a camouflage for the political designs of the leaders. Unionization in the industry lagged behind other industries and wages and related benefits likewise did not keep pace with the leading mass production industries.

WAGE POLICY OF UE DURING WORLD WAR II

In the early period of the Second World War the UE wage program included:

1. Industry-wide wage stabilization;
2. Opposition to wage freezing;
3. Collective bargaining for all matters affecting wages;
4. Effective control over prices, profits and rationing;
5. Correction of inequalities and substandard wage rates.[13]

The UE fought for economic stabilization in the economy during 1942 and 1943. The union was keenly disappointed in the failure of the government to prevent rising prices under the economic stabilization law in October 1942, while the workers were being subjected to a wage freeze.[14] During 1942-1943 wage gains were negotiated under the "Little Steel Formula" by the UE on a plant-wide basis affecting 155,000 workers. The union also extended night bonuses, paid holidays, and many other benefits. Important guarantees affecting wage rates, job classification, time values were secured by the union through direct negotiation.[15]

The UE at its 1944 convention passed two significant resolutions. First, the UE urged industry-wide collective bargaining in order to attain job security, minimum wages and other improvements. Concomitantly, the resolution advocated an intensification of the effort to organize all workers within its jurisdiction. In the second resolution the union adopted the policy that it should advance contract demands for life, accident, sickness, hospital and surgical insurance, the premiums to be paid by the companies.[16]

Prior to the termination of the war the UE was continually pressing for economic improvements within the bounds of wage stabilization policies. In the Westinghouse Electric Company (Pittsburgh Division) the union demanded a 17 cents wage increase to compensate for the rise in living costs, a cost-of-living escalator clause and a 40-hour work-week guarantee for the duration of the contract. The

union's position in support of its demands encompassed the follow
ing arguments:

1. That the basic wage rates of Westinghouse employees have
remained unchanged since May 31, 1942;
2. With increased living costs on the one hand and frozen wages
on the other, the real earnings of the workers are insufficient to
maintain their living standards;
3. The employees' share of the national income has declined in
respect to other groups;
4. The Bureau of Labor Statistics price index is inadequate to
measure the workers' wartime costs.

In its decision in this case the National War Labor Board denied
any wage increase and the escalator clause, because it was not per-
missible under the "Little Steel Formula." Although refusing the
union's request for a guaranteed weekly wage, the Board did recommend that the proposed government study of the guaranteed wage
question include the electrical manufacturing industry.[17]

In the General Electric and Westinghouse companies and the
United Electrical, Radio and Machine Workers of America case before the National War Labor Board in September 1945, the principal
issue in dispute was equal pay for equal work. The two firms had
separate evaluation and wage rate systems for men's and women's
jobs. The Board recommended that the parties concerned negotiate a
formula for narrowing unreasonable wage rate differentials and approved the principle of a single evaluation system for all jobs in a
plant regardless of sex.[18]

Other concessions which the union tried to win from the Westinghouse and General Electric companies were:

1. 72 cents per hour minimum wage for common labor:
2. Payment for six holidays;
3. Severance pay for hourly and salaried employees on the basis
of accumulated service;.
4. A more liberal group insurance plan;
5. Double time after twelve hours;
6. Sick leave for salaried employees.[19]

In the 1,843 labor dispute cases involving the UE before the regional war labor boards during the Second World War the UE won
many contract improvements such as modification of policy on the
question of automatic progression, 10 per cent shift differential pre-

mium, graduated vacation plans. In the New York region six paid holidays became the established rule in all UE shops. For Westinghouse salaried workers the UE obtained the Board's approval for merit increases as well as an automatic 10 per cent increase after six months. For the General Electric Company a new step-rate plan for salaried workers was negotiated by the UE.[20]

### UE WAGE POLICY AFTER VJ DAY

With the ending of the Second World War and the accompanying drop in the workers' take-home pay, the UE in September 1945 demanded a wage increase of $2 a day. When it became apparent that the employers would not make any offer, the workers voted to strike. Upon a continued refusal of the employers to bargain, the UE went on strike in January 1946. Shortly, the government announced the new wage policy, permitting a maximum increase of 18½ cents an hour. After a number of weeks of idleness the UE workers in the electrical division of General Motors and in General Electric Company settled for the 18½ cents hourly increase. As a result of these two victories, the UE was successful in having the Wage Stabilization Board set a pattern for the electrical industry at 18½ cents per hour.[21]

The termination of the war necessitated a statement from the union regarding the incentive wage question. The union wage policy had traditionally favored a straight hourly basis of pay. In order to facilitate maximum production during the war, the UE approved the use of incentive systems but insisted on guarantees against rate cutting. At the end of the war the union opposed the installation of incentive plans in plants where the UE had straight day-work. In plants where the union membership opposed existing incentive wage plans, the union assisted locals in making a change to day-work.[22]

The wage policy of the UE in 1946 may be gleaned from the resolutions that were approved at the 1946 convention. The following are pertinent:

1. Guaranteed annual wage—In this resolution the UE called for a fulfillment of the pledges made by the leaders of our government to establish the four freedoms and a new economic bill of rights which would guarantee security to the people. To achieve this goal, the UE would work for an annual, living wage, guarantee clause in collective bargaining contracts.*

* It is interesting to note that in 1954 the UE opposed the guaranteed wage.

2. Minimum requirements in UE contracts—The union recognized that a number of UE contracts failed to provide the minimum requirements. To correct this problem, no local union in the future would be permitted to submit a proposed collective bargaining contract which did not comply with the union minimum contract requirements, nor could any contract be signed without such minimum requirements.

3. Organizing the unorganized—Recognizing that the unorganized plants in the industry are a threat to the wages and working conditions of the organized companies and that the full benefits of collective bargaining could not be achieved without uniform contracts, the UE was prompted to intensify and extend its organizational work.

4. Increased wages—The union believed that wages must be substantially increased because the weekly earnings of the workers had been drastically cut since VJ Day and because recent wage gains had been wiped out by soaring prices. The union thought that cooperation with the steel workers, automobile workers and other CIO unions would be most effective. In addition to wage increases, the resolution charged the union to press for increased security, paid holidays, increased vacation periods and allowances, health and welfare safeguards, adequate old age pensions, and higher minimum wage rates.[23]

UE WAGE ARBITRATION CASES

The following arbitration cases in 1946 and 1947 reveal the demands of the UE and the arguments used to support their cases. From the National Electronics Corporation the union demanded a 20 cents an hour increase retroactive to October 4, 1946. The union's line of reasoning is apparent in the following points developed to support its case. An increase is necessary to meet the rise in the cost of living as reflected in the 18½ cents increase granted in the basic industries. The wage rates of the workers are considerably below those awarded by the War Labor Board prior to its termination. Wage rates are below those paid by several related companies contracted by the National Electronics Company and in the radio parts field. The wage rates are below those paid by other radio parts producers. The arbitrator awarded the workers a 15 cents an hour increase retroactive to October 4, 1945, on the basis of: 1) the increased cost of living since the last wage contracts, 2) rates paid in electrical and radio trades within the local labor market area.[24]

In the case of the Veloco Machine Company (Benton Harbor, Michigan) and the UE, the union asked for a general wage increase of 25 cents an hour in the fall of 1945 to compensate workers for loss in take-home pay. It later amended its request to 18½ cents. An agreement was reached on April 1, 1946, whereby the company increased wages by 11 cents, and the parties agreed to submit to arbitration any additional increase which might be granted. The union's position hinged on the fact that the company is part of an industry that has been granted a pattern wage increase of 18.5 cents per hour by the Wage Stabilization Board. The arbitrator's award granted the employees a 5.5 cents an hour additional increase so as to meet "pattern of increases" established in the local labor market. Increases granted by the employer to a small group of employees were permitted to be offset against the general increase. The general increase should be applied to starting rates to bring increases up to those granted by comparable companies since VJ Day.[25]

In the Camburn, Inc., and UE case the union demanded a general wage increase of 25 cents per hour, effective as of December 1, 1946. It stated that the cost of living between March 16, 1941, the date of the last agreement between the parties, and December 1, 1946, rose 18 per cent. It further argued that the workers were entitled to 6½ cents for the year 1946 since the national pattern of wage increases was 18½ cents at the time the last wage increase of 12½ cents was given. The union is justified in demanding 25 cents an hour, adding 6½ cents to 16.2 cents for a total of 22.7 cents per hour. The union also said that the company is part of the radio and parts industry and should follow the wage pattern of the Electronics Manufacturers Association, Inc. In rebuttal, the company declared that it was not a part of the radio and parts industry and that it was not financially able to pay the wage request. The arbitrator granted the employees a 15 cents general wage increase to compensate them for the rise in the cost of living and to correct for inequities between the Camburn Company wage rates and the pattern for the association and the industry in which it is a part.[26]

In the case of the Moeller Instrument Company, Inc., and the UE, the union requested a wage increase in July 1946, but rejected the general increase of five cents an hour offered by the company. In the arbitration case the union's principal argument was based on the rise in the cost of living and the contention that the company paid lower rates than competitors. The company pleaded inability to pay the wage increase because of losses sustained in 1946 and said that only one out of the four companies that the union held out for comparison was a competitor. The award requested the company to pay, in addition to the five cents increase given in October 1946, a general wage increase of five cents per hour, effective retroactively to August 25, 1946, on the grounds of increased living costs between February 25 and August 25, 1946, of 11.7 per cent. In view of the unfavorable financial condition of the employer, the union's request for larger increases to eliminate inequity between the company's rates and those of competing firms in the area was denied.[27]

In the case of the Watson Elevator Company and the UE, the union asked for a general wage increase. It stated that in October 1946 it had asked the company for a 6½ cents per hour increase to complete the 18½ cents pattern for the industry. An agreement was reached in December 1946 to pay one week's bonus and a general increase of three cents effective January 1, 1947. Under a wage reopening clause, the union on March 1, 1947, endeavored to obtain a needed increase. The union demanded a 20 cents per hour increase across the board for the following reasons:

1. Five cents due for "arrearage" owed by the company in 1946 adjustment;
2. Fifteen cents per hour due the workers to bring the company's employees in line with the general wage pattern;
3. Increased cost of living;
4. Rates paid by the Watson Company are much lower than for comparable jobs at the Otis Elevator Company and the Westinghouse Company.

The employer argued that he should not be required to pay the requested wage increase, because the per capita output of his employees was far below that of competing companies. In his decision the arbitrator said that the efficiency and output of the employees in the Watson Company were largely under the control of the company and advised the company to put into effect an incentive system for the entire working force. The employees should be granted an overall increase of .115 cents per hour principally because of the pattern wage rates established by the other major producers. The union's claim for "arrearage" increase was denied since the previous wage agreement granted one week's bonus plus a prospective three cents increase and wage-reopening privilege.[28]

UNION FIGHT FOR ECONOMIC GAINS IN 1947-1948

With a mandate from the 1946 convention to obtain higher wages in 1947 the UE conducted a planned program to prepare employers and workers for the coming negotiations. Materials were circulated to expose employer arguments against wage increases. The high profits of the electrical manufacturing companies were attacked. According to the union, the large earnings were sufficient proof of the ability of the employer to give substantial wage increases.[29] For the most part, the UE followed the precedent established by the other major CIO unions in 1947 in negotiating for a 15 cents package. The General Electric and Westinghouse package included 11½ cents for wage increases and 3½ cents for improvements in holidays and vacations. Although these contracts looked good on the surface, they seemed to represent a sell-out by those in control of the UE because they deprived the workers of all Saturday holidays. It was not until 1954 that the IUE recaptured this lost ground.

In the following resolutions passed at the 1947 convention the UE reiterated its future objectives on wage policies.

1. Establishment of industry-wide contract provisions providing the best possible working conditions. The new and improved contract provisions established during 1947 should be included as minimum requirements for all firms in the industry;
2. Continued fight for substantial wage increases in 1948 because of the shrinkage of real wages and the ability of employers to pay;
3. The approval of the guaranteed annual wage;
4. The establishment of contract provisions for old age pension plans which afford decent standards of living with voluntary retirement privilege and reduction in existing age limits;
5. Health and welfare provisions should be included in contracts wholly paid for by the company instead of partially paid for by the worker who can ill afford to bear the cost;
6. Increased efforts should be made to strengthen safeguards on piece work and incentive systems where they exist and to oppose the introduction of further piece work or incentive systems in plants where they do not yet exist.[30]

In accordance with the 1948 UE wage policies formulated at the union's twelfth convention, the union proceeded to carry out the wishes of its officers and members. On January 6, 1948, representatives of the workers in General Electric, Westinghouse, Sylvania and the electrical division of General Motors met in conference to map out a wage drive. In addition to wage increases, the delegates voted for adequate pensions, health and welfare plans, severance pay for laid-off workers, improved vacations, additional paid holidays, equal pay for equal work.[31]

Little progress was made in the attainment of the UE goal in negotiation with the leading companies. The General Electric Company stalled, stating that further wage increases would lead to more inflation with resulting hardship to the workers.[32]

The General Motors Conference Board voted in May 1948 to conduct a strike vote after ten weeks of negotiations which failed to bring any offer from the corporation on the union's demands.[33] A few days later the corporation offered an 11 cents an hour increase with an additional raise of three cents for the following year. The same offer was made to the UAW and was accepted by the auto-workers.[34]

The UE made a settlement with the Radio Corporation of America which provided an immediate down payment of four cents an hour on the 1948 wage increase pattern and an improvement in vacation schedules which gave employees with ten years of service a three-week vacation. According to the union, this represented the first three-week vacation period for ten years of service in any major company in the United States.[35]

Four months of negotiation with the General Electric Company finally brought forth the corporation's first counter-proposal on wages. The offer, accepted by the union locals, included an eight per cent increase in total earnings for each worker with a minimum raise of nine cents per hour. Westinghouse was next to make a settlement with a raise from nine to sixteen cents an hour with an additional paid holiday making a total of seven paid holidays. From Sylvania the UE won an eight per cent raise and three weeks' vacation after 15 years of service.[36] In contrast to the major corporations 236 smaller companies in the industry signed contracts with the UE as of April 1948, granting down payment wage increases averaging over 10 cents an hour. Six hundred eighty-eight plants employing 453,000 workers gave increases ranging from 9 cents to 16 cents per hour.[37]

At the annual convention of the UE in September 1948, the union officers severely criticized the corporations in the electrical industry for their failure to compensate the workers, since the termination of war, in proportion to the high profits throughout the industry. As might be expected, the communistic officers condemned the CIO for its weak policies. They accused the CIO of trying to force the Marshall Plan and other political views on the UE and other CIO national unions.[38]

### EXPULSION OF UE FROM THE CIO AND FORMATION OF IUE-CIO

On November 2, 1949, the constitutional convention of the CIO voted to expel the UE because they could no longer tolerate within the CIO the Communist Party masquerading as a labor union. The UE's leaders were charged with "disloyalty to the CIO and dedication to the purposes and program of the Communistic Party. . . "[39] The convention directed the CIO Executive Board to issue a charter of affiliation to a new international union, the International Union of Electrical, Radio and Machine Workers (IUE). The expulsion of the UE from the CIO was a significant event, because it symbolized the beginning of the end of the communistic influence in the American labor movement.

### THE IUE WAGE POLICY, 1949

At the organizational convention of the IUE in November 1949, an economic report of the union administrative committee showed that the electrical workers' wages had lagged in comparison with other major mass-production industries. In September 1949 the average hourly wage in the electrical industry was $1.448 compared with $1.703 for automobiles, $1.652 for steel, $1.667 for transportation equipment, $1.54 for aircraft, $1.62 for railroad equipment, and $1.481 for all durable goods. The electrical industry had enjoyed exceedingly favorable earnings and the outlook for the future was bright. During 1949 most sections of the American labor movement had won some form of a fourth round increase either in wages, pensions or other benefits, but the UE had obtained virtually nothing for its members.[40] In a resolution unanimously approved by the IUE convention in 1949, the delegates pledged that they would bend their efforts to bring about the needed improvements in wages, working conditions and union security.[41] The following program was mapped out and adopted by the convention:

1. Employer-financed minimum monthly pension of $100 including Federal Social Security for all workers with 25 years of service at age 65, with severance pay provisions included;
2. Social security insurance providing medical care, death benefits, hospitalization and surgical care for the worker and his family;
3. Wage adjustments to bring the wages of workers in the electrical manufacturing industry up to that of steel, automobiles and aircraft industries. The adjustments should provide the workers a fair share in increased productivity.[42]

Within a period of ten months after the birth of the IUE the union negotiated and signed agreements with the majority of employers whose plants had been certified by the NLRB as the result of representation elections. In addition, many other contracts were made with companies where no representation election was necessary. The IUE's greatest victories came with signing of agreements with the leading companies in the industry—General Electric, Westinghouse, and General Motors. Following the lead of these companies similar contracts were consummated with many other companies.[43]

The General Motors agreement signed on May 27, 1950, represented the results of cooperative planning and negotiating with the UAW-CIO. Both unions secured a five-year contract, the unique features being: a non-contributory pension of $100 a month including Federal Social Security benefits, the cost-of-living adjustments every three months, and the annual improvement factor of four cents per hour. Also included were increased life insurance and sickness and accident benefits, a hospital and medical insurance plan, improved vacations, and the union shop.[44]

Collective bargaining with the General Electric Company was turbulent from the beginning. Although the elections in May 1950 showed that the IUE had won the right to represent over 55,000 workers against 38,000 for the UE, it was not until September 15, 1950, that a contract was negotiated. The intervening period was marked by reluctance of General Electric to bargain in good faith, by a series of strikes, and finally by the intervention of the U.S. Mediation and Conciliation Service. According to the IUE, the company used the UE as a tool in order to make a satisfactory settlement difficult. The success of General Electric in refusing a ridiculous demand of the UE for a $500 package convinced the company that a more rational IUE demand could be turned down as easily. The General

Electric Company's offer to the IUE included the following: a general wage increase of three per cent and a minimum increase of four cents an hour for all hourly rated and salaried employees, a contributory pension plan with no significant increases in benefits, a group insurance plan which did not cover the worker's dependents nor increase weekly payments for non-occupational sickness and accidents, and an unsatisfactory health and vacation plan. The union was not at all satisfied with the offer.[45] To strengthen its case for a substantial wage increase and a satisfactory pension and group insurance program, the IUE engaged Robert R. Nathan to make a financial analysis of the General Electric Company. The report asserted that in 1949 the General Electric Company had record sales of $1,614 million, almost five times that of 1939 and almost 12 per cent higher than the wartime peak in 1944. Profits after taxes amounted to $125.6 million in 1949, almost triple the pre-war level and more than double the wartime peak. In the first six months of 1950 the company's sales were up 10 per cent over the corresponding period in 1949, and profits after taxes were 66 per cent above the same period of the previous year. The report stated that a substantial wage increase was justified by these factors: 1) The workers have not shared in the phenomenal profits. 2) The company is able to grant an adequate wage increase without raising prices. 3) The General Electric workers have lagged behind other workers in wage increases. 4) The real wages of the workers have not improved.[46]

The final agreement with the General Electric Company on September 15, 1950, included the following gains for the IUE: a flat 10 cents to 15½ cents across-the-board wage increase, minimum pensions of $125 a month, health insurance coverage, a cost-of-living escalator clause to increase wages one cent per hour for every 1.14 per cent increase in the Bureau of Labor Statistics cost-of-living index between September 15, 1950, and March 15, 1951.[47] According to the union, the General Electric agreement showed other companies in the industry that the IUE would use the strike if necessary to obtain the economic benefits needed by its membership. It was believed that the Westinghouse agreement of October 1, 1950, was hastened by the fear of losing its competitive position to General Electric.[48] The new contract brought substantial improvements over the old UE contract of 1948. They included: 1) 10 cents hourly wage increase, 2) a non-contributory minimum pension of $100 a month for workers earning less than $4,800 a year, 3) a social insurance program with life insurance of $2,500 and up, sickness and accident insurance up to $32 a week for 26 weeks, hospital and surgical insurance for both employees and their dependents and in addition maternity and total disability benefits. The company also established a fund of one cent per hour for every employee to adjust to inequities.[49]

The Sylvania agreement of September 11, 1950, was significant because it represented substantial improvement in both wages and fringe provisions in five of the company plants. The total package amounting to 15 cents included a 10 cents hourly wage increase for production and skilled workers, a liberalized vacation program, a company-paid life insurance policy, Blue Cross and Blue Shield insurance, sick leave improvements, two additional holidays, and a union shop.[50]

The RCA agreement brought a five cents an hour across-the-board increase with an additional automatic increase of 4½ cents on June 4, 1951; an extra five cents to adjust for inequities in wage rates; company-paid hospital, surgical and medical benefits for the worker and his dependent.[51]

In conclusion, the 1950 gains of the IUE in the General Electric and Westinghouse companies set the pattern for the industry. The gains were not easily achieved and with the General Electric Company it required many months of negotiation including a strike in several of the company's plants. Pension plans were extended and improved throughout the industry as well as health and welfare benefits. Much to the dislike of the IUE, the UE participated in the same gains that were won by the IUE while contributing nothing to achieve them.

### WAGE POLICIES DURING THE KOREAN WAR

When wage stabilization went into effect after the outbreak of the Korean hostilities, the IUE attempted to advance the needs of its membership under the existing wage controls. To accomplish this objective, the union sought the approval by the Wage Stabilization Board of the following policies: 1) abolition of inequities in the industry, particularly in radio and television production; 2) productivity adjustments which were not in contracts in January 1951; 3) wage increases for those workers making less than one dollar an hour; 4) more adequate pensions and insurance programs; 5) more prompt decisions by the War Stabilization Board.[52]

The 1951 negotiations with the General Electric Company continued to be couched in an antagonistic milieu. In June 1951 the union presented the company its proposals based on its provisions with other companies in the electrical industry. They included: a union shop, assumption by the company of the cost of the check off, an anti-discrimination clause, better overtime provisions, paid lunch-period on multiple shifts, sick leave for salaried workers, improvement in night shift differentials, improvements in call-in and report-in time, greater protection for incentive workers, a better progression sched-ule, improved upgrading and transfer procedures, better holiday pro-visions, three-weeks' vacation after fifteen years of service, etc.

Its economic proposals were: 1) a continuation of the cost-of-living clause expiring March 15, 1951, 2) a profit or productivity bonus,[53] 3) company absorption of the workers two per cent pay-ment for their pensions, 4) an employment security fund to pay part of the cost of temporary layoffs in transition to and from defense work and severance pay to workers with two years seniority follow-ing termination of the defense emergency.

The company officials greeted the proposals with a declaration that they were not prepared to discuss them or to offer any of their own. The IUE met with the company representative 17 days between July 17 to September 26, and it was not until August 21 that the company offered any counter proposals. In respect to the various contractual proposals, the company offered only minor concessions. On the eco-nomic issues, the company offered a 2½ per cent wage increase and a cost-of-living escalator for the periods of March–September 1951 and September 1951–March 1952. All of the other union economic demands were rejected. In return, the union made a number of counter proposals contained in a nine-point program. These in-cluded: 1) acceptance of the cost-of-living escalator with the stipu-lation that the cost-of-living be reviewed every four months instead of six, 2) acceptance of the company's 2½ per cent wage increase, 3) three-weeks vacation after 15 years instead of 20 years, 4) tem-porary deferment of the non-contributory pension demand and substitution of the employment security fund, 5) union shop, 6) anti-discrimination clause to include the word "sex," 7) a better progression schedule, 8) an improved seniority plan, 9) a wage reopener on March 15, 1952, when the cost-of-living escalator ex-pired.

The General Electric Company rejected the IUE nine-point pro-gram and refused to bargain on any point. In order to end the dead-lock and avert a strike, the union agreed to settle for a cost-of-living agreement, a four cents an hour minimum wage increase and three-weeks' vacation after 15 years of service. The proposals were again met by the refusal of the company. Continued negotiations for more than three months and the assistance of the Federal Mediation and Conciliation Service failed to resolve the problems. Finally, after the IUE voted on strike action on October 4, 1951, a General Electric proposal found acceptance by the union. The agreement included: 1) a 2½ per cent wage increase with a 3½ cent minimum retroactive to September 15, 1951, 2) a cost-of-living increase for March 15 to September 15, 3) a wage reopener on March 15, 1952, 4) three-weeks vacation after 15 years service, 5) a September 15, 1952, reopener for pensions insurance discussion. There were also some contractual changes including an increase in reporting pay time and a simplified and clarified grievance procedure.[54]

The Westinghouse-IUE agreement signed on June 1, 1951, included the following gains: 1) a nine cents hourly wage increase retroactive to April 16, 2) a union shop clause, 3) a wage reopener on February 1, 1951, 4) a review of the pension program on October 1, 1951.[55] An additional wage increase from five cents to 15 cents per hour was secured by the IUE in its October 1951 wage reopener.[56] With the Sylvania Electric chain, the IUE won wage increases ranging from 14½ cents to 23½ cents per hour effective September 11, 1951. Nine to 16 cents of the raise was made retroactive to July 30. A cost-of-living escalator clause was also included in the contract.[57]

In conclusion, during the year 1951 the wage gains of the IUE among the leaders were as follows: General Electric 15 cents, Westinghouse 15 cents, General Motors 14 cents, Sylvania 14 cents, RCA 9½ cents, and Philco 9 cents. The union extended pensions to more than 88 per cent of the workers under IUE contracts and group insurance and health security plans were extended to 95 per cent of the IUE membership. Cost-of-living escalator clauses and annual productivity adjustments were incorporated in an increasing number of contracts.[58]

Substantial membership gains were experienced during the year. Membership in the IUE rose from 200,000 in September 1950 to 350,000 by September 1951. Although the big rush of elections in favor of the IUE was over, many new NLRB victories were achieved. Much organizational effort was expended in the South, Midwest, and Far West.[59]

Negotiations with the General Electric Company in 1952 began on March 6. The union demands were: a cost-of-living increase between Spetember 15, 1951, and March 15, 1952, an overhauling of the incentive wage system, a four cents an hour fund to eliminate inequities between men's and women's rates, a wage increase of 25 cents an hour for skilled workers, a 4½ cents an hour fund for removing inequities of clerical and day workers, a profit-sharing plan, company-paid pensions, an anti-discrimination clause, an employment security fund to prevent hardships during defense layoffs. The company agreed to a cost-of-living escalator clause but refused to bargain on the other demands. The IUE rejected the offer, but proposed that the company put into effect the 1.03 per cent wage increase immediately under the cost-of-living adjustments. The General Electric refused to do this.

On August 13 the company made another economic offer providing a cost-of-living increase from September 1951 to September 1952, and a 2½ per cent productivity increase and some improvements in group insurance. Among the contractual proposals, the company tried to move backwards. The IUE rejected the General Electric program and proposed the following seven-point program: 1) continuance of the cost-of-living escalator and an annual four cents an hour productivity increase, with a guarantee of a 10 cents an hour minimum increase each year, 2) an annual wage reopener, 3) seven paid holidays, 4) union shop, 5) company absorption of workers' two per cent contribution for pensions, 6) revision of the incentive system, 7) joint company-union study for restoration of the profit-sharing system. Upon the rejection of the union program, the IUE enlisted the services of the Federal Conciliation Service.

While negotiations were pending, the United Electrical, Radio and Machine Workers of America (UE) accepted the General Electric offer which had been previously made to the IUE. The agreement meant a loss of two paid holidays and company reduction of its pension benefits to the extent of the increase in the Federal Social Security benefits.

The IUE-General Electric Conference Board proposed on September 16, 1952, that the issues in dispute be submitted to arbitration. The company refused to agree to this method of settlement. The IUE then proposed that the company's wage increase offer be put into effect and any action on pensions be withheld until a settlement was reached. The company again refused to effect an agreement.

While the General Electric negotiations were stalemated, the IUE reached a settlement with the Westinghouse Company on September 29, 1952. The agreement provided: 1) a wage increase across-the-board ranging from 7½ cents an hour, 2) a wage reopener on pensions and insurance in January 1953, 3) a substitution of two other holidays for Memorial Day and July 4 which in 1953 fell on Saturday, 4) extension of a modified union shop to all IUE Westinghouse locals where the union shop was not already in effect.

With the signing of the Westinghouse contract, the IUE proposed to the General Electric Company that it agree to a similar contract, but the company would not consent. Finally, on October 27–28 an agreement with the General Electric was reached. It included the following: 1) a wage increase equal to the percentage increase in the cost of living between September 15, 1951, and either September 15, October 15, or November 15, 1952, on option of the union, 2) additional wage increase of 2½ per cent with 3½ cents minimum retroactive to October 13, 1952, 3) reopener on pensions on a date fixed by mutual consent any time prior to expiration of the current pension agreement, September 1955, 4) reopener on wages in March 1953, 5) improvements of contractual and insurance provisions on which agreement was reached earlier in negotiations, 6) termination date for contract set for September 15, 1953.[60]

In the General Motors agreement, the IUE followed the same pattern as the auto workers in their 1952 contract. The agreement included: 1) the inclusion in the base rate of all employees 19 cents of the 24 cents cost-of-living adjustments of the previous years, 2) increase in the annual improvement factor from four cents to five cents an hour, 3) an increase of 10 cents an hour to workers in the skilled trades, 4) improvements in the pension plan so that maximum benefits are $137.50 with additional benefits for a spouse, 5) extension of group insurance and Blue Cross and Blue Shield to pensioners, 6) increases in vacation pay.[61]

In the Philco Company the locals during 1952 won a five cents across-the-board increase. In RCA the 1952 agreement brought a general wage increase of six cents an hour, inequity adjustments ranging from one to 10 cents an hour for more than 2,000 workers on 41 jobs, double time-and-half for work on holidays, two days death-leave for all workers with one year's seniority.[62]

In conclusion, the 1952 wage pattern in the electrical industry was established by Westinghouse on the basis of an average 10 cents hourly increase. The general average for the entire industry amounted to about 7.2 cents an hour. Generally speaking, the gains took care of the increased living costs during the year and an average increase in productivity of 2½ per cent. According to the union, the wage gains compared more than favorably with all manufacturing, durable goods, and non-electrical machinery. Much, however, remained to be done to make up for the years in which the UE failed to win adequate increases.[63]

At the 1953 convention the delegates went on record unanimously supporting the report of the collective bargaining committee calling for substantial wage increases and improvements in fringe benefits. It was believed that such increases were needed to provide the workers a standard of living commensurate with what the American economy could afford and to provide continued prosperity and full employment. More specifically the demands included:

1. Guaranteed annual wage for workers with seniority status;
2. Establishment of an industry-wide minimum wage of $1.25 an hour;
3. Annual improvement adjustments in wages proportionate to yearly increase in productivity;
4. Revision of incentive systems to enable the worker to receive full benefits of his increased production;
5. Removal of intra-plant inequities and injustices through equal pay for equal work;
6. Improvements in pension programs to include non-contributory plans with benefits at the rate of $2 per month for each year of service in addition to social security;
7. Profit-sharing plans provided they are not substitutes for satisfactory wages and pensions;
8. Improvements in insurance and health plans;
9. Additional holidays and vacation benefits;
10. Union security—all employees in a bargaining unit must belong to the union that has representation.[64]

The 1953 IUE convention approved two important resolutions dealing with the subject of incentive wage systems and long-term contracts. Because incentive systems in the electrical industry are too complex and of too many varieties, the convention recommended that an incentive wage survey committee be established to develop a program to correct the inequities or determine whether incentive systems should be eliminated. On the question of long-term contracts, the IUE's position was similar to the UAW, namely, that long-term agreements should be opposed unless they are made living documents. To make them flexible they should provide: 1) reopeners on wages or economic issues at certain intervals, 2) correction of inequities, 3) appropriate changes in contractual language necessitated by changing and unforeseen situations, 4) correction of provisions that have developed into mutual problems.[65]

On March 3, 1953, the IUE made its demands on the General Electric Company which embodied the 1953 program. In respect to wage increases, a request for 21 cents an hour was supported by such factors as comparative wages, productivity and profits. On March 18 the company offered the union two choices. The first was a cost-of-living wage increase, and the second was a straight 1.68 per cent increase based on 1951 wages and equivalent to 1.50 per cent increase in current wages, provided the union would forego wage reopening until March 15, 1954. The General Electric Conference Board rejected the offer and started a campaign for wage and contractual improvements based on the union program adopted by the IUE Executive Board in January 1953. This program demanded a substantial wage increase, the restoration of two Saturday holidays in 1953, a union shop, increased vacations, employee security fund to include severance pay, straight addition of social security increases for General Electric pensioners, an anti-discrimination clause, revision of the incentive system and other miscellaneous improvements. The company refused to modify its wage proposals or to make any substantial changes in the contractual issues. The company contended that its offer was more than the union deserved on the basis of what other companies were paying.

By the end of May 1953 the IUE and the UAW reached an agreement with General Motors and Chrysler to modify their five-year contracts to provide a five cents annual improvement adjustment, a 10-25 cents increase in skilled trades, pension improvements, the factoring of 19 cents of the 24 cents cost-of-living "float" into the wage structure, a continuance of the cost-of-living clause, and other gains. The total package averaged 8 cents an hour. With the signing of the General Motors agreement, the IUE asked General Electric to meet the pattern established by General Motors. In the meantime the IUE obtained a settlement with RCA, which according to the union spokesmen, provided a pattern much superior to the General Electric. The General Electric, however, refused to improve its original offer.

After the IUE locals went on strike at the General Electric plants in Evendale and Syracuse and with mounting unrest in other plants, the company on June 12 reversed its position and offered a general wage increase of 3.15 per cent which averaged about 5.3 cents. The IUE accepted this offer which included additional increases to many day workers of one cent to eight cents, increases for salaried workers, improvements in piece-work payments, termination pay where plants are abandoned, increased vacation benefits, double-time pay after 16 hours on any one shift. The entire package was valued at about seven cents an hour.[66]

The June 1953 agreement with four RCA locals gave the IUE a package which averaged 12½ cents an hour. This included: across-the-board average wage increases of 10 cents, inequity raises for semi-skilled workers, improved sick leave, hospitalization insurance, holidays no matter when they fall, double time for all work over 12 hours, two-weeks severance pay after four-years employment instead of five, and other miscellaneous improvements. The Westinghouse agreement of August 1953 brought across-the-board wage gains which averaged 4.7 cents improvements in pensions for workers with 30 years service, and increased disability payments.[67]

In conclusion, the wage adjustments obtained by the IUE during the first seven months of 1953 were somewhat smaller than those of the comparable period of 1952. The union gains from the independent companies were somewhat greater than from the chain companies. This was particularly true in the area of fringe benefits. In the four years since the IUE was formed, the total package gains for its members in General Electric were 50.01 cents, in General Motors 51 cents, in Westinghouse 50½ cents, and in various independent companies, over 68 cents. In membership gains, the IUE continued to make substantial progress. The total membership by November 2, 1953, was estimated at about 400,000 compared with less than 100,000 for the UE.[68]

The 1954 wage negotiations brought the following across-the-board wage gains: General Electric, five cents per hour average; Westinghouse, five cents per hour average; General Motors, six cents per hour net; Sylvania, 4.5 cents per hour average; RCA, 7.5 cents per hour average; Philco, seven cents per hour average. The IUE finally obtained payment for Saturday holidays from the General

Electric with the choice of alternative days, improvements in up-grading clause, and other minor contractual changes. On the question of job security, the company gave the union a letter containing its position on this matter, but it was not included in the contract. The union bargaining committee was greatly disappointed in the General Electric settlement as it did not meet the needs of the workers. It believed that it represented a bitterly hostile company attitude determined to end collective bargaining and force the IUE into line. The union notified the company on August 19 that there remained many serious unsolved problems. The following problems give a clue to the union's wage objectives with the General Electric Company when negotiations were reopened in 1955:

1. A wage reopener—The union wishes a wage reopener at certain intervals during the period of the contract in order to maintain the real wages of its members. Since the union started negotiations with the General Electric in April 1954, the cost of living has risen nearly .6 per cent. This rise reduces the company's wage increase from 2.68 per cent to about 2 per cent or from five cents to four cents per hour.

2. $1.25 minimum wage—The union believes an increase in the minimum wage is necessary in order to eradicate the wage differentials between the northern urban and the southern and rural plants.

3. Job security—The letter given the union on the subject of job security maintains the company's control over job security and does not provide the necessary protection to the workers. The company has refused to make any commitments concerning the protection of jobs in the older plants, in the decentralization of plants, and the farming out of work.

4. Equal pay for equal work—The company has consistently refused to give women workers equality of pay with male employees.

5. Protection for piece workers—The union fears that the company will violate its contract by retiming jobs in order to reduce workers' earnings. The General Electric has refused to give the union any assurances that it will observe the contract against cutting of piece rates.

6. Unfair labor practice charges—The union feels that the company has used unfair labor practices in the past and wishes to be protected against them. It insists: that if the company discharges workers the union be given the right of arbitration, the com-

pany conform to the NLRB ruling that a union is entitled to information from the company necessary for collective bargaining, the company cease its "take-it-or-leave-it" attitude in negotiations.

7. Retroactive pay—The union claims that the company's refusal to bargain has deprived 100,000 General Electric workers of a wage increase from June 1 to August 2, 1954. The union insists that the company pay its obligation to the workers.

In conclusion, the bargaining relationship between the IUE and the General Electric Company appeared to be at the breaking-point. According to the union, the company's anti-labor offensive was stepped up in 1954 as revealed in its "take-it-or-leave-it" attitude in negotiations, its attempt to prevent or destroy the local unions in its plants, and its anti-labor leadership in Congress. The union feels that the company is planning for more profits at the expense of the workers as revealed in a General Electric conference in April 1954. The company's future plans call for a doubling of production in the next ten years by increasing productivity without additional workers, the decentralization of plants to take advantage of lower labor costs, and a revision of wage incentive values. Lastly, the union criticizes the company's substandard labor conditions. It claims that the General Electric lags behind the industry in working conditions and has become an impediment to the IUE's program of improving labor standards for the industry. Unless the General Electric changes its policy, a showdown with the union appears imminent. To meet this eventuality, the IUE is consolidating its efforts through organization and education.[69] At the October 1954 convention of the IUE, the delegates voted to mobilize the entire union membership to break down General Electric's anti-union campaign. The union strategy will be to adhere to a no-contract, no-work policy.[78]

In the 1955 negotiations with the General Electric Company, the IUE's position was strengthened by its contract with General Motors, which gave IUE employees the same benefits as were obtained by the UAW for its workers. Among the many demands sought from the General Electric were a company-financed layoff plan to provide 52 weeks of full pay for eligible employees; a substantial wage increase; liberalization of pensions, vacations, holidays and insurance; elimination of geographic pay differentials; a full union shop; and an end of "Boulwarism."

Surprisingly, the IUE and the General Electric signed a 5 year contract on August 11, 1955, after less than a month of negotiations. Both sides claimed victory. The General Electric Company defeated the guaranteed wage and was assured of industrial peace for at least three years. Although the IUE lost the guaranteed wage, the contract provides a reopening clause for a review of employment security plans in 1958 at the end of the third year. The union spokesmen appeared jubilant over wage increases and the extension of fringe benefits. James B. Carey termed the contract the biggest settlement ever negotiated between the union and the company. The major provisions included:

1. A general annual wage increase of 3 per cent for each of the first three years with a minimum hourly increase of 4½ cents an hour. In the fourth and fifth years the minimum hourly increase will be 5 cents;

2. Special wage increases for skilled day workers and salaried employees ranging from ½ cent to 6 cents more per hour in the first year;

3. A new health program covering serious and prolonged illness at home or in the hospital;

4. An improved pension plan. The workers' contributions will decline from 2 per cent to 1 per cent of wages in 1955, and by October 1, 1958, there will be no employee contributions for the first $4,200 of earnings and contributions on earnings over that amount will be reduced to 3 per cent;

5. A cost-of-living escalator provision, computed quarterly with a floor based on the September 1955 consumers' price index;

6. Improvement in union security, holidays, vacations, overtime, etc.

According to the IUE, the contract signals a new departure in General Electric-IUE relationships and fulfils many long-sought union demands. The company spokesmen believe that the contract augurs well for stability and harmony.

CONCLUSIONS

The wage policies of the UE from 1936 to 1949 and the IUE from 1949 to 1955 are significant, because these unions represent the principal spokesmen for the workers in the electrical manufacturing industry. The infiltration of the communistic element into the UE in

1941 with the resulting ousting of the president James B. Carey had an adverse effect on the union and its wage policies. The expulsion of the UE from the CIO in 1949 was a major event in the annals of the labor movement, for it represented the first time in the history of American labor that an affiliated union was expelled from a federation on the grounds of Communism. The newly formed non-communistic union, the IUE-CIO, has made phenomenal advances since 1949 in both membership and economic gains, but in spite of its progress, it has not yet fully recovered the losses sustained by the workers under their old communist leaders. Another factor which impedes the economic progress of the IUE is the presence of the rival communist union, the UE. Although it is on the decline (less than 100,000 compared with 400,000 for the IUE), nevertheless some employers have played it off against the IUE in an effort to lower labor standards.

The principal wage policies of the UE from 1936-1949 and the IUE from 1949-1955 are as follows:

## I. *Wage Stabilization*

The unions desired to achieve wage stabilization in order to prohibit any employer from having an advantage in respect to labor costs. They realized that higher standards of living for their membership would be difficult to attain unless there was a degree of stability in the industry wage levels. This program included:

1. Key company bargaining—The unions have sought to obtain agreements first with the large chain companies (General Electric, Westinghouse, General Motors, Sylvania, Philco and RCA.) On the basis of these wage patterns, bargaining with the independent companies follows.
2. Establishment of uniform wage rates—As early as 1939 the UE sought to obtain uniform wage rates throughout the industry. At first the union attempted to achieve this goal on a small scale and chose the General Electric Company as a leader. In 1940–1941 the UE met with committees in the electrical industry for the purpose of setting minimum wages for various trades, classifications and operations.
3. Company-wide agreements—In the early 1940's many company-wide contracts were established which helped to effect uniformity in wage rates on a company basis.
4. Industry-wide bargaining—Although never achieved, the union in 1940 sought to win its demands from all the leading

companies as a group, followed by similar requests on the smaller, independent companies. In 1944 the UE adopted a resolution favoring industry-wide bargaining to help in the attainment of job security, minimum wages and other benefits.

5. Organizing the unorganized—The unions realized that it would be difficult to protect economic gains and union standards so long as unorganized shops prevailed. Efforts were constantly made to carry out this goal. During 1953–1955 the IUE has concentrated its organizing efforts in the Middle West, South and Far West.

6. Equal pay for equal work—The UE always sought this policy but never successfully until the Second World War. In a UE National War Labor Board case against the Westinghouse and General Electric companies, the Board recommended the narrowing of unreasonable wage differentials and establishing a single evaluation system for all jobs regardless of sex. During the postwar period some of the companies have reverted to their former policy of discrimination against women in wage rates. The IUE has attempted to wipe out this practice but as yet has not wholly succeeded.

7. Minimum contract requirements—In 1946 the union adopted a policy which forbade all locals to submit contracts to the union national office for ratification if they did not comply with minimum contract requirements. The IUE has continued this policy. In order to wipe out the lower wage standards of chain company plants in the South and rural sections, it has tried to set a $1.25 minimum wage rate throughout the industry, employer-financed minimum monthly pension, minimum health and welfare benefits and union security in the form of the union shop.

## II. *Raising the Level of Wages*

Even though the union was relatively weak during the depression of 1937-1938, it was able to prevent wage cuts among the larger companies and generally throughout the industry.

With the beginning of the defense program and its accompanying rise in living costs, the locals were urged to raise wages whenever price increases were experienced. The union felt that this sole criterion was insufficient, believing that its policy should ever aim to enlarge the workers' share in the national income. Substantial gains were realized in 1940 and 1941 before the wage freeze went into effect.

During the war the UE worked for effective stabilization of the economy but soon found that, although labor bore its burden through the wage freeze, other interests would not permit their profits to be curtailed. The UE opposition to the "Little Steel Formula" throughout the war was understandable.

Upon the end of hostilities the union strove for a substantial wage adjustment on the ground of a drop in the workers' take-home pay and the continued price inflation. The union demanded a two dollars a day increase. The formulation of a new government wage policy permitting an 18½ cents increase in wages brought a temporary appeasement to the UE.

With the deterioration in the workers' real wage the union soon sought another substantial increment in wages. This time the UE endeavored to get the cooperation of other unions in the basic industries in order to establish a more effective pattern for wage increases. On many occasions the union resorted to arbitration so as to achieve economic benefits for its locals according to the pattern established by the industry.

In 1947 the UE conducted a planned program to prepare both employer and workers for its wage demands. It counterattacked employer propaganda to show why the workers were entitled to wage advances. Ability to pay as revealed by high profits, the reduction in the workers' standard of living because of price rises, and the increased productivity of the employees were the arguments used to back up the demands. The union was successful in obtaining a 15 cents package settlement.

During 1948 the union again pushed for a substantial wage increase. A pattern settlement was effected when General Motors and UAW came to an agreement providing an 11 cents an hour increase with an additional three cents for the following year. This pattern became in turn the basis for a comparable settlement with the UE in its General Electric and Westinghouse agreements.

Chiefly because of the disruption among the electrical employees with the ousting of the UE from the CIO in 1949, the electrical workers were largely omitted in the fourth round increase in wages, pensions, and other fringe benefits. The IUE pledged that it would obtain future wage adjustments to raise the level of wages in the electrical industry to that of steel, automobiles and aircraft.

During the year 1950 the IUE in collaboration with the UAW won a significant victory in a five-year contract with the General Motors

Company. The unique features were a non-contributory pension of $100 a month, a cost-of-living escalator clause, and an annual improvement adjustment of four cents per hour. An agreement with the General Electric Company of 10 cents to 15½ cents wage increase, minimum pensions of $125 and other fringe benefits, set the pattern for Westinghouse and the other major producers for 1950.

During the Korean hostilities the IUE tried to win the approval of the Wage Stabilization Board in abolishing wage inequities, particularly in the radio and television industry, to obtain productivity adjustments which were not in its contracts at the time of the wage freeze, to raise the wage rates of workers receiving less than $1 an hour, and to secure more adequate pensions and insurance programs. Substantial wage increases were won by the IUE in 1951 and 1952. The wage gains for the most part took care of the increased cost of living and a portion of the increased productivity. The gains compared favorably with those in all manufacturing, in durable goods, and in non-electrical manufacturing. Wage gains were again obtained in 1953 but were somewhat smaller than the previous year.

### FRINGE BENEFITS, PENSIONS, HEALTH AND WELFARE BENEFITS

The IUE has insisted upon adequate pensions and health coverage for its membership. At the beginning of 1949 the pension and health insurance plans in the electrical manufacturing business were inadequate. The General Electric provided meager pensions while most of the other concerns had no pensions whatsoever for taking care of their old employees. The unions pressed for $100 to $125 minimum pensions including Social Security on reaching the age of 65 with 25 years of service and complete health insurance for the worker and his family. The cost of all the benefits were to be borne by the company.

Its first success was achieved in the General Motors agreement of 1950. The General Electric Company followed with a contributory minimum pension plan of $125 per month and a health insurance program. Similar gains were obtained from Westinghouse and other major chain companies. Some were financed by both employer and employee contributions, and others were borne entirely by the company. During 1952 and 1953 pension benefits were increased and a large number of the contracts extended hospital and surgical protection to the pensioners. Vast improvements were made in group insurance. Some plans included: company-paid life insurance up to one year's earnings, sickness and accident coverage amounting to two-thirds of the employee's gross pay with a maximum of $40 a week, Blue Cross and Blue Shield insurance, and life insurance of $1,000 for pensioners.

### INCENTIVE WAGES

The UE policy from 1936 to 1949 was to favor the straight day basis of pay, but during World War II incentive wage systems were approved, provided there was a guarantee against rate cutting. During the postwar years the union opposed the installation of incentive plans in plants that were on day work, and if a local wished to change from an incentive system back to the day rate basis, the union gave them assistance.

The IUE from the beginning insisted on an overhauling of the whole incentive wage system. It feels that some companies do not give the workers the full benefit of their increased effort. The systems are too complex and varied, making it difficult for the worker to understand them. The IUE is now making a study of the subject in order to guide future policy.

### ESCALATOR CLAUSES AND PROFIT SHARING

The IUE has favored both the quarterly cost-of-living and annual productivity adjustments in its contracts. Since the General Motors IUE agreement in 1950, an increasing number of IUE contracts have contained these provisions. The union feels that these clauses have been profitable to the workers in protection against inflation and assurance of an increase in real income in proportion to the advance in the nation's productivity.

Because the electrical manufacturing industry has been so profitable, the IUE believes that the workers have shared very inadequately in the fruits of their labor. Attention has been turned to profit-sharing plans in an effort to correct this maladjustment. The union has been successful in negotiating a number of profit-sharing plans in the independent companies.

### GUARANTEED ANNUAL WAGE

In arbitration cases before the National War Labor Board the UE tried to persuade the Board to include the guaranteed weekly wage in collective agreements. In a resolution at the 1946 convention, it recommended that annual wage guarantees should be incorporated in its contracts. The IUE has adopted the following principles for its guidance. All workers with a year's seniority be guaranteed a year-round employment at an adequate annual income. Those with less than one year of employment would obtain a graduated guarantee, but all workers would be allowed some guarantee after acquiring seniority. Responsibility for fulfilling the guarantee would rest upon the employer, but his liability would be limited by agreed-upon contributions to a trust fund. Unemployment compensation payments would be permitted to offset the employer guarantee. To protect workers not eligible for the guaranteed wage, the union would use its efforts to improve unemployment benefits and liberalize eligibility requirements. The IUE is urging its locals to study the guaranteed annual wage jointly with employers so as to develop a body of facts which may become the basis for later bargaining. In the 1955 negotiations the guaranteed wage became one of the major demands, but the union suffered a setback in the new five year contract with the General Electric Company which omitted supplementary pay provisions. However, the union may reopen the contract for review of a wage guarantee plan in 1958.

### IUE AND THE GENERAL ELECTRIC CONFLICT

Because the General Electric Company is the outstanding leader in the electrical manufacturing industry, the union feels that it should assume the leadership in respect to wages and working conditions. The company appears to be hostile to the IUE and is trying to break down the wage standards through attack upon the union. As a result, the independents are surpassing the General Electric in wage standards. The smaller companies are not happy about this trend and are objecting to widening the gap between the General Electric and themselves. This development makes it difficult for the union to continue its policy of raising standards. The 1955 contract appears to have done much to eradicate the bitterness and disharmony which had previously prevailed between the union and company. The marked improvement in wages, fringe benefits, and the absence of anti-unionism in the negotiations place the General Electric Company in a position of leadership in the industry.

Part Five

# SUMMATION

CHAPTER TWELVE

# Implications of the Guaranteed Wage

It seems relevant in the light of the autoworkers' achievement of a modified guaranteed annual wage and the intense public interest in this epochal principle to discuss the implications of the guaranteed wage.[1] The three areas that will be covered briefly are: the worker and the labor movement, the employer, and the economy.

## I. *The Worker and the Labor Movement—Economic Security*

The guaranteed wage will assure for the industrial worker for the first time a considerable degree of protection against a drastic shrinkage in his weekly and yearly income. Under most state laws, unemployment benefits are "shockingly low." In 1954 the average maximum benefit was $27 per week; the average weekly benefit, $23.58; the average potential duration of benefits, 22 weeks; the average duration of benefits, 10 weeks; and the duration for workers who exhausted their benefits, 19 weeks.[2] Although weekly benefits for total unemployment under our unemployment compensation system rose from $20.48 in 1949 to $24.93 in 1954, the ratio of benefit payments to weekly earnings of manufacturing workers has dropped from 37.3 per cent to 34.8 per cent during the same period.[3] It is apparent that the dissatisfaction with our present unemployment compensation program is an important factor in labor's demand for the guaranteed wage.

### SOCIAL POSITION OF THE WORKER

If the guarantee of wages is ultimately placed on a yearly basis, it would substitute payment on a weekly and monthly basis for compensation by the hour. This fundamental change in the nature of wage payments would sever the last link separating the factory

275

worker from the white-collar or salaried employee. The latter class has always received a full week's salary and a full year's income, regardless of daily or seasonal fluctuations in business. The bridging of this last gap by the factory worker will definitely place him in the so-called middle-class group. Daniel Bell, in a recent issue of *Fortune*, believes this is the historic import of the UAW negotiations this year.[4]

EXTENSION OF THE GUARANTEED WAGE

The guaranteed wage may ultimately be expected to become the pattern for the mass-production industries in the United States. The steelworkers are technically bound to wage increases for 1955–1956, but they have already gone on record for the inclusion of the guaranteed wage in June 1956.

In the electrical equipment industry the guaranteed wage is not likely to be an important objective of the IUE until 1958. At that time the IUE–General Electric five year contract may be opened for review and negotiation on the guaranteed wage. Since the General Electric Company is the leader in the industry, it is not likely that the IUE can secure the guarantee from other companies.

In the rubber industry the guaranteed wage has been under study by both management and the United Rubber Workers. Although not an issue in the 1955 negotiations, the union is expected to press for it in the next year's agreements.

The packing house workers have been discussing the guaranteed wage for several years and have formulated a plan which they believe will fit the industry. However, the union did not ask for its inclusion in the 1955 negotiations.

In farm machinery the UAW has already obtained a guarantee in its contracts with the International Harvester and Allis-Chalmers companies. Because of its successful negotiation with these leaders, the guarantee may be expected to embrace the entire industry.

Other mass-production industries which are in line for the guaranteed wage are: aluminum, chemical, aircraft, auto-parts, glass, and the maritime industry. The CIO–Glass, Ceramic and Silica Workers have negotiated plans with the leading companies which follow closely the automobile plan. The CIO National Maritime Union on the East and Gulf Coast recently negotiated a modified guaranteed plan which is similar to that of Ford and General Motors.

In some mass-production industries the guaranteed wage is not likely to be demanded for some time. Many knotty problems must be solved before it becomes feasible. About all that can be expected from the textile industry, for example, is the maintenance of wages, with some exceptions, owing to depressed conditions for a number of years. In the garment industry, the many small concerns and seasonal and style factors, especially in ladies' garments, impede the establishment of the guaranteed wage. The ILGWU recognizes that much study is required before the guaranteed wage can become applicable to the industry.

The shipbuilding, and to a lesser degree the aircraft industry, are not likely to be vulnerable to the guaranteeed wage. These industries are extremely fluctuating and dependent on government contracts to a large extent. A severance wage or dismissal wage has been advanced as a substitute.

In the construction industry the guarantee of wages has not been sought, nor does it seem likely to be. In most sections of the country construction is subject to weather hazards. Workers expect to be idle during the winter season. However, the problem has been met to some extent by the high wage rates which enable the worker to save enough while he is working to carry him over the slack season. To a considerable degree the same holds true for the mining industry.

In conclusion, most mass-production industries are likely to have some form of guaranteed wage in the coming years. However, depressed conditions and wide variation in production preclude a few industries for an indefinite time from the guaranteed wage.

### LABOR'S SHARE IN THE NATIONAL INCOME

Some people believe that the guaranteed wage is just another device by which labor will obtain in a disguised form a larger percentage of the national income. It is important to note that the guaranteed wage may be a substitute for some other form of wage increase such as more fringe benefits or a higher basic wage rate. If that is true, then labor is not gaining any more in its total distributive share. However, union leaders are skillful traders, and they may seek the guaranteed wage partly because through it they can obtain a higher income than through other demands. Although certain groups may increase their economic position through the guaranteed wage, on the whole, it is not likely to increase the proportionate share going to labor but rather represents a change in the character of wage increases. Studies by

Kuznet and others indicate a marked change toward equality of income since 1929.[5] The improved position especially in the lower income groups is undeniable. It is probable that the guaranteed wage will help to strengthen the financial position of this segment of the working population.

### THE DISTRIBUTION OF INCOME BETWEEN LOW-SENIORITY AND HIGHER-SENIORITY EMPLOYEES

The guaranteed wage plan will probably benefit more those most likely to be laid off, namely, the low-seniority workers, although the Ford and General Motors plans have built-in arrangements that recognize the seniority principle. In case of a severe contraction in business, the higher-seniority employee would gain more. In the Ford plan, and to a similar extent in General Motors', the high-seniority employee accumulates credit units at a higher rate during the first two years than do low-seniority workers. Secondly, the number of credit units to be exchanged for a weekly benefit is fewer for high-seniority workers.

Although the automobile companies have recognized an obligation to the older employee during the past few years, workers with a seniority of 30 years or more have lost their jobs permanently through abandonment of plants. Others with equally high seniority rating have been laid off temporarily for as long as ten consecutive weeks or more because of declining sales; while other workers experienced a short work-week of three or four days alternating, over extended periods, with weeks of complete idleness.[6]

With the rapid advance of automation and management's desire for decentralization and the use of new plants, the high-seniority worker cannot look forward to the security which he may have enjoyed at one time. Since inexperienced workers can be used as efficiently as the older workers with mechanized manufacturing processes, management may prefer the inexperienced worker for automatic operations.[7]

Before a conclusion can be reached on whether one group of workers will gain over another under the guaranteed wage, experience culled from the guaranteed wage plans of many companies and industries is needed. Much will depend on the stability of an employer's production and employment.

Will the guaranteed wage tend to freeze employees to the guar-

## MOBILITY OF LABOR

anteeing employer and prevent a rational adjustment of the labor force which is necessary to the maximization of production? Murray Latimer's study of firms under a guaranteed wage shows that more than half of the companies experienced a substantial reduction in the rate of labor turnover. This does not mean that the mobility of labor would drop to a point where it became dangerously inflexible. Such a danger would be prevented by: 1) the employer's desire to eliminate any labor reserve which is normally under-employed, 2) the use of public employment offices to transfer excess labor to suitable jobs. These safeguards should prevent an uneconomical limitation to the mobility of labor.[8]

The Ford and General Motors plans provide built-in provisions which mitigate against immobility. First, they give limited guarantees on the length of time the worker may be eligible to draw supplemental benefits. Secondly, laid-off workers must be available for work with other employers.

Many times the immobility of labor is caused by barriers imposed by employers to hiring qualified available workers. For example, in the automobile industry workers laid off by one company cannot get a job in another company, because they probably will return to their former employer. The UAW-Ford and General Motors plan will help to overcome these employer barriers to labor mobility. The laid-off workers will be required to accept suitable work offered them, and employers in the same area, if they need additional laborers, will be glad to hire them. The original employer is relieved of all or part of the cost of the guarantee due the worker, depending on the level of the worker's earnings. The guaranteed wage, instead of being an impediment to mobility, will actually increase it.[9]

### EMPLOYEES' INCENTIVE

Employers sometimes assert that if the pay to the laid-off worker equals or approximates that of employment, it will destroy his incentive to seek a job. In other words, society will place a premium on idleness. This argument was also used to attack our present unemployment compensation system. The fact is that the majority of Americans are eager to find useful employment and an opportunity for individual success. Our experience under the unemployment compensation system has shown that when jobs became available in the 1940's and 1950's, the ten million or more unemployed in the 1930's found jobs and many additional workers became members of the labor force.[10] According to statistics compiled by the U.S. Labor Department's Bureau of Employment Security, on the whole the unemployed do look for suitable work. In the April-June period of 1954 there were only 23,784 unemployed persons who refused jobs and were denied compensation on this ground. These people made only an infinitesimal fraction of the 62 million employed and even the 2.7 million without jobs.[11]

## II. *Employer Effects—Impact on Cost*

One of the principal objections to the guaranteed wage is the added cost to the employer. Many concerns fear the burden will be so great as to cause bankruptcy. This criticism seems illogical after a careful study of the UAW-Ford and General Motors plans and those prepared for the steel and electrical industries. In these plans the employer's liability is definitely limited. The liability of Ford and General Motors is the maximum amount of their contribution to the reserve fund. Should the reserve fund be depleted, then the guarantee will cease until the reserves are again restored.

Another check on the cost burden is the provision for reduction in the total amount of the employer's contribution into the reserve fund in event of declining sales, etc. During periods of business contraction the number of people actively at work in the company would tend to decrease; therefore, the employer's payroll contribution to the trust fund would diminish.

The incentive given under the guaranteed wage to maintain steady employment will also operate to reduce costs to the employer. Once the maximum limit of reserve funds is established, the employer will not need to add to the funds if he is successful in maintaining steady employment. Under the Ford and General Motors plans as well as the original UAW plan, the aim is to give the employer an incentive. They are based on the premise that the employer faced with the possibility of having to pay idle workers will do everything possible to provide productive work for them. Those who like to base their reasoning on theory, can refer to the marginal productivity theory of wages. Professor Seymour Harris says that, under the guaranteed wage, "the employer taking into account both marginal costs (estimating otherwise idle labor that has to be compensated as zero cost) and marginal revenue (inclusive of losses due to the decline in prices associated with additional output) will be tempted to use otherwise idle labor. So long as marginal revenues exceed marginal costs (thus estimated), he should expand output. This is to say, there would be a special incentive to keep workers on the payrolls."[12]

If management can successfuly plan its work so as to provide regular employment for the working force, much of the criticism against the guaranteed wage would disappear. That management has been irresponsible in planning for steady employment is attested by the Henderson Report on the auto industry in 1935.[13] Although the motor companies have moved a long way since the 1930's in reducing the period of unemployment caused by model changes, the human costs are still neglected for profits in scheduling production. Although the UAW warned the auto companies in 1953 against producing the expected year's output during the first half of the year, management did not heed the union's advice. As a result, it was necessary to recruit additional workers from other parts of the country in order to take care of the feverish production. After a few months of work, not only were the temporary workers released because of a decline in sales, but the regular employees joined the ranks of the unemployed.[14] This is not to infer that all the companies are equally guilty for irresponsible production scheduling. Mr. Ernest R. Breech, chairman of the board of the Ford Motor Company, recently said: "It has been Ford policy for years to stabilize production and employment, to minimize layoffs through better planning and to use overtime pay to meet production peaks rather than hire temporary workers."[15]

What are some of the methods management can use to stabilize production and employment? Some of the techniques include: 1) improved production scheduling, 2) the creation of annual markets for seasonal items through the use of advertising, 3) development of new products to balance decline in sales of others, 4) expansion of markets for already established products, 5) more careful forecasting of sales which requires careful analysis of available government statistics, 6) intelligent personnel policies. The last requirement involves careful estimates of employment needs, training the labor force for greater versatility, interdepartment and interplant transfers, balancing overtime against undertime, union-management cooperation, etc. The adoption of the guaranteed wage will stimulate business planning on all phases of the concern and the industry. Economic intelligence will be increasingly sought. This should mean a much larger role for the technicians, economists and social scientists.

Assuming the worst, namely, that the employer can exercise little control over the stabilization of jobs within his plant, it does not necessarily mean that wage guarantees are impracticable from the cost standpoint. The success of a guaranteed plan for this type of concern would depend largely on three factors. First, the ability of its principal customers to stabilize production is important. For example, if the automobile manufacturers are successful in stabilizing production throughout the entire year, this will help to smooth out fluctuations in the sales of the auto parts producers, the machine tool producers, and myriad other concerns dependent upon the motor-car business. Secondly, purchasing power must be sustained and expanded throughout the economy. The more widespread the guaranteed wage program becomes, the greater will be its potential effect in bolstering purchasing power. The third factor is the government's success in controlling the business cycle.

It is difficult to estimate the costs of the guaranteed wage with any precision. The Latimer report shows that the cost depends upon many factors such as benefits offered, period of service required for workers to become eligible for the guarantee, limits imposed on overtime work, the attrition rate, fluctuations in number of employees under the guarantee, taxes saved, etc. The study represents one of the most reliable analyses of the costs of the guaranteed wage ever made. It was based on a five-year period 1937-1941 and was obtained from an analysis of 47 cases under three benefit schedules. The plan which guaranteed 40 hours a week for 52 weeks for all full-time employees with three months of service showed variations in cost from .4 per cent of actual pay rolls per year to 33 per cent, with an average of 10 per cent. The report points out that if the amount of the guarantee is limited, it will obviously reduce costs to a desired level. Through careful selection of limitations to meet those conditions under which excessive costs arise, it is possible to reduce the cost of the guarantee within reasonable levels and still maintain the maximum level of benefits under all conditions. Following this course of action, Latimer reduced the cost to less than an average of six per cent annually for even the highest cost cases.[16]

According to Professor Harris, if it is assumed that unemployment does not exceed the average of the low levels of the last 15 years and that the guaranteed wage provides benefits equal to wages, the cost would be roughly about three times that of unemployment compensation, or about 4½ per cent of payrolls plus one-half per cent for other items such as longer periods of idleness covered under a guaranteed plan, less strict disqualifications, elimination of waiting periods, etc. "But even if workers are covered for a year, the costs will not necessarily be raised by 52/19 (the numerator being the number of weeks covered by the guaranteed wage and the denominator, the average number of weeks covered prior to exhaustion of benefits under unemployment compensation in 1953), but some allowance must be made for the longer period covered under the guaranteed wage."[17] Harris suggests that one per cent additional cost should be secured for this factor, making a total of about six per cent (4½ plus 1 plus ½) of the payroll.

Employer costs, after the temporary expense involved in creation of the original reserve fund, might be considerably reduced if the unemployment compensation laws were amended to increase benefits and extend their duration. With the increasing spread of the guaranteed wage, the state laws are certain to be liberalized as was the case with old age and survivors insurance. Other changes in legislation suggested by Mr. Latimer that would assist in reducing employers' cost of the guaranteed wage are: 1) amendment of corporation income taxes to permit: a) deduction of corporation income tax against guaranteed wage costs, b) carrying back and carrying forward of guaranteed wage costs, c) exemption from taxation of payments into reserve funds to cover guaranteed wage costs if required standards are met; 2) amendment of the Fair Labor Standards Act to allow employer exemption from penalty-pay requirements up to a maximum of 2,180 annual hours;* 3) amendment of state wage

---

* The Fair Labor Standards Act as amended in 1949 now partially exempts from the overtime requirements certain workers employed under an agreement for the payment of guaranteed wages made by a labor union which has been certified by the National Labor Relations Board as representative of the workers. The agreement must provide either: 1) that no employee should be employed more than 1040 hours during any consecutive 26-week period, or 2) not more than 2240 hours during any consecutive 52-week period. In the latter case, the worker must be guaranteed not less than 1840 and not more than 2080 hours of work during the period. The employee must be paid overtime for all hours worked in the year in excess of the guaranteed number.

payment laws to permit holding back of overtime wage by employers operating guaranteed wage plans with properly certified unions.[18]

A system of reinsurance may be a means of reducing costs of the company guarantee, using the principle involved in lowering the employer cost of the risks against fire, etc. It is less expensive for a company to pay premiums to an insurance company for protection against fire loss to its various plants than to put the money aside in its treasury for this purpose. In the same way, a company would need less in its guaranteed wage reserve fund, if there is a pooled fund upon which it may draw in the event of large layoffs. However, some employers may not want to assume the liability of unemployment of their competitors. If the guaranteed wage becomes widespread, the government might establish and manage a reinsurance scheme.

The cost of the guaranteed wage would obviously be easier to carry in growing industries than in declining ones. In industries susceptible to large cyclical instability or secular declines, it might be necessary to set a limit of payment or a percentage of payrolls using the average annual cost of the whole cycle instead of just one year. In very seasonal industries higher rates of pay may have to be made to compensate the worker for losses in idle periods.[19]

The question is often raised about the marginal producers, or those small employers operating close to the margin. Will they be able to absorb the added cost? If they are already operating at cost and are unable to pass on the added costs in higher prices, the unions may have to exempt them or tailor their demands to each situation. However, the unions should not be expected to subsidize management inefficiency. Union-management cooperation may play an important role in increasing production as exemplified in the garment industry. The UAW last year demonstrated that it is ready to alter its policies in the case of the Studebaker Company by agreeing to lower wages. What may happen in many cases is a continuation and even a hastening of the trend of smaller companies to merge into larger and more efficient operating companies.

### MECHANIZATION AND AUTOMATION

Some critics believe that the guaranteed wage will impede the introduction of technological improvements, because the displacement of workers will add more to the employers' total cost than is offset by the reduced labor costs. This may well be true for the short run and for periods of business decline. Harris says, "There is something to be said for slowing down technological change when the costs of adjustment are heavy."[20] Owing to bearing part of the costs of displacing the worker, the employer may make fewer improvements in the depression periods. In periods of prosperity there is less risk in rapid technological changes, because the displaced workers will soon be absorbed into the working force. The UAW confirms Harris's belief that the guaranteed wage will serve as a regulator of technology. Management is likely to avoid the introduction of automation in times of major layoffs and, conversely, increase automation in periods of business expansion.[21] Weinberg says that, except during periods of depression, the reductions in the labor requirements of a single firm from technological improvements rarely occur at rates too fast to be completely offset by the usual attrition of the labor force through quits, deaths, retirements, etc.[22]

The guaranteed wage may also affect the employer's geographical location of new investments to replace the old plants. The desire to minimize the guaranteed costs for the workers laid off in the abandoned plants might induce the employer to relocate the new plant within accessible distance from the workers' homes.[23] The guaranteed wage is a probable deterrent to employer irresponsibility to his old employees and to the community which has made it possible for him to carry on his business. Ghost towns through the New England region attest to the unequal contest between employers' profits and accountability to the community.

## III. The Effects of the Guaranteed Wage on the Economy

### BUSINESS EXPANSION

Will the guarantee of wages deter expansion in business? If the guarantee imposes a heavy liability on the employer, making the payroll a truly fixed cost, it is possible there might be a slowing down of the upward secular trend of business. An examination of the Ford and General Motors plan, or any of the proposed union plans, indicates that the employer's maximum liability is limited to a relatively small percentage of his total working force. There is provision for a gradation in the guarantee of benefits and the length of time for which an employee is eligible to draw benefits. This gradation is based on the length of the employee's employment. Workers in a new company or plan would have a relatively low guarantee right.

The total amount of dollars liability assumed by the employer is another limit on the fixed costs of the guaranteed wage. In the Ford and General Motors plan the amount is equivalent to the reserve fund. Although it must be replenished if it drops below its stipulated maximum, the company is not liable for more than a definite amount.

Another cushion to the employer's fixed costs under the guarantee is the limitation of the employer's liability as a percentage of his current payroll. This is important, because the cost of the guarantee during periods of substantial layoffs is as variable as the payroll itself. The guarantee of wages under the Ford and General Motors plan includes this feature. The guarantee of wages is therefore unlike such fixed costs as interest, managerial salaries, depreciation, property taxes and many other costs incurred in expansion of business.

### EFFECTS ON PRICES

If the guarantee of wages is limited and there is a definite predictable cost as in the Ford and General Motors plan and the proposed steel and electrical industries' programs, it is probable that the costs can be absorbed by the employer. This is particularly true in the automobile and electrical industries where competition is keen.

The guaranteed wage is essentially no different from an increase in wages, pensions or other fringe benefits in its effect on higher wages. It is a substitution for some other form of employee compensation which the union would seek if it did not choose this demand.

Undoubtedly, a powerful check to increased prices will be management's drive to lower costs in order to balance increased labor expenditures. The speeding up of automation and other labor-saving techniques will be noticeable. Already this is indicated by the announcement in 1955 of General Motors to spend $500,000,000 for capital expansion, the bulk of which is to be spent for labor saving equipment.[24]

Mr. Leland Hazard believes the guaranteed wage will mean higher prices, because the employer pays for non-production. His assumption is based on the premise that the employer will not be able to use all workers continually on his machines.[25] This does not take into account the added incentive of the employer under the guaranteed wage to maintain uninterrupted production and to use his workers efficiently. Ford Motor Company officials have stated that the Ford plan will stimulate the stabilization of employment, because so long as the trust fund is at its maximum funding level, the company ceases to contribute additional amounts to it.[26]

There is little empirical evidence in the shifting of business taxes. If we consider the guaranteed wage payments similar to a payroll tax, the published consensus concludes that the tax will be borne by the worker, but this belief is not unanimous.[27] In the short run, capital may pay the tax, particularly if the workers are unionized. In the long run, the tax, by reducing the returns on capital in the industry subject to the guaranteed wage, may discourage new investment and cause prices to rise or wages to fall. According to Harris, when the guaranteed wage is widely established, the tax will be borne by the workers or (and) consumers, but management and capital may share a portion.[28]

#### STABILIZATION OF THE ECONOMY

It is the opinion of the writer that a wide adoption of the guaranteed wage can contribute to stabilization of the economy, provided that the plans are tailored to fit the peculiarities of each industry and include provisions for limited liability and for augmenting reserves.

In our highly productive society there is danger of imbalance between the ability to create wealth and the inability to consume wealth sufficiently fast because of inadequacy of purchasing power of most people. This is particularly true during peacetime when the insatiable demands of war diminish. As wages and salaries constitute the largest part of the national income, their stabilization will have a powerful influence on the maintenance of consumer expenditures. The regularity of consumer spending will be most directly felt in sustaining the demand for consumer goods, but the repercussions may be much greater. The bolstering of consumer spending may stimulate the demand for investments in consumer and capital goods.

The maintenance of purchasing power will not necessarily assure the constancy of demand in all areas of the economy. Consumer preference is fickle and causes fluctuations in the demand for various products. However, the guaranteed wage is likely to stimulate management planning to maintain and/or increase consumer preference for the company's product. Management will do everything in its power to cater to the consumer if it must compensate idle workers under a guaranteed wage plan.

The influence of the guaranteed wage on key industries also helps to stabilize the economy. The automobile, agricultural implement, and electrical industries are strategic in the economy. If these industries, under the impetus of the guaranteed wage, are successful in sustaining their production, they will influence steel, glass, rubber, textiles, auto parts, tool machines, and, in turn, affect raw materials industries, such as agriculture, mining, etc.

The ramifications of the leveling of production in the strategic industries and the maintenance of purchasing power are difficult to evaluate in a dynamic economy. We have had no experience to show the effect of sustained consumer spending and the stabilization of production of key industries on consumer demand and investments.

The accumulation of trust funds under the guaranteed wage plan may also have an important stabilizing effect on the economy. According to the pattern of the Ford and General Motors plan, the reserves will probably be invested in marketable U.S. government securities. The accretion of the funds would represent a transfer of money which normally might be spent or saved by individuals or reinvested by business for expansion. At any rate, the funds would be less active than in the hands of workers and business firms. The result may be to moderate the rate of consumption and investment which might temper the boom in periods of business prosperity. In the event that funds are built up in a period of considerable unemployment, they might hamper business expansion. However, this consequence could be counterbalanced by a liberal credit policy of the banking system or through fiscal policies of the government, or both. In periods of downswing the disbursement of benefits would have a probable salutary effect. The receipt of money by laid-off workers would tend to maintain consumer expenditures, reduce the amount of dissaving and help meet installment and other fixed expenses.

It must be recognized that the guaranteed wage is not a panacea for maintaining full production and employment, but it may be an important stabilizer in the economy, particularly as more industries embrace supplementary unemployment benefits.

## CHAPTER THIRTEEN

# Conclusions

The amorphous mass of material and the length of the period covered in the study make it difficult for the writer to present conclusions. Summaries have nevertheless been given at proper places in the preceding chapters. This chapter indicates broad trends and major findings and also incorporates some personal observations of the writer.

I.

Labor's wage policies in the United States during the twentieth century as expressed through the channels of the organized labor movement have been largely influenced by many factors. Among them are the needs of the workers, the type of unionism represented by the AFL and the CIO, the extent of union organization, the caliber of union leadership, the length of the period of collective bargaining, the character of the industry, i.e., size of producing units and nature of competition, the demand characteristics of the product, promotion of membership in the union, stage in the business cycle, the effects of war and its aftermath. The writer has touched on all of these factors, but the emphasis has been on the *needs* of the workers.

The wage policies have assumed the following patterns:

1. Improvement of economic position of worker through high wages;
2. Stabilization of wages. This goal is designed to effect stability of wage structure, to make for competitive parity in labor costs among employers, and to bring about equalization of wages among workers. Stabilization of wages is based on the premise that both the worker and the employer prefer stability in the wage structure;
3. Reduction of hours to give worker more leisure and to allocate available work among employees;

289

4. Overtime pay after standard work-day. This policy is designed to encourage the hiring of additional workers because of penalty rates;

5. Fringe benefits—vacations with pay, shift differentials in wage rates, double-time pay rates for Sunday and holidays, pensions, health and welfare benefits, guaranteed annual wage, dismissal pay;

6. The achievement of industrial democracy. The objective is to give the worker a voice in the determination of wages and working conditions. It reveals itself not only through the channels of collective bargaining but also through union-management cooperation;

7. Social objectives. This goal is an integral part of wage policies, because it aims at raising the working and economic standards of all people. Labor legislation, such as the Wagner Act, Fair Labor Standards Act, Social Security Act, is intended to accomplish this end.*

II.

The economic and social conditions of the working class during the first two decades of the twentieth century have been well documented by historians and labor economists. Wages were deplorably low until the First World War. Although there was a small gain in real wages, most of the advance was wiped out by the rising cost of living. The average industrial worker was unable to meet a $700–$900 subsistence family budget. Wages advanced markedly during the First World War, but the cost of living rose faster so that real earnings experienced a severe decline. It was not until after the war that wages finally caught up with prices. During the depression of 1920–1921 prices dropped much more than wages with resulting substantial gain in real wages for those who were employed.

In the intervening years 1922–1930 money wages rose slowly while living costs remained relatively stable with resulting gain in real income.

---

* John T. Dunlop in his *Wage Determination Under Trade Unions*, Macmillan Company, N.Y., 1944, pp. 48–50, mentions two additional union wage policies namely: control of the rate of introduction of technical improvements and the control of the entrance to trades. The writer has touched on union control of technological improvements in Chapter XII, "Implications of the Guaranteed Wage." No reference has been made to union control of entrance to trades because of the paucity of material on this subject for the unions examined.

Labor failed to share proportionately with the other factors of production in the increase in the nation's productivity from 1900–1930. The lag widened markedly in the first postwar depression era. The working conditions of the employees at the turn of the century and through the next twenty years were equally as bad as wages. The 10-hour day and 60-hour week were standard in most establishments, and it was not unusual to find a 12-hour day and 70- or 72-hour work week.

The worker had practically no protection from the vicissitudes of life. Pensions, health and sickness insurance were unknown. Paid vacations were nonexistent. There was practically no security against unemployment unless the worker was fortunate enough to enjoy seniority rights protected by a union contract.

Democratic participation by the worker in the establishment of his wage and working conditions was only rarely permitted. The worker, under these conditions, could be likened to a slave who took orders from his master.

### III.

The American Federation of Labor practiced the following wage policies from 1900–1930. At the turn of the century the Federation placed great emphasis on the reduction of working hours. It appealed to the employers for a standard eight-hour day and worked through legislative channels to seek federal and state laws to attain this goal. To raise and protect the economic standards of the workers, the AFL continually pressed for unionization of the workers, restriction of the power of the courts to issue injunctions against labor, opposition to the employment of convict labor in lieu of free labor, resistance to the use of child labor, promotion of the union label. AFL wage pronouncements or slogans were soon in circulation. The "fair wage" and "living wage" were used interchangeably. A fair day's work for a fair day's pay became the rallying call of several affiliated AFL unions. In a number of railway wage arbitration cases from 1910 to 1912 the demand of the unions was for a "living wage." The "living wage" was first recognized as a subsistence level wage, and it was believed that the payment of this minimum was a responsibility of both the employer and society. The labor movement pressed for state minimum wage laws in its efforts to attain this subsistence standard. The "living wage" principle received its greatest emphasis during the period from 1916 to 1920. It was during these years that real wages deteriorated because of the advancing cost of living. During the First World War the "living wage" was one of the principles that guided the National War Labor Board in administering its wage policies. At this time the "living wage" was not considered a subsistence wage, but one which provided a modest comfort and health level.

In 1919 the AFL expanded the concept of the "living wage" into a new principle, the "cultural wage." This wage would provide a worker and his family not only a modest comfort and health level, but sufficient savings to take care of the workers' needs in old age and develop the cultural and spiritual side of his personality.[1] The Brotherhood of Railway Trainmen associated the cultural wage with its demand for a shorter work-week. In asking for a six-hour day in 1937, the brotherhood believed that it would provide the worker with more leisure to develop the cultural side of life. It was also felt that society would obtain cultural values from providing more jobs for the idle.[2]

During 1925–1926 the AFL adopted the slogan of the "social wage." This wage statement appeared to be a reaction against the tying of wages to the cost of living. Labor worked to advance its standard of living, and the "social wage" with its emphasis on wages linked to productivity was conducive to this objective.

## IV.

In the period from 1930 to 1935 the organized labor movement in the United States underwent a tremendous growth in membership and in power. In the 12 years from 1936 to 1948 trade union membership increased from less than 4 million to approximately 16 million. In 1935 the Congress of Industrial Organizations was formed which represented a new trend in industrial unionism. Starting with only eight unions and a little over a million members, it expanded to more than 30 unions with about six million members. The AFL witnessed a growth from three million members in 1935 to over ten and a half million by 1955. Favorable government labor legislation in the 1930's and the long period of business prosperity beginning in 1939 were important factors in this growth. Concomitant with the expansion in membership was a growth of power that greatly affected labor's wage policies.

During the Great Depression the AFL's wage policy took on several facets. The maintenance of wages was the first demand. The AFL was opposed to the tying of wages to the cost of living and stressed the basing of wages on productivity. The Federation felt that lack of sufficient purchasing power in the hands of the masses during the 1920's was one of the causes of the recession. What was needed were higher wage earnings. The Federation demanded the shortening of the work-week so that more people could be absorbed into jobs provided that the total weekly earnings were not reduced.

The NRA was welcomed by the AFL as an experiment in improving the relations between business and labor. Through cooperation between business and government higher minimum wage rates were established in industrial codes.

From 1933 to the recession of 1937–1938 the laborer's economic position showed marked improvement. Although living costs advanced, hourly and weekly earnings increased more. Wages experienced a spurt in 1936–37 with the improvement in business conditions and through the wage drives of the newly-formed CIO unions in the basic industries. Many enterprises increased wages to forestall union organization.

Both the AFL and CIO insisted on the maintenance of wage rates during the business recession of 1937–1938. The CIO laid much stress on the purchasing power theory of wages. Labor's opposition to wage reduction was largely successful, as wage rates remained firm. However, real weekly earnings deteriorated owing primarily to the shorter work-week.

The stimulus of the defense program in 1939 was reflected in a substantial gain in money wages and in real earnings. In spite of the improvement in labor's economic position, the AFL and CIO were not satisfied. The AFL purported to show that, according to budgetary studies, the vast majority of wage earners did not earn enough to support a family on a standard of health and efficiency. The AFL asked for an equitable sharing of the increased productivity. The CIO likewise demanded a larger share of the national income for its members.

At the beginning of the Second World War both the federations demanded equal sacrifice for all groups. With the freezing of wages in October 1942 and the issuance of the "Little Steel Formula" in May 1943, labor was deprived of further adjustment of wages through collective bargaining. Organized labor soon became hostile to the wage freeze as living costs advanced and profits increased. Labor demanded an elimination of the "Little Steel Formula" or its modification to more realistic conditions. The Bureau of Labor Statistics price index, it was contended, was no longer a reliable criterion of prices because of deficiences. Labor also used the purchasing-power argument to end the wage freeze. Higher wages were indispensable to assure mass purchasing-power after the end of the war.

Although labor was not successful in removing the "Little Steel Formula," it aided in establishing flexibility in the National War Labor Board's wage policies. The Board approved higher minimum wage rates to correct for substandard living conditions and granted certain fringe benefits.

The termination of the war resulted in a decline in the workers' take-home pay. Average weekly earnings in manufacturing dropped from $46.08 in 1944 to $44.39 in 1945 and $43.82 in 1946. Living costs spiraled upward with resulting loss in real weekly earnings. The federations demanded higher wages to preserve living standards. The purchasing-power argument was also used in the struggle for higher wages. It was claimed that more earnings were a *sine qua non* for full employment and prosperity. In addition to wage demands, the CIO placed much emphasis on pensions, health and welfare benefits.

With the emerging business recession in 1949 and the lowering of living costs, labor soft pedalled the cost-of-living argument and placed its major emphasis on pensions. It was believed that as long as the federal government's social security program failed to meet adequately the needs of retired workers, the employer should absorb the additional amount as a legitimate cost of doing business.

During the postwar period 1946-1949, average hourly wage rates in manufacturing advanced from $1.086 to $1.401 or 29 per cent. Weekly earnings rose from $43.82 to $54.92 or 25 per cent. The cost of living, on the other hand, witnessed a rise from 139.5 to 170.2 or 22 per cent. Weekly real earnings just barely maintained parity with living costs, and it was not until 1949–50 that any significant improvement in real wages was achieved. Labor's continued demand for higher wages is understandable when viewed with the shrinking purchasing power of the wage earners' dollar.

Unlike the first twenty years of the twentieth century, organized labor shared more equitably in the increased productivity from 1930 to 1955. Average real weekly earnings in manufacturing increased 91 per cent during this period while average real hourly earnings advanced 105 per cent. Assuming an average annual rise of 2½ per cent in the nation's productivity, organized labor's gain in real earnings more than outdistanced the overall increase in productivity.

Labor's share in the private national income from 1930 to the middle of the century exhibited considerable stability. During the depression years 1930–1933 labor's share increased from 51.1 per cent to 70 per cent while corporate profits were almost extinct. With the improvement in business, labor's share reached approximately 60 per cent in 1940. During the war years labor's share declined while corporate profits rose sharply. In the following postwar period labor's share again approached the 60 per cent level.

At the beginning of the Korean hostilities, the AFL and CIO opposed wage controls, but if, however, events proved that wage controls were necessary, adjustments were to be permitted for rising living costs, for wage inequities within and between industries, and for increases in productivity. With the establishment of a wage freeze in January 1951, labor objected to the Wage Stabilization Board's formula limiting general wage increases to 10 per cent above the levels of January 15, 1950. The objections were based on the following: 1) the invalidation of many existing agreements; 2) the disregard of increased living costs; 3) the inclusion of the costs of fringe benefits; 4) failure to provide adjustments in wages for inequities. The withdrawal of labor representatives from the Wage Stabilization Board, in protest of the Board's policies, led to some modification of its regulations. But dissatisfaction soon expressed itself over the Board's refusal to grant workers a share in increased productivity, its slowness in approving labor contracts, and the government's failure to curtail inflation. Labor felt it was bearing more than its share in the defense effort as evidenced by the sharp increase in profits in contrast to the deterioration in the standard of living. Real hourly and weekly manufacturing earnings, however, did not experience a decline during the Korean war period, but rather kept ahead of the cost of living. Profits enjoyed a spurt from 1949 to 1950, but thereafter declined because of heavier taxes.

With the cessation of the Korean war appearing imminent in the early part of 1953, labor felt that the end of hostilities would be accompanied by a decline in business activity and price levels. In the formulation of wage policies for 1953, the AFL and CIO decided to press for higher wages. Labor justified its demand on the premise that more purchasing power was needed to bolster the economy during the transitional period. Higher wages could be paid because of the increased productivity of the economy. In addition to more take-home pay, the CIO continued to seek improved pensions, health and welfare benefits, and the guaranteed annual wage.

v.

The following pattern is discernible in the wage policies of the affiliated unions:

I. *Improvement of economic position of workers through higher wages.*

The unions examined in this study appeared to be alert to the factors in the industry and the economy which affect wages and standards of living for their members. The International Ladies' Garment Workers' Union and the Amalgamated Clothing Workers of America have realized that the basic problems and sore spots in the industry had to be overcome before higher economic standards could be attained. Hence, they have been outstanding examples of unions that worked with management to prevent cutthroat competition between employers, to strengthen working standards in the industry, to achieve an equitable distribution of work and economies in production. Financial and technical aid has been given employers, and the unions have assisted in promoting the sale of union-made garments. A flexible wage policy has been evidenced in that they have not attempted to impose a single wage formula on the entire trade but instead have determined for each market and each branch of the trade the most advantageous terms. During periods of business recovery the unions have pressed for wage increases to keep wages at parity with living costs and to raise the worker's standard of living. They have succeeded in removing the garment workers from a depressed economic class, placing them on a level comparable with other non-durable manufacturing groups.

Unlike the garment industry, the paper industry has been relatively free from severe competition. Most producers have enjoyed increasing demand for their products, which have resulted in overtime for the worker. It has been the aim of the pulp and sulphite workers and the paper makers to keep the industry a leader in wage earnings, to raise the base rate in the South to the level of the West Coast, and to eliminate wage differentials between Canada and the United States. The brotherhoods have been cognizant of the increased productivity in the industry, the insatiable demand for paper products, and the high return on the employer's investment. Unlike many unions they have not followed the practice of tying wages to the cost of living or to productivity, but negotiate for what they can get. Protection against inflation has been assured through insistence on reopening clauses in their contracts.

The prosperous condition of the steel and automobile industries since 1939 has been reflected in the union demands for an increasing share for the worker. As a result, these two industries have been leaders in setting wage patterns for the economy. The unions have not hesitated to resort to the strike when all other means were exhausted.

The United Automobile Workers have been noted for their aggressive and intelligent wage policy. They have deplored the nickel-in-the-pay-envelope philosophy. The union believes it is necessary to enlarge the area of bargaining to encompass not only wages, but prices and profits. Unlike the steelworkers, the autoworkers have used the escalator clause in their contracts since 1948. It was believed that the cost-of-living escalator clause and the annual improvement adjustments would avoid the necessity for the workers to waste their energies every year to protect their real wages, and permit them to concentrate on the important objective of advancing the economic well-being of the membership. With the threatened downturn in prices in 1953, the UAW demanded that the employees retain a substantial amount gained through the cost-of-living escalation as a part of the workers' permanent base pay. It also sought an increase in its annual productivity adjustments. The steelworkers have opposed the use of escalator clauses, because they believe more substantial gains can be won by yearly bargaining over change in prices and productivity.

The textile industry, long considered substandard in respect to wages, has through the untiring efforts of the Textile Workers Union of America substantially raised the economic well-being of the workers. Suffering from the wage cuts in the recession of 1937–38, the union was successful in restoring the wage reductions in

1939. This represented the first time in the history of the industry that extensive wage increases had been negotiated. During the war years the union pressed the War Labor Board for increases in wages in those branches of the industry considered substandard. Its efforts proved successful, so that by the close of World War II wages in the textile industry more nearly approximated the prevailing wage levels throughout American industry. During the postwar years the union demanded wage increases comparable to the gains obtained in other industries. When negotiation resulted in failure, arbitration was resorted to and in some cases the use of the strike. The union has used cost-of-living escalator clauses in many of its contracts, and in a few cases annual improvement clauses were obtained. During the 1951–1954 textile depression, the union fought against wage reductions. With the exception of the New England cotton-rayon industry, its efforts proved successful.

In the electrical manufacturing industry, the UE, before its capture by Communists in 1941, consistently obtained a larger share in the earnings of the industry. With the ousting of James B. Carey from the presidency of the UE, the union program was diverted from that of fulfilling the needs of the workers to the advancement of the communistic cause. As a result, the electrical workers' wages began to lag behind those employees in the other basic industries. With the revocation of the UE charter by the CIO in 1949 and the formation of the IUE-CIO under the leadership of Carey, substantial progress has been made in raising the level of wages in the industry to that of steel, automobiles and aircraft. The IUE has favored the use of quarterly cost-of-living adjustments, annual productivity provisions, and profit-sharing plans. Many of its contracts contain one or more of these provisions.

## II. *Wage Stabilization*

Wage stabilization objectives have appeared of great importance to all of the unions. The reason for this is that the unions as well as employers desire competitive parity in labor costs and freedom from constant change in wages. The unions want to protect union standards and to achieve a degree of wage security for their members. They realize that if some employers have lower labor costs than others, cutthroat competition may occur which will result in lowering the wage levels of those employers paying the union wage scales.

The employer wants approximate parity in wage costs in order to assure continuation of profitable operations.

In the garment industry a breakdown of labor standards has been one of the chief concerns of the ILGWU and ACWA from the earliest period. They have fought for collective contracts with all employers establishing the preferential and the union shop, uniform wage scales and hours of work, premium pay, holidays, and the use of the union label. The ILGWU has sought to achieve some degree of wage parity between employers. It recognized that the jobber and manufacturer were indirectly the true employers of labor and should accept responsibility for labor conditions in the shops of the contractors and submanufacturers. The coat and suit branch of the women's garment industry achieved wage stabilization in 1933 under the NRA codes. In 1936 stabilization was finally achieved in the dress industry. As a necessary aid in stabilizing dresses, the union demanded and obtained a price settlement of garments on the jobbers' premises, the unit system of price settlement and a limitation of contractors. To accomplish the necessary stabilization of wages in the men's clothing industry, the ACWA sought standardization of labor costs. The union worked out a program whereby a definite total labor cost for the garment was established in a number of popular grades. Piece rates for different operations were agreed upon by the union with each employer. To prevent chiseling among employers and local unions, a stabilization department was established to provide for periodic examination of piece rates, labor costs, and earnings of workers.

In the paper industry the International Brotherhood of Pulp, Sulphite, and Paper Mill Workers and the International Brotherhood of Paper Makers have sought wage stabilization by: (1) the use of union wage scales, (2) extension of union organization and preferential union hiring, (3) multi-employer and key company bargaining, (4) the use of job analysis in setting standard rates of pay and in eradicating wage inequities, (5) the elimination of the North and South, South and West Coast, and Canadian–United States wage differentials.

In the steel industry and the automobile industry the United Steel Workers and the United Automobile Workers have used most of the techniques employed by the brotherhoods in the paper industry. The United Steelworkers have made remarkable progress in the reduction of geographical wage differentials and the equalization of wage rates between various classes of labor and the equalization of wage scales between competing companies. The union has sought industry-wide bargaining but has met the opposition of the industry. However, it has achieved practically the same results through key company bargaining, using the U.S. Steel Corporation as the leader. The United Automobile Workers have used General Motors as the pattern setter on most occasions.

The Textile Workers Union of America, like the garment workers' unions, has had to contend with an industry composed of many small producers with resulting keen competitive conditions. The use of non-union labor, particularly in the South, has been a sore spot. To facilitate wage stabilization it has followed the usual methods of uniform wage scales, extension of union organization, establishment of minimum wage rates, key company bargaining, guarantee of base rates for piece workers, and the establishment of minimum plant rates.

In the electrical manufacturing industry, the UE and IUE have sought stabilization of the wage structure through: extension of organization in the industry, establishment of minimum contract requirements, equal pay for equal work, uniform minimum wage rates for various trades, key company bargaining, company-wide agreements.

## III. *Fringe Benefits*

The labor movement paid little attention to fringe benefits prior to the Second World War. Although some progress was made in obtaining premium pay for the night shifts, paid vacations and holidays, these practices were by no means widespread. The wage freeze of the Second World War gave labor an opportunity to press for fringe benefits on the grounds that they were not payable in cash and therefore were not within the bounds of the wage freeze. The National Labor Relations Board decision of 1949 in the Inland Steel Case, giving approval to pensions for collective bargaining, was a tremendous stimulus to prompt unions in asking for these non-economic benefits.

The garment unions have been pioneers in health and welfare programs. Medical and health care was one of their first objectives, followed by vacations, death benefits and old age pensions. Both unions have established health centers in the principal sectors of their membership. The entire program of health and welfare benefits is now paid for by employer contributions. In an industry rarely providing full-time yearly employment before the Second World War, the unions gave employment guarantee plans their consideration. As far back as 1921, the ILGWU and the employers in the Cleveland area established an agreement providing for limited employment guarantees to the workers. From time to time other guaranteed wage plans have been negotiated on a small scale. The ILGWU is currently studying the subject for its possible application to the industry. The ACWA has not given the guaranteed annual wage high priority. It has preferred to work out various devices for effecting greater regularity of employment, etc. In the New York laundry branch and the journeyman tailors, the Amalgamated has negotiated a limited guarantee of employment.

The paper industry has been a leader in respect to fringe benefits. The brotherhoods were among the first unions to ask for vacations with pay. The majority of workers now enjoy: two-weeks' vacations with pay, six paid holidays per year, six days' sick leave with pay, three days off with pay for death in immediate family, hospitalization, health, accident, life insurance, and old age pensions. In some cases hospitalization and health benefits are extended to the entire family. During the Second World War the United Steelworkers obtained many benefits in the nature of vacations, improvements in holidays and shift provisions. After the war the union demanded a broad social security program including old age benefits, medical and hospitalization benefits, and the guaranteed annual wage. In 1949 the union placed pensions and welfare benefits at the top of its demands. It was successful in winning a non-contributory pension plan and a health and welfare benefit plan with equal division of cost between employer and employee. During the Korean hostilities the union obtained additional improvements in its welfare benefits. Because the steelworkers are still fearful of unemployment in their industry, the guaranteed annual wage has been an objective since World War II. Although the guaranteed wage was not pressed by the steelworkers in their 1955 contract, they have indicated that it will be included in 1956 spring negotiations.

The United Automobile Workers first sought a company-paid social security and pension system in 1946, but little progress was made until 1949. In that year the union gave pensions, health, and welfare benefits priority in its demands. Obstinacy on the part of Chrysler Corporation resulted in one of the longest and costliest strikes in the union's history. In 1950 Chrysler finally agreed to meet the social security package which had previously been given by several other auto producers. The UAW–General Motors agreement of 1950, which was shortly matched by the Ford Motor Company, provided an increase in pensions from $100 to $125 and a substantial increase in hospital and medical and group insurance plans. In 1953 maximum pensions were increased to $137.50 per month, and gains were also made in health and welfare benefits. In 1955 further liberalization was achieved in pensions and other fringe benefits. Maximum pensions, including social security, were raised to $237.80. The principle of vesting of pension rights was also added and is almost certain to be adopted in the other basic industries. The guaranteed annual wage, the most important demand in the 1955 negotiations, was won on a modified basis in the 1955–1957 three-year contract with General Motors and Ford.

In the textile industry the TWUA has made rapid progress in securing fringe benefits since its initial attempt in 1943. By 1946 about 230,000 textile workers were covered by hospitalization, surgical, accident, sickness and medical care benefits, all costs borne by the employers. In 1948 the union turned its attention to pensions for its aged workers and concluded several important agreements providing such benefits. Again in 1950 pensions providing at least $100 were set as a primary goal of the union. Progress was made in the achievement of this goal as witnessed in the negotiation of pension programs covering 60,000 members. In spite of the severe textile depression from 1951–1954 the union negotiated many improvements in pensions and health and welfare benefits. As usual the Southern mills have lagged behind the North in fringe benefits. The guaranteed annual wage has not been a demand of TWUA since the Second World War. The depressed condition of the industry and its lack of complete unionization has made its acceptance unrealistic.

In the electrical manufacturing industry, the UE turned its attention to winning fringe benefits during the Second World War. Although the union was unable to win group insurance to cover the major hazards of life, it was successful in obtaining improvements in vacations, holidays, and premium payments. The IUE has insisted upon an adequate program of social and welfare benefits. Its first success was achieved with the General Motors Corporation in 1950. The General Electric and Westinghouse followed with pension plans paying benefits of $125 a month and group insurance covering hospital, surgical, sickness and life. During 1952 and 1953 further improvements have been made in the area of fringe benefits.

Within recent years the IUE has given increasing attention to the guaranteed annual wage. It has formulated a tentative program to guide the union in exploratory talks with the employers. It is the hope that these joint discussions and studies will develop a body of facts which will later become the basis for the negotiation of a guaranteed wage plan.

## IV. *Industrial Democracy—Union-Management Cooperation*

The right of economic citizenship has been apparent in the wage policies of all the affiliated unions that have been studied. In some cases, this goal has been more apparent than in others. The objective assumes that workers want to participate in the determination of the conditions of their employment, to review these conditions and to share in their establishment. Collective bargaining is not enough. The worker wants to utilize the democratic procedure of group discussion of important problems in industry which affect his employment.

In the garment industry, union-management cooperation has been a keystone of the ILGWU and the ACWA wage policy. As already noted under wage stabilization procedures, the unions early demanded a voice in the industry. This policy has continued through the years to the beneficial interest of both workers and employers. The workers through their union have helped employers to promote efficiency and to solve many of their problems. The unions have furnished engineering service, promoted sales through extensive advertising, and have even lent financial aid to distressed concerns. They have succeeded in obtaining the right to send their own technicians in plants to study jobs and to determine normal production quotas, equitable piece rates and wage systems.

In the steel industry the United Steel Workers have welcomed opportunities to cooperate with management in solving problems. The union has been a pioneer among the CIO unions in cooperating with management. The union has assisted the industry in establishing wage stabilization through job description and classification. It has on several occasions modified its wage rates for companies in financial difficulties.

## V. *Social Objectives*

All the unions studied have given social objectives an important place in their wage policies. The ILGWU, ACWA, and TWUA have perhaps placed more emphasis on this goal than others. Operating in industries which are very highly competitive and where business turnover is high because of smaller capital requirements, these unions have actively sought legislation which would wipe out poverty among their membership and eliminate parasitic businesses. The ILGWU and ACWA pioneered for the adoption of the Fair Labor Standards Act. In recent years the textile workers and garment workers have sought amendments to the federal wage law to increase the minimum wage to more realistic levels. The ACWA has actively worked to raise state minimum wage laws in order to improve the economic position of workers in its more depressed branches such as laundry, cleaning and dyeing.

All the unions have sought amendment to the Federal Social Security laws which would substantially increase old age benefits and extend coverage to all people. They have felt that their crusade for employer-financed pensions would be an opening wedge in raising federal old age benefits. A national health insurance program has received the unions' wholehearted support. The unions believed their demand for employer-paid health insurance benefits would force the government to adopt adequate legislation. Other legislation demanded has included: effective price control and an equitable taxation system giving relief to lower-income groups.

### VI.

The criteria used by labor in support of its wage demands are varied, but a limited number has been used singly or in combination to achieve the desired objective. The following criteria have been favored: cost of living, productivity, ability to pay, comparable wage rates, purchasing-power doctrine, substandards of living, miscellaneous.

### 1. Cost of Living

This criterion has perhaps beeen more frequently advanced than any other. The reason for its prominence rests in part on the fact that the cost of living has been rising during most of the period since unions gained recognition in the mass-production industries.[3] The validity of the cost-of-living criterion rests on the ethical ground that the real wages of the worker should not be impaired by forces beyond his control.

During periods of rapid changes in prices the unions have given the cost-of-living principle priority over others. This was revealed during the First and Second World Wars, the post war periods 1919–20 and 1945–48, and the Korean War 1950–52. In the latter war many unions insisted on cost-of-living escalator clauses in their contracts which automatically adjusted wage-rates to changes in the consumers' price index. Unions have not been willing to base wages solely on the cost of living even during periods of rapid inflation. The principal objection is that it tends to freeze the workers' standard of living rather than to raise it. This was recognized in the 1948 and 1950 General Motors–UAW contract. The UAW was willing to incorporate a cost-of-living escalator clause in its contract when assured that the real wage would increase through an inclusion of an annual improvement clause in the agreement.

In the forepart of 1953 when the cost of living was turning downward, the unions became fearful that the cost-of-living escalator clause would turn against them by reducing much of the wage increase obtained under escalation. To protect itself from this occurrence, the UAW demanded that at least 20 cents of the 25 cents increase through escalation be retained as part of the base pay.

Believing that the consumers' price index did not fully reflect the rise in the price level during World War II and immediate postwar years, the labor movement attacked the Bureau of Labor Statistics consumers' price index. Labor felt that the reliability of the index was impaired through changes in consumption habits, quality deterioration of products, and scarcity of moderate price goods in the market.

2. Productivity

The labor movement has often resorted to the productivity criterion for raising wages. During the mid-1920's the AFL adopted this argument because of the belief that labor shared inequitably in the gains from technology and increased business activity. Again in post-World War II period, labor felt it was not adequately participating in the expanded national output. With the decline in the cost of living in the forepart of 1953, the productivity argument received increasing attention from the labor movement in its demands for higher wages.

The productivity criterion received much attention in the UAW–General Motors contract in 1948. The wage agreement included an annual improvement factor of three cents to be added to all base rates on May 29, 1949. The three cents increase was based on the estimated increase in the productivity for the whole economy.

### 3. Ability to Pay

During periods of prosperity labor has frequently referred to the employers' excellent financial record as evidence for justification in asking for higher wages. In the post World War II period, the unions advanced this criterion in their negotiations, in the public press, in arbitration, and before fact-finding boards. After VJ Day, Walter Reuther in seeking a 30 per cent increase in hourly wage rates for the autoworkers pointed to the high profits of General Motors and its favorable outlook in the future. In its demands for higher wages in 1947–1948, the United Electrical Radio and Machine Workers purported to show that the large earnings of employers in the electrical manufacturing industry were proof of the ability of the companies to give substantial wage increases. The United Steelworkers' brief to support their demand for a general wage increase and welfare benefits in 1948 stressed the high profits of the steel industry.

Employers in opposing union wage demands have not hesitated to plead inability to pay and at times have used this argument in asking for wage reductions. The Moeller Instrument Company pleaded inability to pay wage increases sought by the UE in 1946 because of losses sustained in that year. In 1951 the employers in the Pacific Coast Association of Pulp and Paper Manufacturers, in countering the demands of the unions for higher wages, pointed out the plight of the industry in operating on a profitable basis. During the depression in the textile industry in 1951–1954 the employers sought wage reductions on the grounds of inability to pay existing wage levels.

### 4. Comparable Wage Rates

Another important principle to support a certain wage level is that of comparisons. Ross believes that "the most powerful influence linking together separate wage bargains into an interdependent system is

the force of equitable comparison."[4]

The garment workers in their bargaining negotiations have often referred to wage comparisons to justify their demands. They believe that comparable wages between companies in the same branch of the industry are imperative for effecting competitive parity in labor costs.

In arbitration cases during the post World War II period, a number of locals in the UE pointed to intra-industry comparisons in their effort to justify higher wage demands. For example, the UE union asked the Watson Elevator Company for a wage increase in order to bring its wage level up to the pattern etablished in the industry.

Employers too have sometimes resorted to intra-industry comparisons in an effort to obtain wage reductions. The Bates Manufacturing Company and several smaller employers in the textile industry sought a reduction in wages in 1951–1952 on the grounds that wage rates in the North were higher than in the South.

For several of the national unions, it appeared customary to come to terms first with the leading companies in the industry. The wage pattern thus established was then used for comparion purposes in an effort to obtain equivalent terms with lesser companies.

Occasionally unions have justified their wage demands by inter-industry comparisons. The pulp, sulphite and paper mill workers and the paper makers in their bargaining with the West Coast employers in 1948 purported to show that wages in the paper industry had not followed the pattern of other base industries such as steel and automobiles. Employers likewise have not hesitated to point out to the union that their requests are out of line with unions in key industries.

## 5. The Purchasing Power Doctrine

This principle, dating back to the AFL social wage demand of the 1920's, has been increasingly used by labor whenever it lent itself to the occasion, or when no other argument seemed cogent. The slogan assumes that by keeping wages up or by increasing them, prosperity will be maintained or restored. It received a great impetus under the influence of the late Lord Keynes in his *General Theory* (1936). Keynesian economics stresses that wages are not only a cost of production but the source of income for the largest element in our population. Believing that business depressions are caused by a maldistribution of income, the union movement would correct this situation by increasing the purchasing power of the wage earners.[5]

During the post-World War II period, the purchasing-power criterion found increasing use among the unions to achieve higher wages. The United Steelworkers and United Autoworkers, following VJ Day, strongly emphasized substantial wage increases without price rises in order to restore the economic balance and to prevent a threatened business depression. In 1946 the CIO engaged Robert R. Nathan to strengthen its case for higher wages. The Nathan and Gass report, "A National Wage Policy for 1947," related an adequate purchasing power to prosperity. The analysis endeavored to show that the level of wage rates was too low at existing price levels to sustain high levels of employment.

In 1953 Walter Reuther voiced the thinking of the CIO when he said: "The philosophy of economic scarcity . . . must yield to the broad concept of an ever expanding productive capacity geared to the full development of our natural resources."[6] To achieve this goal Reuther would use collective bargaining to raise the purchasing power of the workers.

### 6. Substandards of Living

The labor movement since early times has related wage rates to what is needed to maintain a minimum standard of health and decency. Budgetary studies and the emergence of state minimum wage laws for women brought to the attention of both labor and management the fact that the vast majority of workers were living under substandard conditions. During the First World War the government adopted as part of its wage policy the payment of living wages. In the 1920's the vogue receded and not much was heard about it until the enactment of the NRA in 1933 and the Fair Labor Standards Act of 1938. In the Second World War and the following postwar period, the substandard wage argument was frequently referred to by the federations and affiliated unions. Comparisons were made of the workers' average income and a budgetary study of the Bureau of Labor Statistics, "City Worker's Family Budget," and of the Heller Committee budget for a wage earner's family in the city of San Francisco. The Textile Workers of America pointed to the substandard wage levels in the cotton-rayon industry in their effort to raise rates. A budgetary study was made by the union in collaboration with the Bureau of Labor Statistics to support the union's claim for higher wages before the War Labor Board.

## 7. Miscellaneous Criteria

Two arguments used particularly during the Second World War and transitional period are: attracting manpower and maintenance of take-home pay.

The Textile Workers Union of America in seeking a wage increase for the cotton textile workers during the war period stated that higher wage rates were necessary to hold and attract workers in the industry. After V J Day with the drop in the work-week from 48 to 40 hours and concomitant reduction in take-home pay, the labor movement demanded higher wage rates to make up for the loss.

# VII

### SOME OBSERVATIONS ON LABOR'S PROGRESS

During the twentieth century the working class in the United States experienced a phenomenal rise in economic well-being. The most spectacular progress has occurred since the latter part of the 1930's. The economic advance for the average worker was painfully slow during the earlier years of the twentieth century. But despite periods of downswings and periods of relatively little change, the general level of money and real wages was upward.

From 1909 to 1929 average hourly earnings in manufacturing increased from 19 cents to approximately 56½ cents representing a 197 per cent advance. Weekly earnings rose from $9.84 to $25.03 or 154 per cent. The increase in the level of money wages was largely due to the inflationary effects of the First World War. The purchasing power of the workers' wage which is a more important criterion of progress was also in his favor. Real hourly earnings rose 50 per cent while real weekly earnings advanced approximately 30 per cent.

The next two decades witnessed a remarkable rise in the workers' standard of living. Average hourly earnings in manufacturing rose from .566¢ in 1929 to $1.81 for 1954 or approximately 220 per cent. Weekly earnings during the same period advanced from $25.03 to $71.64 or 186 per cent. Hourly earnings translated into purchasing power showed a net gain of 105 per cent, while weekly real earnings increased 82 per cent.

Another clue to the economic progress of labor is seen from a study of the changes in income distribution. More people at the middle of the twentieth century were relatively well-to-do than 20 years ago, while the very wealthy and the very poor showed a substantial decline. According to Simon Kuznets, in 1929 the top five per cent of the population received 34 per cent of the total income in the U.S. after deducting taxes. In 1939 the top five percent received only 27 percent, and in 1946 this group received only 18 percent.[7]

The Korean hostilities with its accompanying higher levels of income, employment and prices continued to affect the trend toward a more uniform distribution of income. In 1946, 10 per cent of all spending units in the U.S. had incomes of $5,000 or more, which compared with 26 per cent in 1952. On the other hand, the proportion of consumer-spending units with less than $2,000 declined from 40 to 25 per cent during the same period.[8]

Another measure of labor's rise in its standard of living is seen through the gains in fringe benefits. Wages are no longer an accurate measure of workers' income. Today collective bargaining contracts, covering approximately nine million workers, contain many wage supplements. According to the Chamber of Commerce of the U.S., the average payment among 736 representative companies for fringe benefits in 1951 was 18.7 per cent of the payroll, 31.5 cents for payroll hour, or $644 per year per employee.[9]

The impressive gains in the workers' standard of living were made possible largely by technology and its application to industry, the growth of the organized labor movement, the enactment of labor laws, the personal income tax and government disbursement of tax receipts, labor-management cooperation, and the high level of prosperity from 1939–1955.

Technology is recognized as one of the most important factors in the rise of real incomes. Machines have become the servants of society. Output per man-hour in manufacturing has increased from 48.8 in 1909 to 135.2 in 1940. This represents an increase of nearly 180 per cent in 30 years.[10]

The growth of the labor movement has been an important factor for both union and non-union workers. In the year 1910 there were about 1½ million union members or one out of every 15 workers in the U.S. In 1955 there were 17 million workers in the ranks of organized labor or about one out of every three non-agricultural employees. Trade unions have developed into powerful economic and political institutions.

To what extent they have raised real earnings for their membership is a debatable subject. Ross's study of the influence of unions on earnings from 1933–1945 shows that the percentage increase in real hourly earnings is greater in highly organized industries than in less organized industries.[11] Levinson's study of average hourly earnings in selected union and non-union industries from 1934–1952 reveals that the average increase in hourly earnings in unionized industries from 1934 to 1941 was approximately 30 per cent compared to 20 per cent in the non-union sector. From 1941 to 1952 union earnings rose 130 per cent versus 120 per cent for non-union earnings.[12] On the other hand, Millis and Montgomery believe that unions have not had much influence in raising real earnings.[13]

It is the writer's opinion that the stronger unions, particularly those that have been successful in organizing the majority of workers in their jurisdiction, have been an important influence in raising real earnings for their membership. This has been shown in the northern textile industry in comparison with the southern textiles. Largely because the Textile Union Workers of America have been successful in organizing the northern workers, their wage levels are considerably higher than throughout the South where the extent of unionization is minute. However, the wages of the unorganized workers everywhere have been favorably affected through the key wage patterns set by the stronger unions. Especially since World War II the unions have exerted a powerful influence on non-unionized wages.

The enactment of labor laws has had both a direct and an indirect influence in raising the standards of the worker. The child labor laws have not only prohibited the exploitation of youth but they have stopped competition with adults for jobs, thus helping to raise wage levels. Minimum wage and maximum hour laws have been of particular advantage to the lower-paid workers. By 1952, 30 states and territories had minimum wage laws for women and minors, seven states having extended the laws to men. On the national level, the Fair Labor Standards Act, the Bacon-Davis Act, and the Walsh-Healey Act have been of inestimable value to the worker. The government through the direct purchase of labor has also exerted an influence on increasing wage levels. Perhaps the biggest boon to the worker was the enactment of the National Labor Relations Act of 1935. Following its enactment the labor movement experienced the greatest growth in history. Thirteen states have enacted equal pay laws and eleven states have passed fair employment practice laws. The equal pay laws have helped to prevent exploitation of women workers, while the fair employment practice statutes have helped in stopping discrimination against minority groups in regard to wages, employment, etc.

Other important factors affecting the supply side of labor which have aided the worker in raising his living conditions are: the drop in the ratio of agricultural employment to non-agricultural employment, the decline in immigration, and the decline in the proportion of adult population in the labor force. The decline in the relative size of the agricultural working force has taken from industry a large reservoir of unskilled cheap labor, while the drastic decline in immigration since the enactment of our immigration laws has relieved the labor force of large quantities of cheap labor from abroad. The decline in the proportion of adult population in the labor force has, according to Slichter, been a contributing factor in making for a smaller labor force. The proportion of population ten years of age or over in the labor force dropped markedly from 1910 to 1940. Since 1930 the proportion of young men between the ages of twenty and thirty-four in the labor force has been dropping substantially.[14]

On the demand side for labor, some of the factors which have tended to raise the economic well-being of the workers are: 1) the acceding of employers to labor's demands to prevent closing their plant while competitors remained open, 2) encouragement by public officials of the workers' demand for wage increases as exemplified by President Truman's broadcast in October 1945 urging substantial wage increases to maintain adequate purchasing power and raise the national income, 3) stimulants from the Second World War and the Korean hostilities.

The Federal Government's fiscal policy has been a benefit to the workers through several facets. In the first place, the progressive income tax has tended to effect a more equitable distribution of income. This has been accomplished not only through the tax rates but also through the disbursements of tax receipts which have favored the lower-income groups. In the second place, continued government deficit spending during the post-World War II period has encouraged full employment and business prosperity.

Although union-management cooperation has not been widespread in the labor movement, in those sectors of the economy where it is practiced favorable benefits have flowed to both management and the workers.

The promotion of business activity caused by the Second World War and the Korean hostilities occasioned the most rapid economic gains to labor since the turn of the century. From an economy of underemployment the United States emerged into full employment. Most lines of business activity have enjoyed exceptionally good profits with resulting high money and real wages that were believed impossible of attainment twenty years ago.

VIII

SOME EVALUATIONS OF UNION WAGE POLICIES

## 1. Employment and Prices

Some persons believe that the continuous pressure of wages and almost complete downward rigidity of money rates may have adverse effects on the maintenance of full employment at stable prices.[15] If higher labor costs are passed on to the consumer, they may result in restriction of demand. This may occur in spite of the purchasing-power principle espoused by the labor movement, because organized workers provide only a relatively small percentage of the total working-force in the society. Should employers bear the higher wage-rates, the decline in profits may adversely affect capital expansion which in turn could more than counteract the increase in consumer demand from the union workers obtaining the higher incomes. Professor Slichter holds that the wage-fixing arrangements between the big unions and employers during the post-World War II period have caused an inflationary bias in the economy. The "pattern" settlements in steel, automobiles, oil, and other heavily unionized industries were considerably above the settlements that were being made by the majority of concerns. The general effect was to accelerate the rise in wages. Although advancing labor costs stimulate technological developments that raise labor productivity, they also produce either unemployment or higher prices.[16] Professor Christenson maintains that collective bargaining does not generate an upswing in the general price level, but may be nourished by it. Inflation is originally caused from expanded government or private demand supported by increases in money or a speeding-up of the flow of accumulated reserve balances. When the spiral of inflation begins, collective bargaining may assist in keeping the spiraling of prices in motion.[17] Dunlop points out that unions have very little influence on the wage structure of the economy or on the general wage level. He cites as evidence of this position reliable studies which show: (a) The geographical wage structure of manufacturing industries did not change to any marked degree in the period 1907–46, (b) the occupational wage structure within industries has changed about the same way among various regions, (c) the wage structure by industries in the years 1923–40 appears to have been more responsive to change in productivity and product market conditions than to change in the extent of union organization.[18] Shultz and Myers believe that some unions, faced with a particular set of labor-market and product-market conditions, do take into account the probable effect of wage demands on the level of employment for their membership. These situations are not unusual except in periods of full employment and rising prices.[19] The writer's study of the ILGWU, ACWA, and TWUA confirms this belief. Hildebrand concurs with Dunlop in the belief that unions have little influence in raising the general wage levels of the country. Where the following conditions prevail, the likelihood of the success of the unions in securing wage increases is enhanced: 1) a highly inelastic demand for labor, 2) amelioration of the danger of unemployment by a high wage level, 3) a closed shop and restriction of entry into the trade, 4) the entrance of a new union into an isolated labor market where the labor supply is immobile. Large increases occur most commonly when the demand for labor is advancing.[20] It is the writer's opinion that the trade union movement, on the whole, has not adversely affected prices or employment. It may well be that the gains which organized labor has received since 1946 have been partly at the expense of the fixed-income groups.

## 2. Wage Equalization

Union wage policy of equalization of wages on an industry-wide or regional basis removes the possibility of the individual firm enjoying competitive advantage in respect to wage rates. The ramifications of this policy to both management and the union are significant. What it may eventually lead to is the enhanced role of personnel management and union-management cooperation. Realizing that it is not possible to win competitive advantage over rival firms in wage rates, management may try to reduce labor costs by achieving greater efficiency of the working group. Techniques of personnel management may be used to obtain improved selection of employees, better placement of workers, and the maintenance of interest of the worker on the job. Some labor economists believe that personnel management will not succeed wholeheartedly unless the union becomes a spokesman for the worker. Workers' interests tend to gravitate to the trade union, because it expresses the workers' language as well as the workers' dissatisfaction with the terms of employment.[21] This may well be an important reason why management should encourage cooperation with trade unions. By the establishment of union-management committees at various corporate levels, workers are likely to feel that they have an important role in the success of the enterprise. It is a recognition that production is a joint affair and that the workers are entitled to a voice in the pertinent problems of industry.

### 3. Guaranteed Annual Wage

The demand for the guaranteed annual wage has come largely from the CIO and its affiliated unions, particularly the United Automobile Workers, the United Steelworkers, the International Union of Electrical, Radio and Machine Workers, the United Packinghouse Workers, the National Maritime Union, and the Glass, Ceramic and Silica Sand Workers. The AFL and its unions have, for the most part, remained indifferent toward the guaranteed annual wage, with the exception of some locals of the teamsters' union.

The union leaders in the auto, steel, electrical machinery and appliances, and meat packing industries have been studying the problem of employer-guarantee of wages for some time. In the year 1955 plans were devised to fit their industries. The autoworkers voted to place their plan at the top of their demands in the spring of 1955. The Ford Motor Company was chosen as the test case. After eight weeks of negotiations the UAW won a modified annual wage plan on June 6, 1955. A week later, on June 13, General Motors agreed to a similar plan. Although the union obtained only a maximum guarantee of 26 weeks of unemployment benefits that approximated 60 per cent of a worker's regular wage, including state unemployment compensation benefits, the principle of the guaranteed annual wage has been established in mass-production industries. It is a beginning upon which the labor movement may extend the duration of the benefits to include 52 weeks and to raise the payments to approximate the workers' regular wage. The UAW-Ford and General Motors agreements are historic, because they establish the principle of employer-responsibility for disemployment of workers. This is a concept that was considered revolutionary a few years ago by both capital and labor.[22] The UAW agreements are given added significance, because the guaranteed wage principle has occurred in an industry which has always experienced a considerable degree of fluctuation in production.

It may be expected that the guarantee of wages will meet with resistance from management in many industries, as was the case with pensions and other fringe benefits. Although an opening wedge has been made, it will be a long time before a large proportion of the labor force is covered by some form of private wage guarantee.

The state legislatures are one of the chief obstacles to be overcome. In many states unemployment compensation is reduced or eliminated by law if the worker receives income from his former employer. New administrative rulings or laws must be passed in most states to put into effect supplementary compensation plans. Some employers may be expected to take their opposition of the guaranteed wage to the legislatures to prevent any changes in existing laws. In Michigan legislative approval of private supplementary benefits will probably be easily secured, because of the political influence of General Motors and Ford, whereas in other states such sanction may be gained more slowly.

# Notes

## INTRODUCTION

1. John T. Dunlop, *Wage Determination under Trade Unions*, The Macmillan Company, New York, 1944, pp. 50–51.

## CHAPTER I

1. T. R. Malthus, *The Principle of Population*, The Macmillan Company, New York, 1916.

2. David Ricardo, *Principles of Political Economy and Taxation*, edited by E. C. K. Gonner, G. Bell and Sons, Ltd., 1925, pp. 71–72.

3. J. Stuart Mill, *Principles of Political Economy*, edited by W. J. Ashley, Longmans, Green, and Co., Ltd., New York, 1926, p. 751.

4. Harold G. Moulton, *Controlling Factors in Economic Development*, The Brookings Institution, Washington, D.C., 1949, p. 15.

5. See: William Vogt, *Road to Survival*, William Sloane Associates, New York, 1948, and Elmer Pendell, *Population on the Loose*, Monumental Printing Company, Baltimore, 1950.

6. J. Stuart Mill, *op. cit.*, pp. 343–44, 363.

7. Francis A. Walker, *Political Economy*, 3rd edition, Henry Holt and Co., New York, 1887, pp. 248–50.

8. Dale Yoder, *Manpower Economic and Labor Problems*, 3rd edition, McGraw-Hill Book Co., New York, 1950, pp. 149–50, 154.

9. Marx denied that land and natural resources should receive any contribution, because only when labor was applied to land, did any value arise. He also claimed labor had just as much right to land as people who took a legal title to it; and capital was nothing more than the conversion of the work of labor and land. See Karl Marx, *Capital*, The Modern Library, New York, 1936.

10. Alfred Marshall, *Principles of Economics*, Macmillan and Company, Ltd., London, 1890, p. 619.

11. Eric Roll, *A History of Economic Thought*, Prentice-Hall, Inc., 1942, p. 437.

12. Harry A. Millis and Royal E. Montgomery, *The Economcs of Labor*, Vol. I, "Labor's Progress and Problems," McGraw-Hill Book Co., Inc., N.Y., 1938, p. 176.

13. Orme W. Phelps, *Introduction to Labor Economics*, McGraw-Hill Book Co., Inc., New York, 1950, pp. 101–02.

14. *Ibid.*, pp. 108–09.

15. Moulton, *op. cit.*, p. 27.

16. Sumner H. Slichter, *The Challenge of Industrial Relations*, Cornell University Press, Ithaca, N.Y., 1947, p. 14.

17. *Ibid.*, pp. 20–21.

18. Phelps, *op. cit.*, p. 104.

19. Edward Chamberlin, *The Theory of Monopolistic Competition*, 3rd edition, Harvard University Press, Cambridge, 1933, p. 181.

20. John Ise, *Economics*, Harper and Brothers, New York, 1946, p. 381.

21. Joseph Shister, *Economics of the Labor Market*, J. B. Lippincott Co., Chicago, 1949, pp. 385–88. H. M. Oliver Jr., "Marginal Theory and Business Behavior," *American Economic Review*, v. 37, June, 1947, pp. 381–82.

22. Richard A. Lester and Joseph Shister, *Insights into Labor Issues*, The Macmillan Co., N.Y., 1949, pp. 218–19.

23. Yoder, *op. cit.*, p. 166.

24. Paul H. Douglas, *The Theory of Wages*, The Macmillan Co., N.Y., 1934, pp. 312–14. Richard H. Lester, *Economics of Labor*, The Macmillan Co., N.Y., 1941, pp. 104–09.

25. Phelps, *op. cit.*, pp. 106–08.

26. Adam Smith, *An Inquiry into the Nature and Causes of the Wealth of Nations*, 4th ed. by J. R. McCulloch, Adam and Charles Black, Edinburgh, 1849, p. 30.

27. John Davidson, *The Bargain Theory of Wages*, G. P. Putnam's Son, N.Y., 1898, pp. 127–74.

28. Marshall, *op. cit.*, pp. 627–28. Maurice Dobbs, *Wages*, Harcourt, Brace and Co., 1928, pp. 97–109.

29. J. B. Hicks, *The Theory of Wages*, Macmillan Co., London, 1935.

30. Arthur M. Ross, *Trade Union Wage Policy*, University of California Press, Berkeley and Los Angeles, 1948, p. 3.

31. Ross, *op. cit.*, pp. 12, 43.

32. G. P. Shultz and C. A. Myers, "Union Wage Decisions and Employment," *American Economic Review*, vol. XI, June, 1950, pp. 362–80.

33. John T. Dunlop, *Wage Determinations under Trade Unions*, The Macmillan Company, New York, 1944, pp. 46–51.

34. John T. Dunlop, "The Demand and Supply Functions for Labor," *American Economic Review*, vol. 38, May, 1948, pp. 349–350.

35. John Maynard Keynes, *The General Theory of Employment, Interest and Money*, Harcourt, Brace and Co., N.Y., 1935, p. 267.

36. *Ibid.*, p. 270.

37. Joseph Shister, *Economics of the Labor Market*, pp. 419–20.

38. Walton Hamilton and Stacy May, *The Control of Wages*, The Macmillan Co., N.Y., 1927, p. 103.

39. Lester and Shister, *op. cit.*, p. 197.

## CHAPTER II

1. U.S. Department of Commerce, Bureau of the Census, *Historical Statistics of the United States* 1789–1945. U.S. Government Printing Office, Washington. D.C., 1949, p. 72.

2. *Proceedings*, 2nd Annual Session, Federation of Organized Trades and Labor Unions of United States and Canada, Cleveland, Ohio, 1882, pp. 3–4. *Proceedings*, 4th Annual Session, F.O.T. and L.A., Chicago, 1884, p. 14. *Proceedings*, 5th Annual Session, F.O.T. and L.A., Washington, 1885, pp. 15–17. The Executive Council of AFL, *Textbook of Labor's Political Demands*, Washington, D.C., 1906, pp. 4–7.

3. *Proceedings*, 23rd Annual Convention AFL, Boston, Mass., 1903, pp. 15–16.

4. *Proceedings*, 26th Annual Convention AFL, Minneapolis, Minn., 1906, p. 177.

5. *Proceedings*, 27th Annual Convention AFL, 1907, Norfolk, Va., p. 203.

6. John Mitchell, "The Question of a Maximum Wage," *The Outlook*, March 28, 1903, p. 721.

7. Samuel Gompers, "Fallacy of Wage Reductions," *American Federationist*, XI, Jan., 1904, pp. 41–42.

8. *The Outlook*, 73, March 28, 1903, p. 721.

9. *The Outlook*, 73, March 28, 1903, p. 722.

10. Phillip Snowden, *The Living Wage*, Hodder and Stoughton, London, 1912,

pp. 17–18 and Henry W. Macrosty, "The Recent History of the Living Wage Movement," *Political Science Quarterly*, September, 1898, pp. 413–41.

11. Paul H. Douglas, *Real Wages in the United States 1890–1926*, Houghton Mifflin Co., 1930, pp. 130, 325, 350, 375, 391, 393.

12. U.S. Department of Commerce and Labor, *Eighteenth Annual Report of the Commissioner of Labor*, 1903, Washington, D.C., p. 285.

13. Paul H. Douglas, *Real Wages in the United States 1890–1926, op. cit.*, pp. 60, 391.

14. Samuel Gompers, "A Minimum Living Wage Should Be Recognized as a Principle and Rule of Life," *American Federationist*, 5, March, 1898, p. 25.

15. Scott Nearing, "Wages in the United States," *Annals of the American Academy of Political and Social Science*, 48, July, 1913, pp. 41–42.

16. *Fourth Report of the New York Factory Investigating Commission 1915*, (Albany) vol. IV, pp. 1625, 1671.

17. F. H. Streightoff, *The Standard of Living Among the Industrial People of America*, Houghton Mifflin Co., Boston, 1911, p. 162.

18. Scott Nearing, *Financing the Wage-Earner's Family*, B. W. Huebsch, New York, 1913, p. 97.

19. *Final Report of the Commission on Industrial Relations*, Washington, 1915, p. 99.

20. Millis and Montgomery, "Labor's Progress and Problems," *op. cit.*, p. 302.

21. *Lochner v. N.Y.* 198 U.S. 45, 25 Sup. Ct. 539, (1905).

22. J. Noble Stockett, *The Arbitral Determination of Railway Wages*, Houghton Mifflin Co., Boston, 1918, pp. 54–67.

23. Hugh S. Hanna and W. Jett Lauck, *Wages and the War*, Doyle and Waltz Printing Co., Cleveland, 1918, pp. 3–4.

24. Paul H. Douglas, *Real Wages in the United States 1890–1926, op. cit.*, pp. 60, 140.

25. Harry A. Millis and Royal E. Montgomery, *Labor's Progress and Problems, op. cit.*, p. 391.

26. Paul H. Douglas, *Real Wages in the United States 1890–1926, op. cit.*, p. 391.

27. *Monthly Labor Review*, U.S. Bureau of Labor Statistics, Dec. 1919, pp. 29–41. In 1917 Professor Ogburn estimated that $1,506 was necessary to support a standard family in Tacoma and Seattle, and in 1918, $1,760 was required in the eastern cities of the United States. Bureau of Applied Economics, *Standards of Living, A Compilation of Budgetary Studies*, rev. ed., pp. 92–95, 96–101.

28. *Proceedings*, 28th Annual Convention, National Brotherhood of Operative Potters, Atlantic City, 1918, p. 90.

29. *Proceedings*, 42nd Annual Convention, Glass Blowers Association of United States and Canada, Zanesville, Ohio, 1918, pp. 153–171.

30. *Monthly Labor Review*, U.S. Bureau of Labor Statistics, vol. II, April, 1916, p. 15, and vol. X, June, 1920, p. 204.

31. W. Jett Lauck, *The New Industrial Revolution and Wages*, Funk and Wagnalls Co., *op. cit.*, pp. 26–30 and Bureau of Applied Economics, *Standards of Living, A Compilation of Budgetary Studies, op. cit.*, pp. 96–101.

32. National War Labor Board, *Bulletin No. 287*, pp. 32–33.

## CHAPTER III

1. *Annual Proceedings*, 39th Annual Convention of American Federation of Labor, Atlantic City, December, 1919, p. 85.

2. *Ibid.*, p. 72.

3. *Proceedings,* 40th Annual Convention AFL, Montreal, 1920, pp. 66–67.

4. Paul H. Douglas, *Real Wages in the United States 1890–1926, op. cit.,* pp. 140 and 477.

5. The Philadelphia standard of $1803 was the amount set by the Philadelphia Bureau of Municipal Research in 1919 as the yearly wage necessary for a standard family in the city of Philadelphia.

6. Paul H. Douglas, "An Examination of the Wage Studies of the National Industrial Conference Board," quarterly publication of the American Statistical Association, XVII, Sept., 1921, pp. 902–03.

7. Paul H. Douglas, *Wages and the Family,* University of Chicago Press, Chicago, 1925, pp. 5–6. Some studies have set the minimum health and decency standard slightly higher for certain select cities, while others are slightly lower. The National Industrial Conference Board study of the "Cost of Living in Twelve Industrial Cities" found that the cost of living for a family of two adults and two minor children according to a fair minimum American standard of living varied from $1659.84 per year in New York City to $1441.96 per year in Marion, Ohio. See *The Wage Earner in New York and Other Cities,* The National Industrial Conference Board, New York, 1928, p. 85.

8. Paul H. Douglas, *Real Wages in the United States 1890–1926, op. cit.,* pp. 468, 472, 477.

9. Paul H. Douglas, *Real Wages in the United States 1890–1926, op. cit.,* pp. 272, 292, 296, 307.

10. Paul H. Douglas, *Real Wages in the United States 1890–1926, op. cit.,* pp. 10, 15, 17, 18.

11. Paul H. Douglas and Florence T. Jennison, *The Movement of Money and Real Earnings in the United States, 1926–1928,* University of Chicago Press, 1930, pp. 25–27.

12. *Proceedings,* 41st Annual Convention AFL, Denver, 1921, p. 68.

13. *Proceedings,* 45th Annual Convention AFL, Atlantic City, 1925, p. 271.

14. *Proceedings,* 46th Annual Convention AFL, Detroit, 1926, p. 317.

15. *Proceedings,* 47th Annual Convention AFL, Los Angeles, 1927, p. 37.

16. Aryness Jay, "Index of Production of Manufacturer derived from Census Data," *Journal of the American Statistical Association, vol.* 25, Dec., 1930, p. 457.

17. Charles Bliss, "Recent Changes in Production," National Bureau of Economic Research, Bulletin 51, June 28, 1934, p. 6.

18. Millis and Montgomery, *op. cit.,* p. 154.

19. Paul H. Douglas, *Real Wages in the United States 1890–1926 op. cit.,* p. 510.

20. E. F. Gay and Leo Wolman, *Recent Social Trends,* vol. 1, p. 231.

21. Paul H. Douglas, *Real Wages in the United States 1890–1926, op. cit.,* p. 529.

22. Millis and Montgomery, *op. cit.,* p. 164.

23. Paul H. Douglas, *Real Wages in the United States 1890–1926, op. cit.,* pp. 540–547.

24. Millis and Montgomery, *Labor's Progress and Problems, op. cit.,* p. 170.

25. E. F. Gay and Leo Wolman, *Recent Social Trends, op. cit.,* p. 231.

## CHAPTER IV

1. *Proceedings,* 50th Convention AFL, 1930, p. 59.

2. *Proceedings,* 51st Convention AFL, 1931, pp. 78–81.

3. *Proceedings,* 53rd Convention AFL, 1933, pp. 530–31.

4. *Proceedings,* 55th Convention AFL, 1935, pp. 394–95.
5. *Proceedings,* 53rd Convention AFL, 1933, p. 8.
6. Broadus Mitchell, *Depression Decade,* vol. 9, Rinehart and Co., Inc., N.Y., 1947, pp. 284–85.
7. *Proceedings,* 53rd Convention AFL, 1933, p. 69.
8. *Proceedings,* 54th Convention AFL, 1934, p. 126.
9. *Proceedings,* 55th Convention AFL, 1935, p. 397.
10. Harry A. Millis and Royal E. Montgomery, *Labor's Progress and Problems,* McGraw-Hill Book Co., Inc., N.Y., 1938, pp. 119–22.
11. *Ibid.,* pp. 127–28.
12. *Proceedings,* First Constitutional Convention of Congress of Industrial Organizations, 1938, p. 165.
13. *The CIO News,* vol. 2, Nov. 13, 1939, p. 6.
14. *Ibid.,* p. 7.
15. *Proceedings,* 58th Convention AFL, 1938, p. 109.
16. *Proceedings,* 60th Convention AFL, 1940, pp. 105–557.
17. *Proceedings,* 61st Convention AFL, 1941, p. 72.
18. *Proceedings,* 4th Constitutional Convention CIO, 1941, p. 75.
19. *Proceedings,* 62nd Convention AFL, 1942, p. 118.
20. *Ibid.,* pp. 119–20.
21. *Proceedings,* 5th Constitutional Convention CIO, 1942, pp. 69–70.
22. *Op. cit., Proceedings,* 62nd Convention AFL, 1942, p. 121.
23. *Ibid.,* pp. 180–97, 603–04.
24. *Planning for Democratic Defense,* CIO Publication No. 59, p. 13.
25. *Op. cit., Proceedings,* 62nd Convention AFL, 1942, p. 217.
26. *Ibid.,* pp. 216–18.
27. *Proceedings,* 6th Constitutional Convention CIO, 1943, pp. 44–45.
28. *Ibid.,* pp. 152–53.
29. *Proceedings,* 63rd Convention AFL, 1943, p. 502. *Proceedings,* 6th Constitutional Convention CIO, 1943, pp. 152–53.
30. *Proceedings,* 64th Convention AFL, 1944, p. 133.
31. *Ibid.,* p. 133.
32. *Ibid.,* pp. 136–37.
33. See Chapter VIII, for brief submitted by the United Steelworkers of America (CIO) to panel of National War Labor Board, National War Labor Board case in re: United Steelworkers of America and United States Steel Corporation et al. *Proceedings,* 7th Constitutional Convention CIO, 1944, pp. 36–40, 47.
34. *Op. cit., Proceedings,* 64th Convention AFL, 1944, p. 233.
35. *Ibid.,* pp. 385–86.
36. *Ibid.,* p. 510. *Proceedings,* 7th Constitutional Convention CIO, 1944, pp. 315–17.
37. *Proceedings,* 66th Convention AFL, 1946, pp. 111–12.
38. *Ibid.,* p. 119.
39. *Ibid.,* pp. 537–38.
40. *Ibid.,* p. 179.
41. *Proceedings,* 8th Constitutional Convention CIO, 1946, p. 235.
42. *Ibid.,* pp. 184–85.
43. *Proceedings,* 9th Constitutional Convention CIO, 1947, p. 237. *Proceedings,* 10th Constitutional Convention CIO, 1948, pp. 333–34.
44. *Ibid.,* pp. 52–53.
45. *Ibid.,* p. 327.

46. *Ibid.*, pp. 202–03, 336.
47. *Proceedings*, 11th Constitutional Convention CIO, 1949, pp. 226–27.
48. *Ibid.*, pp. 348–49.
49. *Proceedings*, 69th Convention AFL, 1950, pp. 288, 441, 469.
50. *Proceedings*, 12th Constitutional Convention CIO, 1950, pp. 87–88.
51. *Ibid.*, p. 286.
52. *Ibid.*, p. 405.
53. *Proceedings*, 13th Constitutional Convention CIO, 1951, pp. 389–90.
54. *Proceedings*, 71st Convention AFL, 1952, p. 169.
55. *AFL News-Reporter*, vol. I, Feb. 13, 1952, pp. 1–13.
56. *AFL News Reporter*, vol. I, June 4, 1952, pp. 1 and 3.
57. *Proceedings*, 71st Convention AFL, 1952, p. 170.
58. *The American Federationist*, vol. 60, Feb., 1953, pp. 4–7.
59. *Proceedings*, 72nd Convention AFL, 1953, pp. 284–86, 290–92.
60. *CIO News Release*, January, 1, 1953.
61. *CIO News*, Vol. XVI, January 5, 1953, p. 3.
62. *CIO News Release*, Feb. 3, 1953.
63. *Proceedings*, 14th Constitutional Convention CIO, 1952, p. 44. *Proceedings*, 15th Constitutional Convention CIO, 1953, pp. 615–16.
64. *Guaranteed Annual Wages*, Pamphlet No. 231, reprinted from October, 1953, *Economic Outlook*, CIO.


CHAPTER V

1. Benjamin Stolberg, *Tailor's Progress*, Doubleday, Doran and Co., Inc., Garden City, N.Y., 1944, p. 23.
2. Louis Levine, *The Women's Garment Workers*, B. W. Huebsch, Inc., New York, 1924, pp. 174–76.
3. Dwight E. Robinson *Collective Bargaining and Market Control in the New York Coat and Suit Industry*, Columbia University Press, New York, 1949, p. 13.
4. Governor's Advisory Commission. Cloak, Suit, and Shirt Industry, New York City. *Report of an Investigation* by John Dickinson and Morris Kolchin.
5. Benjamin Stolberg, *Tailor's Progress, op. cit.*, p. 68.
6. *Ibid.*, p. 90.
7. *Report of the General Executive Board to the 17th Convention*, ILGWU, 1924, pp. 39–40.
8. *Report and Proceedings*, 19th Convention, ILGWU, 1928, pp. 10–12.
9. *Report of the General Executive Board to the 17th Convention*, ILGWU, 1924, pp. 16–18; *Report of the General Executive Board to the 18th Convention*, 1925, p. 43.
10. Governor's Advisory Commission. Cloak, Suit, and Shirt Industry, New York City. *Report of an Investigation*, by John Dickinson and Morris Kolchin, p. 158.
11. *Ibid.*, pp. 158–60.
12. Dickinson and Kolchin, *Report of an Investigation, op. cit.*
13. Governor's Advisory Commission. Cloak, Suit and Skirt Industry, New York City. Final Recommendations.
14. Robinson, D. E., *Collective Bargaining and Market Control in the New York Coat and Suit Industry, op. cit.*, p. 54.
15. *Report and Proceedings of 19th Convention*, ILGWU, 1928.

16. *Report of the General Executive Board to the 20th Convention*, ILGWU, 1929, pp. 38–39.

17. *Ibid.*, pp. 43–44.

18. *Report of the General Executive Board of the 21st Convention*, ILGWU, 1932, pp. 5–10.

19. *Report of the General Executive Board to 21st Convention*, ILGWU, 1932, pp. 25–26.

20. *Ibid.*, pp. 29–31.

21. *Report of the General Executive Board to the 22nd Convention*, ILGWU, 1934, pp. 49–50.

22. *Report of the General Executive Board to the 22nd Convention*, ILGWU, 1934, p. 27.

23. *Ibid.*, pp. 30–31.

24. Julius Hochman, *Why This Strike*, Joint Board Dress and Waistmakers' Union, N.Y.

25. *Report of the General Executive Board to 23rd Convention*, ILGWU, 1937, pp. 40–41; Kurt Braun, *Union-Management Co-operation*, The Brookings Institution, Washington, D.C., 1947.

26. *Report of the General Executive Board to 24th Convention*, ILGWU, 1940, pp. 45–46.

27. *Report of the General Executive Board to 25th Convention*, ILGWU, 1944, pp. 67–68.

28. *Ibid.*, p. 69.

29. Sumner H. Slichter, *Union Policies and Industrial Management*, The Brookings Institution, Washington, D.C., 1941, pp. 406–07.

30. *Report of the General Executive Board to 25th Convention*, ILGWU, 1944, p. 48.

31. *ILGWU News-History, 1900–1950*, Absco Press, Inc. N.Y., 1950, p. 102.

32. *Ibid.*, p. 104.

33. *Report of the General Executive Board to the 26th Convention*, ILGWU, 1947, pp. 145–46.

34. *Report and Record*, 27th Convention, ILGWU, 1950, p. 126.

35. *Report and Record*, 26th Convention, ILGWU, 1947, pp. 35–36.

36. *Ibid.*, pp. 19–20, 409–10, 511.

37. *Ibid.*, p. 100.

38. *Report and Record*, 27th Convention, ILGWU, 1950, pp. 12–13.

39. *Report and Record*, 27th Convention, ILGWU, 1950, p. 13.

40. *Report and Record*, 28th Convention, ILGWU, 1953, p. 77.

41. Labor Arbitration Service—New England Sportswear Mfgs. Ass'n. and Int. Ladies' Garment Union, Dec. 28, 1950, vol. 15, pp. 926–27.

42. *Report and Record*, 28th Convention. ILGWU, 1953, pp. 77–78.

43. *Ibid.*, pp. 78–80.

44. *Ibid.*, pp. 92–93.

45. *Justice*, vol. 34, April 1, 1952, p. 12.

46. *Report and Record*, 28th Convention, ILGWU, 1953, p. 297.

47. *Report and Record*, 25th Convention, ILGWU, 1944, p. 447.

48. Health and Welfare Services, International Ladies' Garment Workers' Union, 1953.

## CHAPTER VI

1. *Guaranteed Wages*, Report to the President by the Advisory Board, Office of War Mobilization and Reconversion, Office of Temporary Controls, U.S. Government Printing Office, Washington, 1947, pp. 386–90.

2. ACWA Report of the General Executive Board to the Fourth Biennial Convention, 1920.

3. *ACWA Proceedings,* Fourth Biennial Convention, 1920, p. 297.

4. *ACWA Proceedings,* Fourth Biennial Convention, 1920, pp. 343–52.

5. *ACWA Proceedings,* Eighth Biennial Convention, 1928, p. 28.

6. *ACWA Proceedings,* Fifth Biennial Convention, 1922, pp. 7–83.

7. *ACWA Proceedings,* Ninth Biennial Convention, 1930, p. 64.

8. Kurt Braun, *Union-Management Co-operation,* The Brookings Institution, Washington, D.C., 1947, pp. 95–100.

9. *ACWA Proceedings,* Fifth Biennial Convention, 1922, pp. 82–83.

10. *ACWA Proceedings,* Sixth Biennial Convention, 1924, p. 279.

11. *ACWA Report of the General Executive Board and Proceedings of the Seventh Biennial Convention,* 1926, pp. 12–13.

12. Joel Seidman, *The Needle Trades,* Farrar and Rinehart, Inc., N.Y., 1942, p. 272.

13. Sumner Slichter, *Union Policies and Industrial Management,* The Brookings Institution, Washington, 1941, pp. 522–23.

14. ACWA, *Report of the General Executive Board to Eighth Biennial Convention,* 1928, p. 42.

15. ACWA, *Report of the General Executive Board to the Eighth Biennial Convention,* 1928.

16. *Documentary History of the Amalgamated Clothing Workers of America 1930–1934.* Report of the General Executive Board, Proceedings of the Tenth Convention, 1934.

17. *Documentary History ACWA—1930–1934,* p. 36.

18. *Documentary History ACWA—1936–1938,* p. 171.

19. Bernard Stern, *Wage Policy of the ACWA, 1920–1940*—Paper for Seminar in the Economics of Collective Bargaining, Harvard University, Graduate School of Public Administration, June, 1944.

20. *Documentary History ACWA, 1936–1938,* p. 18.

21. *Ibid.,* p. 375.

22. Kurt Braun, *Union-Management Cooperation,* The Brookings Institution, Washington, D.C., 1947, pp. 103–04.

23. *Ibid.,* pp. 104–05.

24. *Documentary History ACWA, 1938–1940.*

25. *How Collective Bargaining Works,* The Twentieth Century Fund, New York, 1942, p. 436.

26. *Ibid.,* pp. 437–39.

27. *ACWA Report of the General Executive Board and Proceedings of the Fourteenth Biennial Convention,* 1944, p. 18.

28. *The Social Insurance Program of the Amalgamated Clothing Workers of America,* Research Department, ACWA, Sept., 1952.

29. *ACWA Report of the General Executive Board and Proceedings of the Fourteenth Biennial Convention,* 1944, p. 145.

30. *ACWA General Executive Board Report and Proceedings of the 15th Biennial Convention,* 1946, pp. 5–6.

31. *Ibid.,* p. 21.

32. *ACWA General Executive Board Report and Proceedings,* Sixteenth Biennial Convention, 1948.

33. *Ibid.,* pp. 22–23, 254–55.

34. *ACWA General Executive Board Report and Proceedings,* Seventeenth Biennial Convention, 1950, pp. 9–11, *The Social Insurance Program of the*

*Amalgamated Clothing Workers of America*, Research Department, ACWA, Sept., 1952.

35. *ACWA General Executive Board Report and Proceedings, Seventeenth Biennial Convention*, 1950, pp. 14–15, 25–26.

36. *ACWA General Executive Board Report and Proceedings*, 17th Biennial Convention, 1950, pp. 2–3.

37. *Ibid.*, pp. 11–15.

38. Letter from Jacob S. Potofsky to Clothing Manufacturers Association, September 1, 1950.

39. Letter—Re: Negotiations for Wage Increases, September 25, 1950.

40. ACWA, *The Advance*, vol. 38, September 1, 1952, p. 3.

41. News release, ACWA, March 27, 1953; Recent Changes in Social Security Benefits, Research Department, ACWA, June 1, 1953.

## CHAPTER VII

1. *Introducing Your Union*, International Brotherhood of Pulp, Sulphite and Paper Mill Workers, Department of Research and Education, Washington, D.C., p. 8.

2. *Proceedings*, 14th Convention of the International Brotherhood of Pulp, Sulphite and Paper Mill Workers, 1931, p. 10.

3. *Ibid.*, p. 11.

4. *Proceedings*, 16th Convention of the International Brotherhood of Pulp, Sulphite and Paper Mill Workers, 1935, p. 15.

5. *Ibid.*, p. 15.

6. *Proceedings*, 16th Convention of the International Brotherhood of Pulp, Sulphite and Paper Mill Workers, 1935, p. 16.

7. *Ibid.*, pp. 19–23; *Proceedings*, 14th Convention of the International Brotherhood of Paper Makers, 1935, pp. 17–18.

8. *The Pulp, Sulphite and Paper Mill Workers' Journal*, vol. 19, June 1935, p. 2.

9. *Proceedings*, 18th Convention of the International Brotherhood of Pulp, Sulphite and Paper Mill Workers, 1939, pp. 53–55; *Proceedings*, 15th Convention of the International Brotherhood of Paper Makers, 1939, p. 25.

10. *Proceedings*, 18th Convention of the International Brotherhood of Pulp, Sulphite and Paper Mill Workers, 1939, pp. 112, 196; *Proceedings*, 15th Convention of the International Brotherhood of Paper Makers, 1939, p. 134.

11. *Record of the Negotiations between the International Brotherhood of Pulp, Sulphite and Paper Mill Workers, the International Brotherhood of Paper Makers, and the Pacific Coast Association of Pulp and Paper Manufacturers, May 27, 1940, to May 31, 1940*, pp. 204–18.

12. *The Pulp, Sulphite and Paper Mill Workers' Journal*, vol. 28, January–February, 1944, p. 1.

13. *The Pulp, Sulphite and Paper Mill Workers' Journal*, vol. 24, July–August, 1940, p. 1.

14. *Proceedings*, 19th Convention of the International Brotherhood of Pulp, Sulphite and Paper Mill Workers, 1941, p. 85.

15. *Record of the Negotiations between the International Brotherhood of Pulp, Sulphite and Paper Mill Workers, the International Brotherhood of Paper Makers and the Pacific Coast Association of Pulp and Paper Manufacturers, 1942*, pp. 87–93, 170–79.

16. *Proceedings*, 20th Convention of the International Brotherhood of Pulp, Sulphite and Paper Mill Workers, 1944, pp. 151, 153, 165; *Proceedings*, 17th Convention of the International Brotherhood of Paper Makers, 1946, p. 11.

17. *The Paper Makers' Journal*, vol. 43, April, 1944, pp. 3–4.

18. Minutes of the Joint Board Meetings of the International Brotherhood of Paper Makers and the International Brotherhood of Pulp, Sulphite and Paper Mill Workers, January 8, 1948.

19. *Record of the Negotiations between the International Brotherhood of Pulp, Sulphite and Paper Mill Workers, the International Brotherhood of Paper Makers and the Pacific Coast Association of Pulp and Paper Manufacturers*, April, 1948, pp. 76–78, 118–19, 164, 214.

20. Minutes of the Executive Boards of the International Brotherhood of Paper Makers and the International Brotherhood of Pulp, Sulphite and Paper Mill Workers, January 13, 1949, p. 7.

21. *The Paper Makers' Journal*, vol. 51, March, 1952, p. 3.

22. Minutes of the Meeting of the Joint Board of the International Brotherhood of Paper Makers and the International Brotherhood of Pulp, Sulphite and Paper Mill Workers, January 12, 1950.

23. *News Letters* from the International Office of the International Brotherhood of Pulp, Sulphite and Paper Mill Workers, June 22, 1950, p. 20.

24. *Proceedings*, 22nd Convention of the International Brotherhood of Pulp, Sulphite and Paper Mill Workers, 1950, p. 58.

25. *The Paper Makers' Journal*, vol. 51, March, 1952, p. 3.

26. *The Paper Maker*, vol. 4, January 31, 1952, p. 8.

27. *Record of Negotiations between the International Brotherhood of Pulp, Sulphite and Paper Mill Workers, the International Brotherhood of Paper Makers and the Pacific Coast Association of Pulp and Paper Manufacturers*, May, 1951, pp. 33, 49, 51–52, 103, 105, 111–55, 273–81, 308–28.

28. *The Paper Maker*, vol. 4, January 31, 1952, p. 1.

29. *Record of Negotiations between the International Brotherhood of Pulp, Sulphite and Paper Mill Workers, the International Brotherhood of Paper Makers and the Pacific Coast Association of Pulp and Paper Manufacturers*, April, May, 1953, pp. 21–22, 34–43, 161, 174, 195, 230, 355, 360, 364.

30. *Record of Negotiations between the International Brotherhood of Pulp, Sulphite and Paper Mill Workers, the International Brotherhood of Paper Makers and The Pacific Coast Association of Pulp and Paper Manufacturers*, May, 1954, pp. 171–85.

*News Letter* from the International Office of the International Brotherhood of Pulp, Sulphite and Paper Mill Workers, July 27, 1954.

## CHAPTER VIII

1. Vincent D. Sweeney, *The First Ten Years*, The United Steelworkers of America.

2. Frederick H. Harbison, *Steel, How Collective Bargaining Works*, Twentieth Century Fund, New York, 1945, pp. 529–30.

3. *Proceedings*, Second International Wage and Policy Convention of the SWOC, 1940, p. 24.

4. *How Collective Bargaining Works, op. cit.*, p. 533.

5. *Proceedings*, Second International Wage and Policy Convention of the SWOC, May, 1940, pp. 210–14, 238.

6. Clinton S. Golden and Harold J. Ruttenberg, *The Dynamics of Industrial Democracy*, Harper and Bros., N.Y., pp. 152–55.

7. *How Collective Bargaining Works, op. cit.*, pp. 560–63.

8. National War Labor Board—in the matter of the Steelworkers Organizing Committee and Bethlehem Steel Co., Republic Steel Co., Youngstown Sheet and

Tube Co., and Inland Steel Co. Submitted by SWOC, 1942. (Unbound copy—Industrial Relations Library, Harvard University.)

9. John T. Dunlop, *An Appraisal of Wage Stabilization Policies*, Reprint from Bulletin 1009, U.S. Dept. of Labor, p. 163.

10. Vol. 1, *War Labor Reports*, The Bureau of National Affairs, Washington, D.C., 1942, p. 329.

11. Resolutions adopted by the International Executive Board and the National Wage and Policy Conference at its meetings on November 30 to December 2, 1943—United Steelworkers of America (Unbound personal copy).

12. Vol. 13, *War Labor Reports*, Bureau of National Affairs, Washington, D.C., 1944, p. 203.

13. Vol. 19, *War Labor Reports*, Bureau of National Affairs, Washington, D.C., 1945, p. 583. National War Labor Board in re: United Steelworkers of America and United States Steel Corporation et al. Brief submitted by the United Steelworkers of America to panel of National War Labor Board, Case No. 111–623 OD 14–1, 1944. Industrial Relations Library, Harvard University.

14. Vol. 19. *War Labor Reports*, Bureau of National Affairs, Washington, D.C., 1945, p. 577.

15. *Wartime Wage Control and Dispute Settlement: Laws, Regulations, Directives, General Orders, etc.*, Bureau of National Affairs, Washington, D.C., 1945, pp. 20–21. Vol. 19, *War Labor Reports*, Bureau of National Affairs, Washington, D.C., 1945, pp. 680–81.

16. Philip Murray, *Steelworkers Need a $2.00 a Day Wage Increase*, United Steelworkers of America.

17. *Proceedings*, Third Constitutional Convention of the United Steelworkers of America, 1946, pp. 22–34.

18. Letter by Secretary and Treasurer David J. McDonald of the United Steelworkers of America to all district directors, staff representatives and local unions of United Steelworkers of America, December 19, 1946.

19. Robert Tilove, *Collective Bargaining in the Steel Industry*, University of Pennsylvania Press, 1948, pp. 15, 22, 23. Letter to author from Otis Brubaker, Director of Research, United Steelworkers of America, April 1, 1954.

20. *Proceedings*, Fourth Constitutional Convention of the United Steelworkers of America, 1948, pp. 46–47.

21. *Proceedings*, Fourth Constitutional Convention of the United Steelworkers of America, 1948, pp. 159–160.

22. 1949 Wage Policy for the United Steelworkers of America, letter from McDonald, Secretary-Treasurer, United Steelworkers, May 5, 1949.

23. *Proceedings*, Fifth Constitutional Convention of the United Steelworkers of America, 1950, p. 31.

24. *The Steelworkers' Case for Wages, Pensions and Social Insurance*, as presented to President Truman's Steel Industry Board by Philip Murray, United Steelworkers, 1949, pp. 18–21.

25. *Ibid.*, p. 19.

26. Report to the President of the United States on the labor dispute in the basic steel industry by the steel industry board appointed by the President, July 15, 1949.

27. *Proceedings*, Fifth Constitutional Convention of the United Steelworkers of America, 1950, pp. 35–39.

28. United States of America—Wage Stabilization Board, Washington, D.C., Case No. D—18C—In the matter of United Steelworkers of America and various Steel and Iron Ore Companies—The Economic Documentation of the Steel-

workers' Demand-Union Exhibit No. 9, Otis Brubaker, Research Director, United Steelworkers of America, p. 5.

29. *Ibid.*, pp. 12–69.

30. U.S. of America. Wage Stabilization Board–Case No. D–18-C. In matter of United Steelworkers of America and various steel and iron ore companies–Union Exhibit No. 22. Statement of Philip Murray on the Guaranteed Annual Wage.

31. *Labor Arbitration Reports*, vol. 18, 1952, Bureau of National Affairs. In re: Basic Steel Industry and United Steelworkers of America, Case No. D–18-C, March 12, 1952.

32. *New York Times,* July 25, 1952, pp. 1 and 6.

33. Robert R. R. Brooks, *As Steel Goes,* Yale University Press, New Haven, Conn., 1940, pp. 212–13.

34. The Empire rates were and still are somewhat lower than the major portion of the industry. In 1943 the Company's minimum labor rate was 5½ cents lower than for most of the industry. By 1948 this differential was narrowed to five cents and remains the same at the present time. In addition, labor jobs at Empire are at the plant minimum rate; whereas, in the industry generally, they are in Class 2 or more. (Class 2 is 5½ cents higher than the minimum plant rate.) This means that for most labor jobs Empire is 10½ cents below most of the industry. This arises from both the earlier lag in rates and from the fact that Empire has never installed a job classification program similar to that in common use in the industry.

35. *Proceedings,* First Constitutional Convention of the United Steelworkers of America and the Third Consecutive Convention of the SWOC, vol. I, 1942, p. 70.

36. *Proceedings,* Fourth Constitutional Convention of the United Steelworkers of America, 1948.

37. National Planning Association–Causes of Industrial Peace under Collective Bargaining. Sharon Steel Corporation and United Steelworkers of America. Case Studies 5 by J. Wade Miller Jr., National Planning Association, Washington, D.C., 1949.

## CHAPTER IX

1. *How Collective Bargaining Works,* Chapter 11, "Automobiles," by W. H. McPherson and Anthony Luchek, Twentieth Century Fund, New York, 1945, pp. 573–78.

2. *Ibid.,* p. 587.

3. Financial Statement, Secretary Treasurer UAW, May, 1954.

4. Robert W. Dunn, *Labor and Automobiles,* International Publishers, N.Y., 1929, pp. 117, 120. William H. McPherson, *Labor Relations in the Automobile Industry,* The Brookings Institution, Washington, D.C., 1940, p. 98.

5. Edward Levinson, *Rise of the Auto Workers,* UAW-CIO, p. 9.

6. William H. McPherson, *Labor Relations in the Automobile Industry, op. cit,.* pp. 78–79.

7. Edward Levinson, *Rise of the Auto Workers, op. cit.,* pp. 10–17.

8. *Proceedings,* 1941 Convention of the International Union, United Automobile Workers of America, p. 225.

9. McPherson, *Labor Relations in the Automobile Industry, op. cit.,* pp. 85–86.

10. *Proceedings,* Fifth Annual Convention of the International United Automobile Workers of America, 1940, p. 277.

11. McPherson, *Labor Relations in the Automobile Industry, op cit.*, pp. 103–108.

12. *Proceedings,* Eighth Convention of the UAW-CIO, 1943, pp. 228, 231.

13. Statement of Nat Weinberg, Research Director, UAW-CIO.

14. The Wage Chronology Series General Motors Corp., 1939—Series 4, no. 9. The Wage Chronology Series Chrysler Corp., 1939—Series 4, no. 5. The Wage Chronology Series Ford Motor Co., 1941—Series 4, no. 14. U.S. Department of Labor, Bureau of Labor Statistics.

15. R. J. Thomas, *Automobile Unionism,* A Report submitted to the 1943 Convention of the UAW-CIO, October 4, 1943, p. 82.

16. *Ibid.,* p. 83.

17. *Ibid.,* pp. 88–91.

18. Frederick H. Harbison and Robert Dubin, *Patterns of Union-Management Relations,* Science Research Associates, Chicago, 1947, p. 34.

19. *Proceedings,* Ninth Convention of the United Automobile, Aircraft and Agricultural Implement Workers of America, 1944, pp. 382–383.

20. In matter—International Union UAW and General Motors, Dec. 21, 1945. The Case for Maintaining Take-Home Pay without Increasing Prices—(unbound copy) Industrial Relations Library, Harvard University, p. 1.

21. General Motors Corporation and the UAW, Jan. 10, 1946, *Labor Arbitration Reports,* vol. 1, Bureau of National Affairs, Washington, D.C., 1946, pp. 128–29, 136.

22. Harbison and Dubin, Patterns of Union-Management Relations, *op. cit.,* pp. 87–88.

23. *Wages, Prices, Profits—The Automobile Workers' Case for a 23½c Wage Increase,* International Union, United Automobile, Aircraft and Agricultural Implement Workers of America, March, 1947, pp. 1–2.

24. Harbison and Dubin, *Patterns of Union-Management Relations, op. cit.,* p. 92.

25. *Report of the President* UAW-CIO, Part II, Report from Administrative Department submitted by Walter P. Reuther to the Eleventh Convention of the UAW-CIO, November 9, 1947, p. 8.

26. *Proceedings,* Eleventh Convention UAW-CIO, 1947, pp. 54–55.

27. *UAW-CIO Press Release,* UAW Public Relations Department, February 29, 1948.

28. *UAW-CIO Press Release,* UAW Public Relations Department, March 9, 1948, p. 3.

29. *UAW-CIO Press Release,* UAW Public Relations Department, April 30, 1948, May 8, 1948, May 13, 1948.

30. *UAW-CIO Press Release,* UAW Public Relations Department, May 25, 1948.

31. *UAW Press Release,* UAW Public Relations Dept., May 25, 1948. Statement issued by John W. Livingston, UAW Vice President and T. A. Johnston, Assistant Director of Union's General Motors Department, pp. 1–4.

32. *UAW Press Release,* UAW Public Relations Dept., May 28, 1948, p. 2.

33. *UAW Press Release,* UAW Public Relations Dept., July 21, 1948.

34. *UAW Press Release,* UAW Public Relations Dept., Jan. 16, 1949.

35. *Proceedings,* Twelfth Convention UAW 1949, pp. 231–32.

36. The Wage Chronology Series Ford Motor Co. 1941—Series 4, no. 14, U.S. Dept. of Labor, Bureau of Labor Statistics.

37. Statement by Frank Winn, Director of Public Relations UAW-CIO, made to author.

38. *UAW Press Release,* UAW Public Relations Department, May 4, 1950.

39. Letter Addressed to All Chrysler Workers—UAW-CIO, May 8, 1950, p. 1.

40. The Wage Chronology Series, General Motors Corp., 1939—Series 4, no. 9, U.S. Department of Labor, Bureau of Labor Statistics.

41. *UAW Press Release,* UAW Public Relations Department, May 23, 1950.

42. Frederick H. Harbison, "The General Motors—United Auto Workers Agreement of 1950," The Journal of Political Economy, vol. LVIII., Oct., 1950, p. 410.

43. The Wage Chronology Series Chrysler Corp. 1939—Series 4, no. 5, U.S. Department of Labor, Bureau of Labor Statistics.

44. The Wage Chronology Series Ford Motor Co. 1941—Series 4, no. 14, U.S. Department of Labor, Bureau of Labor Statistics.

45. *UAW Press Release,* UAW Public Relations Dept., August 22, Oct. 24, Nov. 14, 1950, Jan. 21, Feb. 11, 1951.

46. *The United Automobile Worker UAW-CIO,* vol. 16, May, 1952, pp. 8–9.

47. Wage Chronology No. 9, General Motors Corp. Supplement No. 2, *Monthly Labor Review,* Aug., 1953, vol. 76, U.S. Department of Labor, Bureau of Labor Statistics, p. 845.

48. *UAW Press Release,* UAW Public Relations Dept., Feb. 28, 1953. *The Wall Street Journal,* March 21, 1953, pp. 1–2.

49. Wage Chronology no. 9 General Motors Corp., Supplement no. 2, *Monthly Labor Review,* August 1953, vol. 76. U.S. Dept. of Labor, Bureau of Labor Statistics, *op. cit.,* pp. 485–87.

50. Wage Chronology no. 14 Ford Motor Co., Supplement no. 1, *Monthly Labor Review,* January 1954, vol. 77, U.S. Dept. of Labor BLS, pp. 56–57. Wage Chronology no. 5 Chrysler Corp., Supplement no. 2, *Monthly Labor Review,* November 1953, vol. 76, U.S. Department of Labor BLS, pp. 1201–1203.

51. *The United Automobile Worker,* UAW-CIO, vol. 16, April 1952, p. 3.

52. Report of Walter P. Reuther to Fourteenth Convention UAW-CIO 1953, pp. 8–13.

53. *Proceedings,* Fourteenth Constitutional Convention UAW-CIO 1953, pp. 143–49.

54. *Preparing a Guaranteed Employment Plan,* An Explanation of the UAW-CIO Annual Wage Study Committee's Proposed Plan for Guaranteed Employment in Industries in the Jurisdiction of the UAW-CIO, Publication 321.

55. *The New York Times,* June 7, 1955, p. 24.

56. *Ibid.,* p. 24.

57. General Motors Corporation Press Release, June 12, 1955. Collective Bargaining Agreement between Ford Motor Company and UAW-CIO, June 8, 1955. *The United Automobile Worker,* June 1955.

## CHAPTER X

1. Solomon Barkin, "The Regional Significance of the Integration Movement in the Southern Textile Industry," *The Southern Economic Journal,* Vol. XV, April 1949, pp. 395, 409.

2. *Building a Union of Textile Workers*—Report of Two Years' Progress to the Convention of United Textile Workers of America and the Textile Workers Organizers Committee, 1939, pp. 26–28.

3. *Executive Council Report,* Second Biennial Convention, TWUA, 1941, pp. 5–11.

4. Solomon Barkin, "Industrial Union Wage Policies," Reprint from *Plan Age*, January, 1940, p. 7.

5. *Executive Council Report* 1939–41, Second Biennial Convention, TWUA, 1941, p. 16.

6. *Ibid.*, pp. 16–64.

7. *Ibid.*, p. 61.

8. Statement of Textile Workers Union of America before the War Labor Board on April 29, 1942, on Proposed Wage Increases for New England and New York Cotton and Rayon Workers (unbound), Harvard University Graduate School of Public Administration, November 20, 1942.

9. *Executive Council Report*, Fourth Biennial Convention, TWUA, 1946, pp. 59–60.

10. *Substandard Conditions of Living*, A Study of the Cost of the Emergency Sustenance Budget in Five Textile Manufacturing Communities in January–February, 1944, Research Department, TWUA, 1944.

11. U.S. of America before the NWLB—In matter of 23 Southern Cotton Textile Mills, 25 New England Cotton Rayon Companies, and six New York and Pennsylvania Rayon Companies and the TWUA, Washington, Oct. 6, 1944 (unbound copy), Industrial Relations Library, Harvard University.

12. *Executive Council Report*, Fourth Biennial Convention, TWUA, 1946, p. 62.

13. TWUA "Firsts," Research Department, TWUA, August, 1951.

14. *Executive Council Report*, Fourth Biennial Convention, TWUA, 1946, p. 63.

15. The Wage Chronology Series, American Woolen Co., 1939, Series 4, No. 1, U.S. Department of Labor, B.L.S.

16. *Executive Council Report*, Fourth Biennial Convention, TWUA, 1946, pp. 68–71.

17. *Textile Labor*, Vol. 8, No. 11, June 7, 1947, pp. 1–2.

18. *Executive Council Report*, Fifth Biennial Convention, TWUA, 1948, pp. 58–60.

19. *Executive Council Report*, Sixth Biennial Convention, TWUA, 1950, p. 50.

20. Fall River Textile Manufacturers' Association, New Bedford Cotton Manufacturers' Association, and Textile Workers Union of America—*Labor Arbitration Reports*, v. 11, 1949, pp. 985–991.

21. Statement of the Textile Workers Union of America in the matter of Arbitration with the American Woolen Company, January 26, 1949, Research Department, TWUA, January 24, 1949.

22. TWUA "Firsts," Research Department, TWUA, August 30, 1951.

23. *Executive Council Report*, Fifth Biennial Convention, TWUA, 1948, pp. 66–67.

24. *Ibid.*, p. 68.

25. *Proceedings*, Fifth Biennial Convention, TWUA, 1948, p. 216.

26. *Proceedings*, Sixth Biennial Convention, TWUA, 1950, p. 181.

27. *Executive Council Report*, Fifth Biennial Convention, TWUA, 1948, pp. 68–70.

28. Solomon Barkin, "The Application of Quality Control Techniques in Determining Work Assignments and Standards." (Reproduced from the Eighth Annual Conference, American Society For Quality Control), June, 1954, TWUA Publication, No. T–117.

29. *Executive Council Report*, Seventh Biennial Convention, TWUA, 1952, p. 13.

30. *Ibid.*, p. 50.
31. *Ibid.*, p. 50.
32. *Ibid.*, p. 51.
33. *Ibid.*, pp. 53–59.
34. Ibid., pp. 60–61.
35. *Executive Council Report*, Eighth Biennial Convention, TWUA, 1954, pp. 19–23.
36. *Ibid.*, pp. 25–26.
37. *Textile Labor*, Jan. 12, 1952, pp. 1–2; Jan. 26, 1952, pp. 1 and 3; Feb. 9, 1952, pp. 1 and 3.
38. *Textile Labor*, June 7, 1952, p. 8.
39. *Ibid.*, p. 8.
40. *Textile Labor*, June 21, 1952, pp. 1 and 3.
41. *Textile Labor*, July 26, 1952, pp. 1 and 2.
42. *Executive Council Report*, Eighth Biennial Convention, TWUA, 1954, p. 58.
43. *Ibid.*, p. 61.
44. *Ibid.*, p. 58.
45. *Ibid.* p. 59.
46. *Ibid.*, p. 61.
47. *Ibid.*, pp. 62–63.

## CHAPTER XI

1. Milton Derber, "Electrical Products," Chapter 14, *How Collective Bargaining Works*, Twentieth Century Fund, New York, 1945, pp. 744–746.
2. *Ibid.*, pp. 760–761.
3. *The UE Record*, United Electrical, Radio and Machine Workers of America, 1947, New York, p. 20.
4. *Proceedings*, Fifth Convention of United Electrical, Radio and Machine Workers of America, 1939, pp. 76, 198.
5. *The UE Record, op. cit.*, p. 20.
6. *Proceedings*, Fifth Convention of UE, 1939, *op. cit.*, p. 104.
7. *Proceedings*, Sixth Convention of Electrical, Radio and Machine Workers of America, 1940, p. 170.
8. James B. Carey, "United Electrical, Radio and Machine Workers Union," *Labor Information Bulletin*, U.S. Dept. of Labor, May, 1940, vol. 7, p. 3.
9. *Proceedings*, Sixth Convention, UERMWA, 1940, *op. cit.*, pp. 32–33.
10. *Proceedings*, Seventh Convention of the United Electrical, Radio and Machine Workers of America, 1941, pp. 4–5.
11. *Ibid.*, p. 183.
12. *Ibid.*, p. 202.
13. *Proceedings*, Eighth Convention of United Electrical, Radio and Machine Workers of America, 1942, p. 47.
14. *Proceedings*, Ninth Convention of United Electrical, Radio and Machine Workers of America, 1943, p. 53.
15. *Ibid.*, pp. 86–88.
16. *Proceedings*, Tenth Convention of United Electrical, Radio and Machine Workers of America, 1944, p. 226.
17. *War Labor Reports*, vol. 23, Bureau of National Affairs, Wash., D.C., 1945, Westinghouse Electric Co. (Pittsburgh) and UERMWA (CIO), Case no. 111-8213-D, April 11, 1945, pp. 153–66.
18. *War Labor Reports*, vol. 28, Bureau of National Affairs, Wash., D.C.,

1946, General Electric Co. and Westinghouse and UERMWA (CIO), Cases No. 111–17208-D and 111–17209-D, Nov. 27, 1945, pp. 357–59.

19. National War Labor Board, Westinghouse Electric Corp. vs. UERMWA Case No. 111-17209-D, Sept. 21, 1945. Verbatim transcript, unbound copy, Industrial Relations Library, Harvard University.

20. *Report of General Officers,* Eleventh Convention of United Electrical, Radio and Machine Workers of America, 1946, p. 15.

21. *Ibid.,* pp. 9–13.

22. *Ibid.,* p. 18, and *UE Policy*—Resolutions and Reports of Eleventh Convention, UERMWA, 1946, p. 28.

23. *UE Policy Resolutions and Reports,* Eleventh Convention, 1946, *op. cit.,* pp. 9–26.

24. *Labor Arbitration Reports,* Bureau of National Affairs, Washington, D.C., vol. 5, 1947, National Electronics Corporation and United Electrical, Radio and Machine Workers of America, Local 452, Dec. 2, 1946, pp. 500–504.

25. *Labor Arbitration Reports,* Bureau of National Affairs, Washington, D.C., vol. 3, 1946, Veloco Machine Co. (Benton Harbor, Michigan) and United Electrical, Radio and Machine Workers of America, Local 931, July 20, 1946, pp. 867–73.

26. *Labor Arbitration Reports,* Bureau of National Affairs, Washington, D.C., vol. 6, 1947, pp. 636–639. Camburn, Inc., and UERMWA Local 430 (CIO), Feb. 27, 1947.

27. *Labor Arbitration Reports,* Bureau of National Affairs, Washington, D.C., vol. 6, 1947. Moeller Instrument Co., Inc., and UERMWA Local 1227, Jan. 23, 1947, pp. 639–44.

28. *Labor Arbitration Reports,* Bureau of National Affairs, Washington, D.C., vol. 8, 1948. Watson Elevator Co. and UERMWA Local 423 (CIO) Case No. 47–A–363, July 22, 1947, pp. 386–89.

29. *Proceedings,* 12th Convention of United Electrical, Radio and Machine Workers of America, 1947, pp. 22–28.

30. *Proceedings,* 12th Convention of UERMWA, *op. cit.,* pp. 22–28, 31–33, 226–27, 128, 190, 251–52.

31. *UE News,* vol. X, January 10, 1948, p. 7.

32. *UE News,* vol. X, April 10, 1948, p. 1.

33. *UE News,* vol. X, May 22, 1948, p. 2.

34. *UE News,* vol. X, May 29, 1948, p. 2.

35. *Ibid.,* p. 4.

36. *UE News,* vol. X, June 12, 1948, p. 1; June 19, 1948, p. 1; June 26, 1948, p. 1.

37. *UE News,* vol. X, Sept. 11, 1948, p. 6.

38. *Proceedings,* 13th Convention, United Electrical, Radio and Machine Workers of America, 1948, p. 22.

39. *Proceedings,* 2nd Annual Convention, IUE–CIO, 1950, p. 353.

40. *Ibid.,* p. 351.

41. *Proceedings,* Organizational Convention of the IUE–CIO, 1949, p. 108.

42. *Ibid.,* pp. 76–77.

43. *Ibid.,* p. 357.

44. *Proceedings,* Second Annual Convention, IUE, 1950, pp. 359–360.

45. *Ibid.,* pp. 360–361.

46. *The IUE-CIO News,* vol. I, July 31, 1950, pp. 1 and 11.

47. *A Short History of Collective Bargaining between IUE-CIO and the General Electric Company,* Research Dept., IUE-CIO.

48. *Proceedings,* IUE Convention, 1950, p. 361.

49. *Ibid.,* pp. 362–63.

50. *Ibid.*, p. 363.

51. *Ibid.*, p. 364.

52. *Proceedings*, 2nd Annual Convention, IUE-CIO, 1950, pp. 324–25. *Proceedings*, 3rd Annual Convention, IUE-CIO, 1951, pp. 349–50.

53. The General Electric Company and the old UE had a profit-sharing plan in previous years, but the UE requested its termination before the Second World War. With the greatly increased profits during the postwar years the IUE computed the workers' loss in profit-sharing about $300 per worker. During the year 1950 the company shared $10 million of profits with its executives. —*The IUE News*, Vol. 2, July 16, 1951, p. 3.

54. *A Short History of Collective Bargaining between IUE-CIO and the General Electric Company*, Research Dept., IUE-CIO.

55. *Proceedings*, 3rd Annual Convention, IUE-CIO, 1951, p. 330.

56. *Proceedings*, 4th Annual Convention, IUE-CIO, 1952, p. 377.

57. *Ibid.*, pp. 380–81.

58. *Proceedings*, 3rd Annual Convention, IUE-CIO, 1951, pp. 349–50. *Proceedings*, 4th Annual Convention, IUE-CIO, 1952, p. 362.

59. *Proceedings*, 3rd Annual Convention, IUE-CIO, 1951, pp. 299–300.

60. *A Short History of Collective Bargaining between the IUE-CIO and the General Electric Company*, Research Dept., IUE-CIO.

61. *Proceedings*, 5th Annual Convention, IUE-CIO, 1953, pp. 383–84.

62. *Proceedings*, 4th Annual Convention, IUE-CIO, 1952, p. 383.

63. *Ibid.*, pp. 256, 423.

64. *Proceedings*, 5th Annual Convention, IUE-CIO, 1953, pp. 213–17, 231–32.

65. *Ibid.*, pp. 238–40.

66. *A Short History of Collective Bargaining between the IUE-CIO and the General Electric Company*, Research Dept., IUE-CIO.

67. *Proceedings*, 5th Annual Convention, IUE-CIO, 1953, pp. 381, 388–89.

68. *Ibid.*, pp. 333–34, 359–60.

69. Report of General Electric Negotiating Committee to General Electric Conference Board, September 2, 1954, Research Dept., IUE-CIO.

70. *Wall Street Journal*, November 3, 1954, p. 2.

## CHAPTER XII

1. Other terms currently in use to express the guaranteed wage are guaranteed employment and supplemental unemployment benefits. The writer will use the phrase, guaranteed wage.

2. Seymour E. Harris, "Economics of the Guaranteed Wage," *Monthly Labor Review*, vol. 78, February 1955, p. 159.

3. *Social Security Bulletin*, U.S. Department of Health, *Education and Welfare*, vol. 13, September 1950, p. 44, vol. 17, May–Dec., 1954, vol. 18, April 1955.

4. Daniel Bell, "Beyond the Annual Wage," *Fortune*, May 1955, p. 93.

5. The study of the "Size Distribution of Income" by Goldsmith, *et al*, confirms Kuznet's findings. Between 1929 and 1950 the percentage share of income received by the top five per cent of the population with the highest income dropped from 30 per cent to 20.4 per cent or from one-third to less than one-fifth of the total. The share of family income received from wages, salaries, and transfer payments (pensions and unemployment benefits) increased from 61.1 per cent to 70.6 per cent. In contrast, there was a marked reduction in the share of interest, dividends, and rent from 22.3 per cent to 12.3 per cent. It is this type of income that is concentrated in the wealthier families.

Goldsmith, Jaszi, Kaitz, and Liebenberg, "Size Distribution of Income since the Mid-Thirties," *Review of Economics and Statistics*, February 1954, pp. 16–18.

6. Nat Weinberg, "The Thinking Behind the UAW-CIO Guaranteed Employment Plan," *Michigan Business Review*, vol. VII, March 1955, pp. 6–7.

7. *Ibid.*, p. 7.

8. *Guaranteed Wages*, Report to the President by the Advisory Board, Office of War Mobilization and Reconversion, Washington, 1947, Chapter 13, "Wage Guarantees and Industrial Relations," p. 172.

9. Nat Weinberg, "The Thinking Behind the UAW-CIO Guaranteed Employment Plan," *Michigan Business Review*, *op. cit.*, vol. VII, March 1955, p. 8.

10. Seymour E. Harris, "Economics of the Guaranteed Wage," *Monthly Labor Review, op. cit.*, vol. 78, February 1955, p. 164.

11. *U.S. News and World Report*, "How Many Jobless are Rejecting Jobs?" November 5, 1954, pp. 35–36.

12. Nat Weinberg, "UAW Defends Guaranteed Annual Wage," *Wall Street Journal*, April 14, 1955, p. 12.

13. See *Monthly Labor Review*, March 1935, for summary of the report.

14. *United Automobile Worker*, vol. 18, March 1955, p. 4.

15. *New York Times*, June 12, 1955, p. 52.

16. *Guaranteed Wages*, Report to the President by the Advisory Board, Office of War Mobilization and Reconversion, Washington, D.C., 1947, *op. cit.*, Chapter VIII, pp. 70–75.

17. *Op. cit.*, Seymour E. Harris, "Economics of the Guaranteed Wage," *Monthly Labor Review*, vol. 78, February 1955, p. 62.

18. *Op. cit.*, *Guaranteed Wages*, Report to the President by the Advisory Board, Office of War Mobilization and Reconversion, Washington, D.C., 1947, p. 418.

19. *Op. cit.*, Seymour E. Harris, "Economics of the Guaranteed Wage," *Monthly Labor Review*, February 1955, p. 163, vol. 78.

20. *Ibid.*, p. 161.

21. *Automation*, A Report to the UAW-CIO Economic and Collective Bargaining Conference, Nov. 12, 13, 1954, p. 3.

22. *Op. cit.*, Nat Weinberg, "The Thinking Behind the UAW-CIO Guaranteed Employment Plan," *Michigan Business Review*, vol. VII, March 1955, p. 5.

23. The decision to move to other regions or to remain within the same community would depend, of course, on many factors such as lower labor costs, proximity to sources of raw materials, taxes, etc.

24. *New York Times*, June 23, 1955, pp. 1, 18.

25. Leland Hazard, "Can We Afford a Guaranteed Wage," *The Atlantic*, March 1955, vol. 195, p. 55.

26. *Detroit Free Press*, June 7, 1955, p. 33.

27. Harold M. Groves, *Financing Government*, Henry Holt and Co., 3rd Ed., 1950, p. 138.

28. *Op. cit.*, Seymour E. Harris, "Economics of the Guaranteed Wage," *Monthly Labor Review*, Feb. 1955, vol. 78, p. 162.

## CHAPTER XIII

1. Matthew Woll, *Labor, Industry and Government*, D. Appleton-Century Co., N.Y., 1935, pp. 150–151.

2. The Brotherhood of Railway Trainmen, "Shorter Workday—A Plea in the Public Interest," March 1937, p. 7.

3. Edwin E. Witte, "Criteria in Wage Rate Determinations," *Washington University Law Quarterly*, 1949, p. 29.

4. Arthur M. Ross, *Trade Union Wage Policy*, Institute of Industrial Rela-

tions, University of California, University of California Press, Berkeley and Los Angeles, 1948, p. 6.

5. Millis and Montgomery, *Organized Labor*, "The Economics of Labor," Part III, *op. cit.*, pp. 410–12.

6. *CIO News Release*, Jan. 1, 1953.

7. Simon Kuznets, "Shares of Upper Income Groups in Income and Savings," *31st Annual Report*, National Bureau of Economic Research, May 1951, p. 4.

8. *1953 Survey of Consumer Finances*, Reprint from Federal Reserve Bulletin, June 1953, p. 2. A consumer-spending unit is defined as all persons living in the same dwelling and belonging to the same family who pooled their income to meet their major expenses.

9. Chamber of Commerce of the United States, *Fringe Benefits 1951*, Washington, D.C., p. 6.

10. Public Affairs Pamphlet No. 142, *Power, Machines, and Plenty*, by Gloria Waldrow and J. Frederic Dewhurst, Twentieth Century Fund, p. 15. Index numbers based on output in 1930 = 100.

11. Arthur M. Ross, *Trade Union Wage Policy, op. cit.*, p. 122.

12. Harold M. Levinson, "Collective Bargaining and Income Distribution," *American Economic Review, Papers and Proceedings*, vol. XLIV, May 1954, p. 312.

13. Harry A. Millis and R. E. Montgomery, *Labor's Progress and Some Basic Labor Problems, op. cit.*, p. 213.

14. Sumner H. Slichter, "Do the Wage-Fixing Arrangements in the American Labor Market Have an Inflationary Bias?" *American Economic Review, Papers and Proceedings*, Vol. XLIV, May 1954, pp. 328–29.

15. See "Impact of Labor Unions," Chapter 11, *Wage Policy, Employment and Economic Stability* by Gottfried Haberler, Harcourt, Brace and Co., N.Y., 1951, pp. 56–57; Lindblom, *Unions and Capitalism*, Yale University Press, New Haven, 1949; Fritz Machlup, "Monopolistic Wage Determination as a Part of the General Problem of Monopoly," in *Wage Determination and the Economics of Liberalism*, Chamber of Commerce of the United States, January 11, 1947; Leo Wolman, *Industry-Wide Bargaining*, The Foundation for Economic Education, 1948.

16. Sumner H. Slichter, "Do the Wage-Fixing Arrangements in the American Labor Market Have an Inflationary Bias?" *op. cit.*, pp. 339, 345.

17. C. L. Christenson, "Variations in the Inflationary Force of Bargaining," *American Economic Review, Papers and Proceedings*, Vol. XLIV, May, 1954, p. 358.

18. Review of *Unions and Capitalism, American Economic Review*, vol. XL, June 1950, p. 465.

19. G. P. Shultz and C. A. Myers, "Union Wage Decisions and Employment," *Americaan Economic Review*, vol. XL, June 1950, p. 379.

20. George H. Hildebrand, "American Unionism, Social Stratification, and Power," *American Journal of Sociology*, vol. LVIII, January 1953, pp. 384–85.

21. Solomon Barkin, "Labor's Code for a Private Enterprise Economy," *Labor Law Journal*, Dec. 1952, vol. 3, No. 16, pp. 480–85.

22. An exception to this rule was found in the employer-initiated guaranteed wage plans of Proctor and Gamble Co., Hormel and Co., Nunn-Bush and Co., William Wrigley Co., and a few scattered union agreements which provided guarantees of one year or less.

# Index